CASE CLOSED™

VOLUME 39

Gosho Aoyama

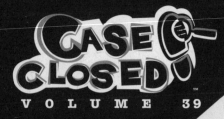

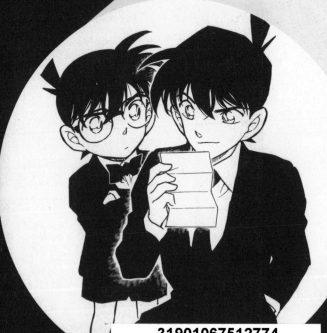

Case Briefing:

Subject:
Occupation:
Special Skills:
Equipment:

Jimmy Kudo, a.k.a. Conan Edogawa
High School Student/Detective
Analytical thinking and deductive reasoning, Soccer
Bow Tie Voice Transmitter, Super Sneakers,
Homing Glasses, Stretchy Suspenders

The subject is hot on the trail of a pair of suspicious men in black when he is attacked from behind and administered a strange substance which physically transforms him into a first grader. When the subject confides in the eccentric inventor Dr. Agasa, they decide to keep the subject's true identity a secret for the safety of everyone around him. Assuming the new identity of first-grader Conan Edogawa, the subject continues to assist the police force on their most baffling cases. The only problem is that most crime-solving professionals won't take a little kid's advice!

Table of Contents

CONFIDEN

CASE CLOSED
Volume 39
Shonen Sunday Edition

Story and Art by GOSHO AOYAMA

MEITANTEI CONAN Vol. 39
by Gosho AOYAMA
© 1994 Gosho AOYAMA
All rights reserved.
Original Japanese edition published by SHOGAKUKAN.
English translation rights in the United States of America, Canada,
the United Kingdom and Ireland arranged with SHOGAKUKAN.

Translation
Tetsuichiro Miyaki

Touch-up & Lettering
Freeman Wong

Cover & Graphic Design
Andrea Rice

Editor
Shaenon K. Garrity

Printed in Canada

Published by VIZ Media, LLC
P.O. Box 77010
San Francisco, CA 94107

10 9 8 7 6 5 4 3 2
First printing, July 2011
Second printing, July 2016

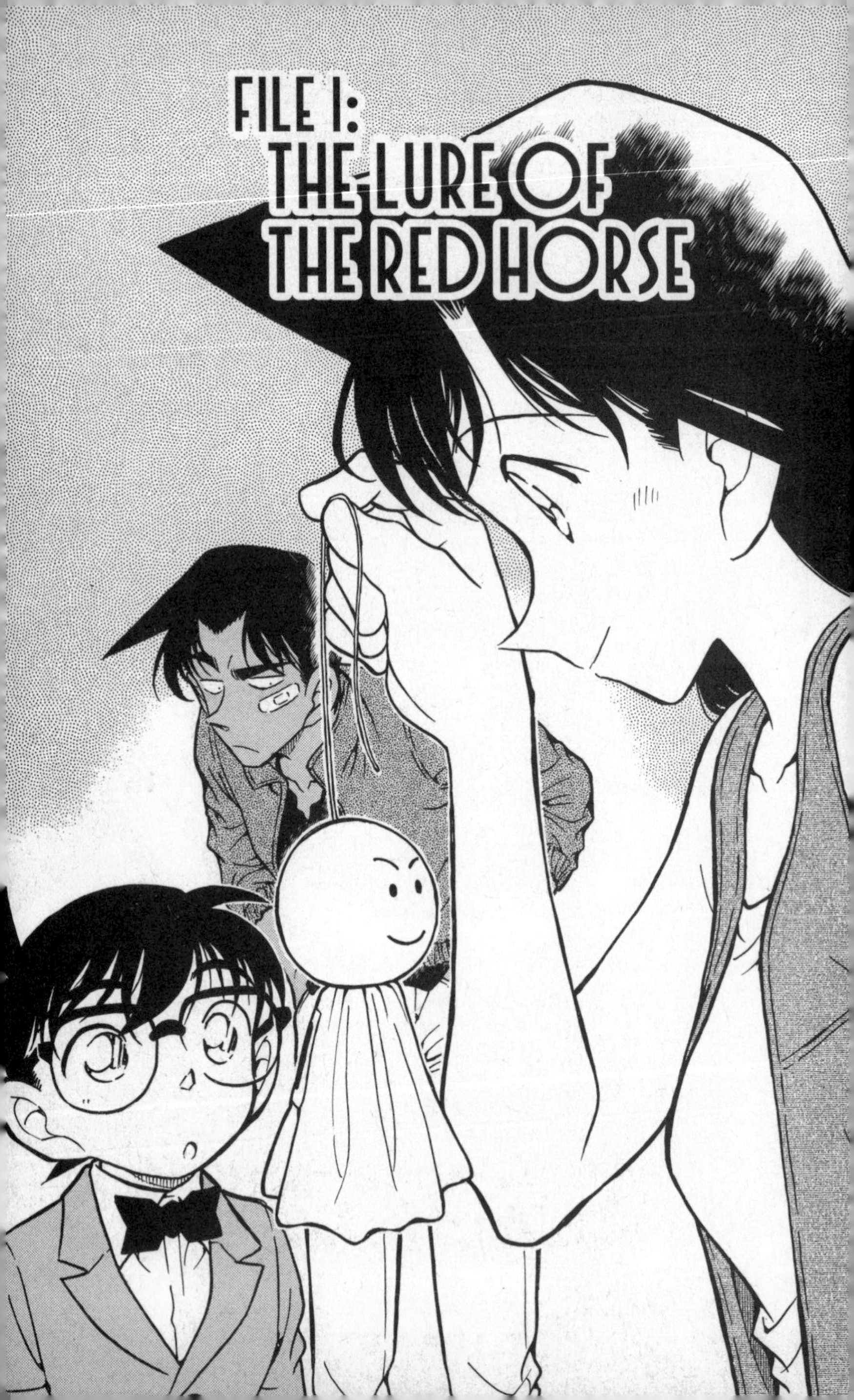
FILE 1:
THE LURE OF
THE RED HORSE

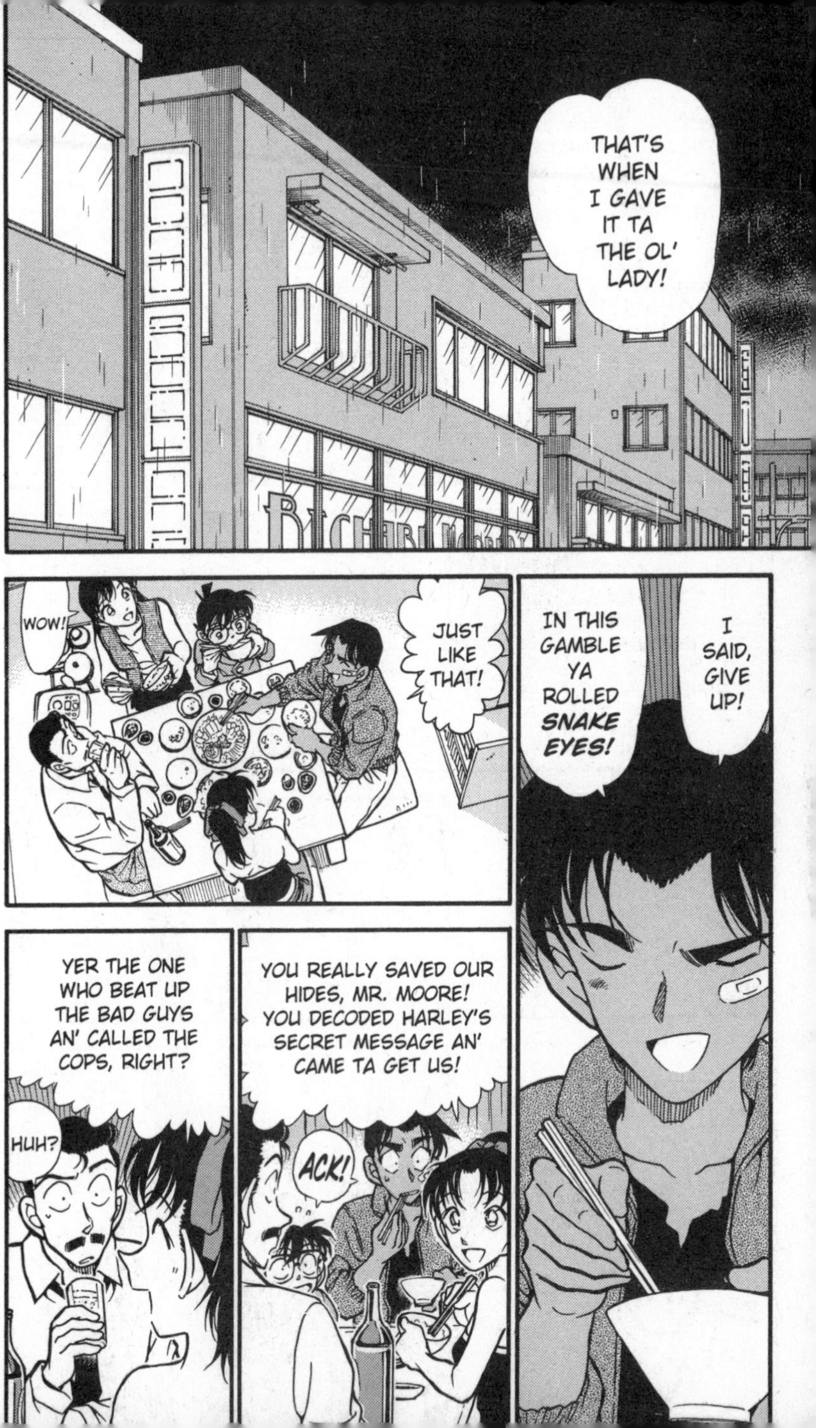
THAT'S WHEN I GAVE IT TA THE OL' LADY!
I SAID, GIVE UP!
IN THIS GAMBLE YA ROLLED SNAKE EYES!
JUST LIKE THAT!
WOW!
YOU REALLY SAVED OUR HIDES, MR. MOORE! YOU DECODED HARLEY'S SECRET MESSAGE AN' CAME TA GET US!
ACK!
YER THE ONE WHO BEAT UP THE BAD GUYS AN' CALLED THE COPS, RIGHT?
HUH?

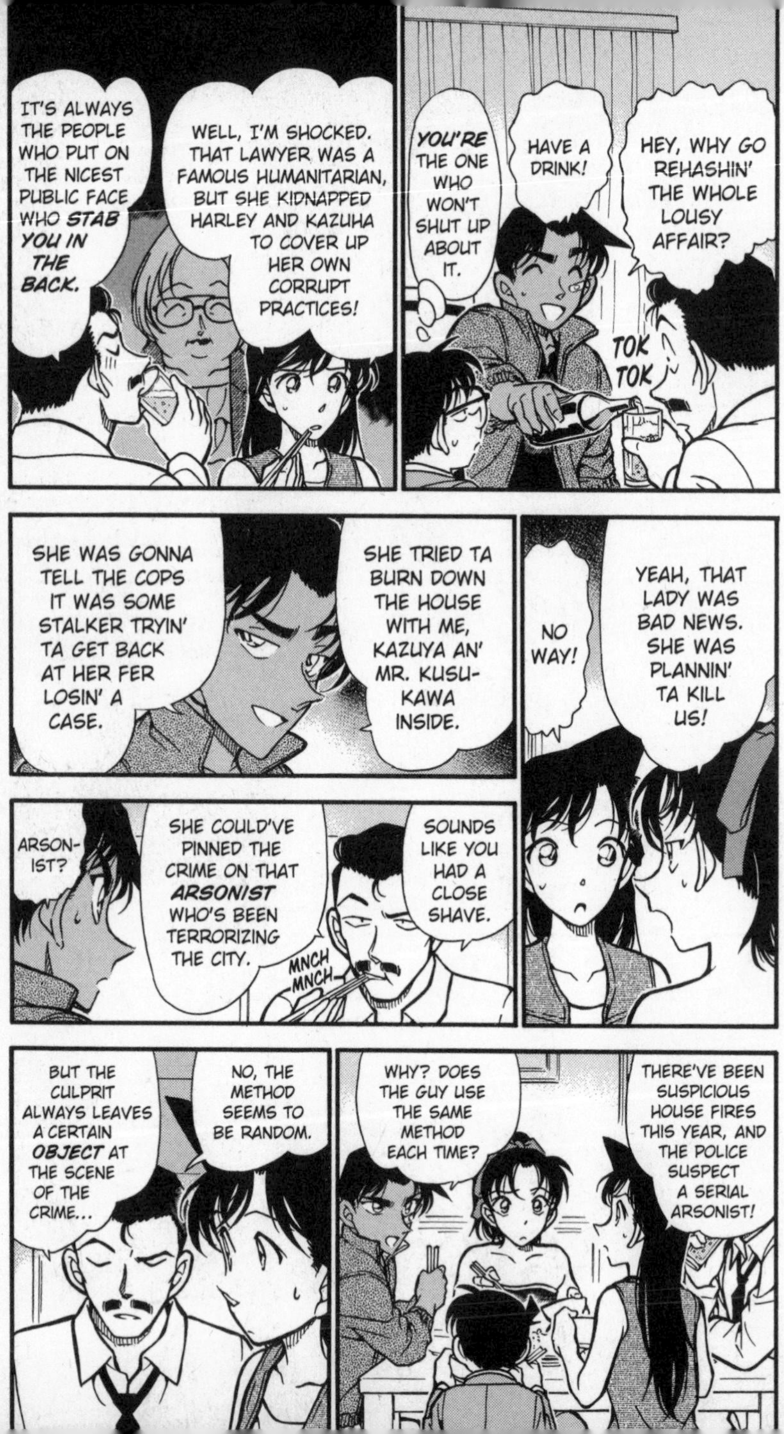
HEY, WHY GO REHASHIN' THE WHOLE LOUSY AFFAIR?
HAVE A DRINK!
YOU'RE THE ONE WHO WON'T SHUT UP ABOUT IT.
TOK TOK
WELL, I'M SHOCKED. THAT LAWYER WAS A FAMOUS HUMANITARIAN, BUT SHE KIDNAPPED HARLEY AND KAZUHA TO COVER UP HER OWN CORRUPT PRACTICES!
IT'S ALWAYS THE PEOPLE WHO PUT ON THE NICEST PUBLIC FACE WHO STAB YOU IN THE BACK.
YEAH, THAT LADY WAS BAD NEWS. SHE WAS PLANNIN' TA KILL US!
NO WAY!
SHE TRIED TA BURN DOWN THE HOUSE WITH ME, KAZUYA AN' MR. KUSU-KAWA INSIDE.
SHE WAS GONNA TELL THE COPS IT WAS SOME STALKER TRYIN' TA GET BACK AT HER FER LOSIN' A CASE.
SOUNDS LIKE YOU HAD A CLOSE SHAVE.
SHE COULD'VE PINNED THE CRIME ON THAT ARSONIST WHO'S BEEN TERRORIZING THE CITY.
MNCH MNCH
ARSON-IST?
THERE'VE BEEN SUSPICIOUS HOUSE FIRES THIS YEAR, AND THE POLICE SUSPECT A SERIAL ARSONIST!
WHY? DOES THE GUY USE THE SAME METHOD EACH TIME?
NO, THE METHOD SEEMS TO BE RANDOM.
BUT THE CULPRIT ALWAYS LEAVES A CERTAIN OBJECT AT THE SCENE OF THE CRIME...

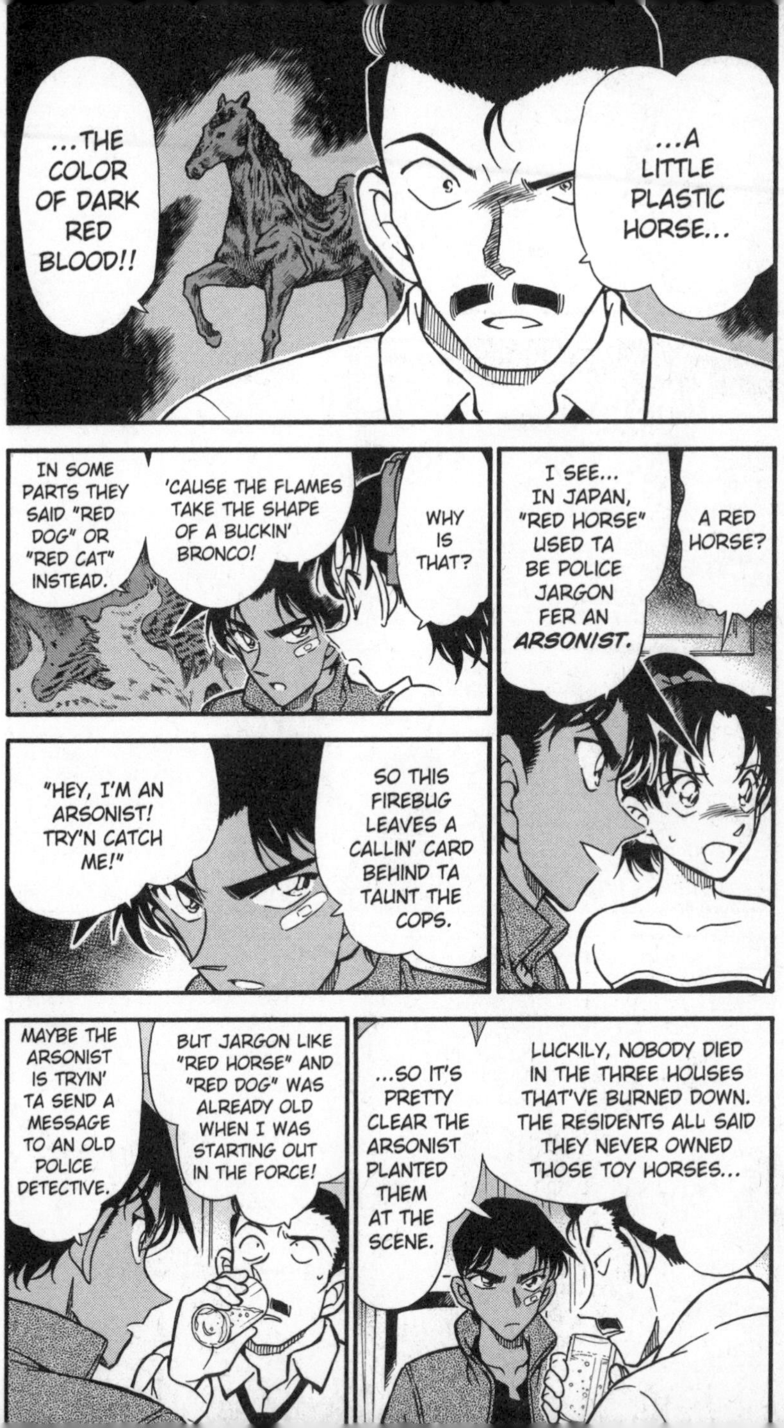
...A LITTLE PLASTIC HORSE...
...THE COLOR OF DARK RED BLOOD!!
A RED HORSE?
I SEE... IN JAPAN, "RED HORSE" USED TA BE POLICE JARGON FER AN ARSONIST.
WHY IS THAT?
'CAUSE THE FLAMES TAKE THE SHAPE OF A BUCKIN' BRONCO!
IN SOME PARTS THEY SAID "RED DOG" OR "RED CAT" INSTEAD.
SO THIS FIREBUG LEAVES A CALLIN' CARD BEHIND TA TAUNT THE COPS.
"HEY, I'M AN ARSONIST! TRY'N CATCH ME!"
LUCKILY, NOBODY DIED IN THE THREE HOUSES THAT'VE BURNED DOWN. THE RESIDENTS ALL SAID THEY NEVER OWNED THOSE TOY HORSES...
...SO IT'S PRETTY CLEAR THE ARSONIST PLANTED THEM AT THE SCENE.
BUT JARGON LIKE "RED HORSE" AND "RED DOG" WAS ALREADY OLD WHEN I WAS STARTING OUT IN THE FORCE!
MAYBE THE ARSONIST IS TRYIN' TA SEND A MESSAGE TO AN OLD POLICE DETECTIVE.

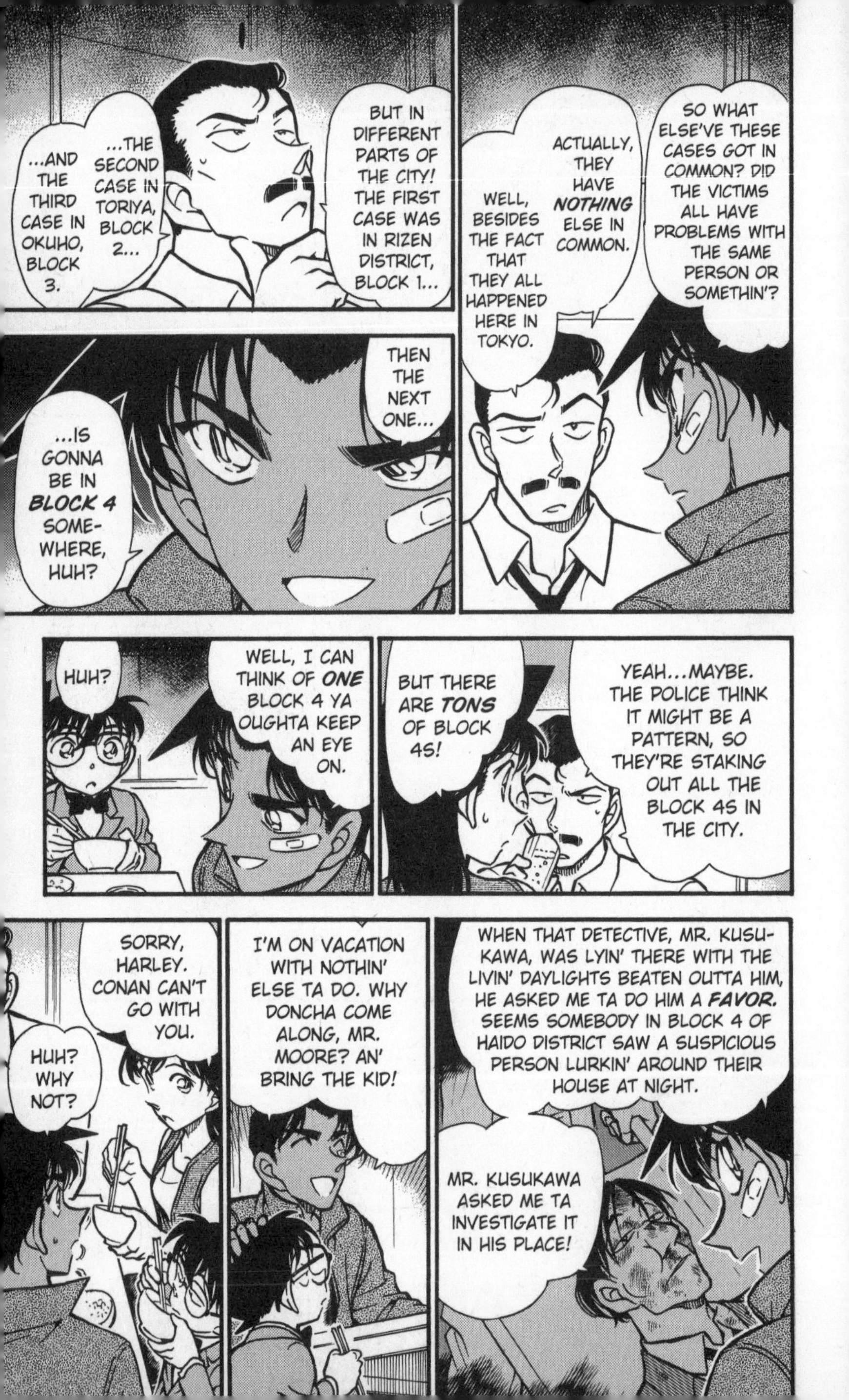
SO WHAT ELSE'VE THESE CASES GOT IN COMMON? DID THE VICTIMS ALL HAVE PROBLEMS WITH THE SAME PERSON OR SOMETHIN'?
ACTUALLY, THEY HAVE NOTHING ELSE IN COMMON.
WELL, BESIDES THE FACT THAT THEY ALL HAPPENED HERE IN TOKYO.
BUT IN DIFFERENT PARTS OF THE CITY! THE FIRST CASE WAS IN RIZEN DISTRICT, BLOCK 1...
...THE SECOND CASE IN TORIYA, BLOCK 2...
...AND THE THIRD CASE IN OKUHO, BLOCK 3.
THEN THE NEXT ONE...
...IS GONNA BE IN BLOCK 4 SOMEWHERE, HUH?
YEAH...MAYBE. THE POLICE THINK IT MIGHT BE A PATTERN, SO THEY'RE STAKING OUT ALL THE BLOCK 4S IN THE CITY.
BUT THERE ARE TONS OF BLOCK 4S!
WELL, I CAN THINK OF ONE BLOCK 4 YA OUGHTA KEEP AN EYE ON.
HUH?
WHEN THAT DETECTIVE, MR. KUSUKAWA, WAS LYIN' THERE WITH THE LIVIN' DAYLIGHTS BEATEN OUTTA HIM, HE ASKED ME TA DO HIM A FAVOR. SEEMS SOMEBODY IN BLOCK 4 OF HAIDO DISTRICT SAW A SUSPICIOUS PERSON LURKIN' AROUND THEIR HOUSE AT NIGHT.
MR. KUSUKAWA ASKED ME TA INVESTIGATE IT IN HIS PLACE!
I'M ON VACATION WITH NOTHIN' ELSE TA DO. WHY DONCHA COME ALONG, MR. MOORE? AN' BRING THE KID!
SORRY, HARLEY. CONAN CAN'T GO WITH YOU.
HUH? WHY NOT?

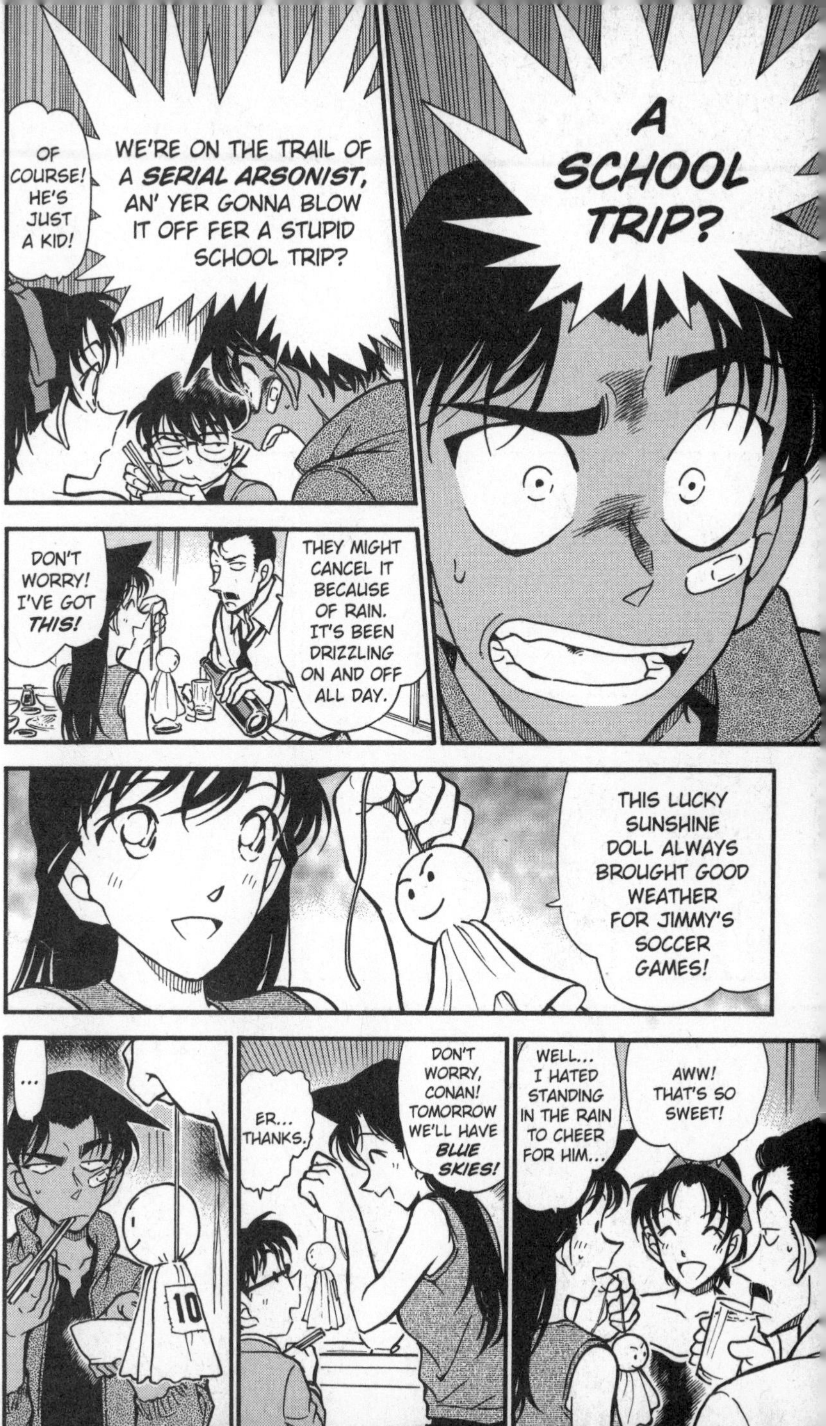
A SCHOOL TRIP?
WE'RE ON THE TRAIL OF A SERIAL ARSONIST, AN' YER GONNA BLOW IT OFF FER A STUPID SCHOOL TRIP?
OF COURSE! HE'S JUST A KID!
THEY MIGHT CANCEL IT BECAUSE OF RAIN. IT'S BEEN DRIZZLING ON AND OFF ALL DAY.
DON'T WORRY! I'VE GOT THIS!
THIS LUCKY SUNSHINE DOLL ALWAYS BROUGHT GOOD WEATHER FOR JIMMY'S SOCCER GAMES!
AWW! THAT'S SO SWEET!
WELL... I HATED STANDING IN THE RAIN TO CHEER FOR HIM...
DON'T WORRY, CONAN! TOMORROW WE'LL HAVE BLUE SKIES!
ER... THANKS.
...
10

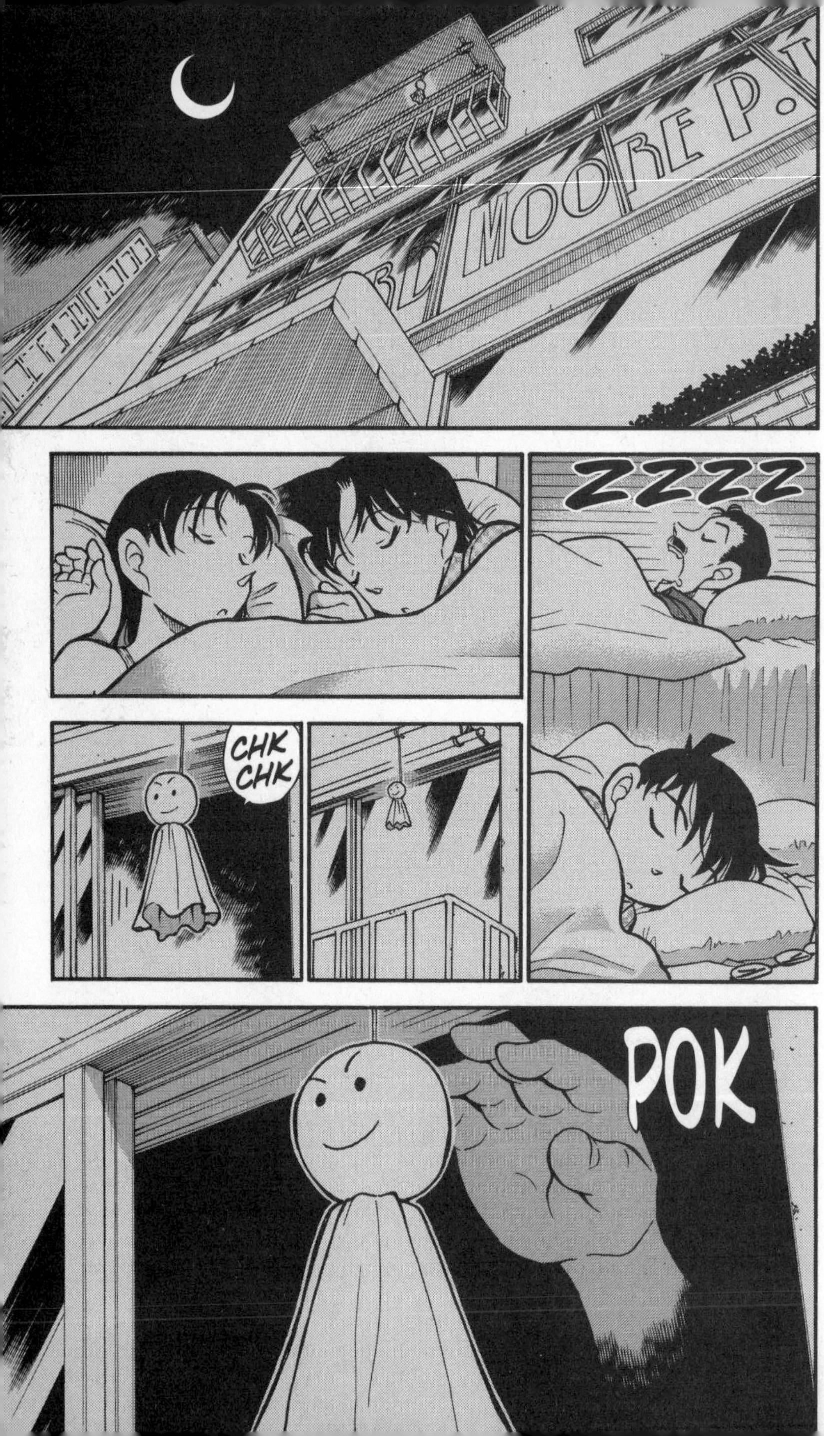

MOORE P.
ZZZZ
CHK CHK
POK

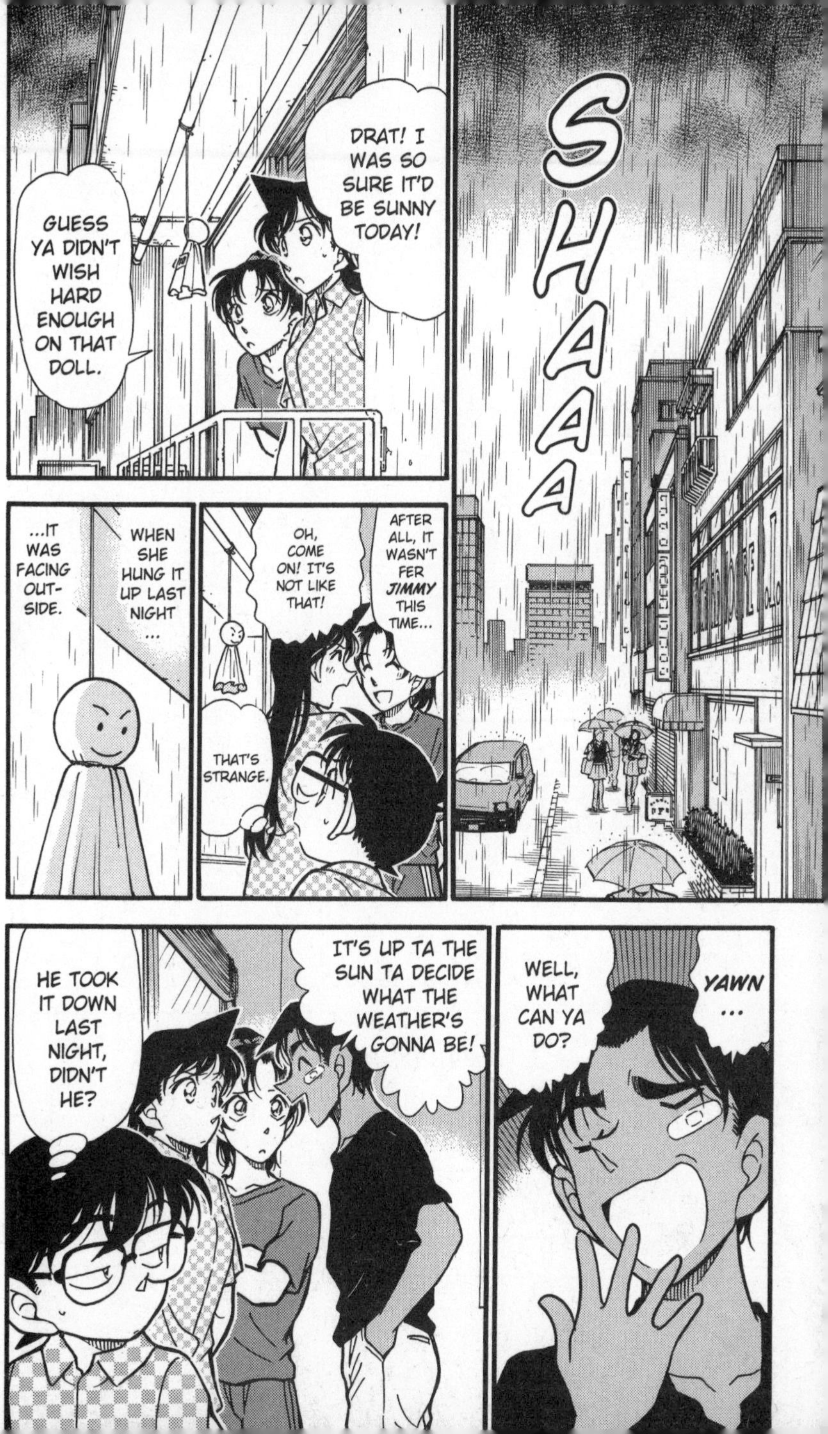
SHAAAA
DRAT! I WAS SO SURE IT'D BE SUNNY TODAY!
GUESS YA DIDN'T WISH HARD ENOUGH ON THAT DOLL.
AFTER ALL, IT WASN'T FER *JIMMY* THIS TIME...
OH, COME ON! IT'S NOT LIKE THAT!
THAT'S STRANGE.
WHEN SHE HUNG IT UP LAST NIGHT...
...IT WAS FACING OUTSIDE.
YAWN...
WELL, WHAT CAN YA DO?
IT'S UP TA THE SUN TA DECIDE WHAT THE WEATHER'S GONNA BE!
HE TOOK IT DOWN LAST NIGHT, DIDN'T HE?

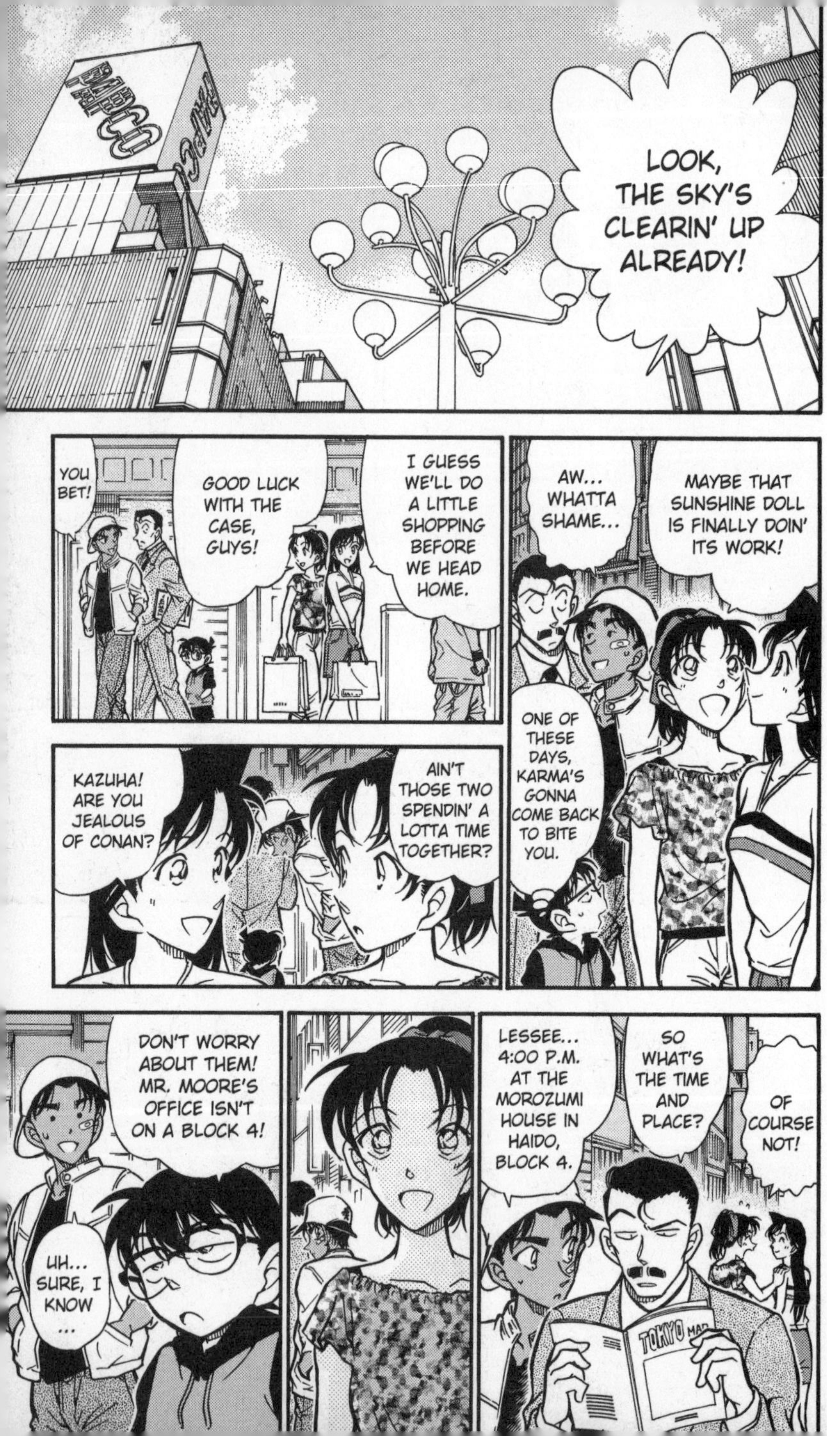
LOOK, THE SKY'S CLEARIN' UP ALREADY!
MAYBE THAT SUNSHINE DOLL IS FINALLY DOIN' ITS WORK!
AW... WHATTA SHAME...
ONE OF THESE DAYS, KARMA'S GONNA COME BACK TO BITE YOU.
I GUESS WE'LL DO A LITTLE SHOPPING BEFORE WE HEAD HOME.
GOOD LUCK WITH THE CASE, GUYS!
YOU BET!
AIN'T THOSE TWO SPENDIN' A LOTTA TIME TOGETHER?
KAZUHA! ARE YOU JEALOUS OF CONAN?
SO WHAT'S THE TIME AND PLACE?
LESSEE... 4:00 P.M. AT THE MOROZUMI HOUSE IN HAIDO, BLOCK 4.
OF COURSE NOT!
TOKYO MAP
DON'T WORRY ABOUT THEM! MR. MOORE'S OFFICE ISN'T ON A BLOCK 4!
UH... SURE, I KNOW ...

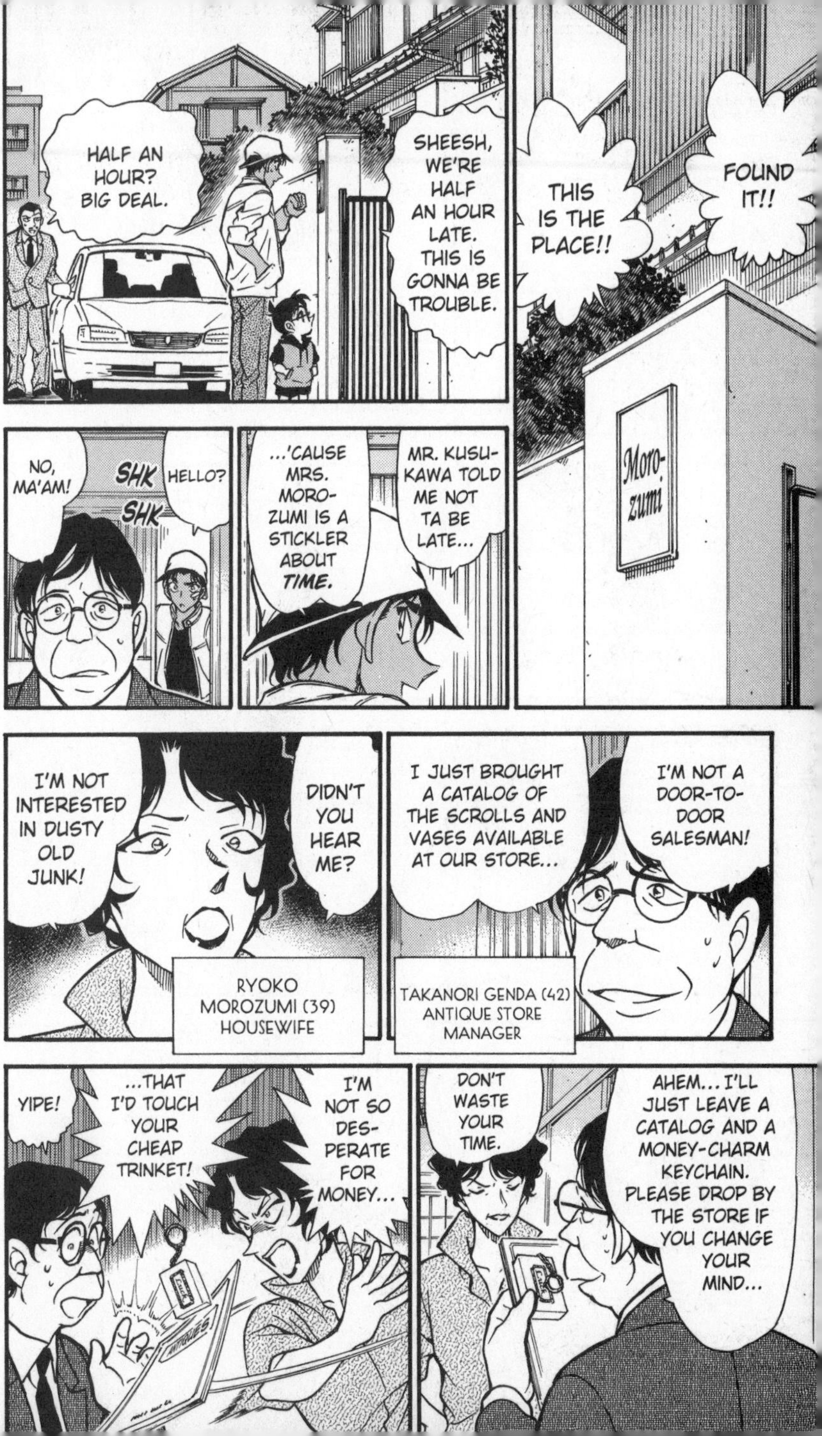
FOUND IT!!
THIS IS THE PLACE!!
Moro-zumi
SHEESH, WE'RE HALF AN HOUR LATE. THIS IS GONNA BE TROUBLE.
HALF AN HOUR? BIG DEAL.
MR. KUSU-KAWA TOLD ME NOT TA BE LATE...
...'CAUSE MRS. MORO-ZUMI IS A STICKLER ABOUT *TIME.*
HELLO?
SHK SHK
NO, MA'AM!
I'M NOT A DOOR-TO-DOOR SALESMAN!
I JUST BROUGHT A CATALOG OF THE SCROLLS AND VASES AVAILABLE AT OUR STORE...
TAKANORI GENDA (42) ANTIQUE STORE MANAGER
DIDN'T YOU HEAR ME?
I'M NOT INTERESTED IN DUSTY OLD JUNK!
RYOKO MOROZUMI (39) HOUSEWIFE
AHEM... I'LL JUST LEAVE A CATALOG AND A MONEY-CHARM KEYCHAIN. PLEASE DROP BY THE STORE IF YOU CHANGE YOUR MIND...
DON'T WASTE YOUR TIME.
I'M NOT SO DES-PERATE FOR MONEY...
...THAT I'D TOUCH YOUR CHEAP TRINKET!
YIPE!
ANTIQUES

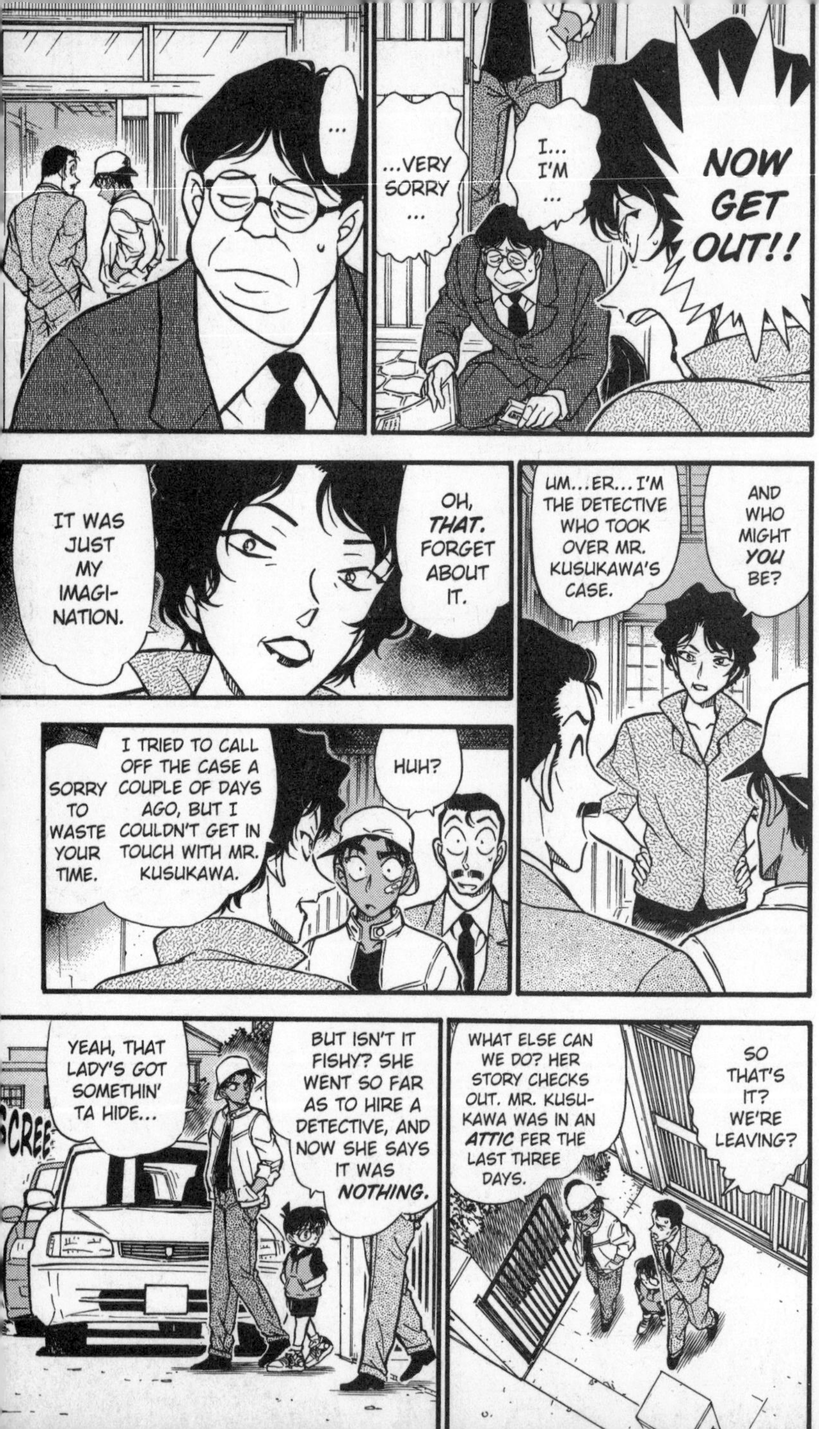
NOW GET OUT!!
I... I'M ...
...VERY SORRY ...
...
AND WHO MIGHT YOU BE?
UM...ER...I'M THE DETECTIVE WHO TOOK OVER MR. KUSUKAWA'S CASE.
OH, THAT. FORGET ABOUT IT.
IT WAS JUST MY IMAGINATION.
HUH?
I TRIED TO CALL OFF THE CASE A COUPLE OF DAYS AGO, BUT I COULDN'T GET IN TOUCH WITH MR. KUSUKAWA.
SORRY TO WASTE YOUR TIME.
SO THAT'S IT? WE'RE LEAVING?
WHAT ELSE CAN WE DO? HER STORY CHECKS OUT. MR. KUSUKAWA WAS IN AN ATTIC FER THE LAST THREE DAYS.
BUT ISN'T IT FISHY? SHE WENT SO FAR AS TO HIRE A DETECTIVE, AND NOW SHE SAYS IT WAS NOTHING.
YEAH, THAT LADY'S GOT SOMETHIN' TA HIDE...
SCREE

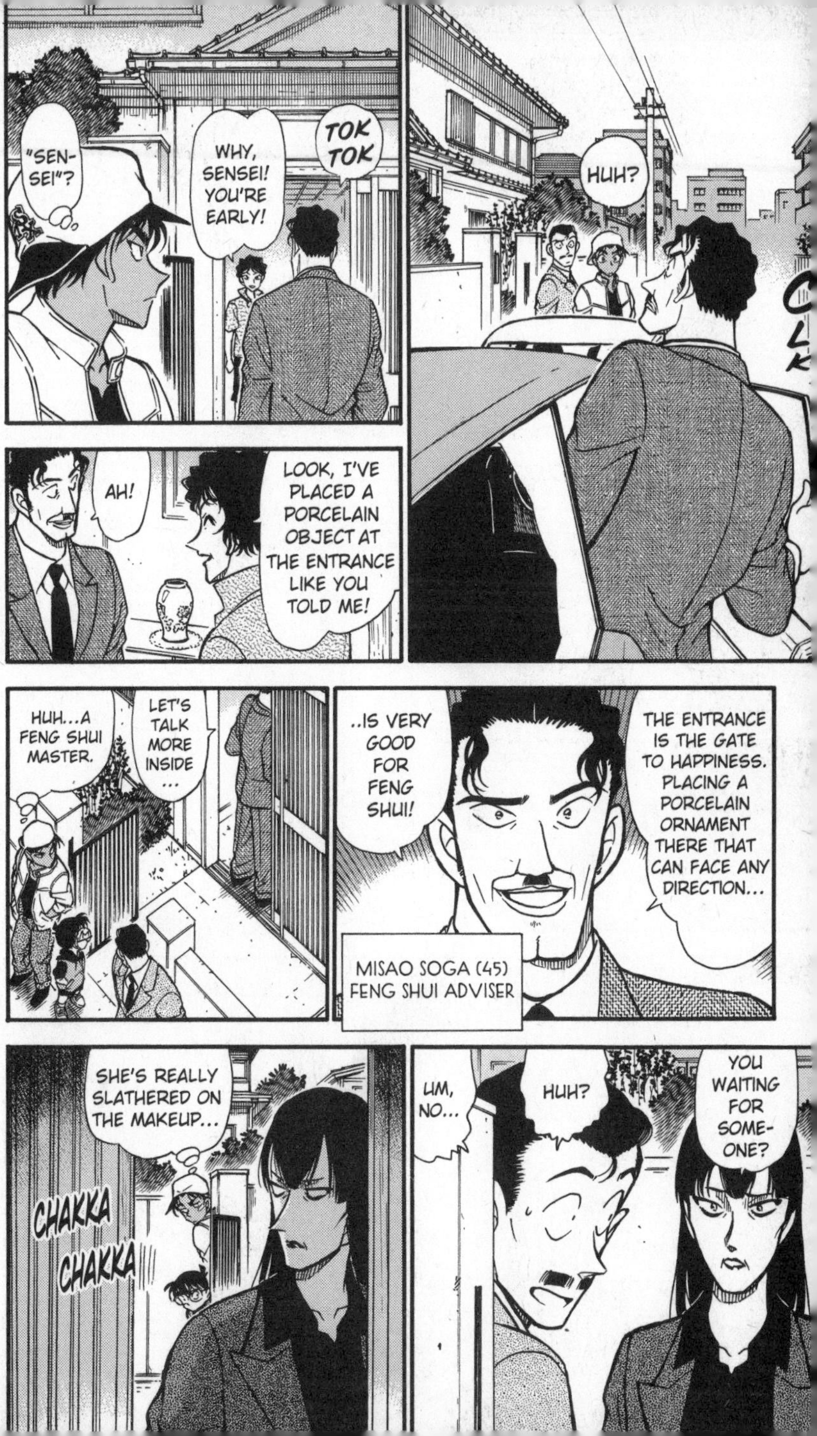
HUH?
CLK
TOK TOK
WHY, SENSEI! YOU'RE EARLY!
"SEN-SEI"?
LOOK, I'VE PLACED A PORCELAIN OBJECT AT THE ENTRANCE LIKE YOU TOLD ME!
AH!
THE ENTRANCE IS THE GATE TO HAPPINESS. PLACING A PORCELAIN ORNAMENT THERE THAT CAN FACE ANY DIRECTION...
..IS VERY GOOD FOR FENG SHUI!
MISAO SOGA (45) FENG SHUI ADVISER
LET'S TALK MORE INSIDE...
HUH...A FENG SHUI MASTER.
YOU WAITING FOR SOMEONE?
HUH?
UM, NO...
SHE'S REALLY SLATHERED ON THE MAKEUP...
CHAKKA CHAKKA

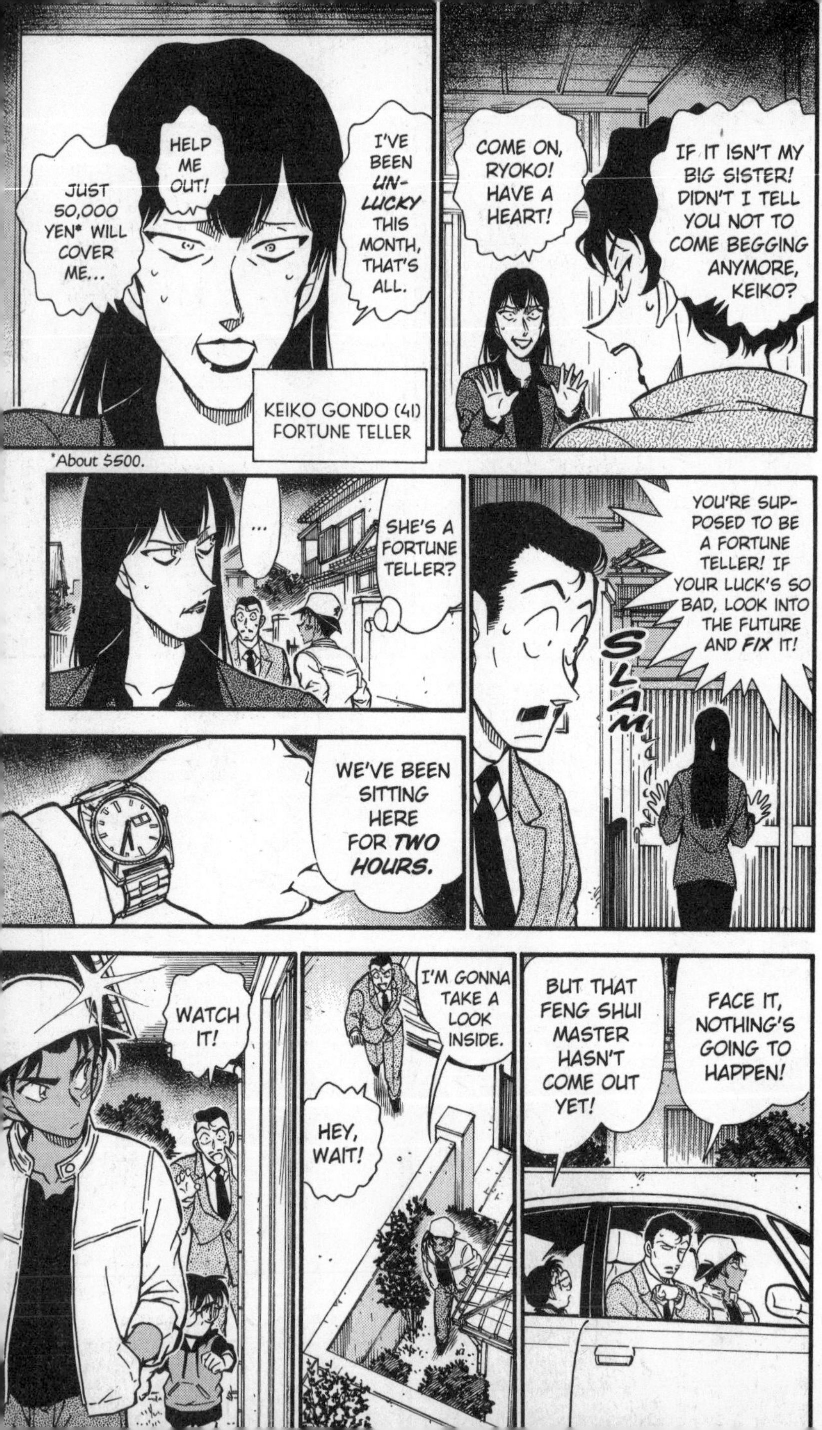
IF IT ISN'T MY BIG SISTER! DIDN'T I TELL YOU NOT TO COME BEGGING ANYMORE, KEIKO?
COME ON, RYOKO! HAVE A HEART!
I'VE BEEN *UN-LUCKY* THIS MONTH, THAT'S ALL.
HELP ME OUT!
JUST 50,000 YEN* WILL COVER ME...
KEIKO GONDO (41) FORTUNE TELLER
*About $500.
YOU'RE SUP-POSED TO BE A FORTUNE TELLER! IF YOUR LUCK'S SO BAD, LOOK INTO THE FUTURE AND *FIX* IT!
SLAM
SHE'S A FORTUNE TELLER?
...
WE'VE BEEN SITTING HERE FOR *TWO HOURS.*
FACE IT, NOTHING'S GOING TO HAPPEN!
BUT THAT FENG SHUI MASTER HASN'T COME OUT YET!
I'M GONNA TAKE A LOOK INSIDE.
HEY, WAIT!
WATCH IT!

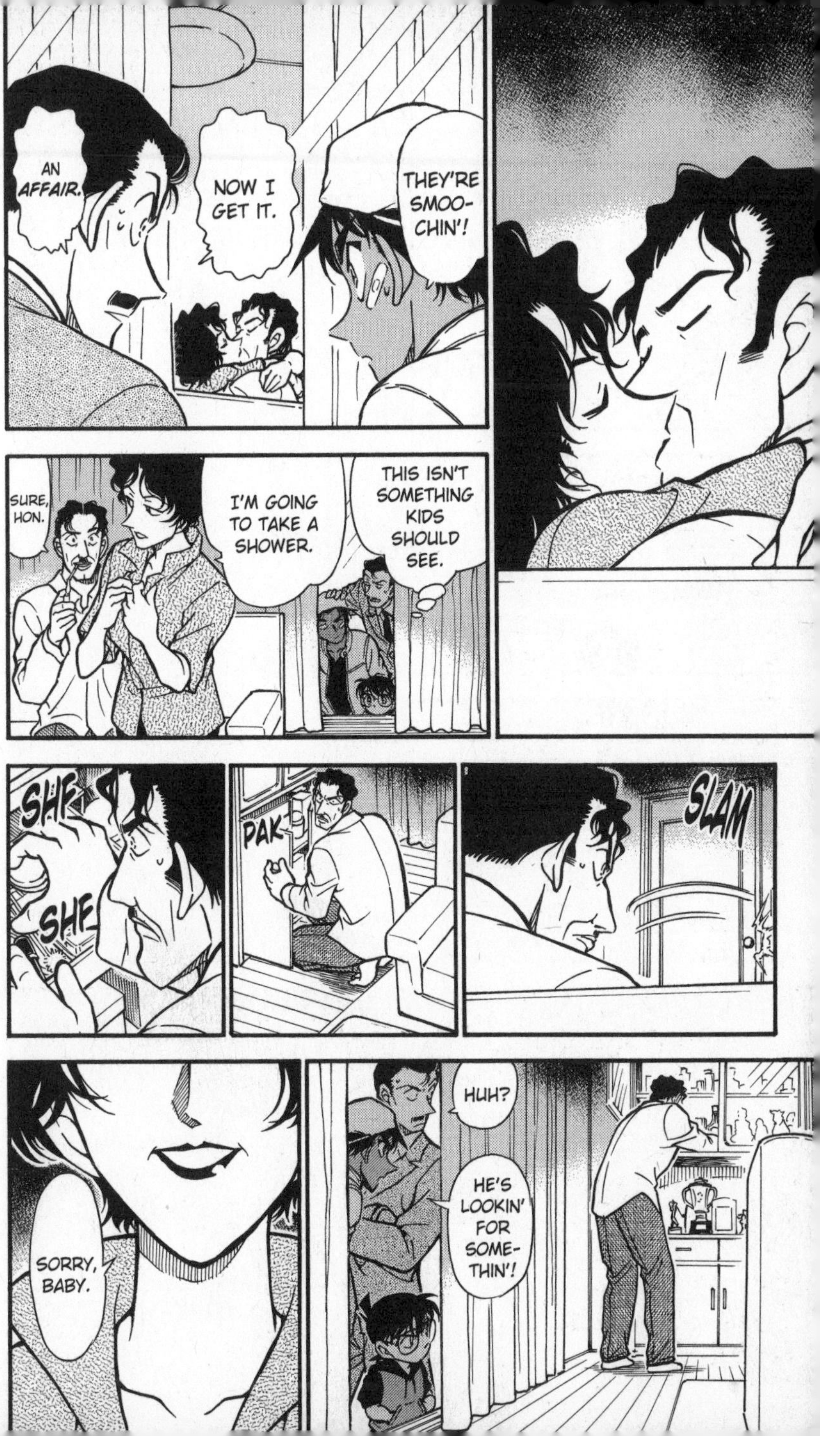
THEY'RE SMOOCHIN'!
NOW I GET IT.
AN AFFAIR.
THIS ISN'T SOMETHING KIDS SHOULD SEE.
I'M GOING TO TAKE A SHOWER.
SURE, HON.
SLAM
PAK
SHF
SHF
HUH?
HE'S LOOKIN' FOR SOMETHIN'!
SORRY, BABY.

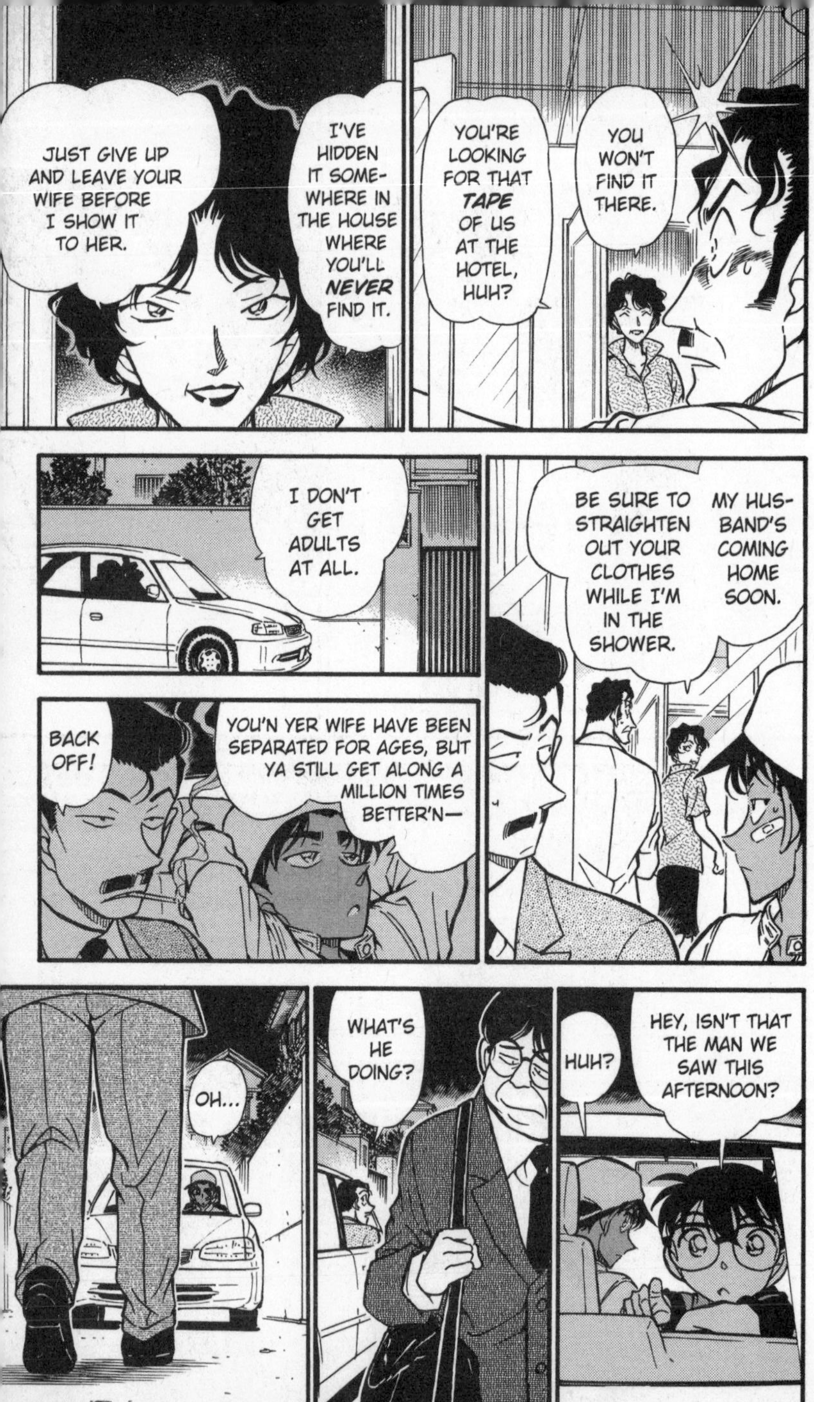
YOU WON'T FIND IT THERE.
YOU'RE LOOKING FOR THAT TAPE OF US AT THE HOTEL, HUH?
I'VE HIDDEN IT SOME-WHERE IN THE HOUSE WHERE YOU'LL NEVER FIND IT.
JUST GIVE UP AND LEAVE YOUR WIFE BEFORE I SHOW IT TO HER.
MY HUS-BAND'S COMING HOME SOON.
BE SURE TO STRAIGHTEN OUT YOUR CLOTHES WHILE I'M IN THE SHOWER.
I DON'T GET ADULTS AT ALL.
YOU'N YER WIFE HAVE BEEN SEPARATED FOR AGES, BUT YA STILL GET ALONG A MILLION TIMES BETTER'N—
BACK OFF!
HEY, ISN'T THAT THE MAN WE SAW THIS AFTERNOON?
HUH?
WHAT'S HE DOING?
OH...

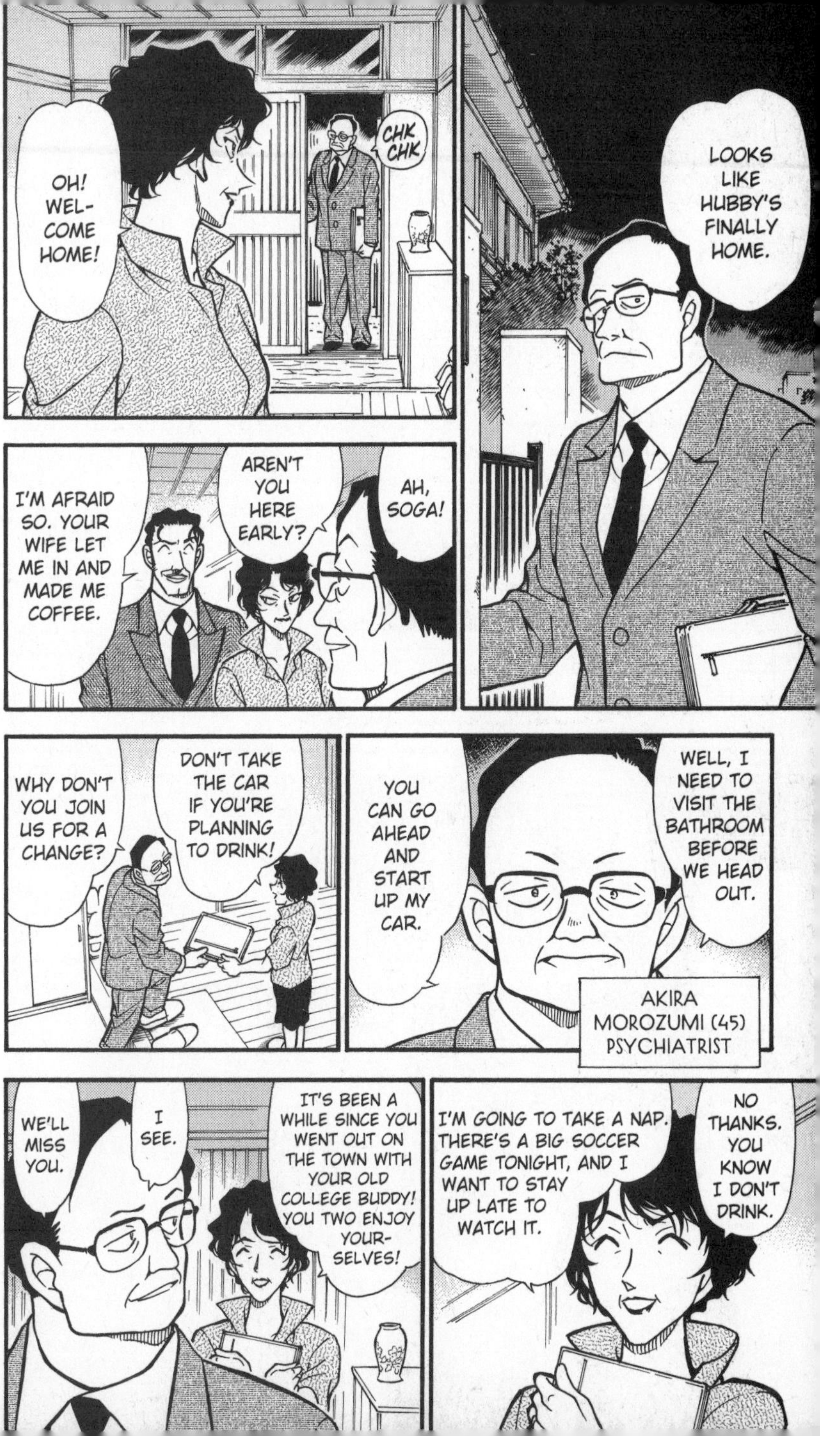
LOOKS LIKE HUBBY'S FINALLY HOME.
CHK CHK
OH! WEL-COME HOME!
AH, SOGA!
AREN'T YOU HERE EARLY?
I'M AFRAID SO. YOUR WIFE LET ME IN AND MADE ME COFFEE.
WELL, I NEED TO VISIT THE BATHROOM BEFORE WE HEAD OUT.
YOU CAN GO AHEAD AND START UP MY CAR.
AKIRA MOROZUMI (45) PSYCHIATRIST
DON'T TAKE THE CAR IF YOU'RE PLANNING TO DRINK!
WHY DON'T YOU JOIN US FOR A CHANGE?
NO THANKS. YOU KNOW I DON'T DRINK.
I'M GOING TO TAKE A NAP. THERE'S A BIG SOCCER GAME TONIGHT, AND I WANT TO STAY UP LATE TO WATCH IT.
IT'S BEEN A WHILE SINCE YOU WENT OUT ON THE TOWN WITH YOUR OLD COLLEGE BUDDY! YOU TWO ENJOY YOUR-SELVES!
I SEE.
WE'LL MISS YOU.

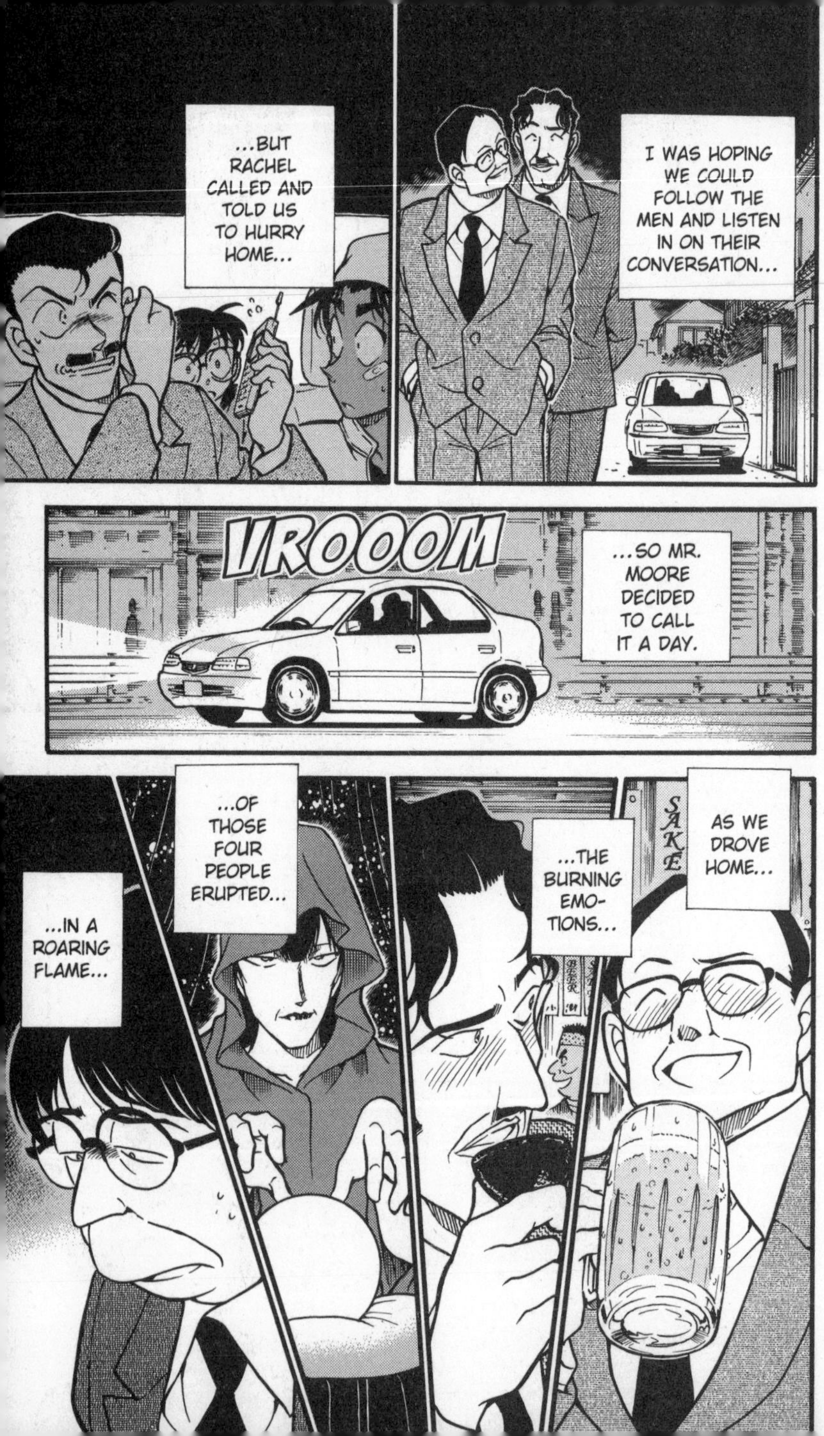
I WAS HOPING WE COULD FOLLOW THE MEN AND LISTEN IN ON THEIR CONVERSATION...
...BUT RACHEL CALLED AND TOLD US TO HURRY HOME...
VROOOM
...SO MR. MOORE DECIDED TO CALL IT A DAY.
AS WE DROVE HOME...
SAKÉ
...THE BURNING EMO-TIONS...
...OF THOSE FOUR PEOPLE ERUPTED...
...IN A ROARING FLAME...

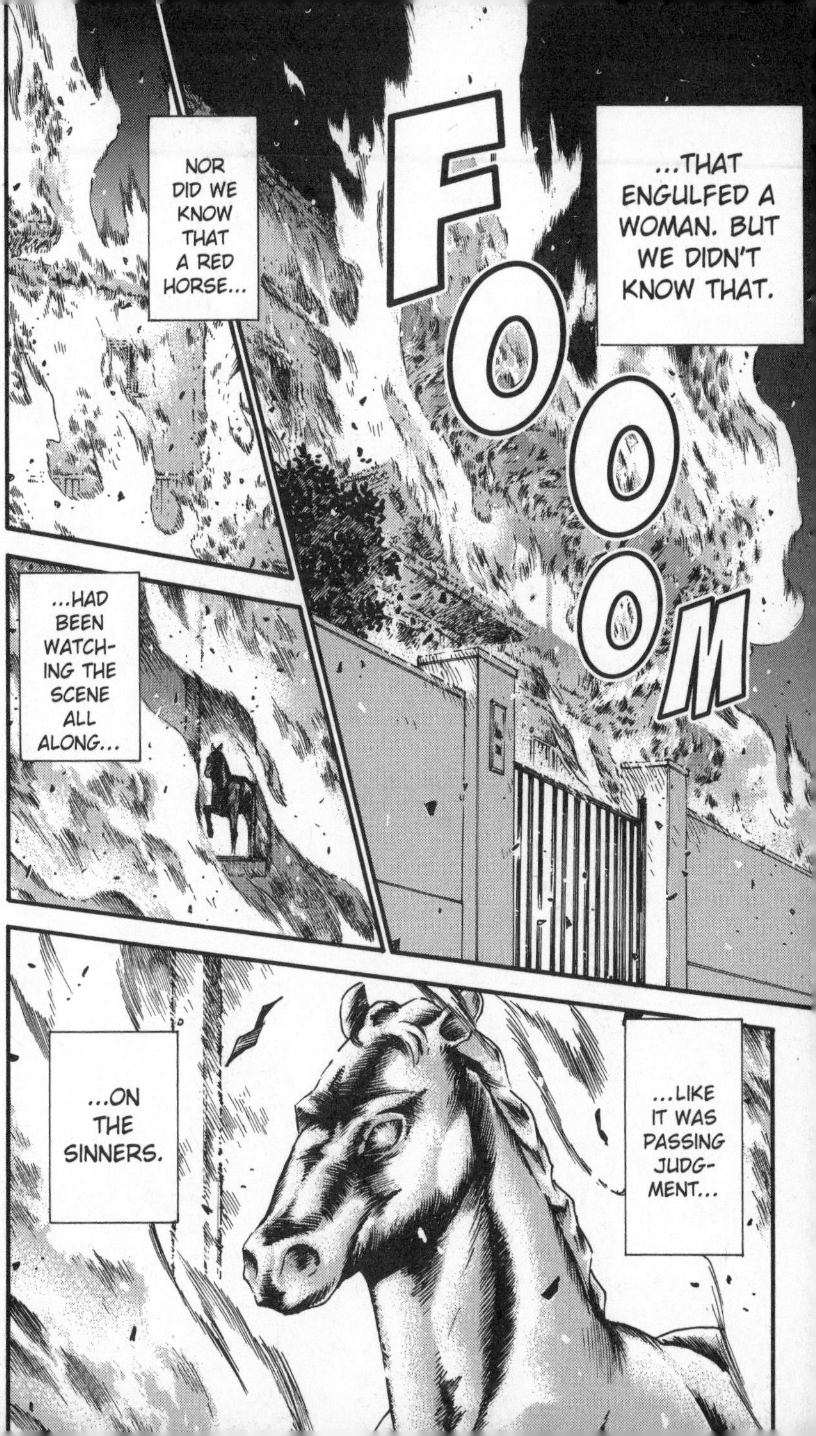
...THAT ENGULFED A WOMAN. BUT WE DIDN'T KNOW THAT.
FOOOM
NOR DID WE KNOW THAT A RED HORSE...
...HAD BEEN WATCHING THE SCENE ALL ALONG...
...LIKE IT WAS PASSING JUDGMENT...
...ON THE SINNERS.

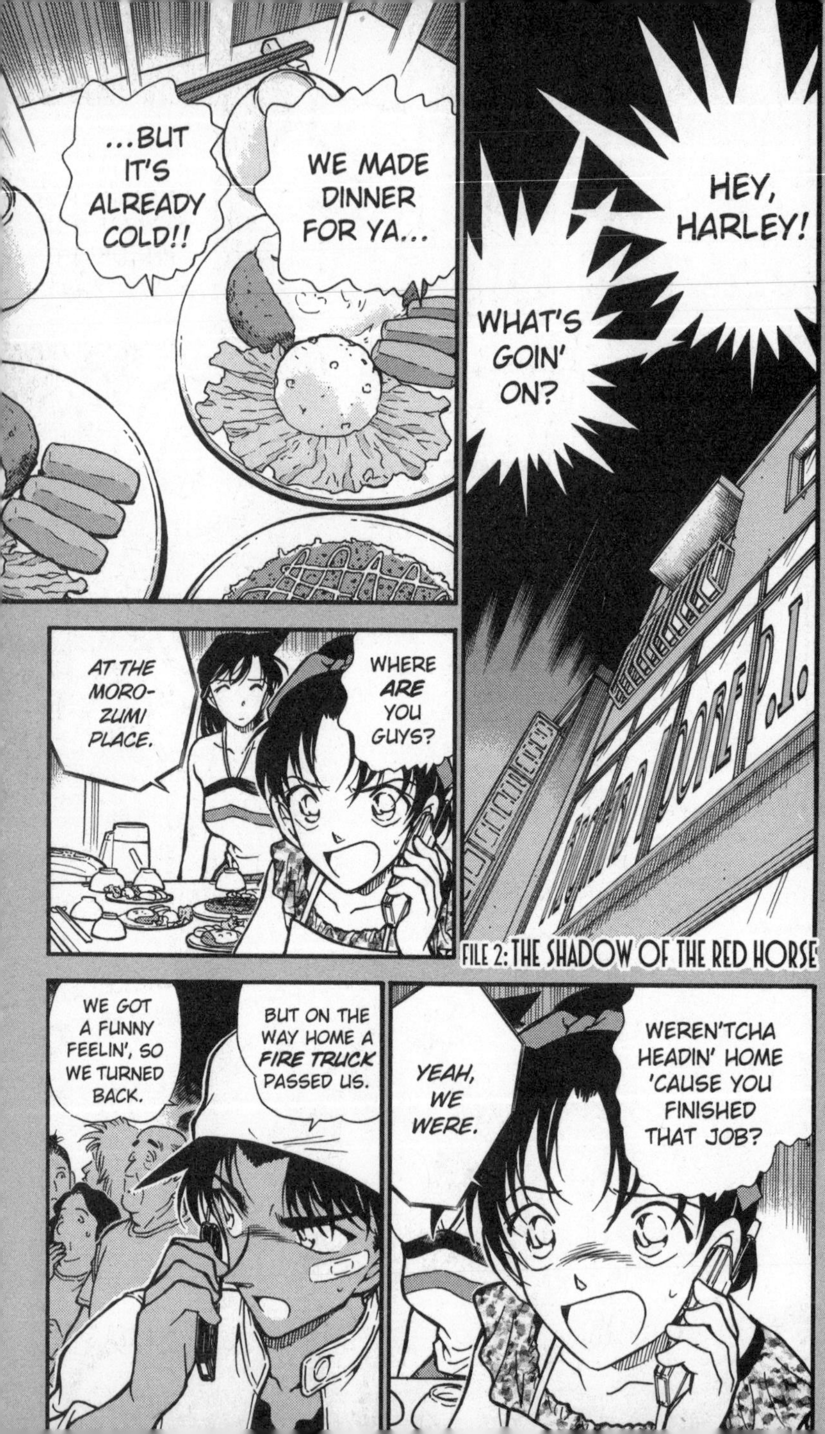
HEY, HARLEY!
WHAT'S GOIN' ON?
WE MADE DINNER FOR YA...
...BUT IT'S ALREADY COLD!!
WHERE *ARE* YOU GUYS?
AT THE MORO-ZUMI PLACE.
FILE 2: THE SHADOW OF THE RED HORSE
WEREN'TCHA HEADIN' HOME 'CAUSE YOU FINISHED THAT JOB?
YEAH, WE WERE.
BUT ON THE WAY HOME A *FIRE TRUCK* PASSED US.
WE GOT A FUNNY FEELIN', SO WE TURNED BACK.

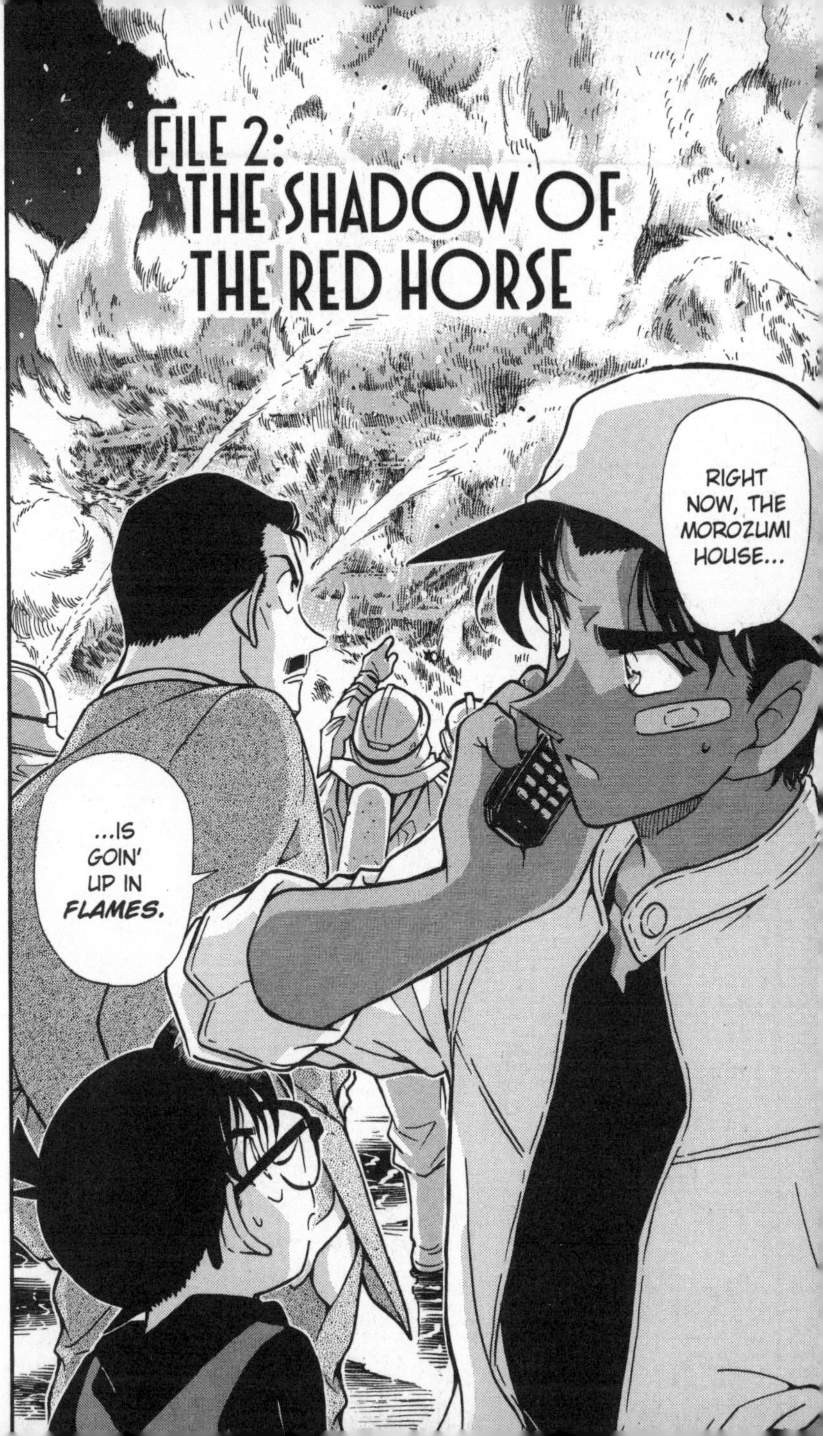
FILE 2:
THE SHADOW OF THE RED HORSE
RIGHT NOW, THE MOROZUMI HOUSE...
...IS GOIN' UP IN FLAMES.

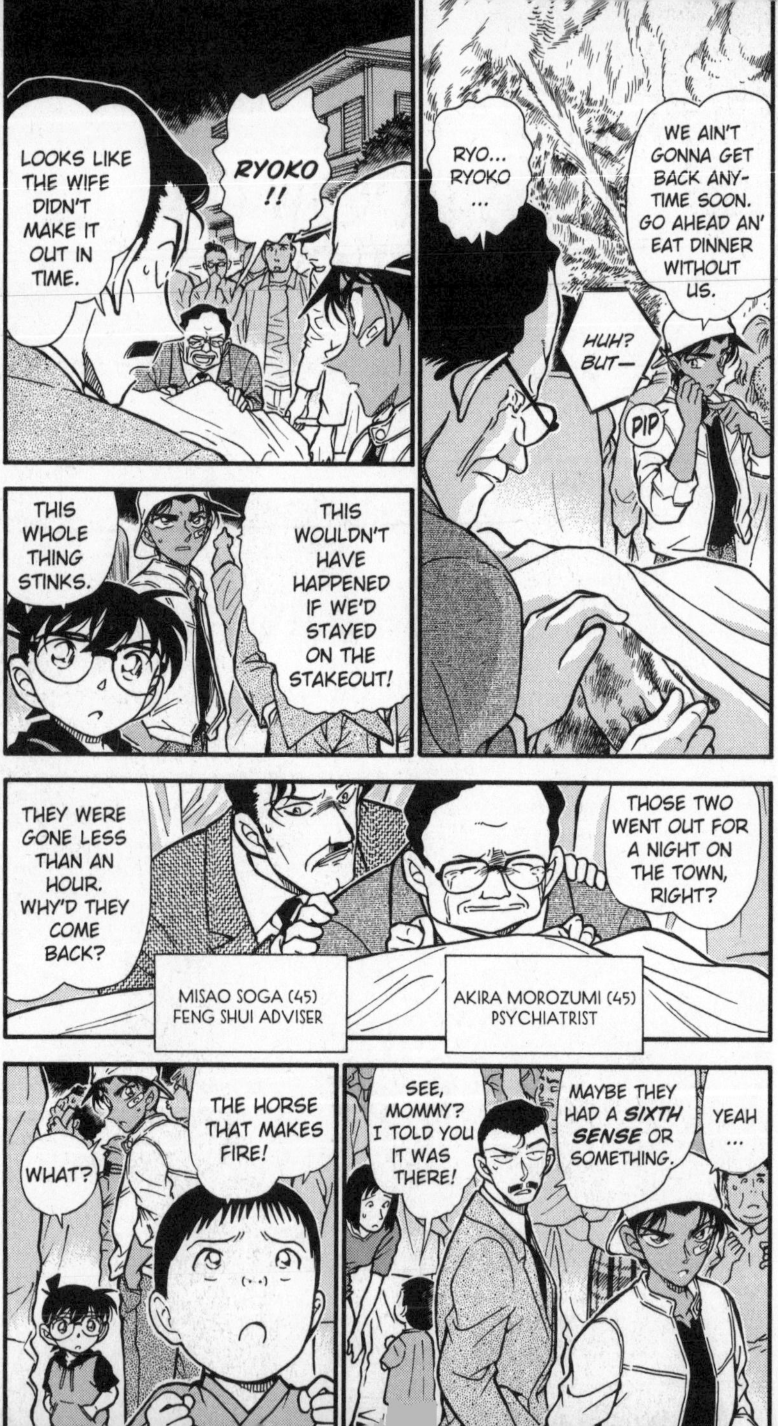
WE AIN'T GONNA GET BACK ANY-TIME SOON. GO AHEAD AN' EAT DINNER WITHOUT US.
RYO... RYOKO ...
HUH? BUT—
PIP
RYOKO !!
LOOKS LIKE THE WIFE DIDN'T MAKE IT OUT IN TIME.
THIS WOULDN'T HAVE HAPPENED IF WE'D STAYED ON THE STAKEOUT!
THIS WHOLE THING STINKS.
THOSE TWO WENT OUT FOR A NIGHT ON THE TOWN, RIGHT?
THEY WERE GONE LESS THAN AN HOUR. WHY'D THEY COME BACK?
AKIRA MOROZUMI (45) PSYCHIATRIST
MISAO SOGA (45) FENG SHUI ADVISER
YEAH ...
MAYBE THEY HAD A *SIXTH SENSE* OR SOMETHING.
SEE, MOMMY? I TOLD YOU IT WAS THERE!
THE HORSE THAT MAKES FIRE!
WHAT?

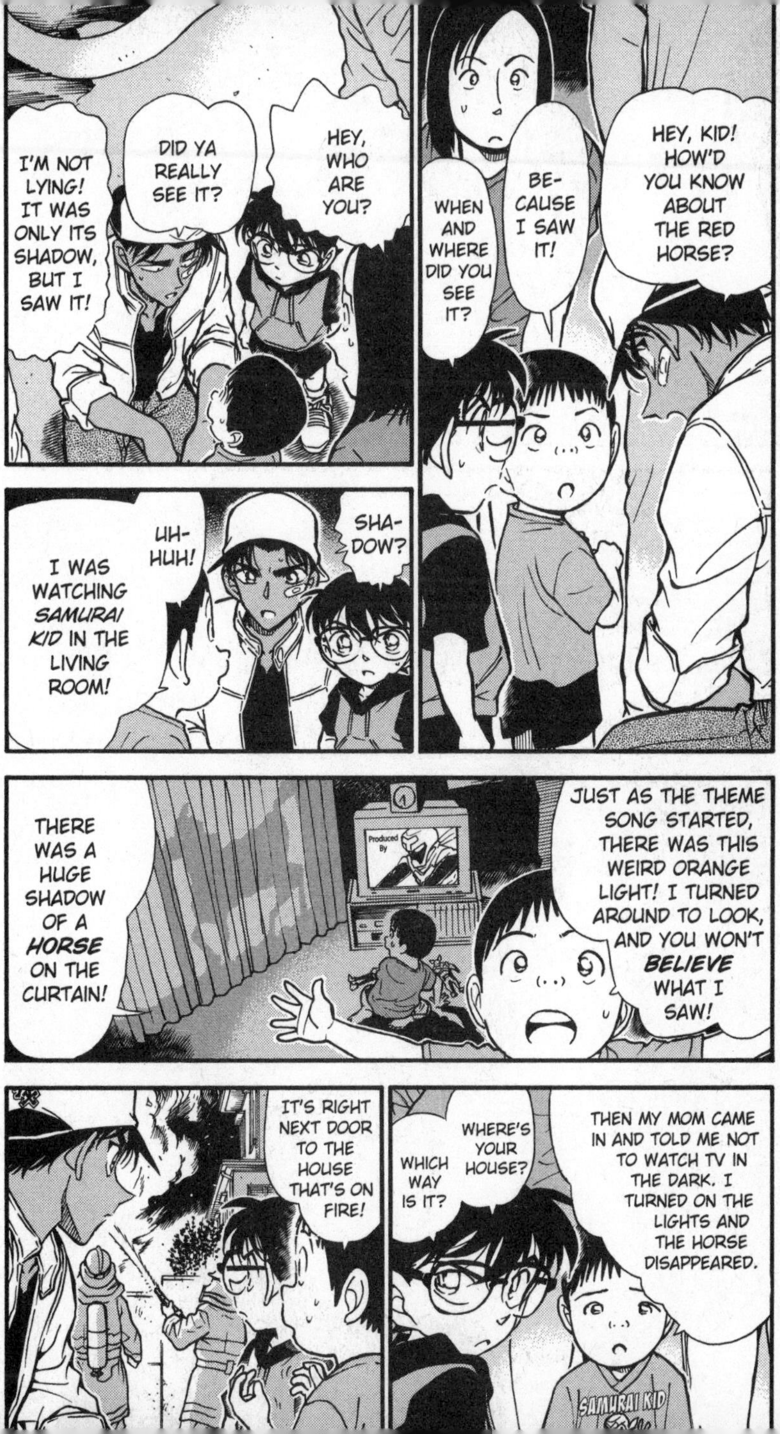
HEY, KID! HOW'D YOU KNOW ABOUT THE RED HORSE?
BE-CAUSE I SAW IT!
WHEN AND WHERE DID YOU SEE IT?
HEY, WHO ARE YOU?
DID YA REALLY SEE IT?
I'M NOT LYING! IT WAS ONLY ITS SHADOW, BUT I SAW IT!
SHA-DOW?
UH-HUH!
I WAS WATCHING *SAMURAI KID* IN THE LIVING ROOM!
JUST AS THE THEME SONG STARTED, THERE WAS THIS WEIRD ORANGE LIGHT! I TURNED AROUND TO LOOK, AND YOU WON'T **BELIEVE** WHAT I SAW!
Produced By
THERE WAS A HUGE SHADOW OF A **HORSE** ON THE CURTAIN!
THEN MY MOM CAME IN AND TOLD ME NOT TO WATCH TV IN THE DARK. I TURNED ON THE LIGHTS AND THE HORSE DISAPPEARED.
WHERE'S YOUR HOUSE?
WHICH WAY IS IT?
SAMURAI KID
IT'S RIGHT NEXT DOOR TO THE HOUSE THAT'S ON FIRE!

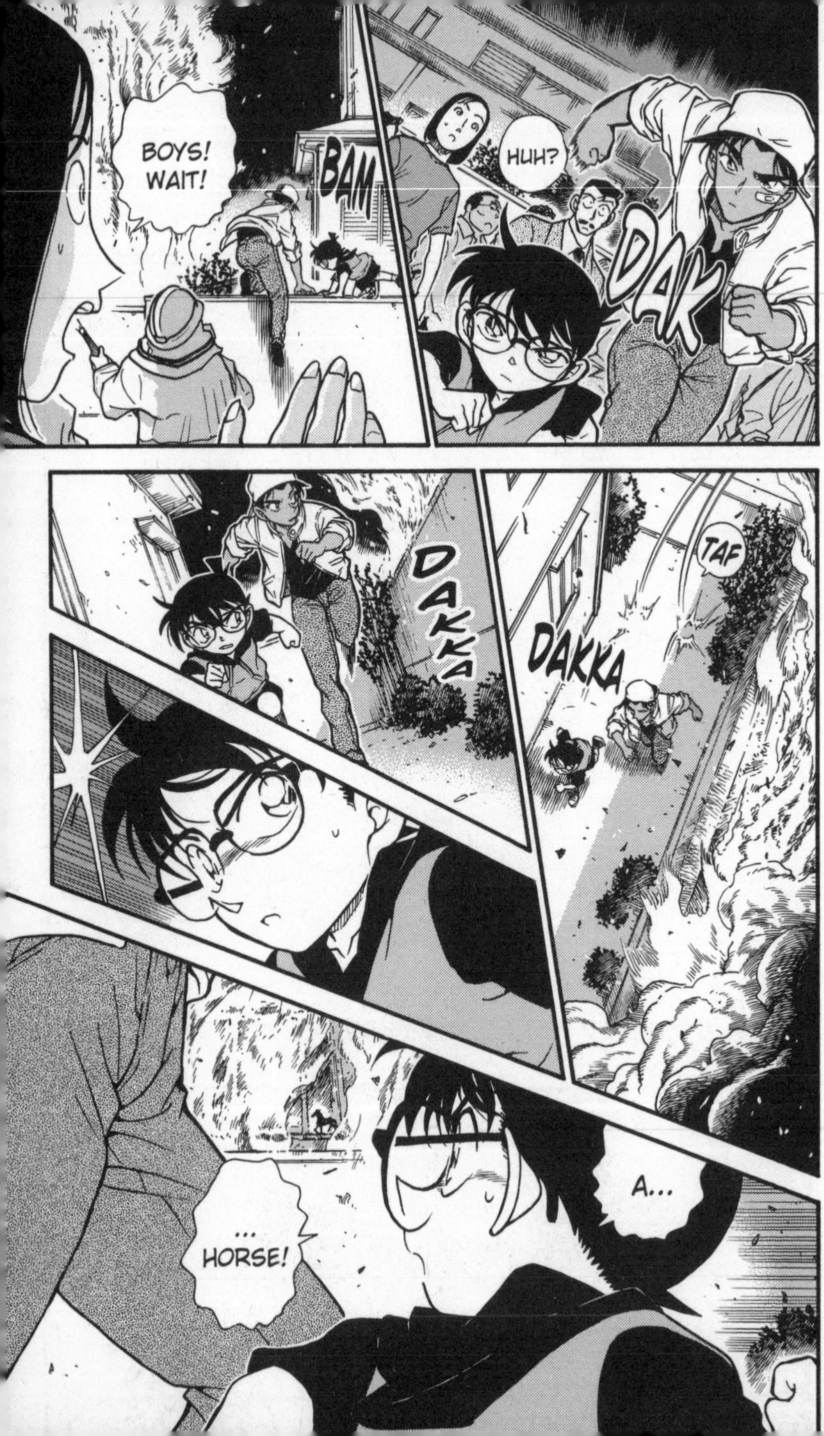
HUH?
DAK
BOYS! WAIT!
BAM
TAF
DAKKA
DAKKA
A...
... HORSE!

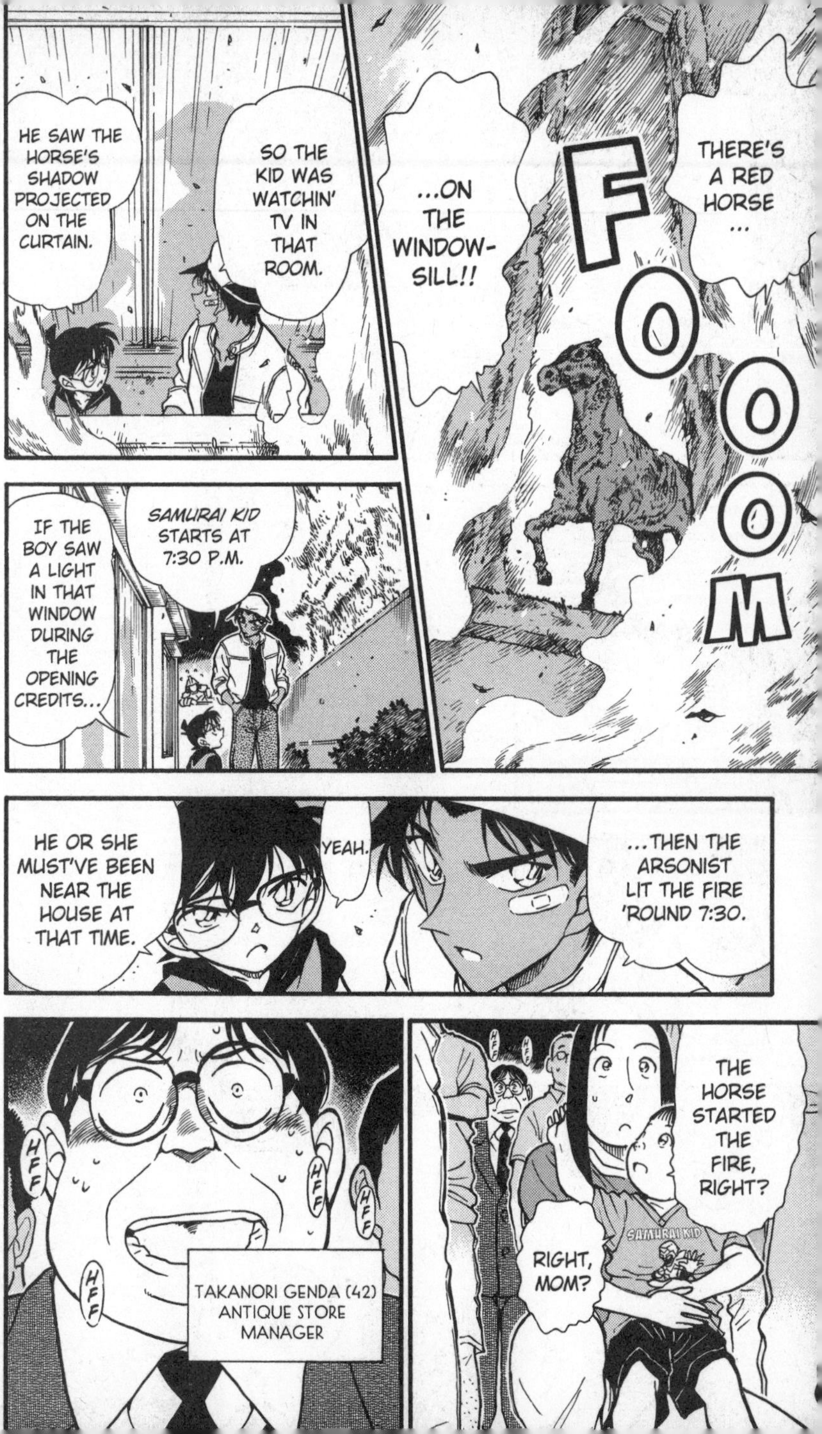
THERE'S A RED HORSE ...
FOOOOM
...ON THE WINDOW-SILL!!
SO THE KID WAS WATCHIN' TV IN THAT ROOM.
HE SAW THE HORSE'S SHADOW PROJECTED ON THE CURTAIN.
SAMURAI KID STARTS AT 7:30 P.M.
IF THE BOY SAW A LIGHT IN THAT WINDOW DURING THE OPENING CREDITS...
...THEN THE ARSONIST LIT THE FIRE 'ROUND 7:30.
YEAH.
HE OR SHE MUST'VE BEEN NEAR THE HOUSE AT THAT TIME.
THE HORSE STARTED THE FIRE, RIGHT?
RIGHT, MOM?
HFF
HFF
SAMURAI KID
HFF HFF HFF
TAKANORI GENDA (42) ANTIQUE STORE MANAGER

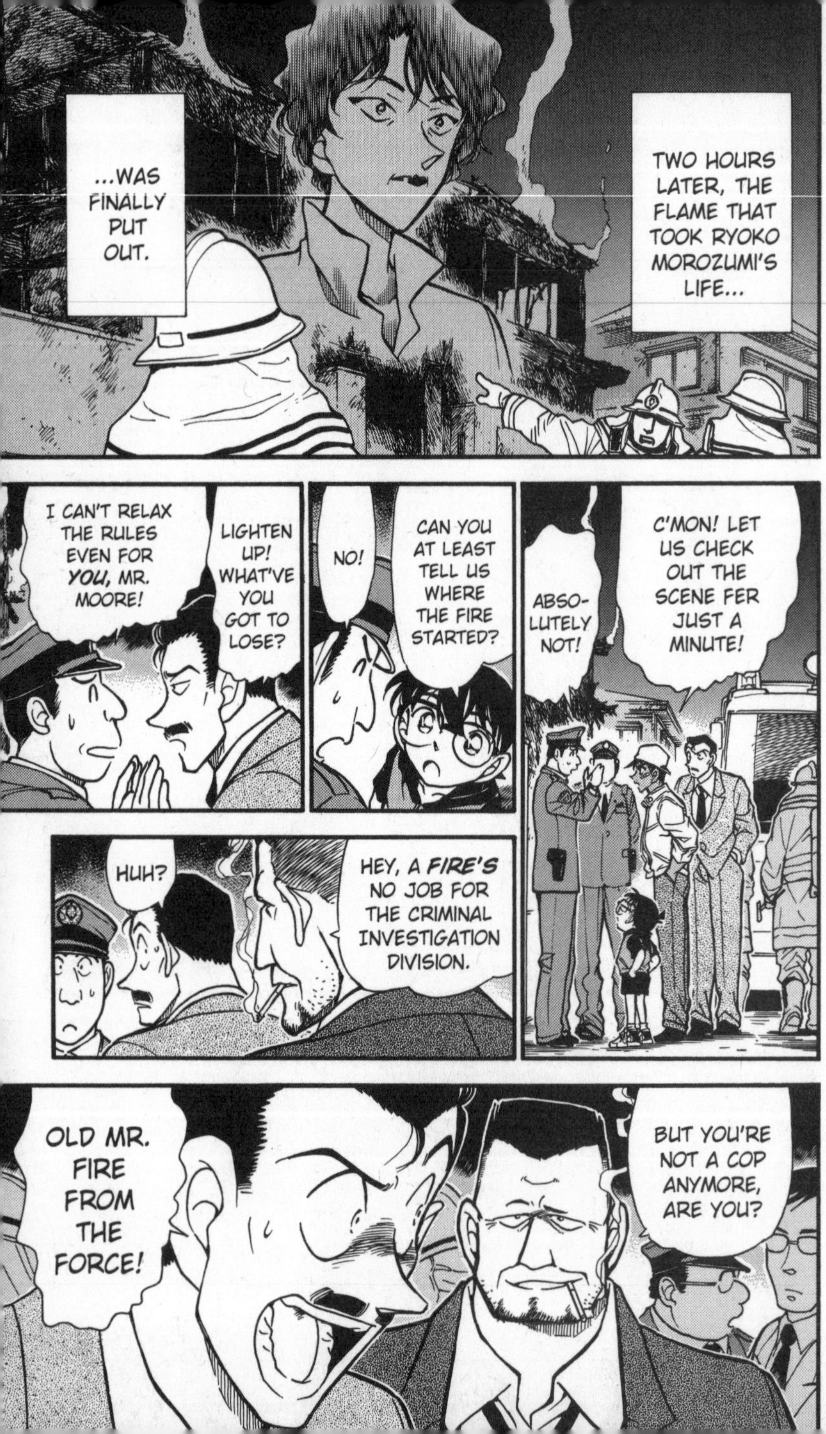
TWO HOURS LATER, THE FLAME THAT TOOK RYOKO MOROZUMI'S LIFE...
...WAS FINALLY PUT OUT.
C'MON! LET US CHECK OUT THE SCENE FER JUST A MINUTE!
ABSO-LUTELY NOT!
CAN YOU AT LEAST TELL US WHERE THE FIRE STARTED?
NO!
LIGHTEN UP! WHAT'VE YOU GOT TO LOSE?
I CAN'T RELAX THE RULES EVEN FOR *YOU*, MR. MOORE!
HEY, A *FIRE'S* NO JOB FOR THE CRIMINAL INVESTIGATION DIVISION.
HUH?
BUT YOU'RE NOT A COP ANYMORE, ARE YOU?
OLD MR. FIRE FROM THE FORCE!

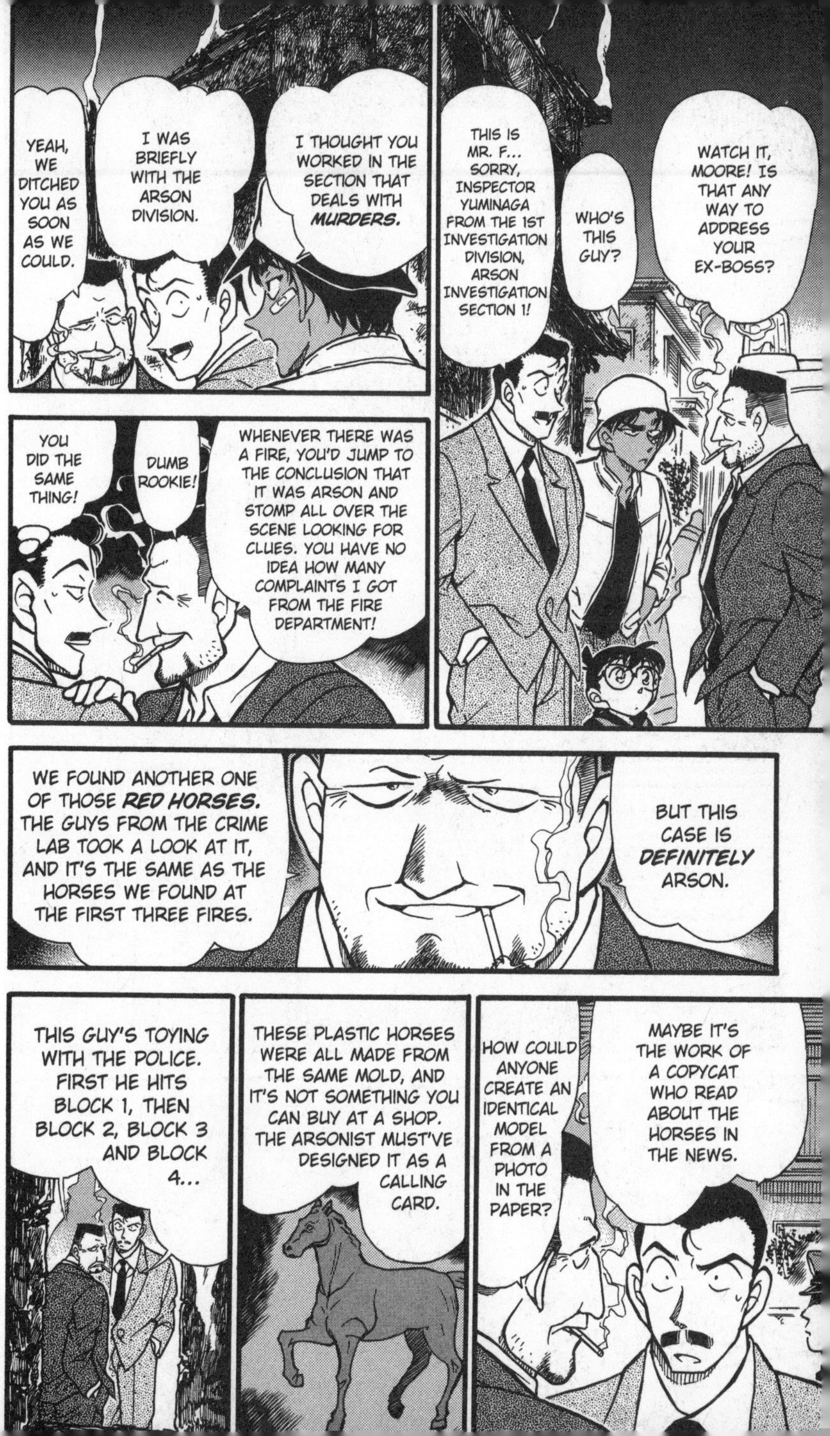
WATCH IT, MOORE! IS THAT ANY WAY TO ADDRESS YOUR EX-BOSS?
WHO'S THIS GUY?
THIS IS MR. F... SORRY, INSPECTOR YUMINAGA FROM THE 1ST INVESTIGATION DIVISION, ARSON INVESTIGATION SECTION 1!
I THOUGHT YOU WORKED IN THE SECTION THAT DEALS WITH *MURDERS.*
I WAS BRIEFLY WITH THE ARSON DIVISION.
YEAH, WE DITCHED YOU AS SOON AS WE COULD.
WHENEVER THERE WAS A FIRE, YOU'D JUMP TO THE CONCLUSION THAT IT WAS ARSON AND STOMP ALL OVER THE SCENE LOOKING FOR CLUES. YOU HAVE NO IDEA HOW MANY COMPLAINTS I GOT FROM THE FIRE DEPARTMENT!
DUMB ROOKIE!
YOU DID THE SAME THING!
BUT THIS CASE IS *DEFINITELY* ARSON.
WE FOUND ANOTHER ONE OF THOSE *RED HORSES.* THE GUYS FROM THE CRIME LAB TOOK A LOOK AT IT, AND IT'S THE SAME AS THE HORSES WE FOUND AT THE FIRST THREE FIRES.
MAYBE IT'S THE WORK OF A COPYCAT WHO READ ABOUT THE HORSES IN THE NEWS.
HOW COULD ANYONE CREATE AN IDENTICAL MODEL FROM A PHOTO IN THE PAPER?
THESE PLASTIC HORSES WERE ALL MADE FROM THE SAME MOLD, AND IT'S NOT SOMETHING YOU CAN BUY AT A SHOP. THE ARSONIST MUST'VE DESIGNED IT AS A CALLING CARD.
THIS GUY'S TOYING WITH THE POLICE. FIRST HE HITS BLOCK 1, THEN BLOCK 2, BLOCK 3 AND BLOCK 4...

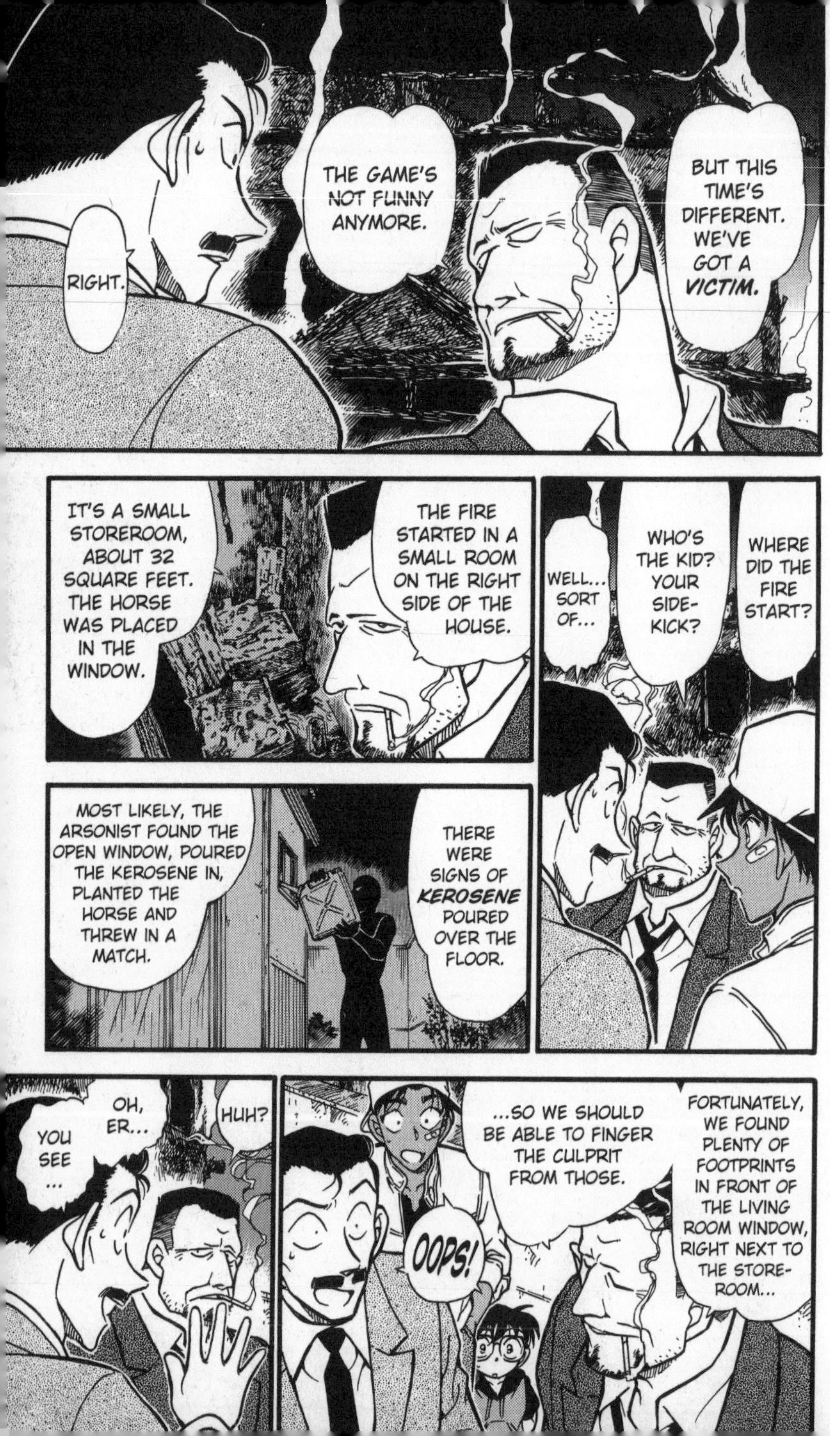
BUT THIS TIME'S DIFFERENT. WE'VE GOT A **VICTIM.**
THE GAME'S NOT FUNNY ANYMORE.
RIGHT.
WHERE DID THE FIRE START?
WHO'S THE KID? YOUR SIDE-KICK?
WELL... SORT OF...
THE FIRE STARTED IN A SMALL ROOM ON THE RIGHT SIDE OF THE HOUSE.
IT'S A SMALL STOREROOM, ABOUT 32 SQUARE FEET. THE HORSE WAS PLACED IN THE WINDOW.
THERE WERE SIGNS OF **KEROSENE** POURED OVER THE FLOOR.
MOST LIKELY, THE ARSONIST FOUND THE OPEN WINDOW, POURED THE KEROSENE IN, PLANTED THE HORSE AND THREW IN A MATCH.
FORTUNATELY, WE FOUND PLENTY OF FOOTPRINTS IN FRONT OF THE LIVING ROOM WINDOW, RIGHT NEXT TO THE STORE-ROOM...
...SO WE SHOULD BE ABLE TO FINGER THE CULPRIT FROM THOSE.
OOPS!
HUH?
OH, ER...
YOU SEE ...

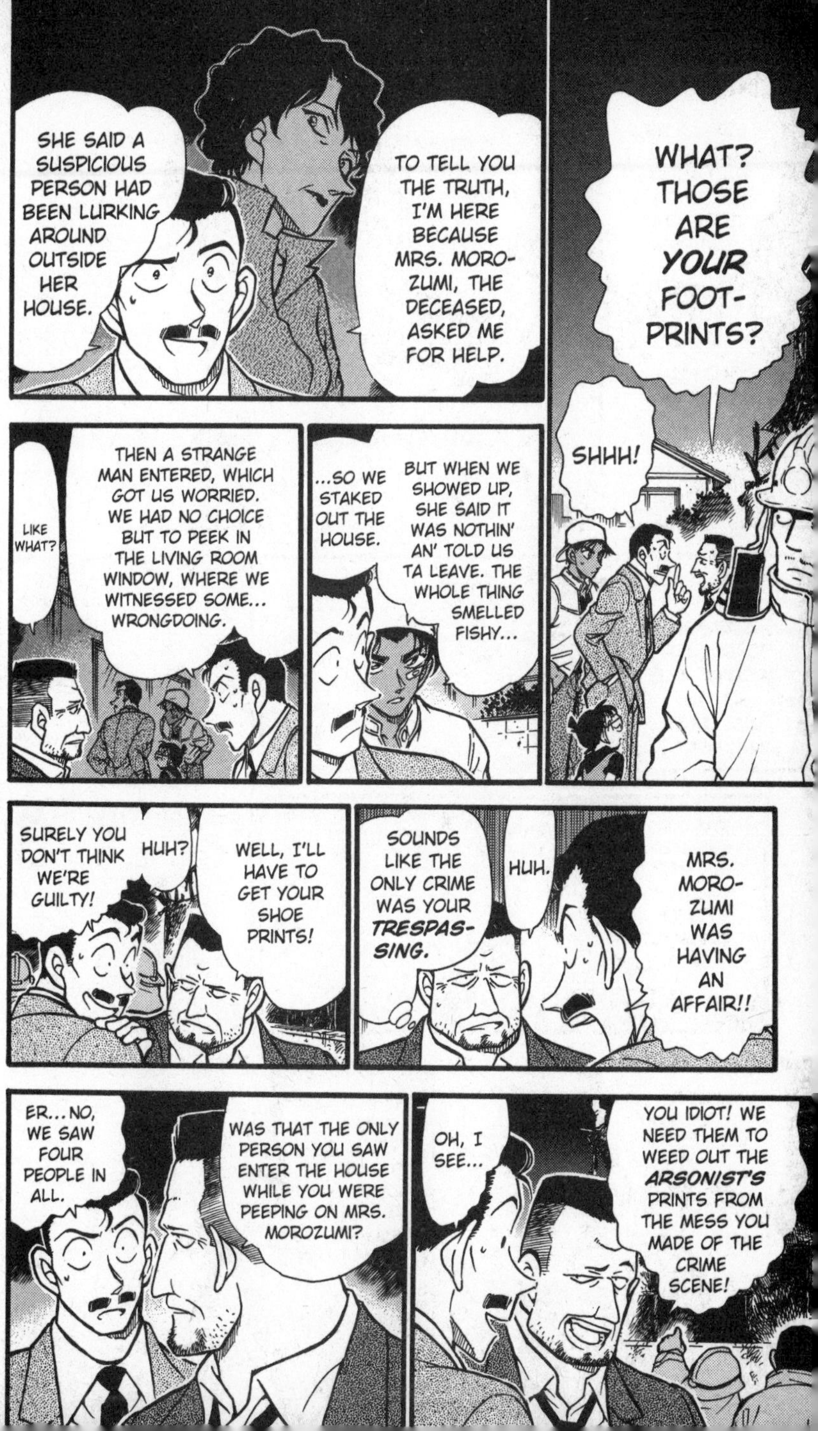
WHAT? THOSE ARE *YOUR* FOOT-PRINTS?
SHHH!
TO TELL YOU THE TRUTH, I'M HERE BECAUSE MRS. MORO-ZUMI, THE DECEASED, ASKED ME FOR HELP.
SHE SAID A SUSPICIOUS PERSON HAD BEEN LURKING AROUND OUTSIDE HER HOUSE.
BUT WHEN WE SHOWED UP, SHE SAID IT WAS NOTHIN' AN' TOLD US TA LEAVE. THE WHOLE THING SMELLED FISHY...
...SO WE STAKED OUT THE HOUSE.
THEN A STRANGE MAN ENTERED, WHICH GOT US WORRIED. WE HAD NO CHOICE BUT TO PEEK IN THE LIVING ROOM WINDOW, WHERE WE WITNESSED SOME... WRONGDOING.
LIKE WHAT?
MRS. MORO-ZUMI WAS HAVING AN AFFAIR!!
HUH.
SOUNDS LIKE THE ONLY CRIME WAS YOUR *TRESPAS-SING.*
WELL, I'LL HAVE TO GET YOUR SHOE PRINTS!
HUH?
SURELY YOU DON'T THINK WE'RE GUILTY!
YOU IDIOT! WE NEED THEM TO WEED OUT THE *ARSONIST'S* PRINTS FROM THE MESS YOU MADE OF THE CRIME SCENE!
OH, I SEE...
WAS THAT THE ONLY PERSON YOU SAW ENTER THE HOUSE WHILE YOU WERE PEEPING ON MRS. MOROZUMI?
ER...NO, WE SAW FOUR PEOPLE IN ALL.

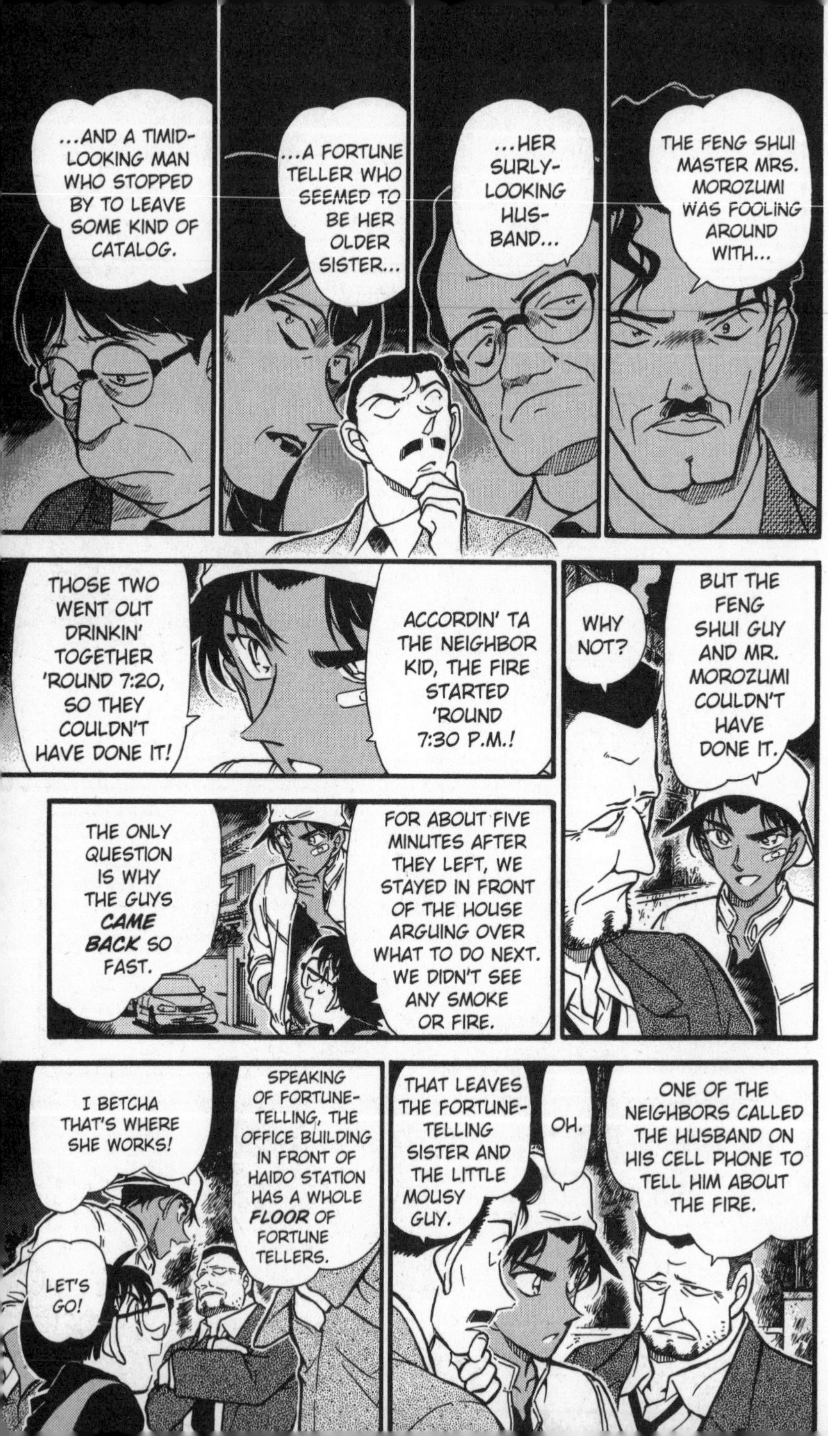
THE FENG SHUI MASTER MRS. MOROZUMI WAS FOOLING AROUND WITH...
...HER SURLY-LOOKING HUSBAND...
...A FORTUNE TELLER WHO SEEMED TO BE HER OLDER SISTER...
...AND A TIMID-LOOKING MAN WHO STOPPED BY TO LEAVE SOME KIND OF CATALOG.
BUT THE FENG SHUI GUY AND MR. MOROZUMI COULDN'T HAVE DONE IT.
WHY NOT?
ACCORDIN' TA THE NEIGHBOR KID, THE FIRE STARTED 'ROUND 7:30 P.M.!
THOSE TWO WENT OUT DRINKIN' TOGETHER 'ROUND 7:20, SO THEY COULDN'T HAVE DONE IT!
FOR ABOUT FIVE MINUTES AFTER THEY LEFT, WE STAYED IN FRONT OF THE HOUSE ARGUING OVER WHAT TO DO NEXT. WE DIDN'T SEE ANY SMOKE OR FIRE.
THE ONLY QUESTION IS WHY THE GUYS *CAME BACK* SO FAST.
ONE OF THE NEIGHBORS CALLED THE HUSBAND ON HIS CELL PHONE TO TELL HIM ABOUT THE FIRE.
OH.
THAT LEAVES THE FORTUNE-TELLING SISTER AND THE LITTLE MOUSY GUY.
SPEAKING OF FORTUNE-TELLING, THE OFFICE BUILDING IN FRONT OF HAIDO STATION HAS A WHOLE *FLOOR* OF FORTUNE TELLERS.
I BETCHA THAT'S WHERE SHE WORKS!
LET'S GO!

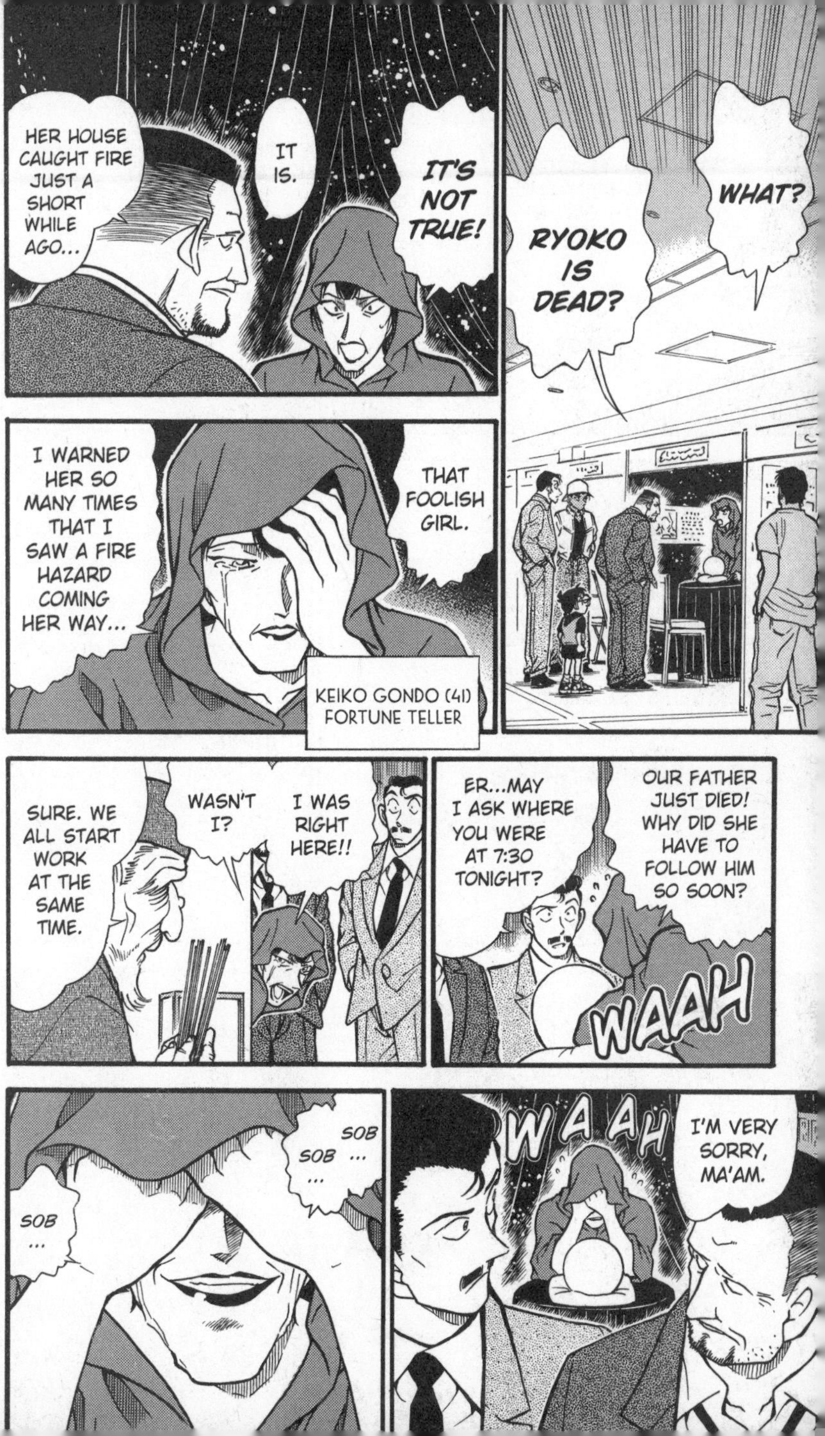
WHAT?
RYOKO IS DEAD?
IT'S NOT TRUE!
IT IS.
HER HOUSE CAUGHT FIRE JUST A SHORT WHILE AGO...
THAT FOOLISH GIRL.
I WARNED HER SO MANY TIMES THAT I SAW A FIRE HAZARD COMING HER WAY...
KEIKO GONDO (41) FORTUNE TELLER
OUR FATHER JUST DIED! WHY DID SHE HAVE TO FOLLOW HIM SO SOON?
ER...MAY I ASK WHERE YOU WERE AT 7:30 TONIGHT?
WAAH
I WAS RIGHT HERE!!
WASN'T I?
SURE. WE ALL START WORK AT THE SAME TIME.
I'M VERY SORRY, MA'AM.
WAAH
SOB SOB ... ...
SOB ...

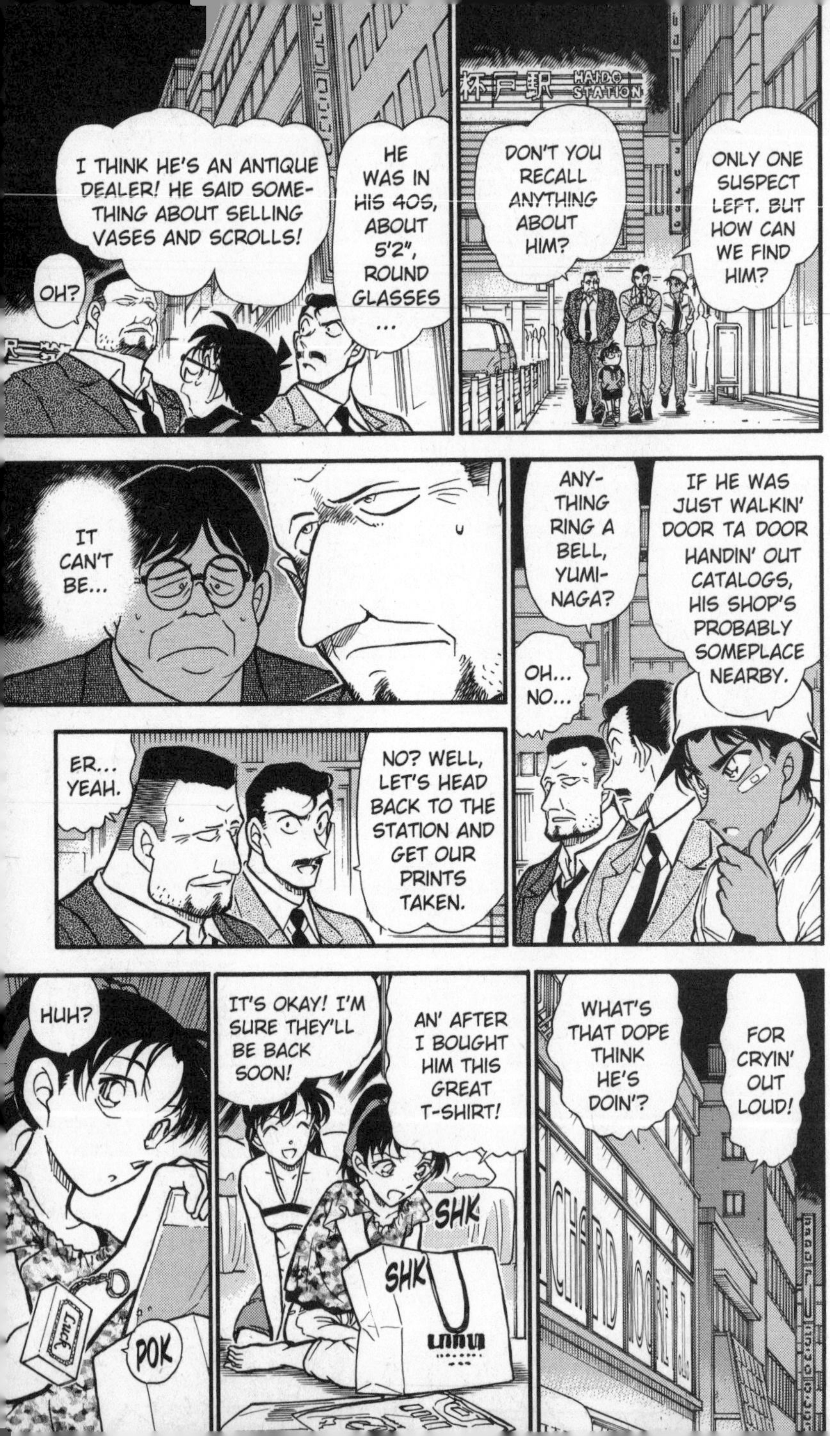
HAIDO STATION
ONLY ONE SUSPECT LEFT. BUT HOW CAN WE FIND HIM?
DON'T YOU RECALL ANYTHING ABOUT HIM?
HE WAS IN HIS 40S, ABOUT 5'2", ROUND GLASSES ...
I THINK HE'S AN ANTIQUE DEALER! HE SAID SOMETHING ABOUT SELLING VASES AND SCROLLS!
OH?
IF HE WAS JUST WALKIN' DOOR TA DOOR HANDIN' OUT CATALOGS, HIS SHOP'S PROBABLY SOMEPLACE NEARBY.
ANYTHING RING A BELL, YUMINAGA?
OH... NO...
IT CAN'T BE...
NO? WELL, LET'S HEAD BACK TO THE STATION AND GET OUR PRINTS TAKEN.
ER... YEAH.
FOR CRYIN' OUT LOUD!
WHAT'S THAT DOPE THINK HE'S DOIN'?
AN' AFTER I BOUGHT HIM THIS GREAT T-SHIRT!
IT'S OKAY! I'M SURE THEY'LL BE BACK SOON!
SHK
SHK
HUH?
POK

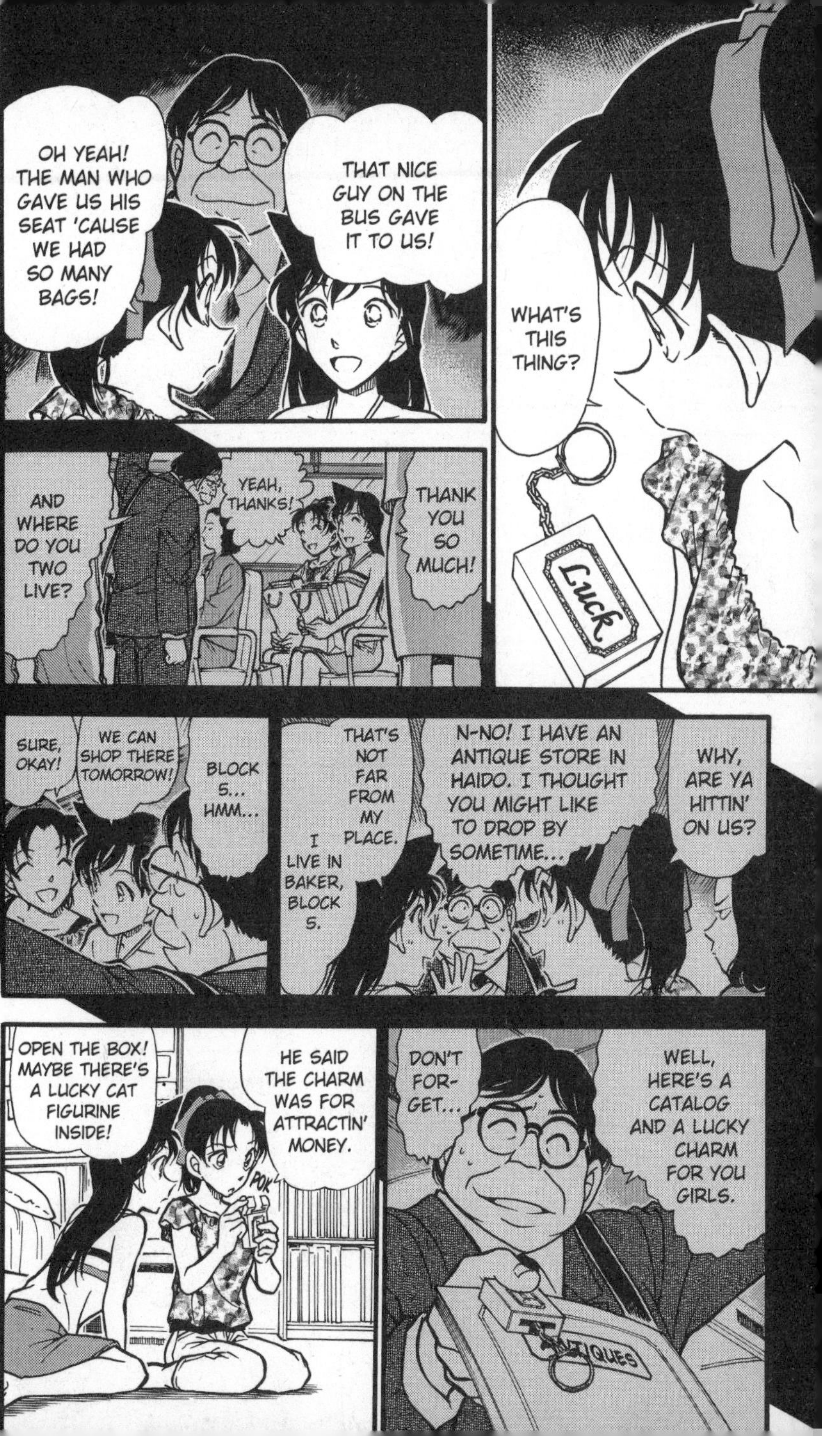

WHAT'S THIS THING?
Luck
THAT NICE GUY ON THE BUS GAVE IT TO US!
OH YEAH! THE MAN WHO GAVE US HIS SEAT 'CAUSE WE HAD SO MANY BAGS!
THANK YOU SO MUCH!
YEAH, THANKS!
AND WHERE DO YOU TWO LIVE?
WHY, ARE YA HITTIN' ON US?
N-NO! I HAVE AN ANTIQUE STORE IN HAIDO. I THOUGHT YOU MIGHT LIKE TO DROP BY SOMETIME...
THAT'S NOT FAR FROM MY PLACE.
I LIVE IN BAKER, BLOCK 5.
BLOCK 5... HMM...
WE CAN SHOP THERE TOMORROW!
SURE, OKAY!
WELL, HERE'S A CATALOG AND A LUCKY CHARM FOR YOU GIRLS.
DON'T FOR-GET...
ANTIQUES
HE SAID THE CHARM WAS FOR ATTRACTIN' MONEY.
POK
OPEN THE BOX! MAYBE THERE'S A LUCKY CAT FIGURINE INSIDE!

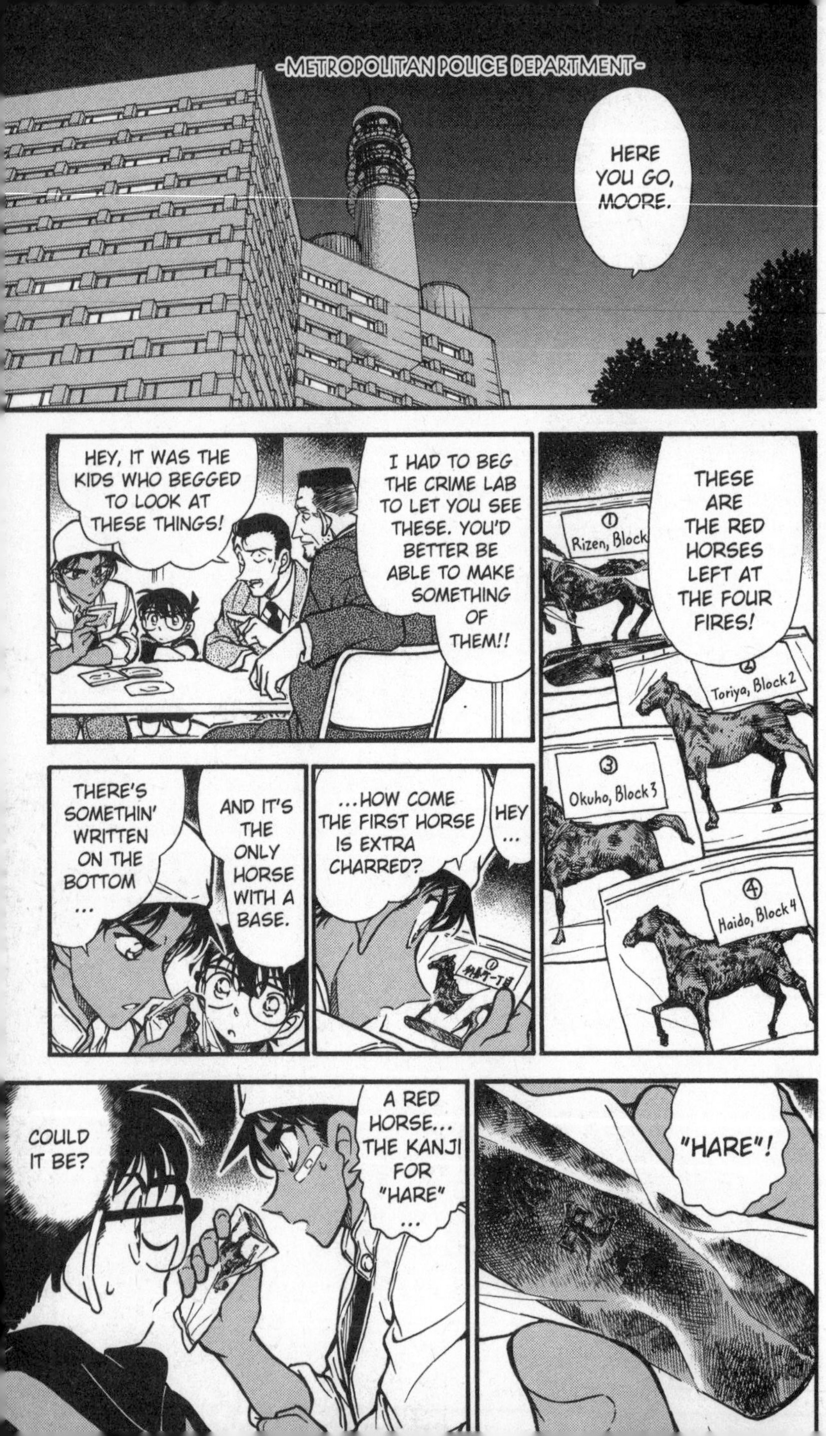
-METROPOLITAN POLICE DEPARTMENT-
HERE YOU GO, MOORE.
THESE ARE THE RED HORSES LEFT AT THE FOUR FIRES!
1 Rizen, Block
2 Toriya, Block 2
3 Okuho, Block 3
4 Haido, Block 4
I HAD TO BEG THE CRIME LAB TO LET YOU SEE THESE. YOU'D BETTER BE ABLE TO MAKE SOMETHING OF THEM!!
HEY, IT WAS THE KIDS WHO BEGGED TO LOOK AT THESE THINGS!
HEY...
...HOW COME THE FIRST HORSE IS EXTRA CHARRED?
AND IT'S THE ONLY HORSE WITH A BASE.
THERE'S SOMETHIN' WRITTEN ON THE BOTTOM...
"HARE"!
A RED HORSE... THE KANJI FOR "HARE"...
COULD IT BE?

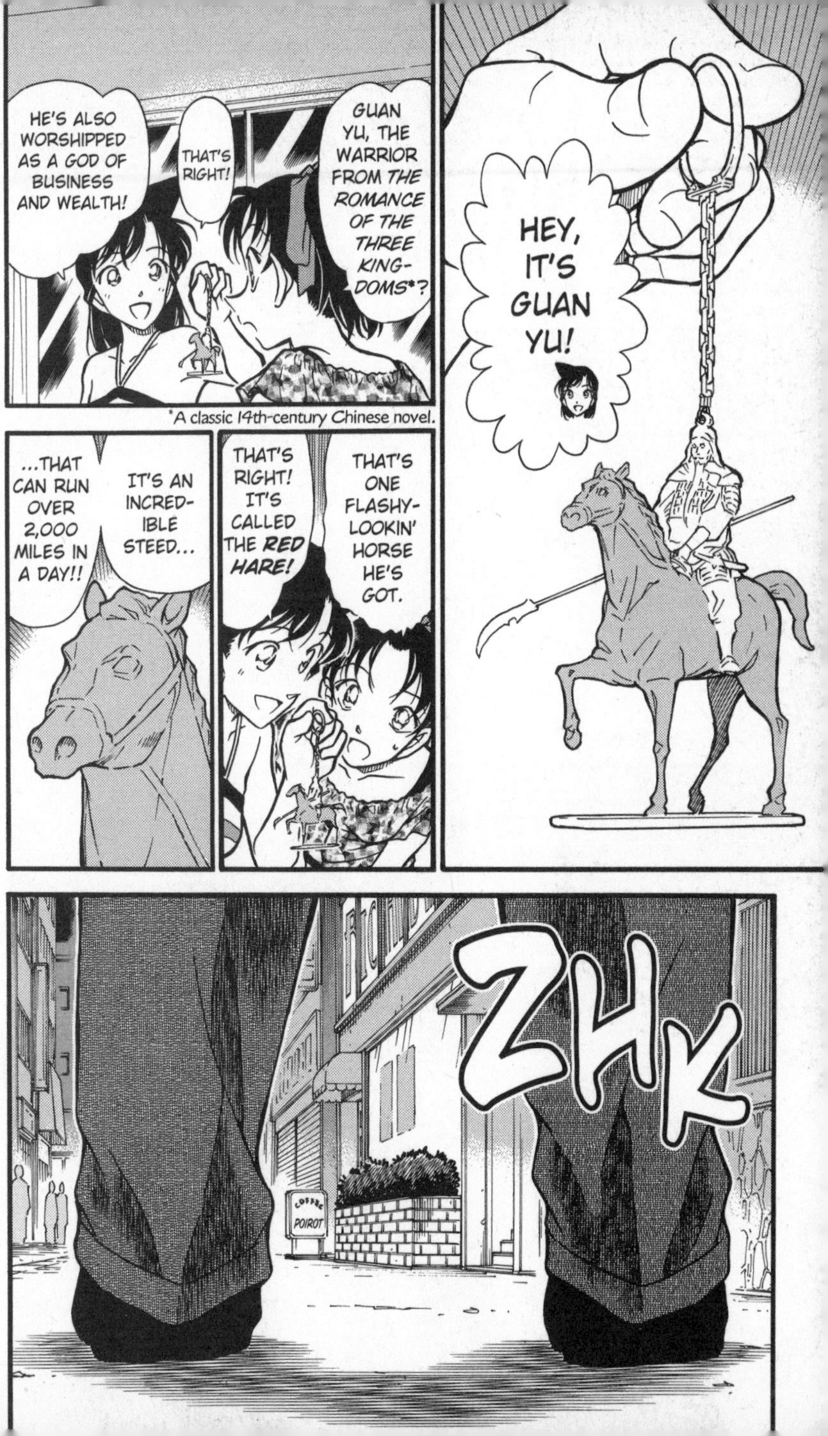
HEY, IT'S GUAN YU!
GUAN YU, THE WARRIOR FROM *THE ROMANCE OF THE THREE KINGDOMS**?
THAT'S RIGHT!
HE'S ALSO WORSHIPPED AS A GOD OF BUSINESS AND WEALTH!
THAT'S ONE FLASHY-LOOKIN' HORSE HE'S GOT.
THAT'S RIGHT! IT'S CALLED THE **RED HARE**!
IT'S AN INCREDIBLE STEED...
...THAT CAN RUN OVER 2,000 MILES IN A DAY!!
ZHK
COFFEE
POIROT

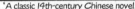

*A classic 14th-century Chinese novel.

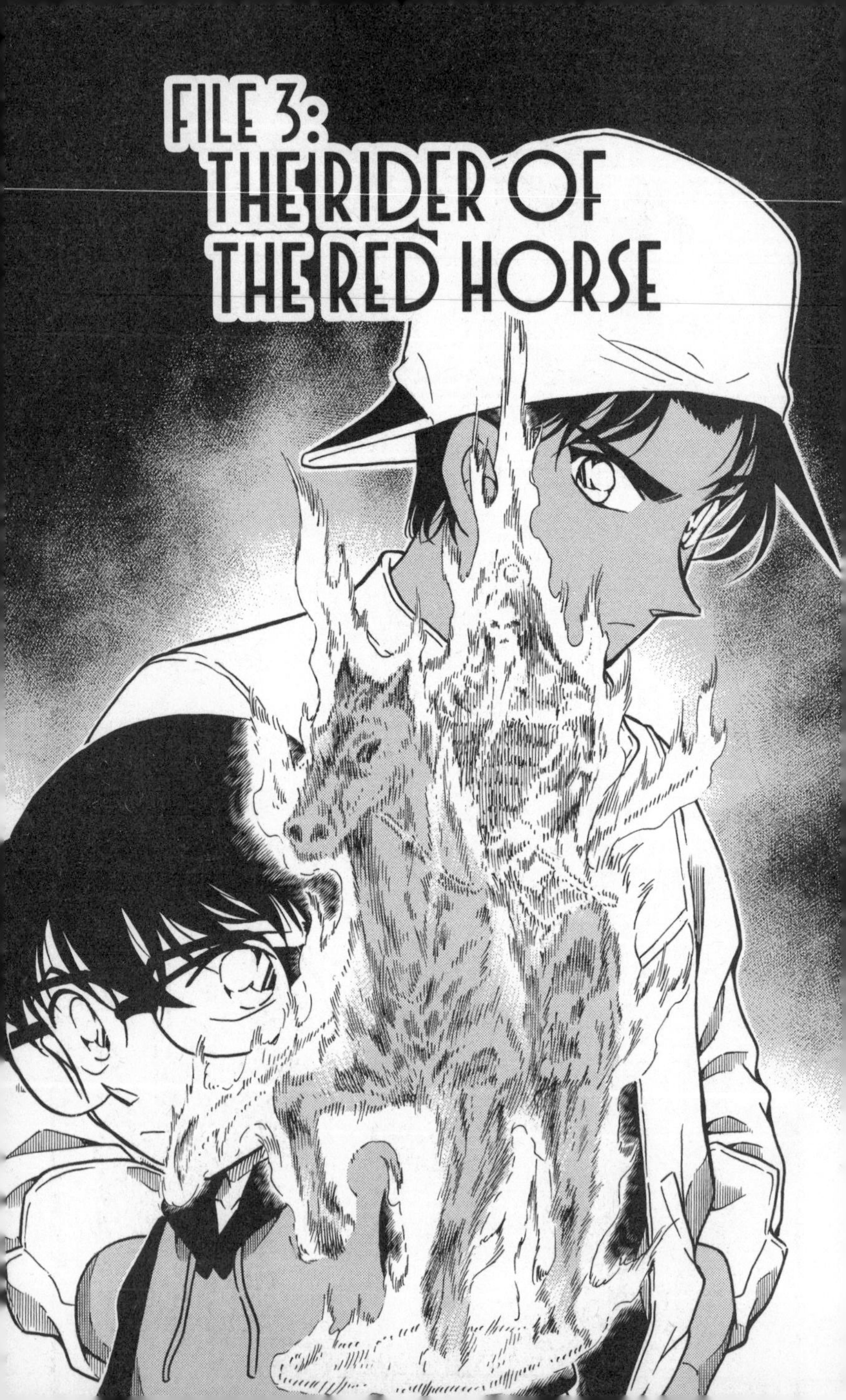
FILE 3:
THE RIDER OF
THE RED HORSE

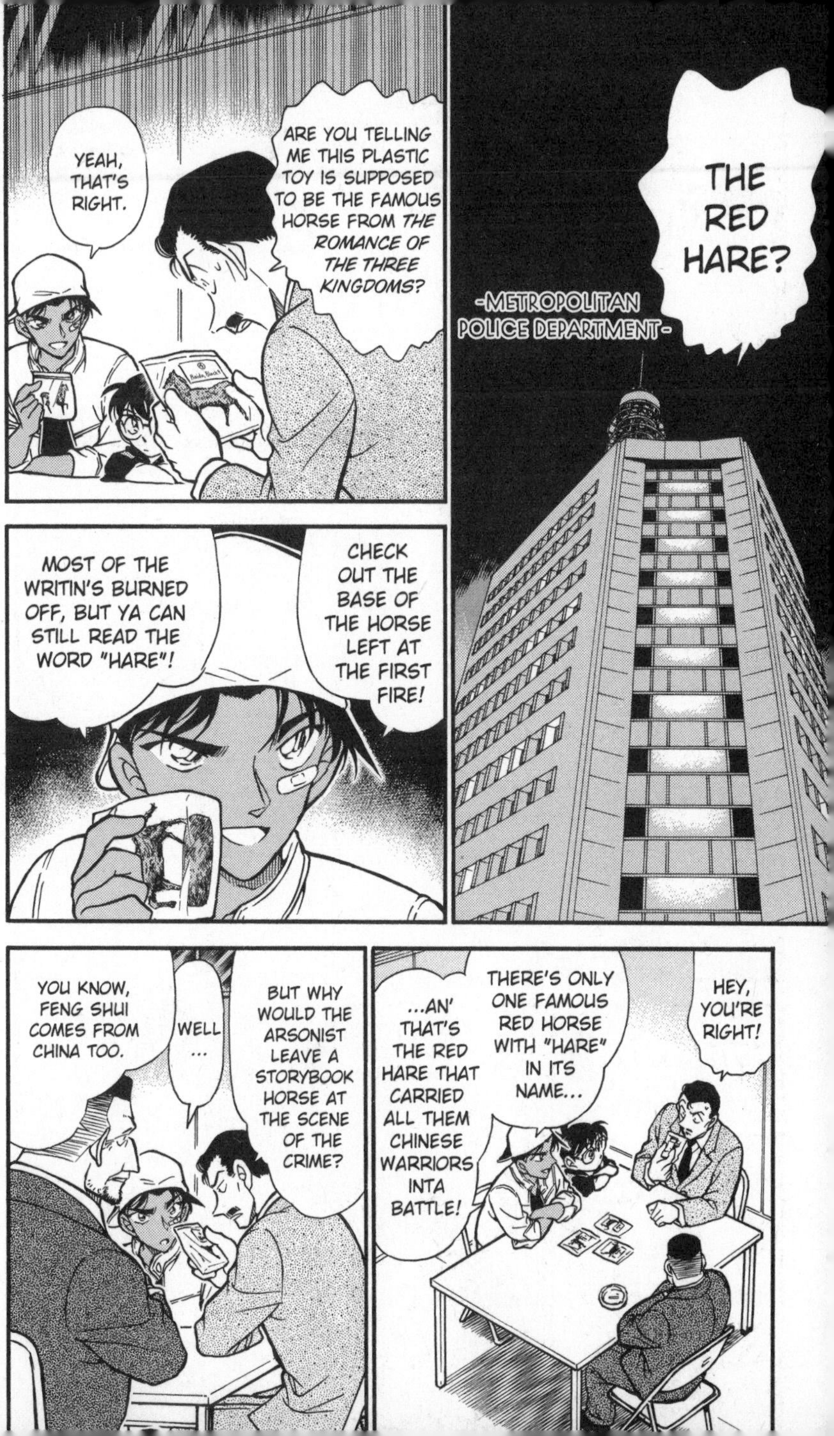
THE RED HARE?
-METROPOLITAN POLICE DEPARTMENT-
ARE YOU TELLING ME THIS PLASTIC TOY IS SUPPOSED TO BE THE FAMOUS HORSE FROM *THE ROMANCE OF THE THREE KINGDOMS*?
YEAH, THAT'S RIGHT.
CHECK OUT THE BASE OF THE HORSE LEFT AT THE FIRST FIRE!
MOST OF THE WRITIN'S BURNED OFF, BUT YA CAN STILL READ THE WORD "HARE"!
HEY, YOU'RE RIGHT!
THERE'S ONLY ONE FAMOUS RED HORSE WITH "HARE" IN ITS NAME...
...AN' THAT'S THE RED HARE THAT CARRIED ALL THEM CHINESE WARRIORS INTA BATTLE!
BUT WHY WOULD THE ARSONIST LEAVE A STORYBOOK HORSE AT THE SCENE OF THE CRIME?
WELL...
YOU KNOW, FENG SHUI COMES FROM CHINA TOO.

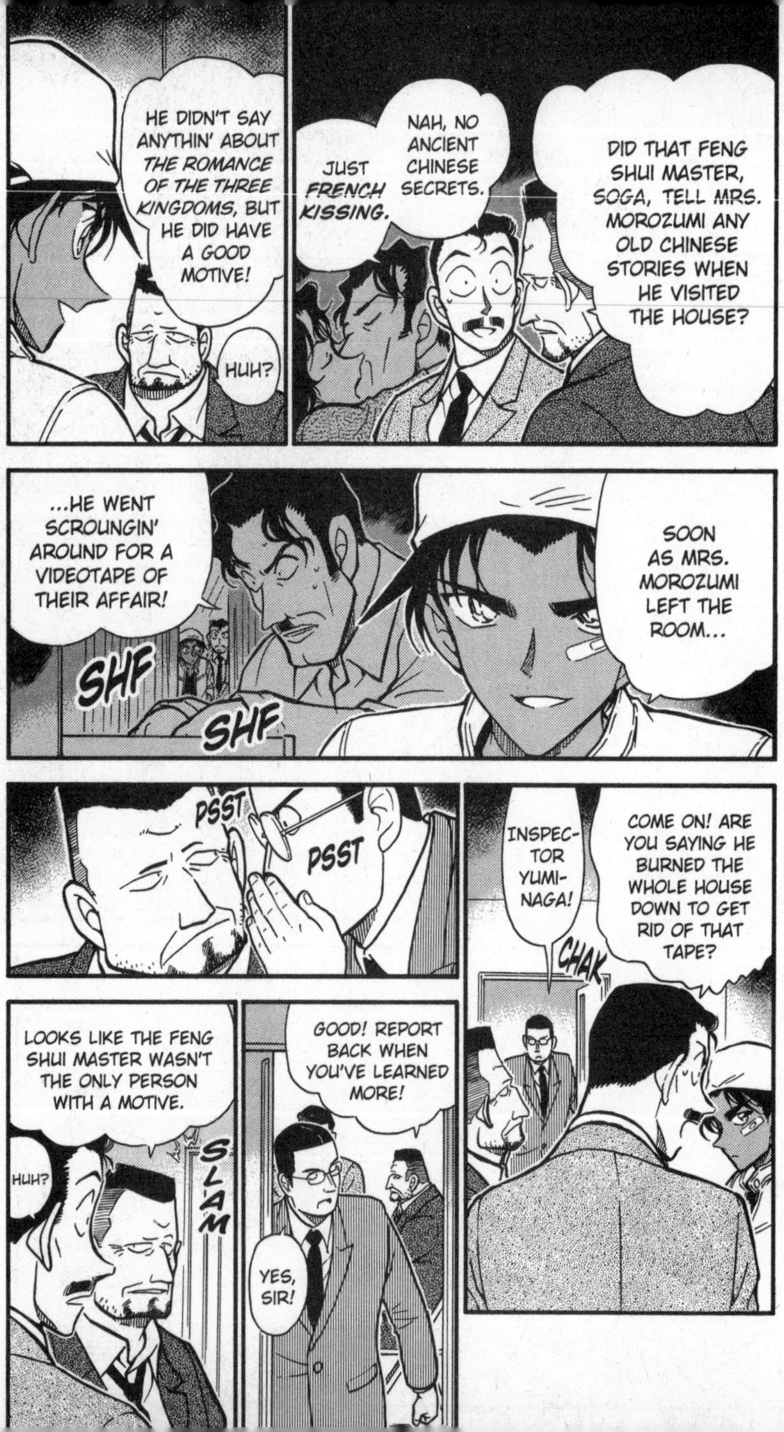
DID THAT FENG SHUI MASTER, SOGA, TELL MRS. MOROZUMI ANY OLD CHINESE STORIES WHEN HE VISITED THE HOUSE?
NAH, NO ANCIENT CHINESE SECRETS.
JUST FRENCH KISSING.
HE DIDN'T SAY ANYTHIN' ABOUT THE ROMANCE OF THE THREE KINGDOMS, BUT HE DID HAVE A GOOD MOTIVE!
HUH?
SOON AS MRS. MOROZUMI LEFT THE ROOM...
...HE WENT SCROUNGIN' AROUND FOR A VIDEOTAPE OF THEIR AFFAIR!
SHF
SHF
COME ON! ARE YOU SAYING HE BURNED THE WHOLE HOUSE DOWN TO GET RID OF THAT TAPE?
INSPEC-TOR YUMI-NAGA!
CHAK
PSST
PSST
GOOD! REPORT BACK WHEN YOU'VE LEARNED MORE!
YES, SIR!
SLAM
LOOKS LIKE THE FENG SHUI MASTER WASN'T THE ONLY PERSON WITH A MOTIVE.
HUH?

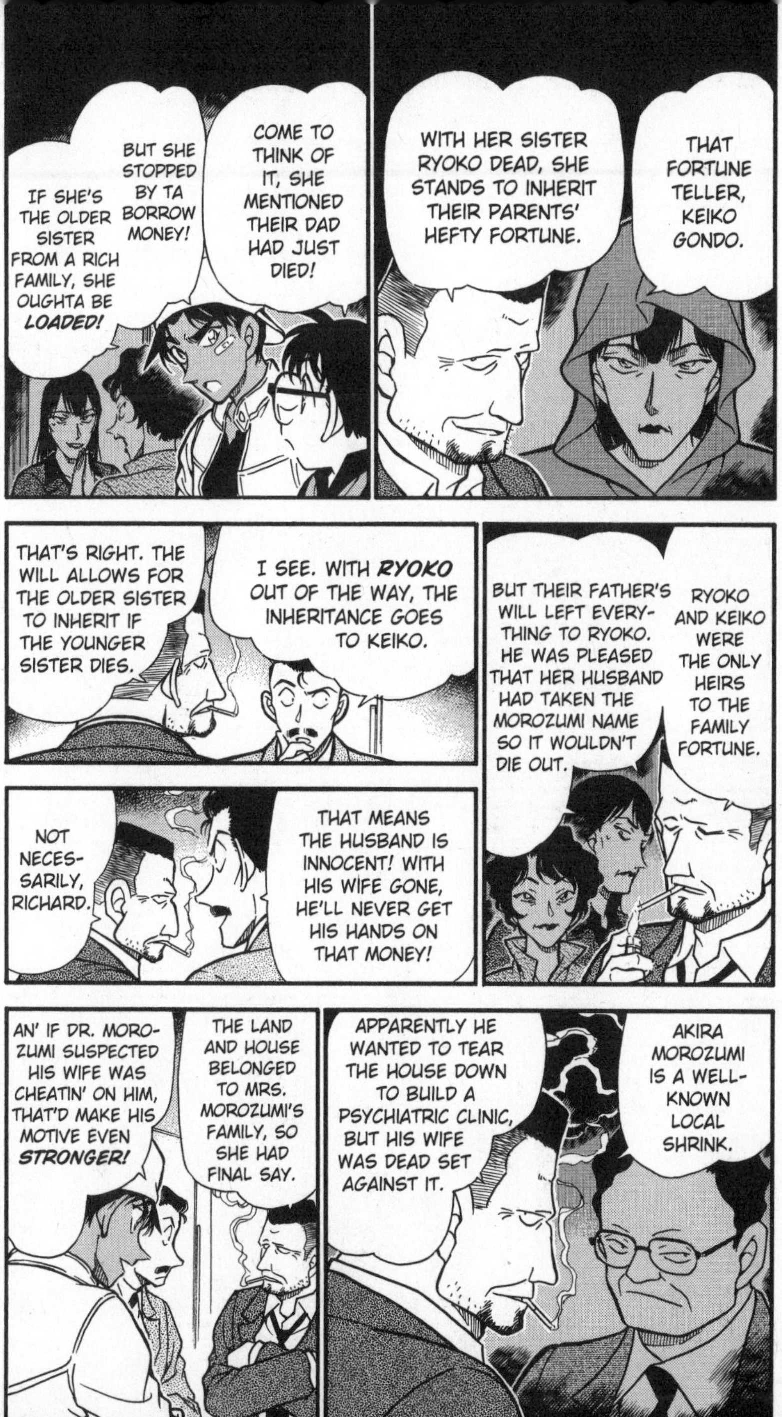
THAT FORTUNE TELLER, KEIKO GONDO.
WITH HER SISTER RYOKO DEAD, SHE STANDS TO INHERIT THEIR PARENTS' HEFTY FORTUNE.
COME TO THINK OF IT, SHE MENTIONED THEIR DAD HAD JUST DIED!
BUT SHE STOPPED BY TA BORROW MONEY!
IF SHE'S THE OLDER SISTER FROM A RICH FAMILY, SHE OUGHTA BE ***LOADED!***
RYOKO AND KEIKO WERE THE ONLY HEIRS TO THE FAMILY FORTUNE.
BUT THEIR FATHER'S WILL LEFT EVERY-THING TO RYOKO. HE WAS PLEASED THAT HER HUSBAND HAD TAKEN THE MOROZUMI NAME SO IT WOULDN'T DIE OUT.
I SEE. WITH ***RYOKO*** OUT OF THE WAY, THE INHERITANCE GOES TO KEIKO.
THAT'S RIGHT. THE WILL ALLOWS FOR THE OLDER SISTER TO INHERIT IF THE YOUNGER SISTER DIES.
THAT MEANS THE HUSBAND IS INNOCENT! WITH HIS WIFE GONE, HE'LL NEVER GET HIS HANDS ON THAT MONEY!
NOT NECES-SARILY, RICHARD.
AKIRA MOROZUMI IS A WELL-KNOWN LOCAL SHRINK.
APPARENTLY HE WANTED TO TEAR THE HOUSE DOWN TO BUILD A PSYCHIATRIC CLINIC, BUT HIS WIFE WAS DEAD SET AGAINST IT.
THE LAND AND HOUSE BELONGED TO MRS. MOROZUMI'S FAMILY, SO SHE HAD FINAL SAY.
AN' IF DR. MORO-ZUMI SUSPECTED HIS WIFE WAS CHEATIN' ON HIM, THAT'D MAKE HIS MOTIVE EVEN ***STRONGER!***

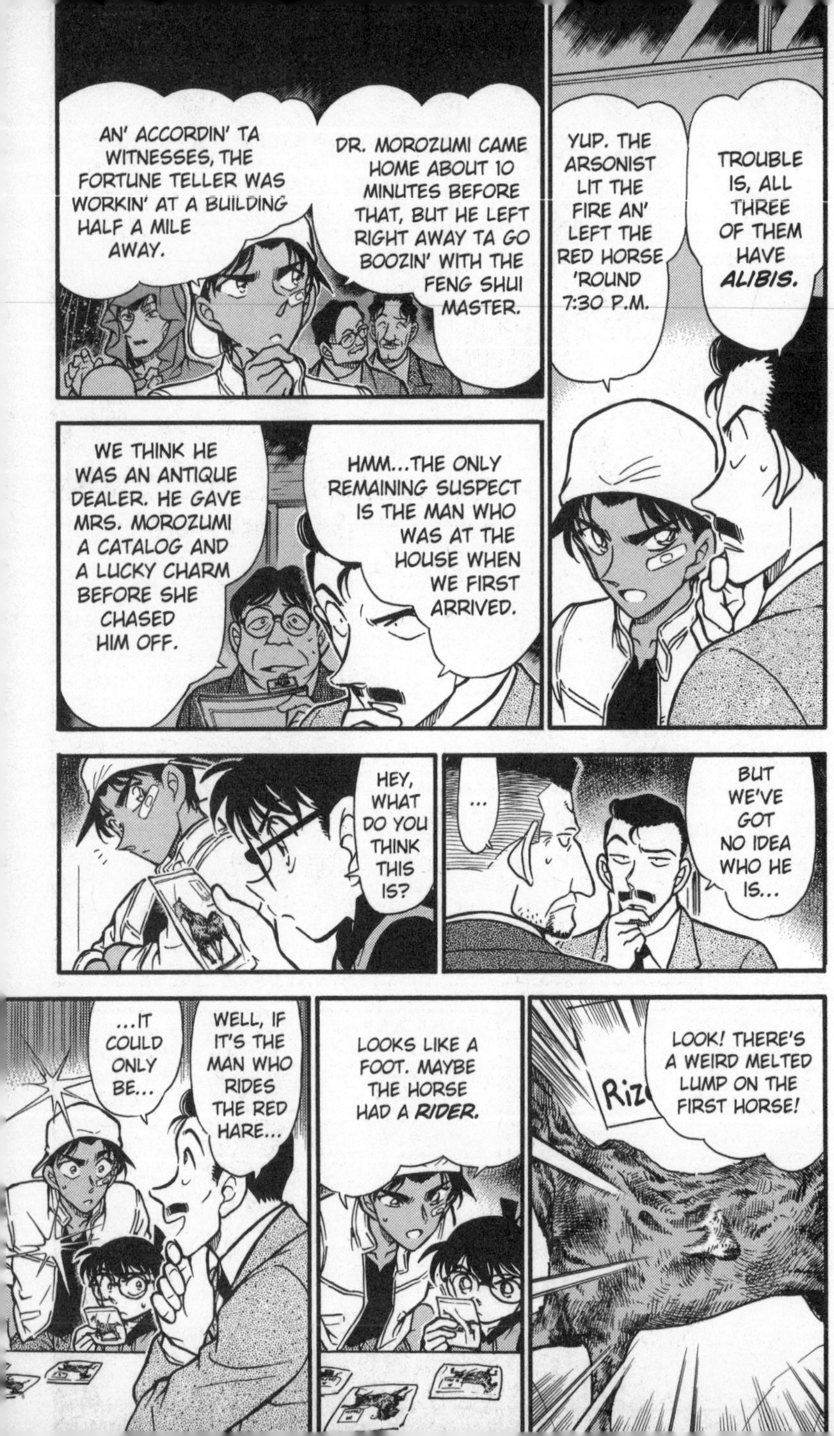
TROUBLE IS, ALL THREE OF THEM HAVE *ALIBIS.*
YUP. THE ARSONIST LIT THE FIRE AN' LEFT THE RED HORSE 'ROUND 7:30 P.M.
DR. MOROZUMI CAME HOME ABOUT 10 MINUTES BEFORE THAT, BUT HE LEFT RIGHT AWAY TA GO BOOZIN' WITH THE FENG SHUI MASTER.
AN' ACCORDIN' TA WITNESSES, THE FORTUNE TELLER WAS WORKIN' AT A BUILDING HALF A MILE AWAY.
HMM...THE ONLY REMAINING SUSPECT IS THE MAN WHO WAS AT THE HOUSE WHEN WE FIRST ARRIVED.
WE THINK HE WAS AN ANTIQUE DEALER. HE GAVE MRS. MOROZUMI A CATALOG AND A LUCKY CHARM BEFORE SHE CHASED HIM OFF.
BUT WE'VE GOT NO IDEA WHO HE IS...
...
HEY, WHAT DO YOU THINK THIS IS?
LOOK! THERE'S A WEIRD MELTED LUMP ON THE FIRST HORSE!
Rize
LOOKS LIKE A FOOT. MAYBE THE HORSE HAD A *RIDER.*
WELL, IF IT'S THE MAN WHO RIDES THE RED HARE...
...IT COULD ONLY BE...

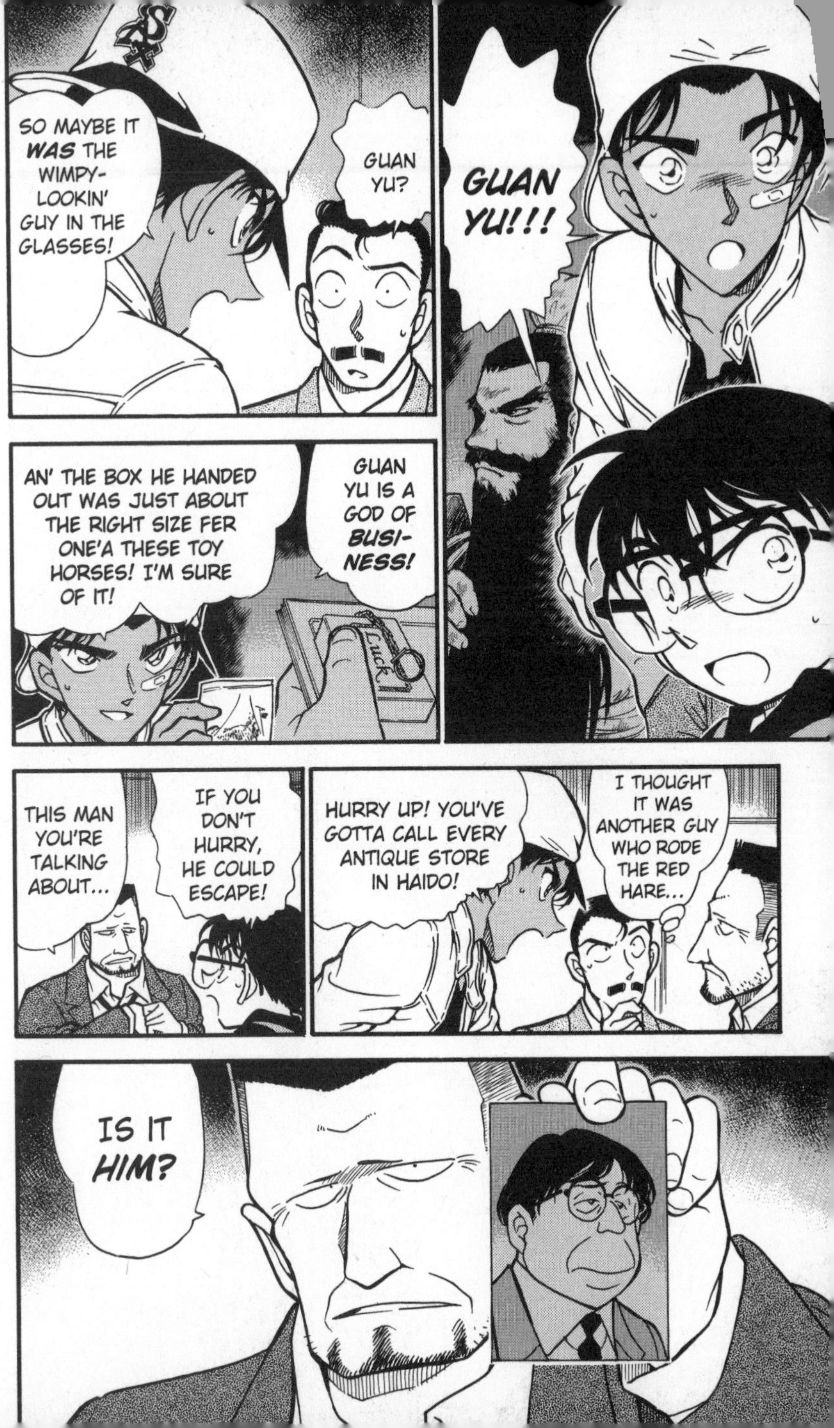
GUAN YU!!!
GUAN YU?
SO MAYBE IT WAS THE WIMPY-LOOKIN' GUY IN THE GLASSES!
GUAN YU IS A GOD OF BUSI-NESS!
AN' THE BOX HE HANDED OUT WAS JUST ABOUT THE RIGHT SIZE FER ONE'A THESE TOY HORSES! I'M SURE OF IT!
LUCK
I THOUGHT IT WAS ANOTHER GUY WHO RODE THE RED HARE...
HURRY UP! YOU'VE GOTTA CALL EVERY ANTIQUE STORE IN HAIDO!
IF YOU DON'T HURRY, HE COULD ESCAPE!
THIS MAN YOU'RE TALKING ABOUT...
IS IT HIM?

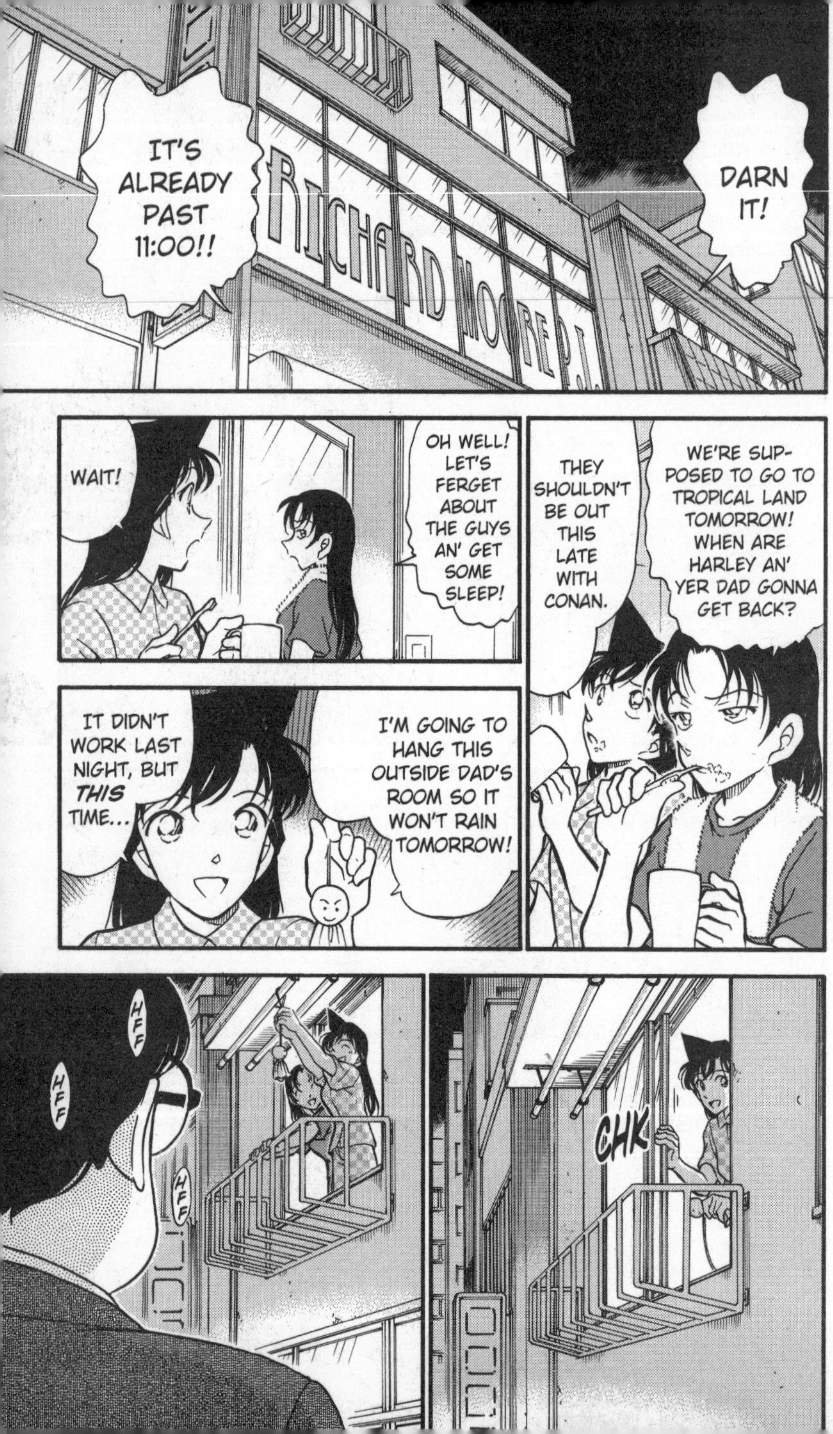
DARN IT!
RICHARD MOORE
IT'S ALREADY PAST 11:00!!
WE'RE SUP-POSED TO GO TO TROPICAL LAND TOMORROW! WHEN ARE HARLEY AN' YER DAD GONNA GET BACK?
THEY SHOULDN'T BE OUT THIS LATE WITH CONAN.
OH WELL! LET'S FERGET ABOUT THE GUYS AN' GET SOME SLEEP!
WAIT!
I'M GOING TO HANG THIS OUTSIDE DAD'S ROOM SO IT WON'T RAIN TOMORROW!
IT DIDN'T WORK LAST NIGHT, BUT *THIS* TIME...
CHK
HFF
HFF
HFF

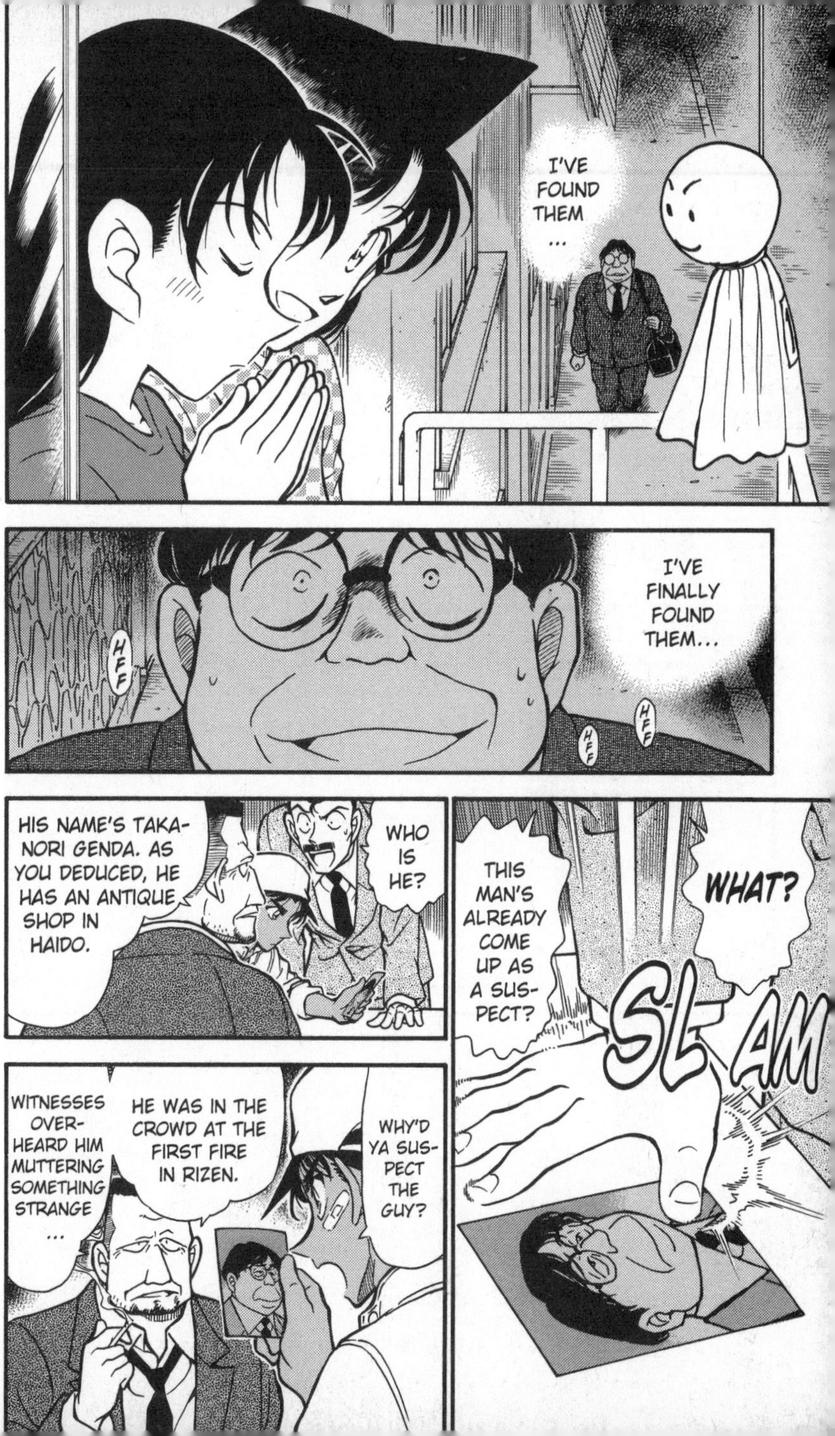
I'VE FOUND THEM ...
I'VE FINALLY FOUND THEM...
HFF
HFF
HFF
WHAT?
THIS MAN'S ALREADY COME UP AS A SUSPECT?
SL AM
WHO IS HE?
HIS NAME'S TAKANORI GENDA. AS YOU DEDUCED, HE HAS AN ANTIQUE SHOP IN HAIDO.
WHY'D YA SUSPECT THE GUY?
HE WAS IN THE CROWD AT THE FIRST FIRE IN RIZEN.
WITNESSES OVERHEARD HIM MUTTERING SOMETHING STRANGE ...

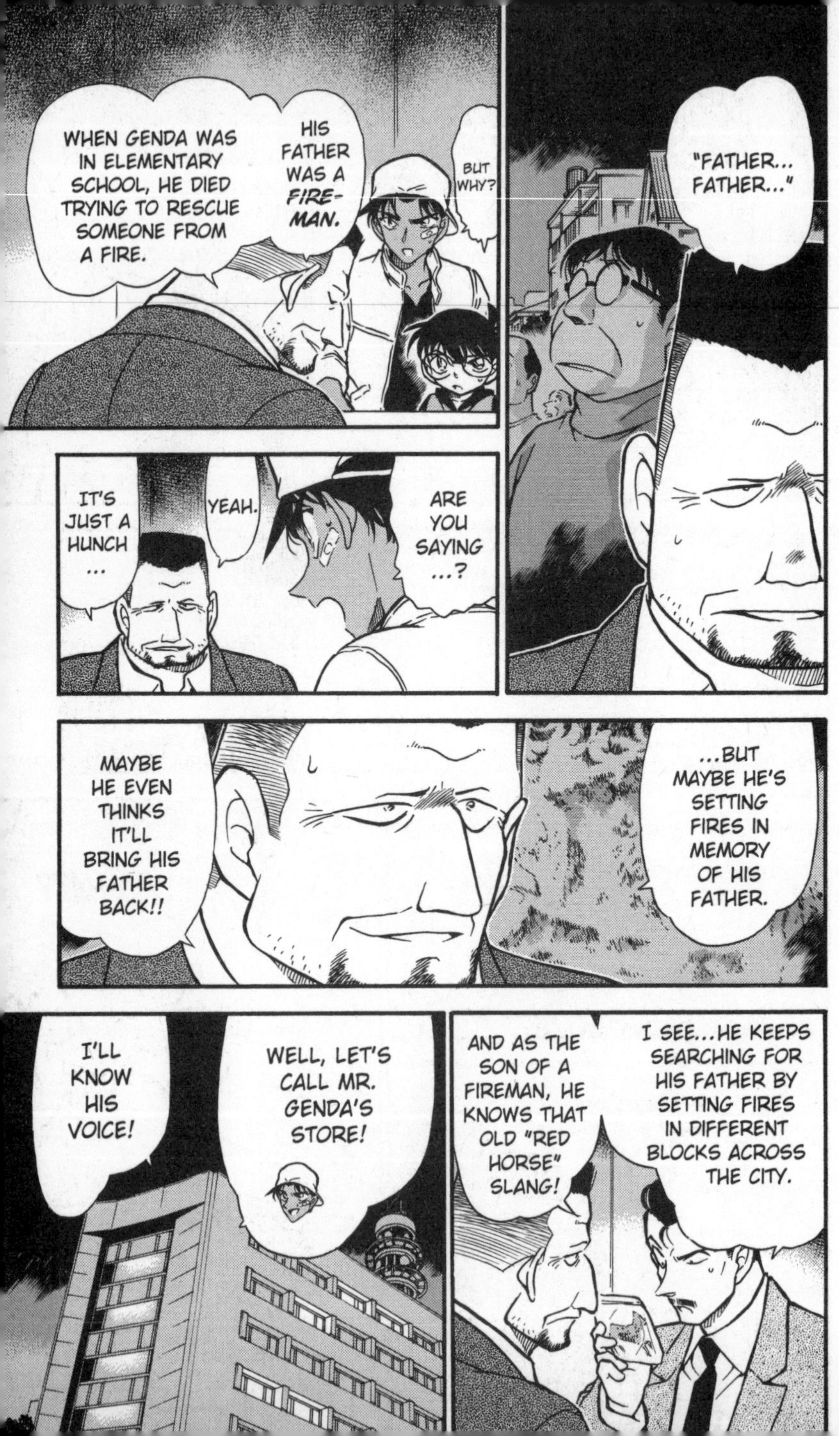
"FATHER... FATHER..."
BUT WHY?
HIS FATHER WAS A FIREMAN.
WHEN GENDA WAS IN ELEMENTARY SCHOOL, HE DIED TRYING TO RESCUE SOMEONE FROM A FIRE.
ARE YOU SAYING...?
YEAH.
IT'S JUST A HUNCH...
...BUT MAYBE HE'S SETTING FIRES IN MEMORY OF HIS FATHER.
MAYBE HE EVEN THINKS IT'LL BRING HIS FATHER BACK!!
I SEE...HE KEEPS SEARCHING FOR HIS FATHER BY SETTING FIRES IN DIFFERENT BLOCKS ACROSS THE CITY.
AND AS THE SON OF A FIREMAN, HE KNOWS THAT OLD "RED HORSE" SLANG!
WELL, LET'S CALL MR. GENDA'S STORE!
I'LL KNOW HIS VOICE!

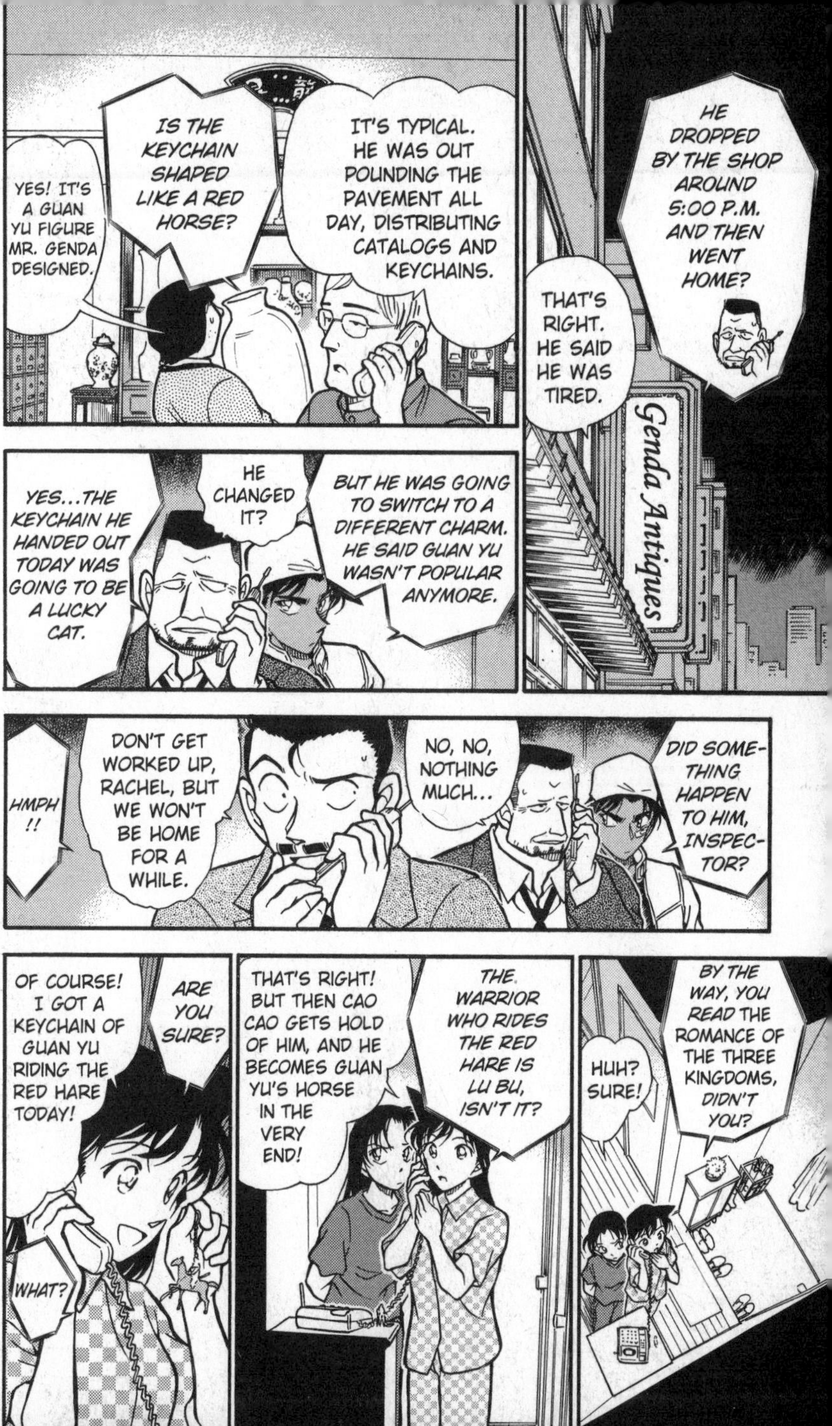
HE DROPPED BY THE SHOP AROUND 5:00 P.M. AND THEN WENT HOME?
THAT'S RIGHT. HE SAID HE WAS TIRED.
Genda Antiques
IT'S TYPICAL. HE WAS OUT POUNDING THE PAVEMENT ALL DAY, DISTRIBUTING CATALOGS AND KEYCHAINS.
IS THE KEYCHAIN SHAPED LIKE A RED HORSE?
YES! IT'S A GUAN YU FIGURE MR. GENDA DESIGNED.
BUT HE WAS GOING TO SWITCH TO A DIFFERENT CHARM. HE SAID GUAN YU WASN'T POPULAR ANYMORE.
HE CHANGED IT?
YES...THE KEYCHAIN HE HANDED OUT TODAY WAS GOING TO BE A LUCKY CAT.
DID SOME-THING HAPPEN TO HIM, INSPEC-TOR?
NO, NO, NOTHING MUCH...
DON'T GET WORKED UP, RACHEL, BUT WE WON'T BE HOME FOR A WHILE.
HMPH!!
BY THE WAY, YOU READ THE ROMANCE OF THE THREE KINGDOMS, DIDN'T YOU?
HUH? SURE!
THE WARRIOR WHO RIDES THE RED HARE IS LU BU, ISN'T IT?
THAT'S RIGHT! BUT THEN CAO CAO GETS HOLD OF HIM, AND HE BECOMES GUAN YU'S HORSE IN THE VERY END!
ARE YOU SURE?
OF COURSE! I GOT A KEYCHAIN OF GUAN YU RIDING THE RED HARE TODAY!
WHAT?

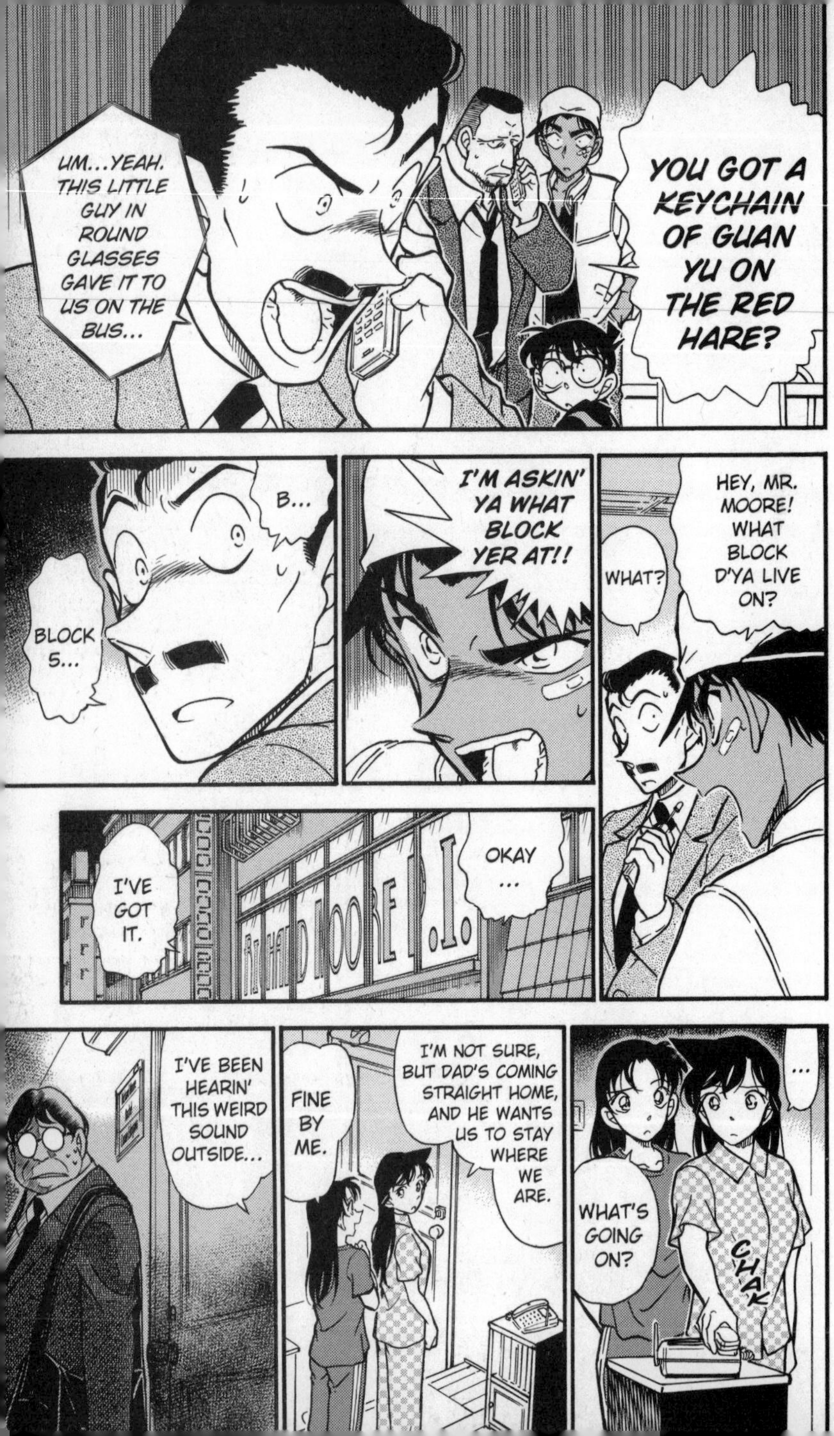
YOU GOT A KEYCHAIN OF GUAN YU ON THE RED HARE?
UM...YEAH. THIS LITTLE GUY IN ROUND GLASSES GAVE IT TO US ON THE BUS...
HEY, MR. MOORE! WHAT BLOCK D'YA LIVE ON?
WHAT?
I'M ASKIN' YA WHAT BLOCK YER AT!!
B...
BLOCK 5...
OKAY ...
RICHARD MOORE P.I.
I'VE GOT IT.
...
WHAT'S GOING ON?
CHAK
I'M NOT SURE, BUT DAD'S COMING STRAIGHT HOME, AND HE WANTS US TO STAY WHERE WE ARE.
FINE BY ME.
I'VE BEEN HEARIN' THIS WEIRD SOUND OUTSIDE...

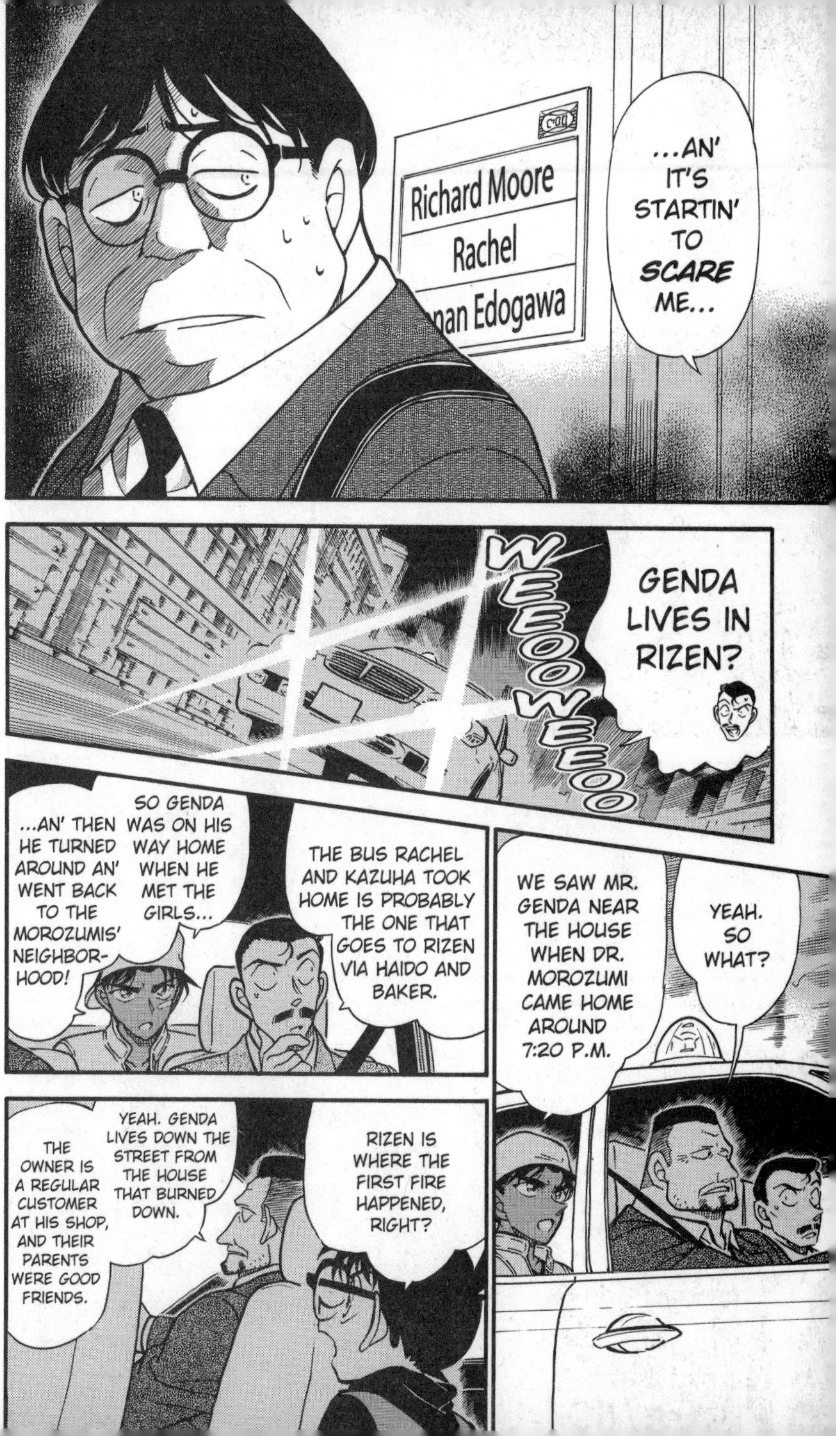
Richard Moore
Rachel
onan Edogawa
...AN' IT'S STARTIN' TO SCARE ME...
GENDA LIVES IN RIZEN?
WEEOOWEEOO
YEAH. SO WHAT?
WE SAW MR. GENDA NEAR THE HOUSE WHEN DR. MOROZUMI CAME HOME AROUND 7:20 P.M.
THE BUS RACHEL AND KAZUHA TOOK HOME IS PROBABLY THE ONE THAT GOES TO RIZEN VIA HAIDO AND BAKER.
SO GENDA WAS ON HIS WAY HOME WHEN HE MET THE GIRLS...
...AN' THEN HE TURNED AROUND AN' WENT BACK TO THE MOROZUMIS' NEIGHBOR-HOOD!
RIZEN IS WHERE THE FIRST FIRE HAPPENED, RIGHT?
YEAH. GENDA LIVES DOWN THE STREET FROM THE HOUSE THAT BURNED DOWN.
THE OWNER IS A REGULAR CUSTOMER AT HIS SHOP, AND THEIR PARENTS WERE GOOD FRIENDS.

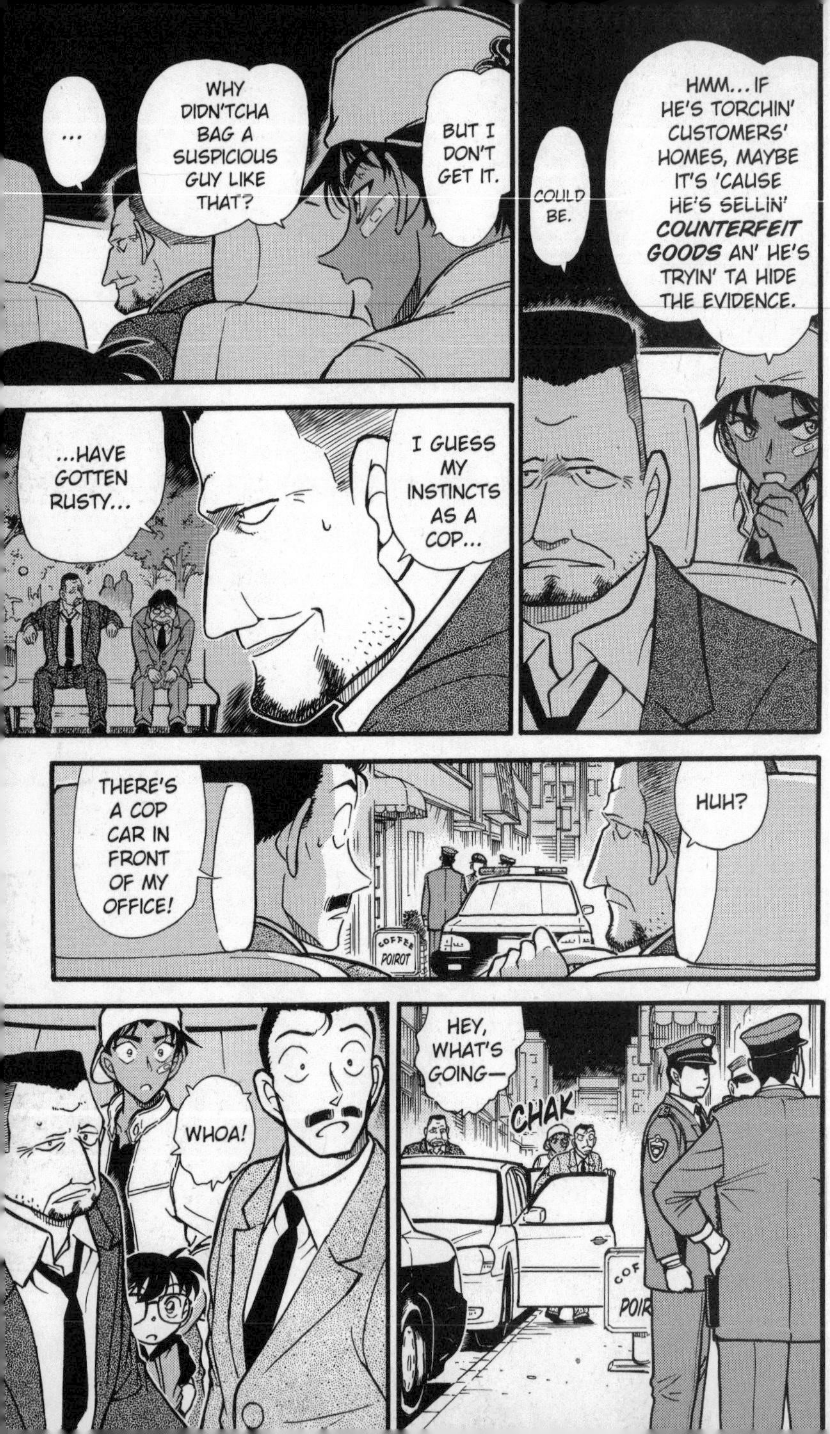
HMM... IF HE'S TORCHIN' CUSTOMERS' HOMES, MAYBE IT'S 'CAUSE HE'S SELLIN' **COUNTERFEIT GOODS** AN' HE'S TRYIN' TA HIDE THE EVIDENCE.
COULD BE.
BUT I DON'T GET IT.
WHY DIDN'TCHA BAG A SUSPICIOUS GUY LIKE THAT?
...
I GUESS MY INSTINCTS AS A COP...
...HAVE GOTTEN RUSTY...
HUH?
THERE'S A COP CAR IN FRONT OF MY OFFICE!
COFFEE POIROT
HEY, WHAT'S GOING—
CHAK
WHOA!

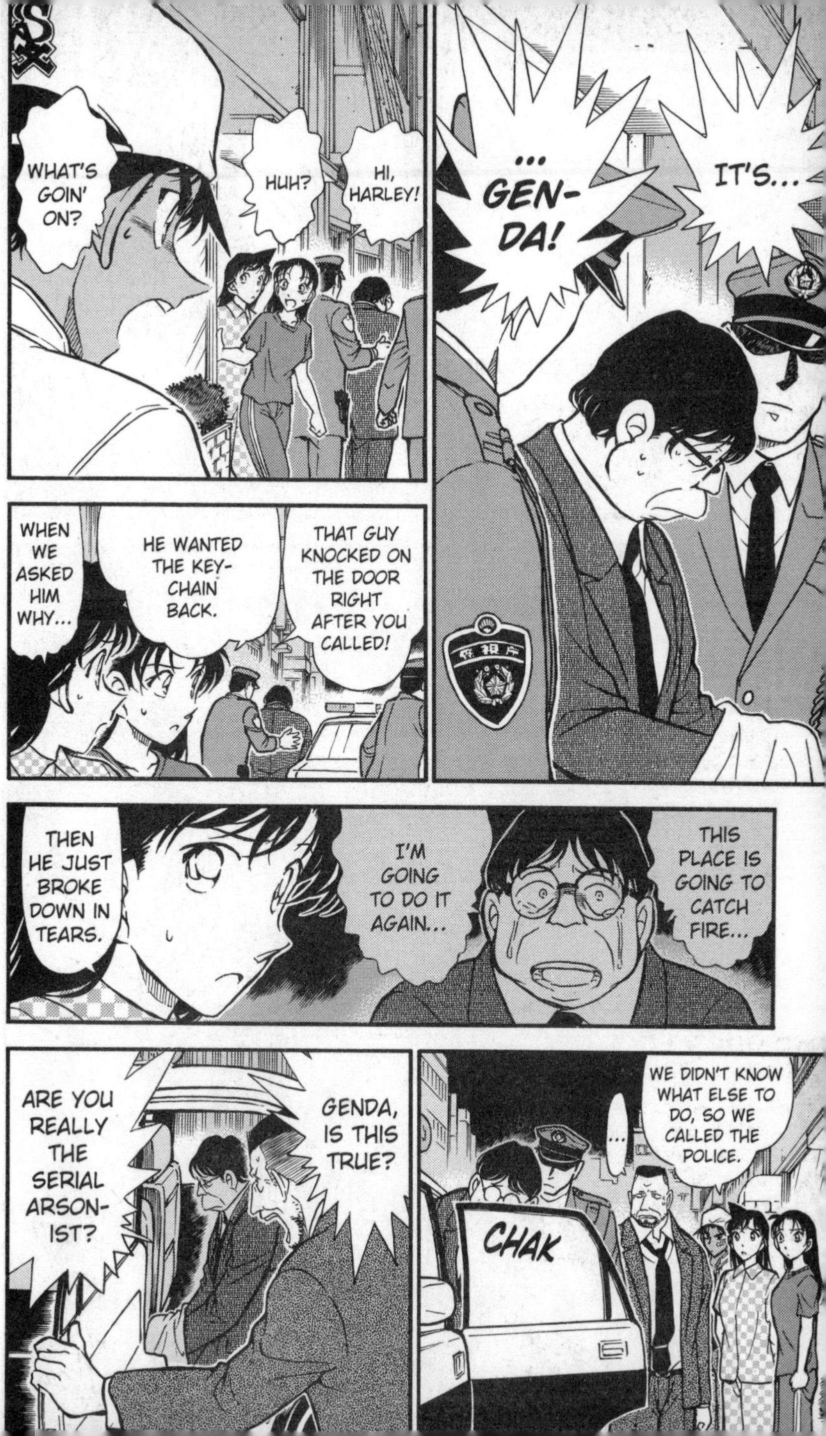
IT'S...
...GEN-DA!
HI, HARLEY!
HUH?
WHAT'S GOIN' ON?
THAT GUY KNOCKED ON THE DOOR RIGHT AFTER YOU CALLED!
HE WANTED THE KEY-CHAIN BACK.
WHEN WE ASKED HIM WHY...
THIS PLACE IS GOING TO CATCH FIRE...
I'M GOING TO DO IT AGAIN...
THEN HE JUST BROKE DOWN IN TEARS.
WE DIDN'T KNOW WHAT ELSE TO DO, SO WE CALLED THE POLICE.
...
CHAK
GENDA, IS THIS TRUE?
ARE YOU REALLY THE SERIAL ARSON-IST?

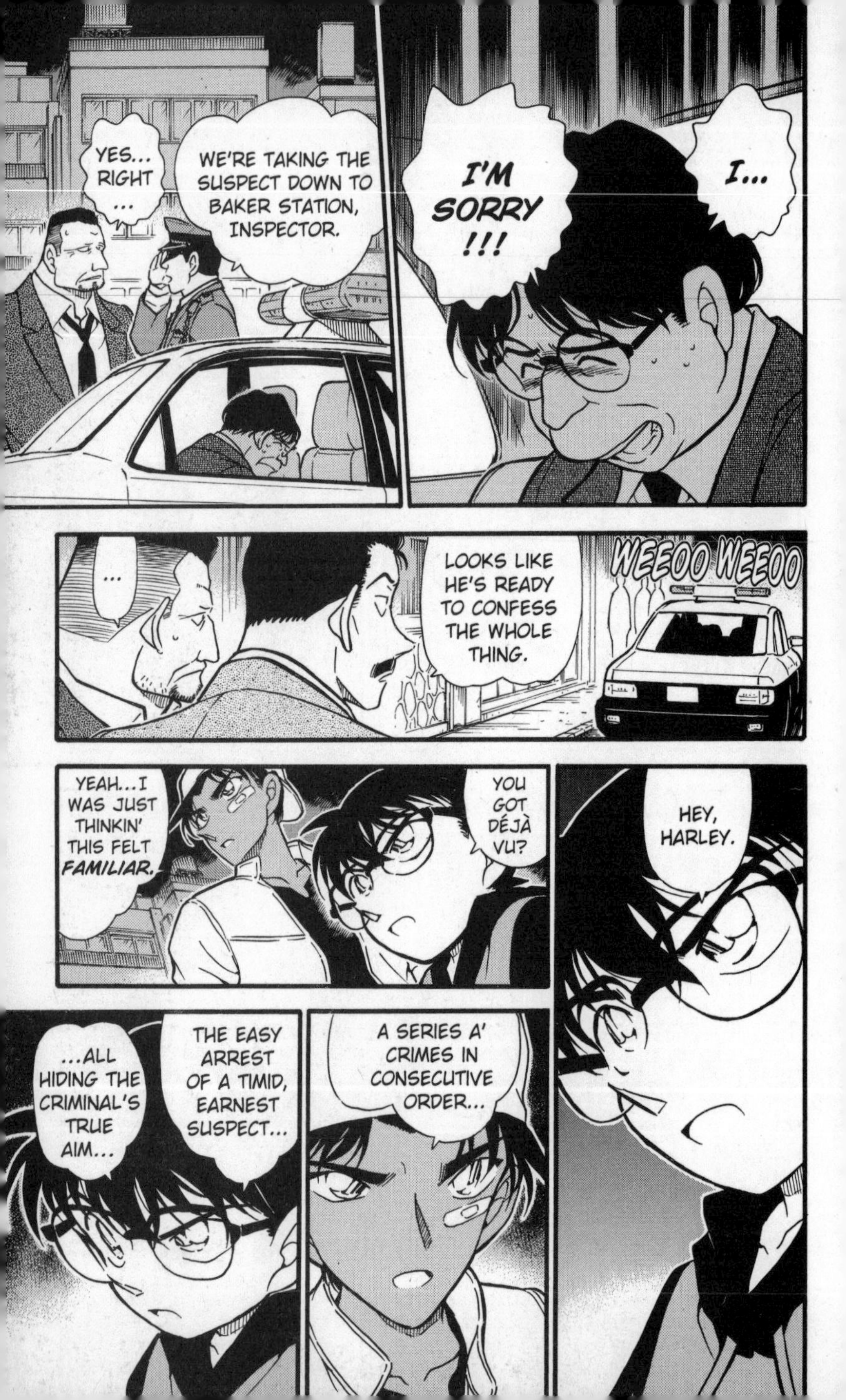
I...
I'M SORRY!!!
WE'RE TAKING THE SUSPECT DOWN TO BAKER STATION, INSPECTOR.
YES... RIGHT ...
WEEOO WEEOO
LOOKS LIKE HE'S READY TO CONFESS THE WHOLE THING.
...
HEY, HARLEY.
YOU GOT DÉJÀ VU?
YEAH...I WAS JUST THINKIN' THIS FELT FAMILIAR.
A SERIES A' CRIMES IN CONSECUTIVE ORDER...
THE EASY ARREST OF A TIMID, EARNEST SUSPECT...
...ALL HIDING THE CRIMINAL'S TRUE AIM...

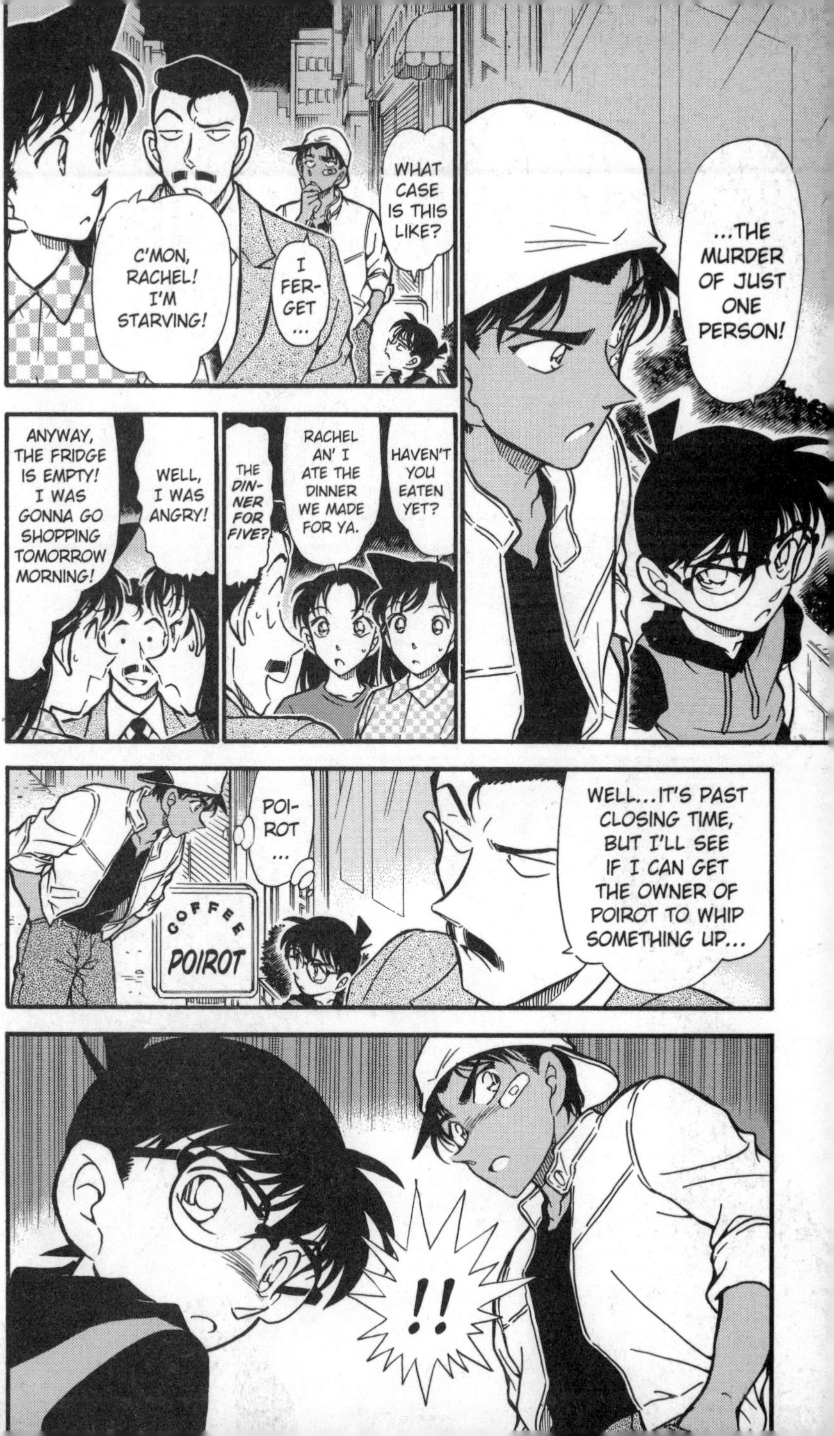
...THE MURDER OF JUST ONE PERSON!
WHAT CASE IS THIS LIKE?
I FER-GET ...
C'MON, RACHEL! I'M STARVING!
HAVEN'T YOU EATEN YET?
RACHEL AN' I ATE THE DINNER WE MADE FOR YA.
THE *DINNER FOR FIVE*?
WELL, I WAS ANGRY!
ANYWAY, THE FRIDGE IS EMPTY! I WAS GONNA GO SHOPPING TOMORROW MORNING!
WELL...IT'S PAST CLOSING TIME, BUT I'LL SEE IF I CAN GET THE OWNER OF POIROT TO WHIP SOMETHING UP...
POI-ROT ...
COFFEE
POIROT
!!

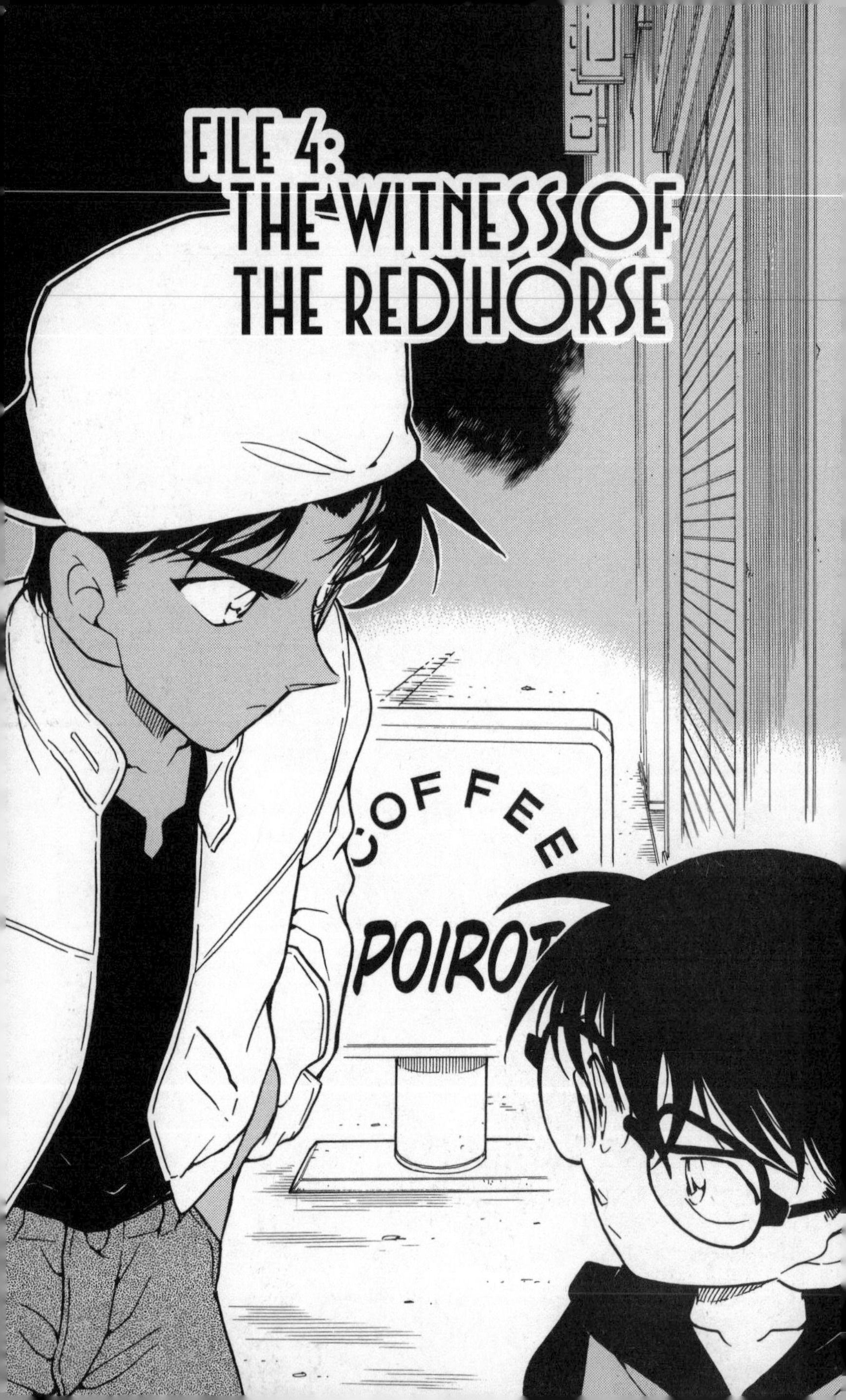
FILE 4:
THE WITNESS OF THE RED HORSE
COFFEE
POIROT

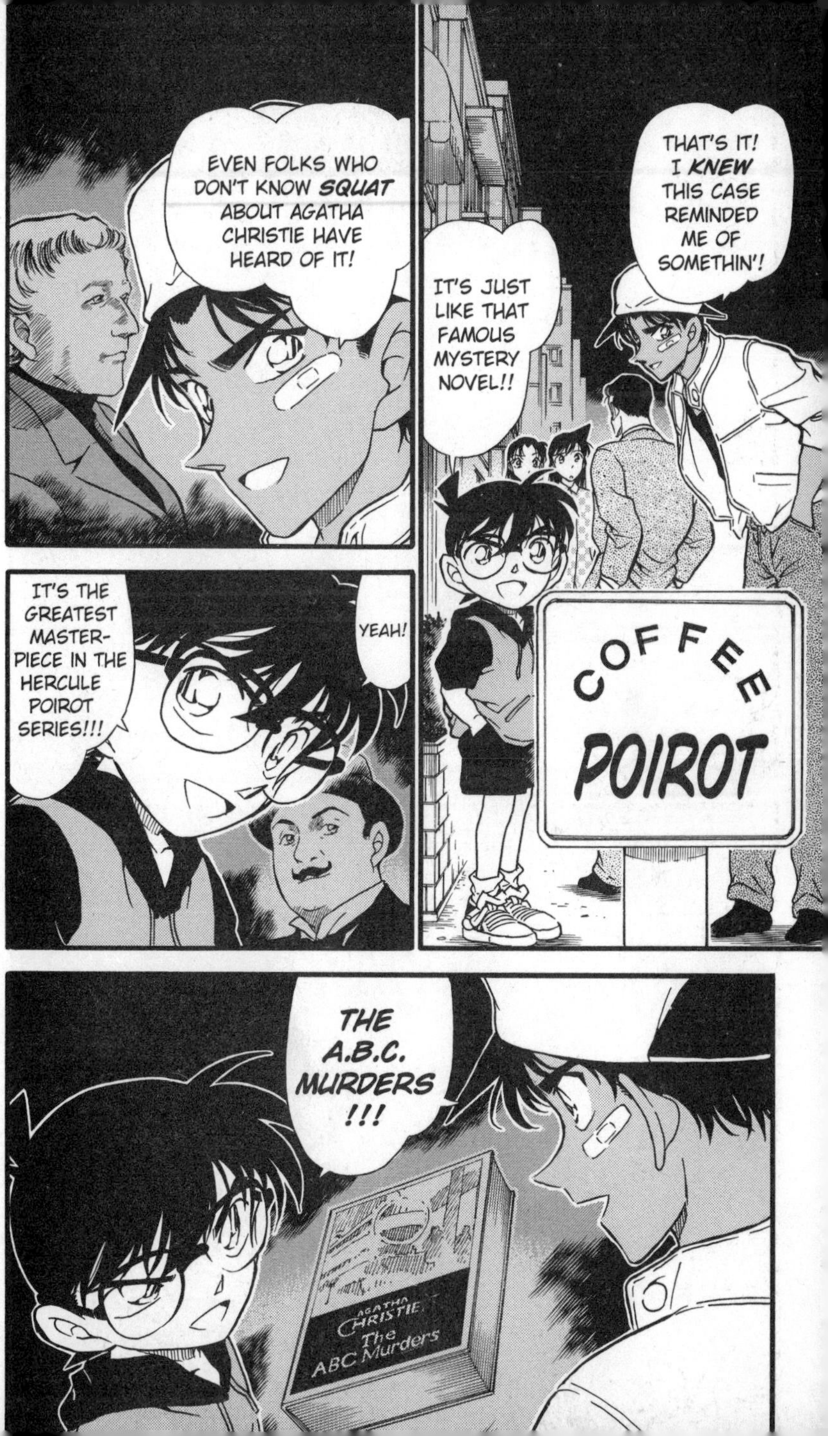
THAT'S IT! I KNEW THIS CASE REMINDED ME OF SOMETHIN'!
IT'S JUST LIKE THAT FAMOUS MYSTERY NOVEL!!
COFFEE POIROT
EVEN FOLKS WHO DON'T KNOW SQUAT ABOUT AGATHA CHRISTIE HAVE HEARD OF IT!
IT'S THE GREATEST MASTERPIECE IN THE HERCULE POIROT SERIES!!!
YEAH!
THE A.B.C. MURDERS!!!
AGATHA CHRISTIE The ABC Murders

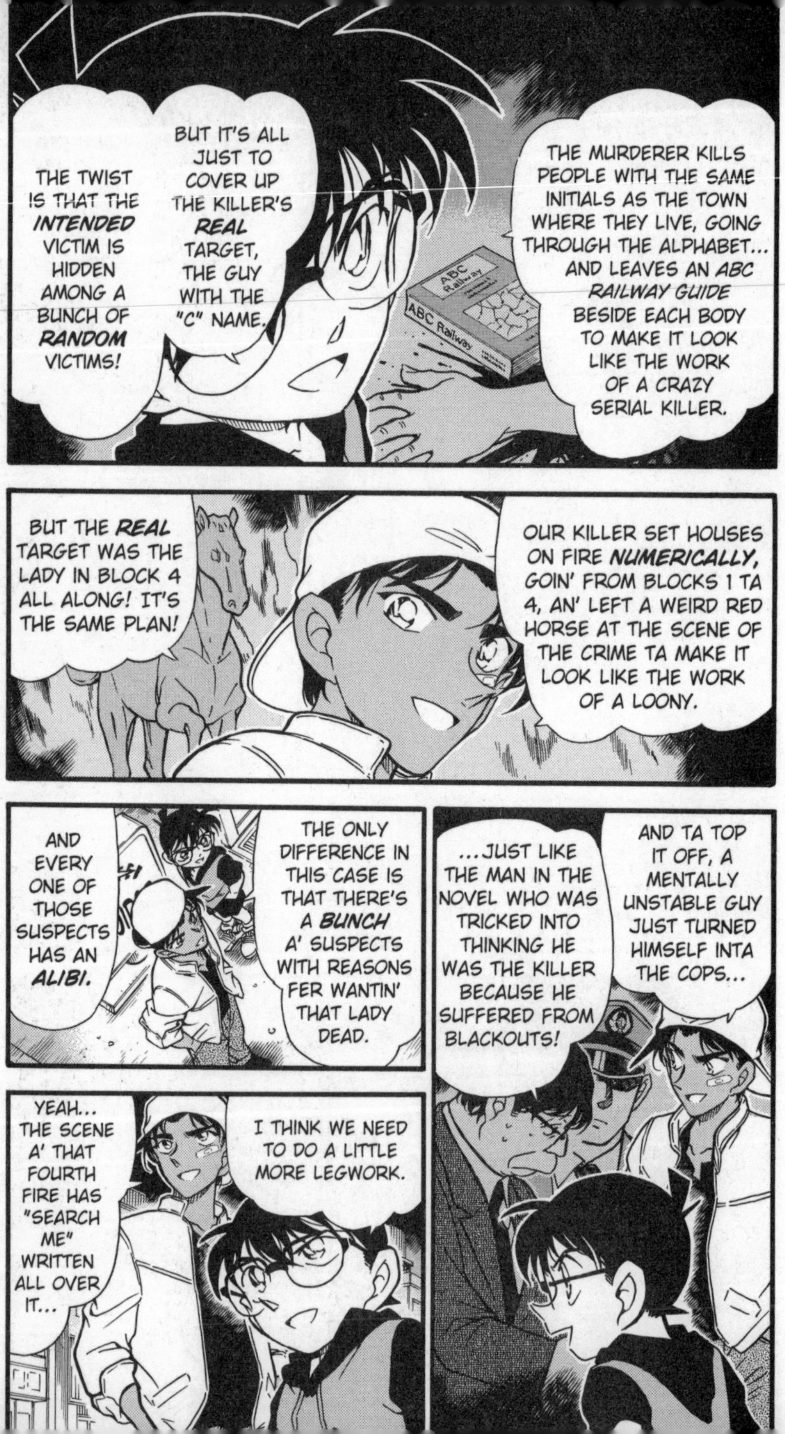
THE MURDERER KILLS PEOPLE WITH THE SAME INITIALS AS THE TOWN WHERE THEY LIVE, GOING THROUGH THE ALPHABET... AND LEAVES AN *ABC RAILWAY GUIDE* BESIDE EACH BODY TO MAKE IT LOOK LIKE THE WORK OF A CRAZY SERIAL KILLER.
ABC Railway
ABC Railway
BUT IT'S ALL JUST TO COVER UP THE KILLER'S ***REAL*** TARGET, THE GUY WITH THE "C" NAME.
THE TWIST IS THAT THE ***INTENDED*** VICTIM IS HIDDEN AMONG A BUNCH OF ***RANDOM*** VICTIMS!
OUR KILLER SET HOUSES ON FIRE ***NUMERICALLY,*** GOIN' FROM BLOCKS 1 TA 4, AN' LEFT A WEIRD RED HORSE AT THE SCENE OF THE CRIME TA MAKE IT LOOK LIKE THE WORK OF A LOONY.
BUT THE ***REAL*** TARGET WAS THE LADY IN BLOCK 4 ALL ALONG! IT'S THE SAME PLAN!
AND TA TOP IT OFF, A MENTALLY UNSTABLE GUY JUST TURNED HIMSELF INTA THE COPS...
...JUST LIKE THE MAN IN THE NOVEL WHO WAS TRICKED INTO THINKING HE WAS THE KILLER BECAUSE HE SUFFERED FROM BLACKOUTS!
THE ONLY DIFFERENCE IN THIS CASE IS THAT THERE'S A ***BUNCH*** A' SUSPECTS WITH REASONS FER WANTIN' THAT LADY DEAD.
AND EVERY ONE OF THOSE SUSPECTS HAS AN ***ALIBI.***
I THINK WE NEED TO DO A LITTLE MORE LEGWORK.
YEAH... THE SCENE A' THAT FOURTH FIRE HAS "SEARCH ME" WRITTEN ALL OVER IT...

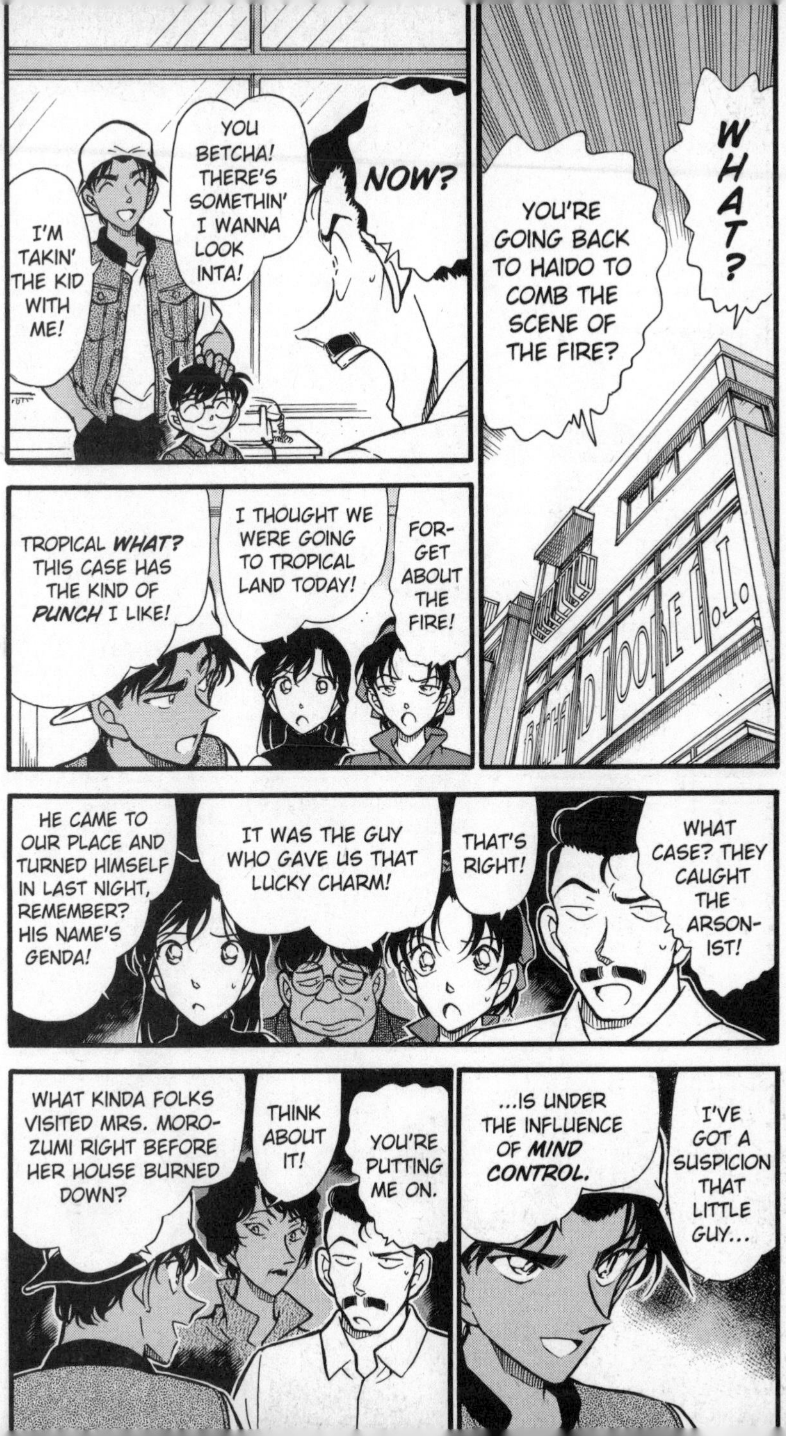
WHAT?
YOU'RE GOING BACK TO HAIDO TO COMB THE SCENE OF THE FIRE?
NOW?
YOU BETCHA! THERE'S SOMETHIN' I WANNA LOOK INTA!
I'M TAKIN' THE KID WITH ME!
FOR-GET ABOUT THE FIRE!
I THOUGHT WE WERE GOING TO TROPICAL LAND TODAY!
TROPICAL WHAT? THIS CASE HAS THE KIND OF PUNCH I LIKE!
WHAT CASE? THEY CAUGHT THE ARSON-IST!
THAT'S RIGHT!
IT WAS THE GUY WHO GAVE US THAT LUCKY CHARM!
HE CAME TO OUR PLACE AND TURNED HIMSELF IN LAST NIGHT, REMEMBER? HIS NAME'S GENDA!
I'VE GOT A SUSPICION THAT LITTLE GUY...
...IS UNDER THE INFLUENCE OF MIND CONTROL.
YOU'RE PUTTING ME ON.
THINK ABOUT IT!
WHAT KINDA FOLKS VISITED MRS. MORO-ZUMI RIGHT BEFORE HER HOUSE BURNED DOWN?

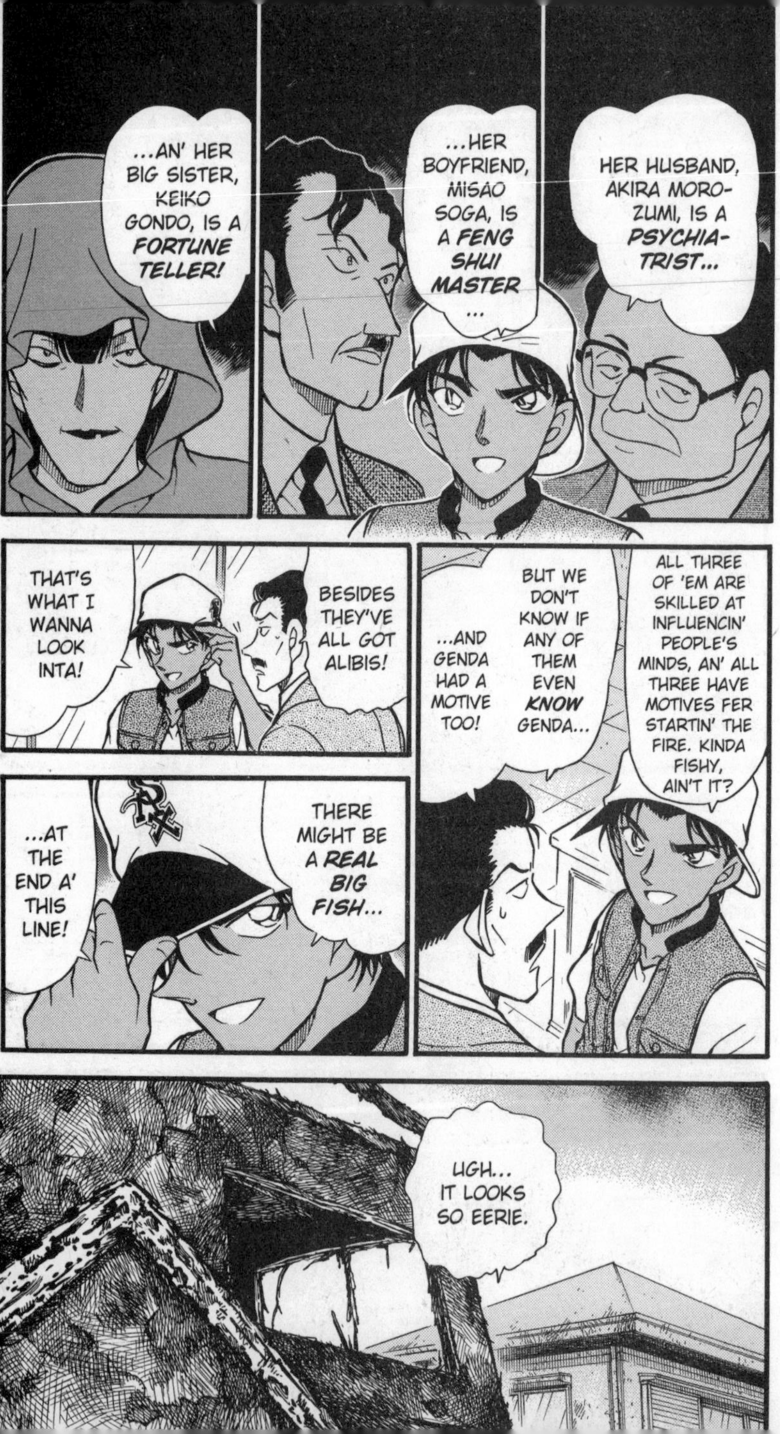
HER HUSBAND, AKIRA MORO-ZUMI, IS A PSYCHIATRIST...
...HER BOYFRIEND, MISAO SOGA, IS A FENG SHUI MASTER ...
...AN' HER BIG SISTER, KEIKO GONDO, IS A FORTUNE TELLER!
ALL THREE OF 'EM ARE SKILLED AT INFLUENCIN' PEOPLE'S MINDS, AN' ALL THREE HAVE MOTIVES FER STARTIN' THE FIRE. KINDA FISHY, AIN'T IT?
BUT WE DON'T KNOW IF ANY OF THEM EVEN KNOW GENDA...
...AND GENDA HAD A MOTIVE TOO!
BESIDES THEY'VE ALL GOT ALIBIS!
THAT'S WHAT I WANNA LOOK INTA!
THERE MIGHT BE A REAL BIG FISH...
...AT THE END A' THIS LINE!
UGH... IT LOOKS SO EERIE.

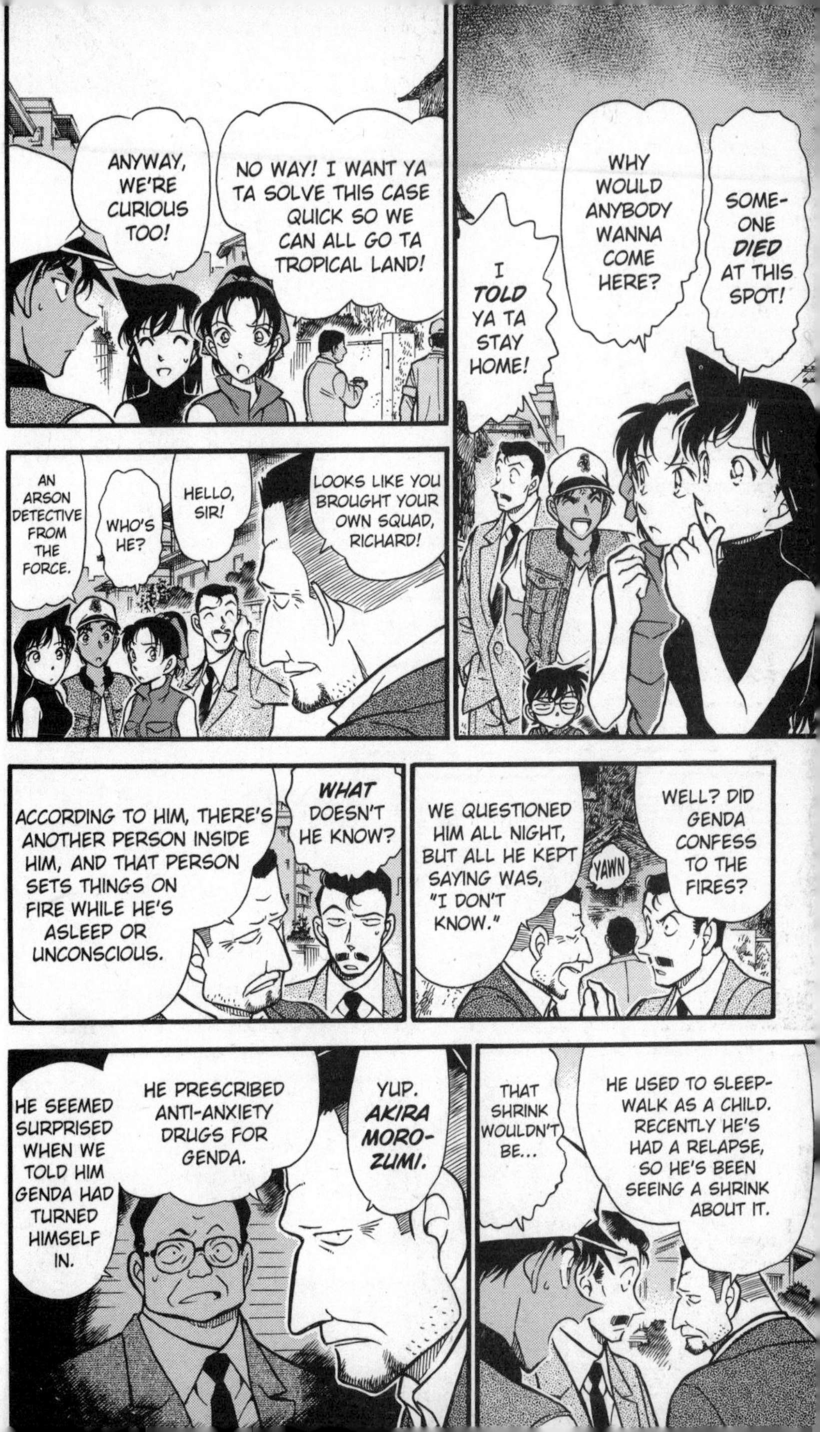
SOME-ONE DIED AT THIS SPOT!
WHY WOULD ANYBODY WANNA COME HERE?
I TOLD YA TA STAY HOME!
NO WAY! I WANT YA TA SOLVE THIS CASE QUICK SO WE CAN ALL GO TA TROPICAL LAND!
ANYWAY, WE'RE CURIOUS TOO!
LOOKS LIKE YOU BROUGHT YOUR OWN SQUAD, RICHARD!
HELLO, SIR!
WHO'S HE?
AN ARSON DETECTIVE FROM THE FORCE.
WELL? DID GENDA CONFESS TO THE FIRES?
YAWN
WE QUESTIONED HIM ALL NIGHT, BUT ALL HE KEPT SAYING WAS, "I DON'T KNOW."
WHAT DOESN'T HE KNOW?
ACCORDING TO HIM, THERE'S ANOTHER PERSON INSIDE HIM, AND THAT PERSON SETS THINGS ON FIRE WHILE HE'S ASLEEP OR UNCONSCIOUS.
HE USED TO SLEEP-WALK AS A CHILD. RECENTLY HE'S HAD A RELAPSE, SO HE'S BEEN SEEING A SHRINK ABOUT IT.
THAT SHRINK WOULDN'T BE...
YUP. AKIRA MORO-ZUMI.
HE PRESCRIBED ANTI-ANXIETY DRUGS FOR GENDA.
HE SEEMED SURPRISED WHEN WE TOLD HIM GENDA HAD TURNED HIMSELF IN.

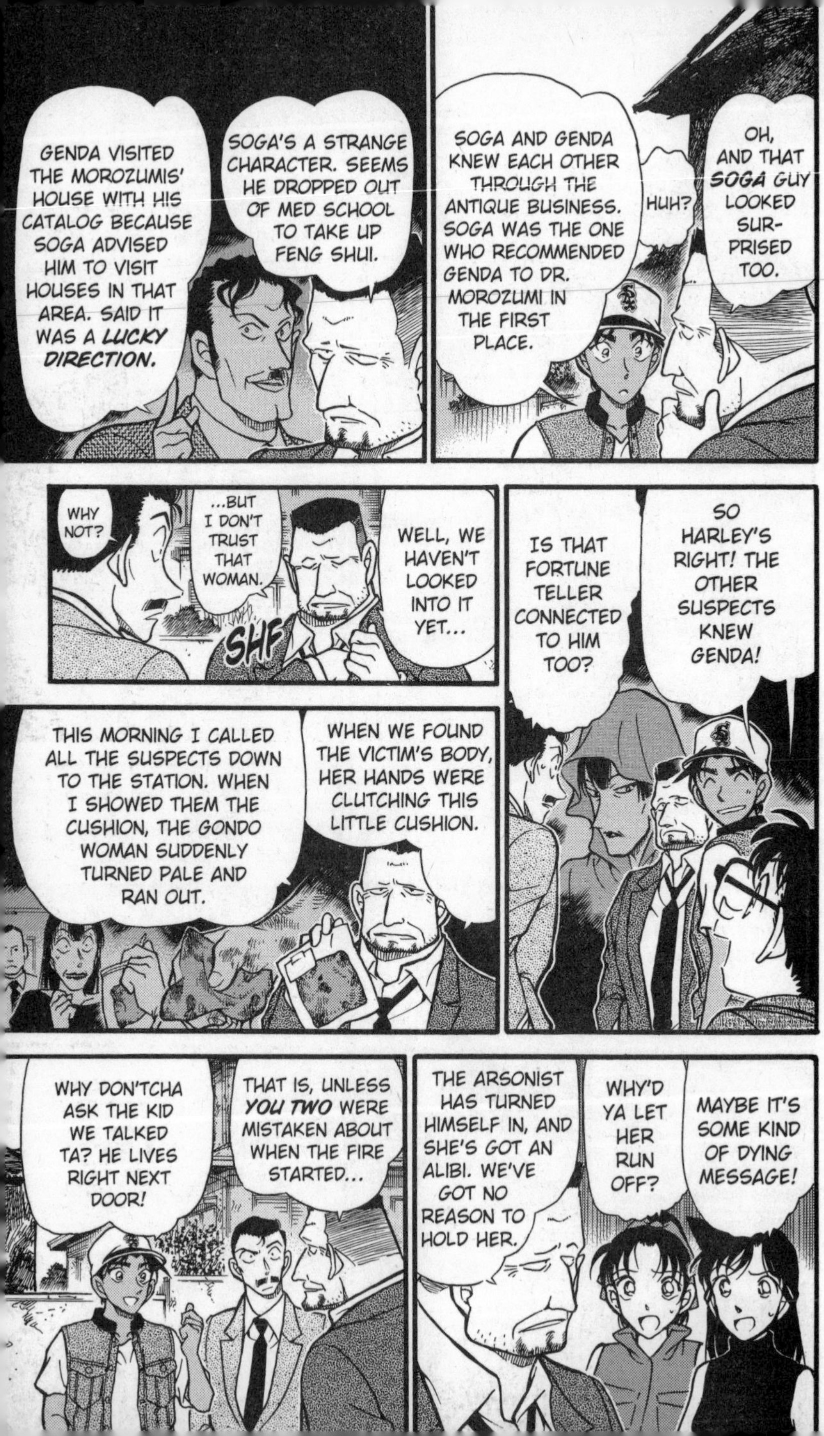
OH, AND THAT SOGA GUY LOOKED SUR-PRISED TOO.
HUH?
SOGA AND GENDA KNEW EACH OTHER THROUGH THE ANTIQUE BUSINESS. SOGA WAS THE ONE WHO RECOMMENDED GENDA TO DR. MOROZUMI IN THE FIRST PLACE.
SOGA'S A STRANGE CHARACTER. SEEMS HE DROPPED OUT OF MED SCHOOL TO TAKE UP FENG SHUI.
GENDA VISITED THE MOROZUMIS' HOUSE WITH HIS CATALOG BECAUSE SOGA ADVISED HIM TO VISIT HOUSES IN THAT AREA. SAID IT WAS A LUCKY DIRECTION.
SO HARLEY'S RIGHT! THE OTHER SUSPECTS KNEW GENDA!
IS THAT FORTUNE TELLER CONNECTED TO HIM TOO?
WELL, WE HAVEN'T LOOKED INTO IT YET...
...BUT I DON'T TRUST THAT WOMAN.
SHF
WHY NOT?
WHEN WE FOUND THE VICTIM'S BODY, HER HANDS WERE CLUTCHING THIS LITTLE CUSHION.
THIS MORNING I CALLED ALL THE SUSPECTS DOWN TO THE STATION. WHEN I SHOWED THEM THE CUSHION, THE GONDO WOMAN SUDDENLY TURNED PALE AND RAN OUT.
MAYBE IT'S SOME KIND OF DYING MESSAGE!
WHY'D YA LET HER RUN OFF?
THE ARSONIST HAS TURNED HIMSELF IN, AND SHE'S GOT AN ALIBI. WE'VE GOT NO REASON TO HOLD HER.
THAT IS, UNLESS YOU TWO WERE MISTAKEN ABOUT WHEN THE FIRE STARTED...
WHY DON'TCHA ASK THE KID WE TALKED TA? HE LIVES RIGHT NEXT DOOR!

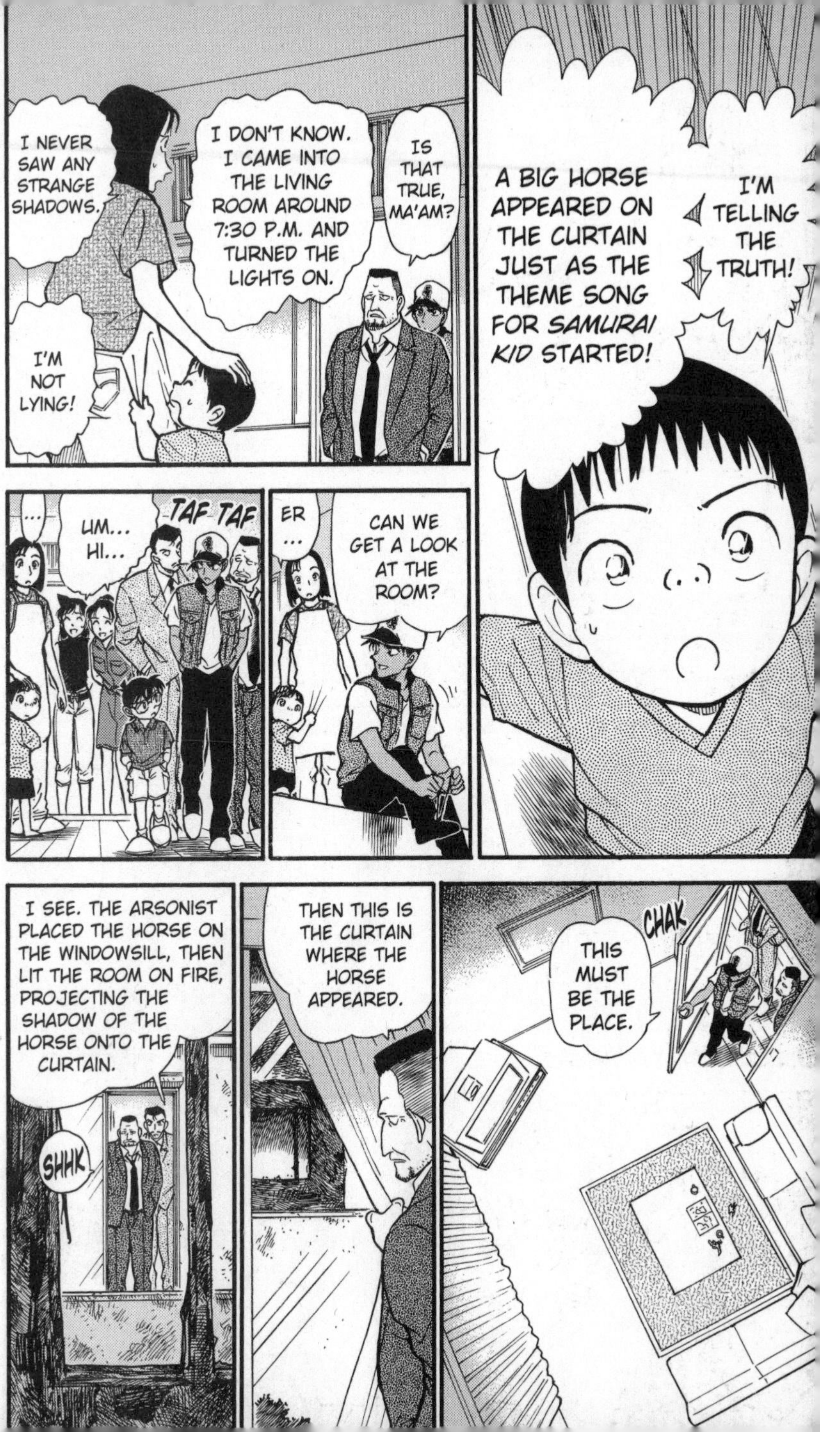

I'M TELLING THE TRUTH!
A BIG HORSE APPEARED ON THE CURTAIN JUST AS THE THEME SONG FOR *SAMURAI KID* STARTED!
IS THAT TRUE, MA'AM?
I DON'T KNOW. I CAME INTO THE LIVING ROOM AROUND 7:30 P.M. AND TURNED THE LIGHTS ON.
I NEVER SAW ANY STRANGE SHADOWS.
I'M NOT LYING!
ER...
CAN WE GET A LOOK AT THE ROOM?
TAF TAF
UM... HI...
...
CHAK
THIS MUST BE THE PLACE.
THEN THIS IS THE CURTAIN WHERE THE HORSE APPEARED.
I SEE. THE ARSONIST PLACED THE HORSE ON THE WINDOWSILL, THEN LIT THE ROOM ON FIRE, PROJECTING THE SHADOW OF THE HORSE ONTO THE CURTAIN.
SHHK

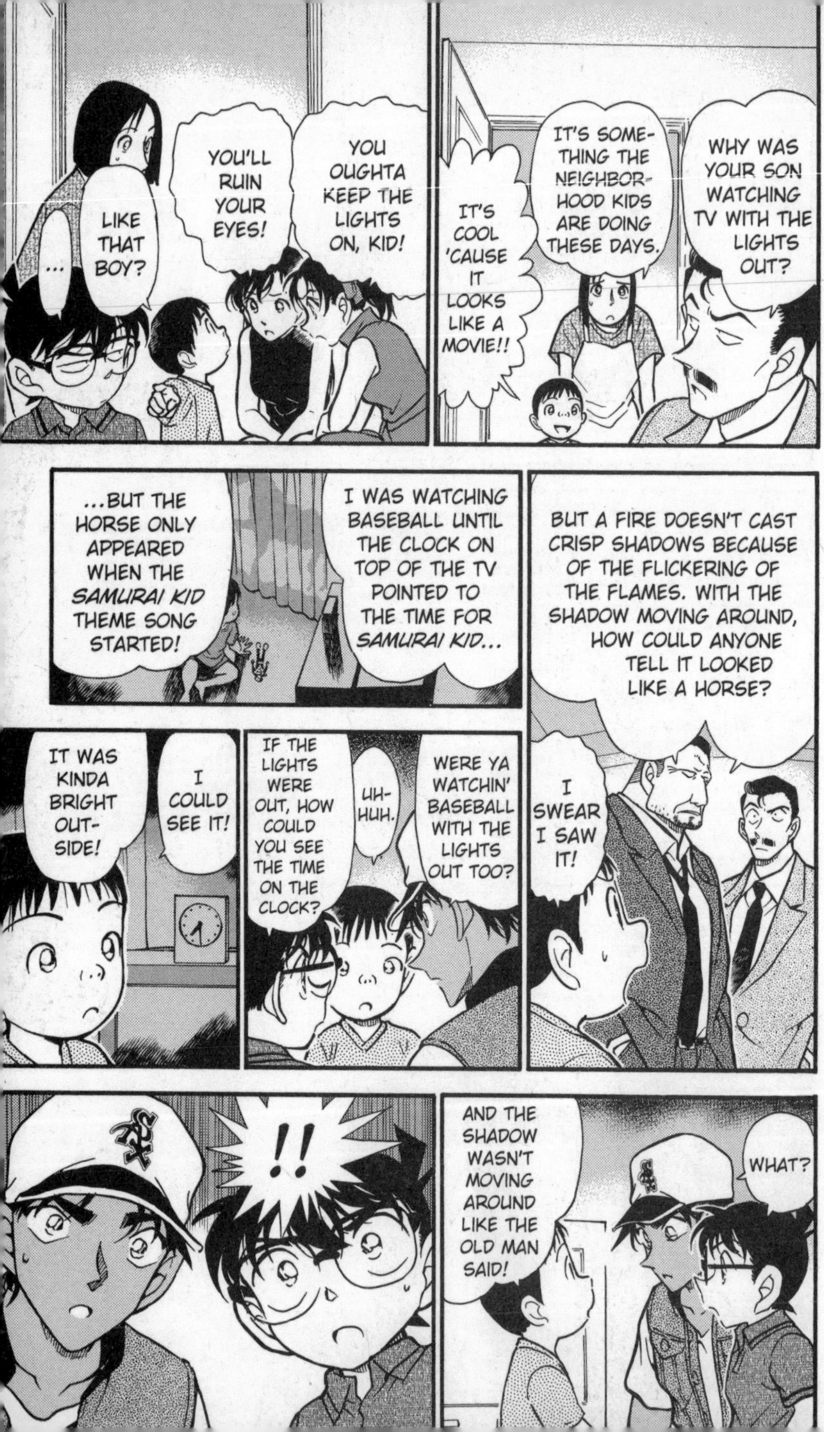
WHY WAS YOUR SON WATCHING TV WITH THE LIGHTS OUT?
IT'S SOMETHING THE NEIGHBORHOOD KIDS ARE DOING THESE DAYS.
IT'S COOL 'CAUSE IT LOOKS LIKE A MOVIE!!
YOU OUGHTA KEEP THE LIGHTS ON, KID!
YOU'LL RUIN YOUR EYES!
LIKE THAT BOY?
...
BUT A FIRE DOESN'T CAST CRISP SHADOWS BECAUSE OF THE FLICKERING OF THE FLAMES. WITH THE SHADOW MOVING AROUND, HOW COULD ANYONE TELL IT LOOKED LIKE A HORSE?
I SWEAR I SAW IT!
I WAS WATCHING BASEBALL UNTIL THE CLOCK ON TOP OF THE TV POINTED TO THE TIME FOR *SAMURAI KID*...
...BUT THE HORSE ONLY APPEARED WHEN THE *SAMURAI KID* THEME SONG STARTED!
WERE YA WATCHIN' BASEBALL WITH THE LIGHTS OUT TOO?
UH-HUH.
IF THE LIGHTS WERE OUT, HOW COULD YOU SEE THE TIME ON THE CLOCK?
I COULD SEE IT!
IT WAS KINDA BRIGHT OUTSIDE!
WHAT?
AND THE SHADOW WASN'T MOVING AROUND LIKE THE OLD MAN SAID!
!!

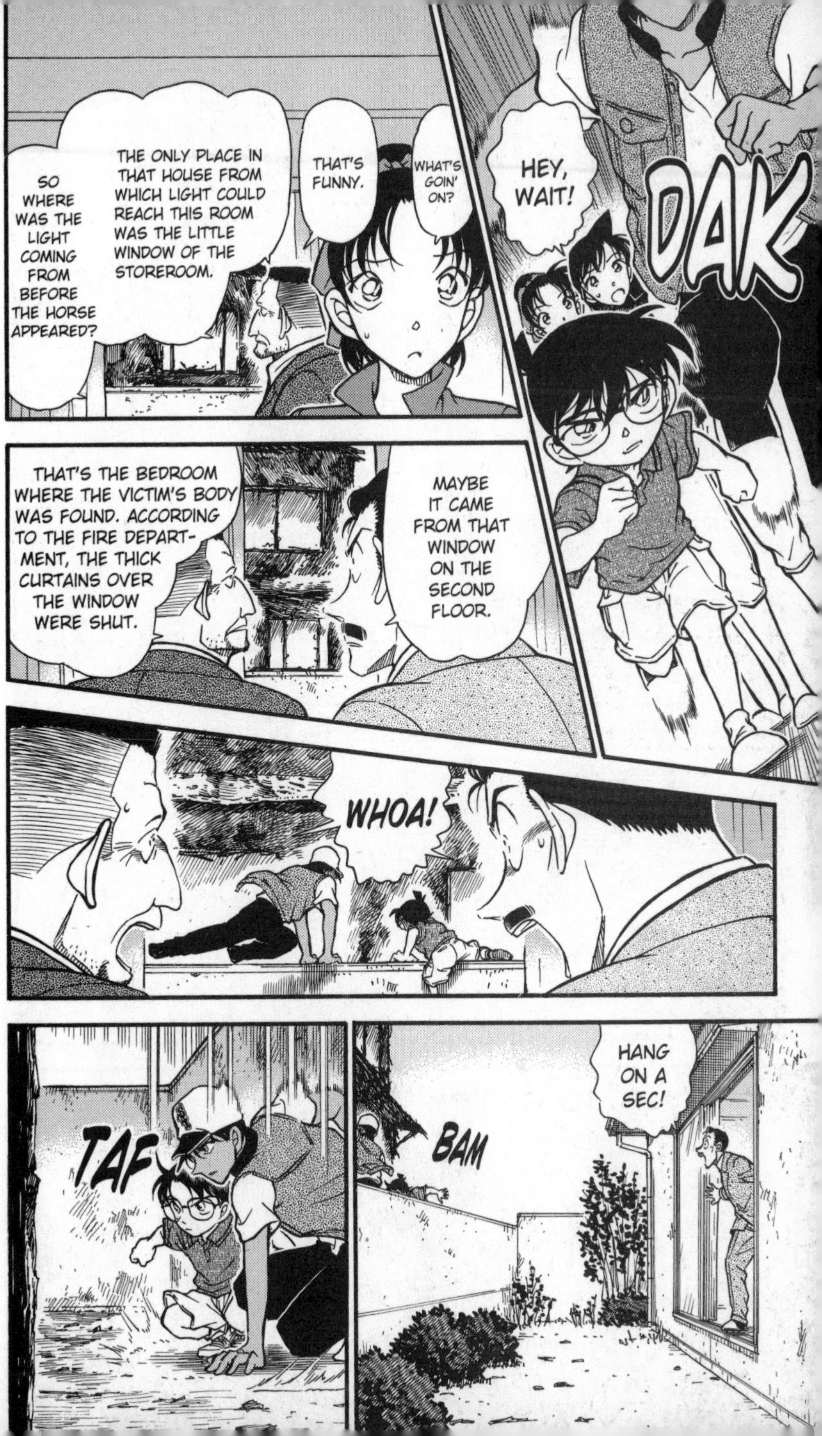
HEY, WAIT!
DAK
WHAT'S GOIN' ON?
THAT'S FUNNY.
THE ONLY PLACE IN THAT HOUSE FROM WHICH LIGHT COULD REACH THIS ROOM WAS THE LITTLE WINDOW OF THE STOREROOM.
SO WHERE WAS THE LIGHT COMING FROM BEFORE THE HORSE APPEARED?
MAYBE IT CAME FROM THAT WINDOW ON THE SECOND FLOOR.
THAT'S THE BEDROOM WHERE THE VICTIM'S BODY WAS FOUND. ACCORDING TO THE FIRE DEPARTMENT, THE THICK CURTAINS OVER THE WINDOW WERE SHUT.
WHOA!
HANG ON A SEC!
BAM
TAF

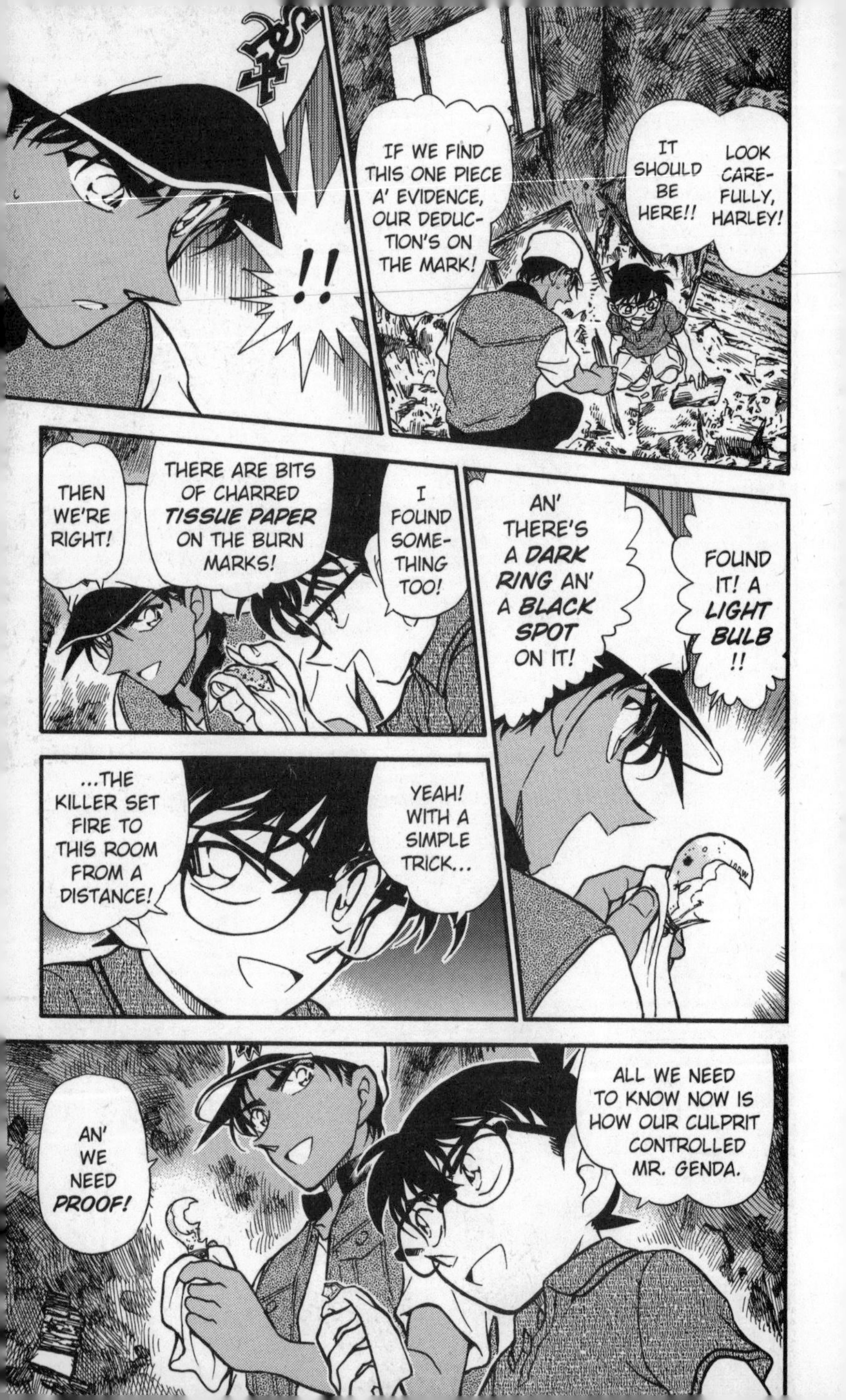
LOOK CAREFULLY, HARLEY!
IT SHOULD BE HERE!!
IF WE FIND THIS ONE PIECE A' EVIDENCE, OUR DEDUCTION'S ON THE MARK!
!!
FOUND IT! A **LIGHT BULB**!!
AN' THERE'S A **DARK RING** AN' A **BLACK SPOT** ON IT!
I FOUND SOMETHING TOO!
THERE ARE BITS OF CHARRED **TISSUE PAPER** ON THE BURN MARKS!
THEN WE'RE RIGHT!
YEAH! WITH A SIMPLE TRICK...
...THE KILLER SET FIRE TO THIS ROOM FROM A DISTANCE!
ALL WE NEED TO KNOW NOW IS HOW OUR CULPRIT CONTROLLED MR. GENDA.
AN' WE NEED **PROOF**!

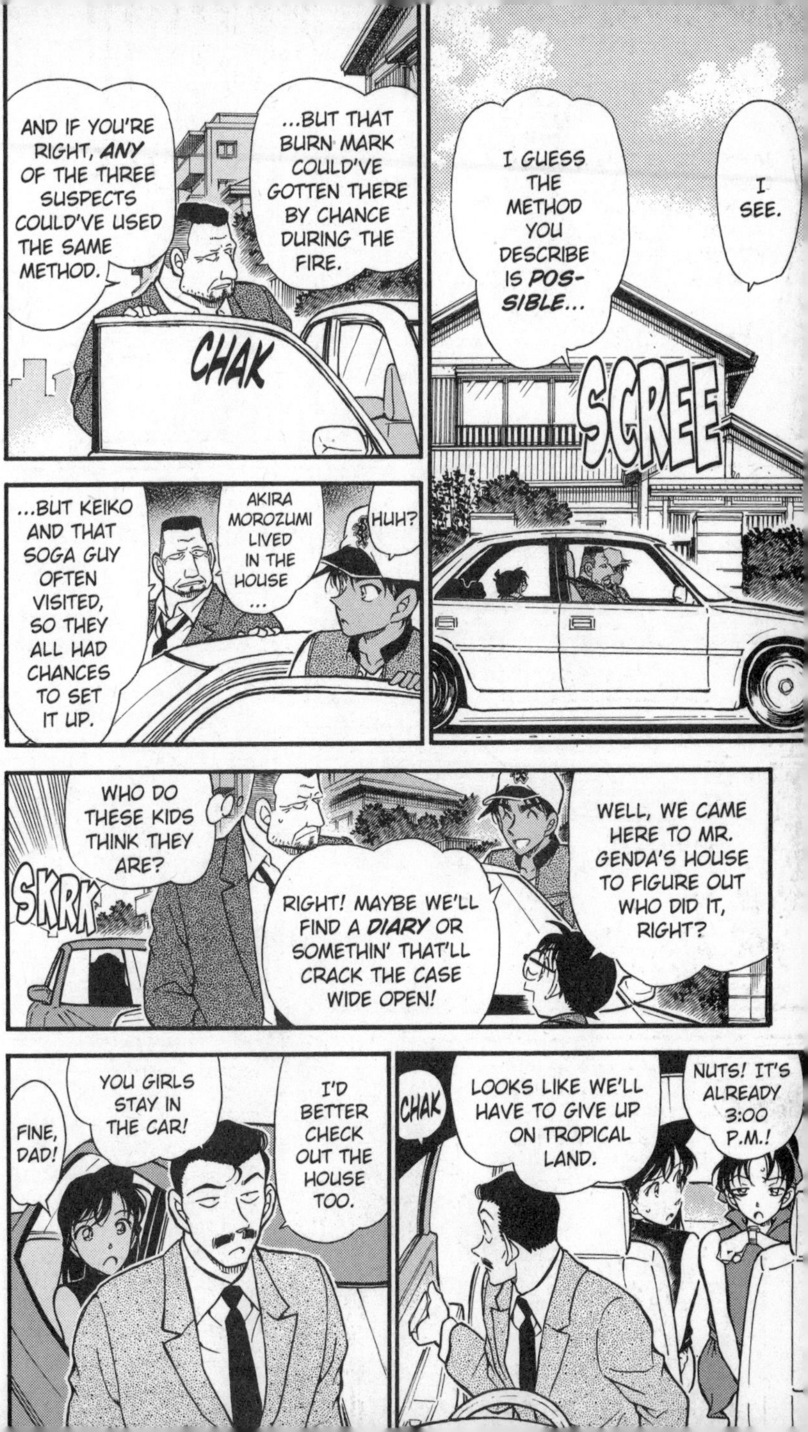
I SEE.
I GUESS THE METHOD YOU DESCRIBE IS ***POSSIBLE***...
SCREE
...BUT THAT BURN MARK COULD'VE GOTTEN THERE BY CHANCE DURING THE FIRE.
AND IF YOU'RE RIGHT, ***ANY*** OF THE THREE SUSPECTS COULD'VE USED THE SAME METHOD.
CHAK
HUH?
AKIRA MOROZUMI LIVED IN THE HOUSE...
...BUT KEIKO AND THAT SOGA GUY OFTEN VISITED, SO THEY ALL HAD CHANCES TO SET IT UP.
WELL, WE CAME HERE TO MR. GENDA'S HOUSE TO FIGURE OUT WHO DID IT, RIGHT?
RIGHT! MAYBE WE'LL FIND A ***DIARY*** OR SOMETHIN' THAT'LL CRACK THE CASE WIDE OPEN!
WHO DO THESE KIDS THINK THEY ARE?
SKRK
NUTS! IT'S ALREADY 3:00 P.M.!
LOOKS LIKE WE'LL HAVE TO GIVE UP ON TROPICAL LAND.
CHAK
I'D BETTER CHECK OUT THE HOUSE TOO.
YOU GIRLS STAY IN THE CAR!
FINE, DAD!

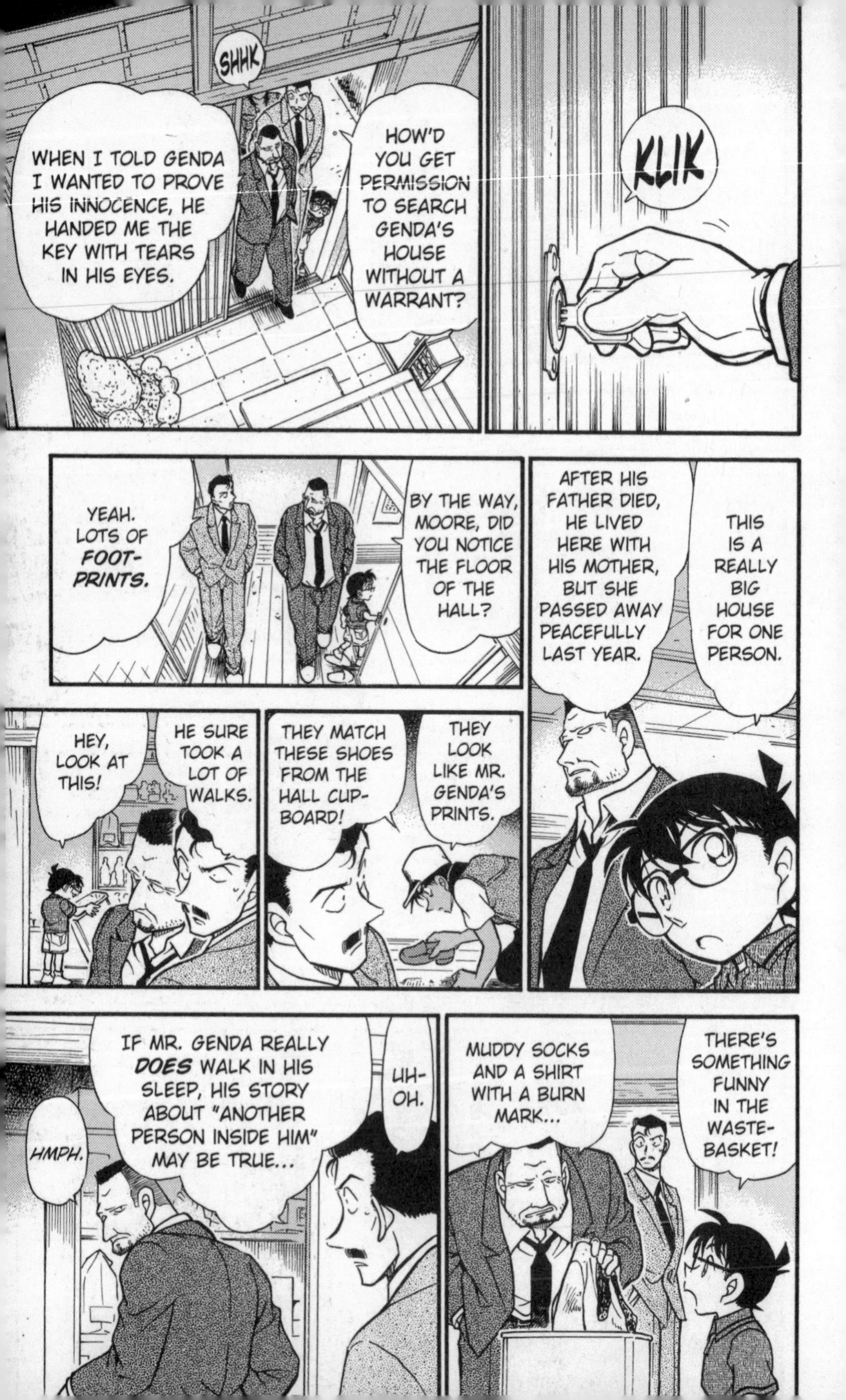

KLIK
SHHK
HOW'D YOU GET PERMISSION TO SEARCH GENDA'S HOUSE WITHOUT A WARRANT?
WHEN I TOLD GENDA I WANTED TO PROVE HIS INNOCENCE, HE HANDED ME THE KEY WITH TEARS IN HIS EYES.
THIS IS A REALLY BIG HOUSE FOR ONE PERSON.
AFTER HIS FATHER DIED, HE LIVED HERE WITH HIS MOTHER, BUT SHE PASSED AWAY PEACEFULLY LAST YEAR.
BY THE WAY, MOORE, DID YOU NOTICE THE FLOOR OF THE HALL?
YEAH. LOTS OF FOOTPRINTS.
THEY LOOK LIKE MR. GENDA'S PRINTS.
THEY MATCH THESE SHOES FROM THE HALL CUPBOARD!
HE SURE TOOK A LOT OF WALKS.
HEY, LOOK AT THIS!
THERE'S SOMETHING FUNNY IN THE WASTEBASKET!
MUDDY SOCKS AND A SHIRT WITH A BURN MARK...
UH-OH.
IF MR. GENDA REALLY DOES WALK IN HIS SLEEP, HIS STORY ABOUT "ANOTHER PERSON INSIDE HIM" MAY BE TRUE...
HMPH.

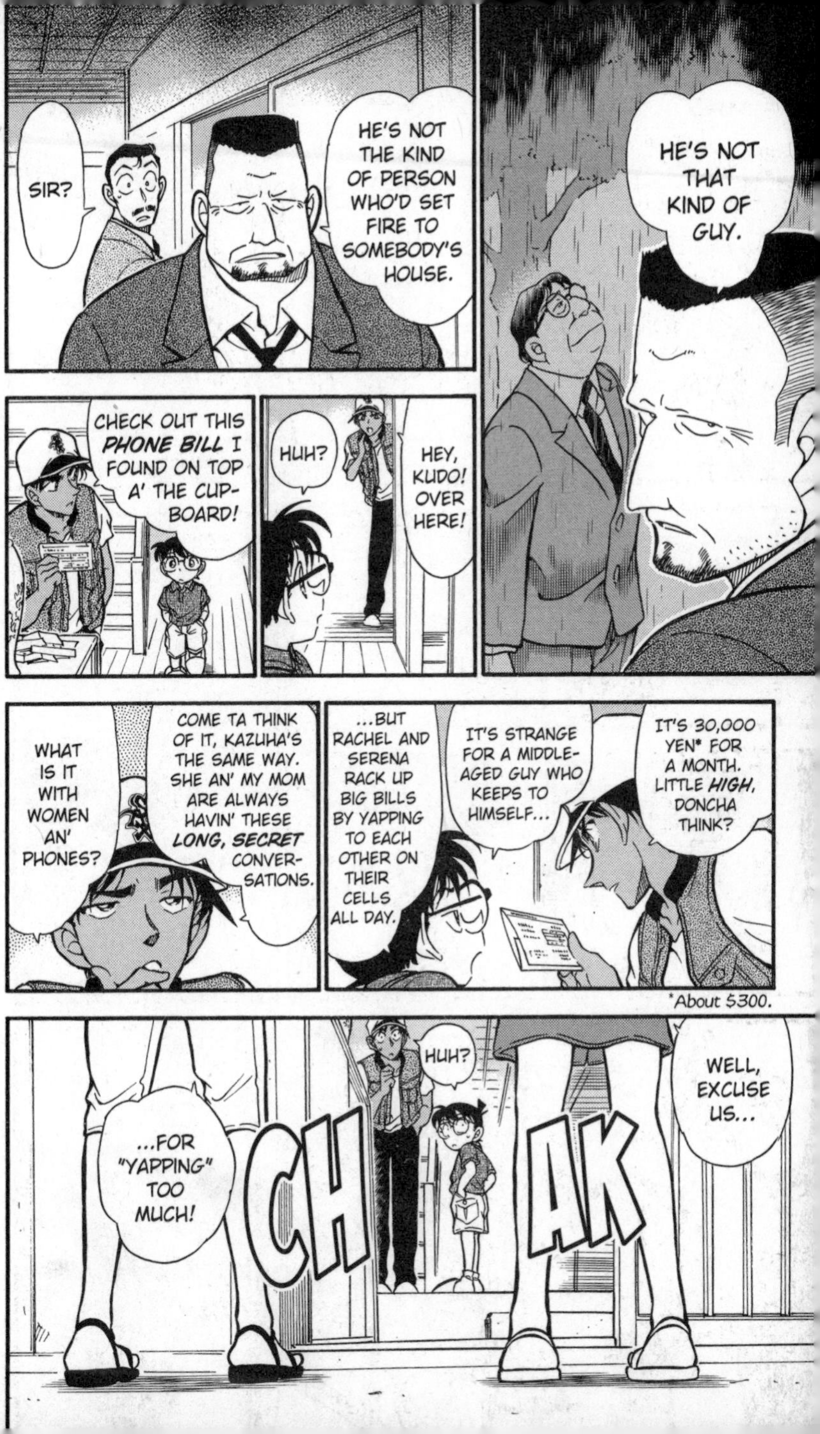
HE'S NOT THAT KIND OF GUY.
HE'S NOT THE KIND OF PERSON WHO'D SET FIRE TO SOMEBODY'S HOUSE.
SIR?
HEY, KUDO! OVER HERE!
HUH?
CHECK OUT THIS PHONE BILL I FOUND ON TOP A' THE CUP-BOARD!
IT'S 30,000 YEN* FOR A MONTH. LITTLE HIGH, DONCHA THINK?
IT'S STRANGE FOR A MIDDLE-AGED GUY WHO KEEPS TO HIMSELF...
...BUT RACHEL AND SERENA RACK UP BIG BILLS BY YAPPING TO EACH OTHER ON THEIR CELLS ALL DAY.
COME TA THINK OF IT, KAZUHA'S THE SAME WAY. SHE AN' MY MOM ARE ALWAYS HAVIN' THESE LONG, SECRET CONVER-SATIONS.
WHAT IS IT WITH WOMEN AN' PHONES?
*About $300.
WELL, EXCUSE US...
HUH?
CHAK
...FOR "YAPPING" TOO MUCH!

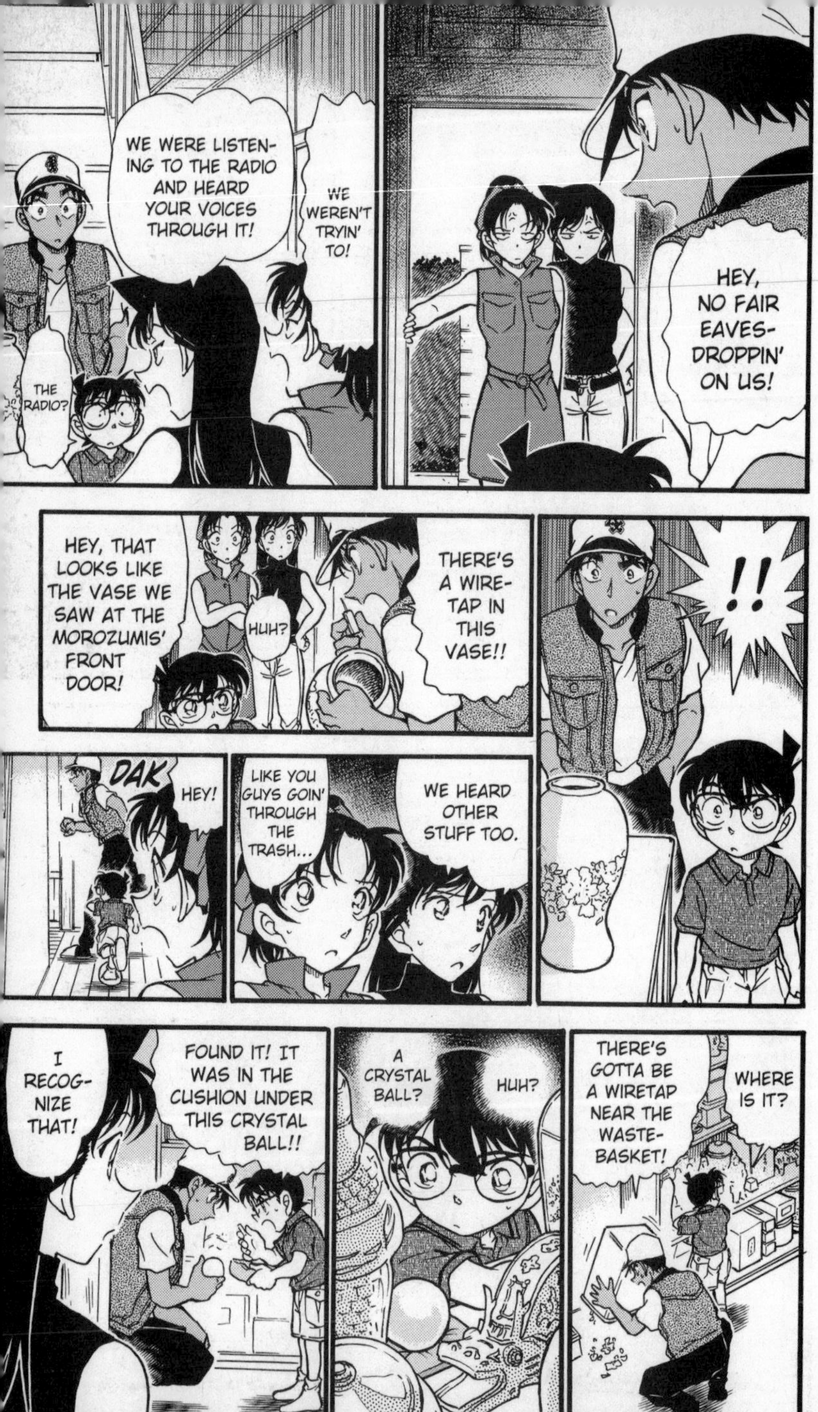
HEY, NO FAIR EAVESDROPPIN' ON US!
WE WEREN'T TRYIN' TO!
WE WERE LISTENING TO THE RADIO AND HEARD YOUR VOICES THROUGH IT!
THE RADIO?
!!
THERE'S A WIRETAP IN THIS VASE!!
HUH?
HEY, THAT LOOKS LIKE THE VASE WE SAW AT THE MOROZUMIS' FRONT DOOR!
WE HEARD OTHER STUFF TOO.
LIKE YOU GUYS GOIN' THROUGH THE TRASH...
HEY!
DAK
WHERE IS IT?
THERE'S GOTTA BE A WIRETAP NEAR THE WASTEBASKET!
HUH?
A CRYSTAL BALL?
FOUND IT! IT WAS IN THE CUSHION UNDER THIS CRYSTAL BALL!!
I RECOGNIZE THAT!

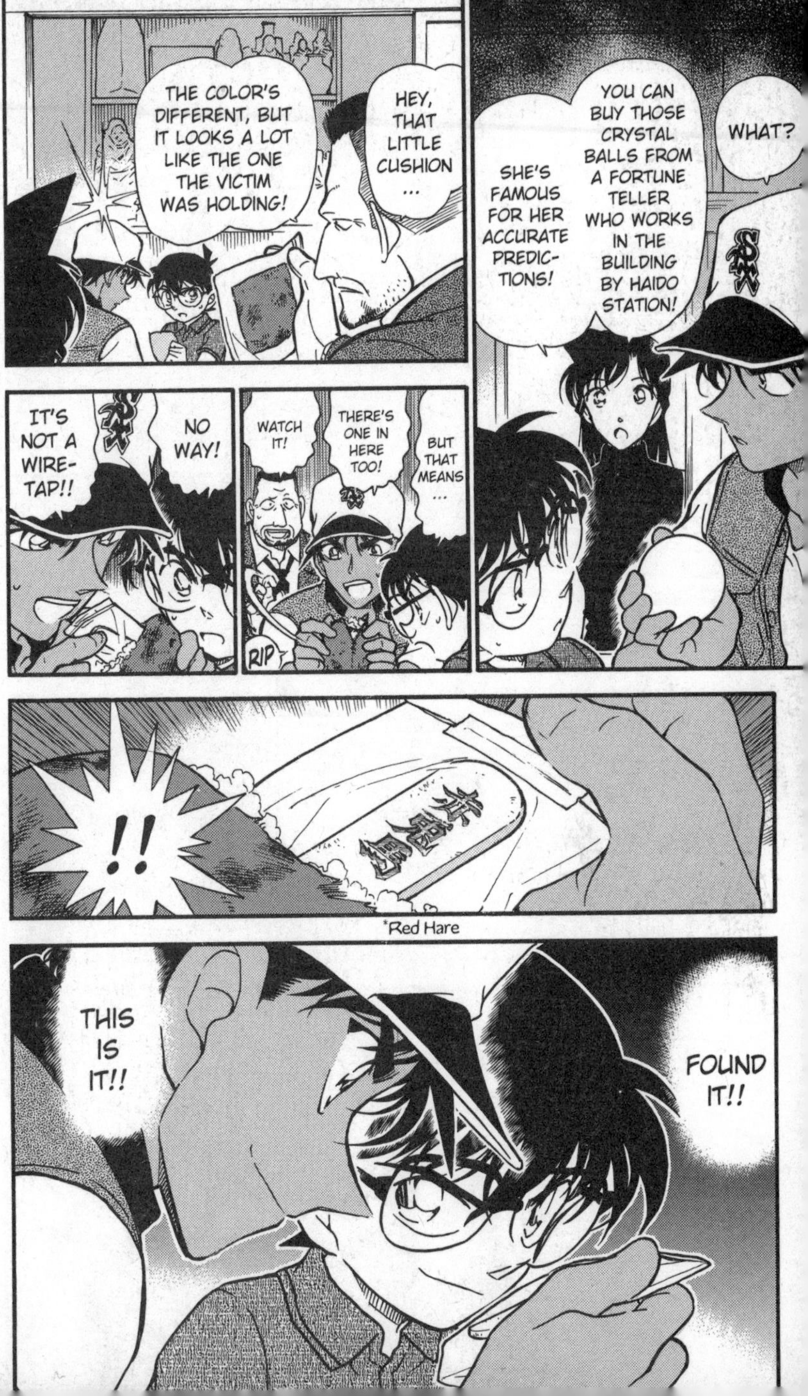
WHAT?
YOU CAN BUY THOSE CRYSTAL BALLS FROM A FORTUNE TELLER WHO WORKS IN THE BUILDING BY HAIDO STATION!
SHE'S FAMOUS FOR HER ACCURATE PREDIC-TIONS!
HEY, THAT LITTLE CUSHION ...
THE COLOR'S DIFFERENT, BUT IT LOOKS A LOT LIKE THE ONE THE VICTIM WAS HOLDING!
BUT THAT MEANS ...
THERE'S ONE IN HERE TOO!
WATCH IT!
RIP
NO WAY!
IT'S NOT A WIRE-TAP!!
!!
FOUND IT!!
THIS IS IT!!
*Red Hare

FILE 5: THREE OF A KIND

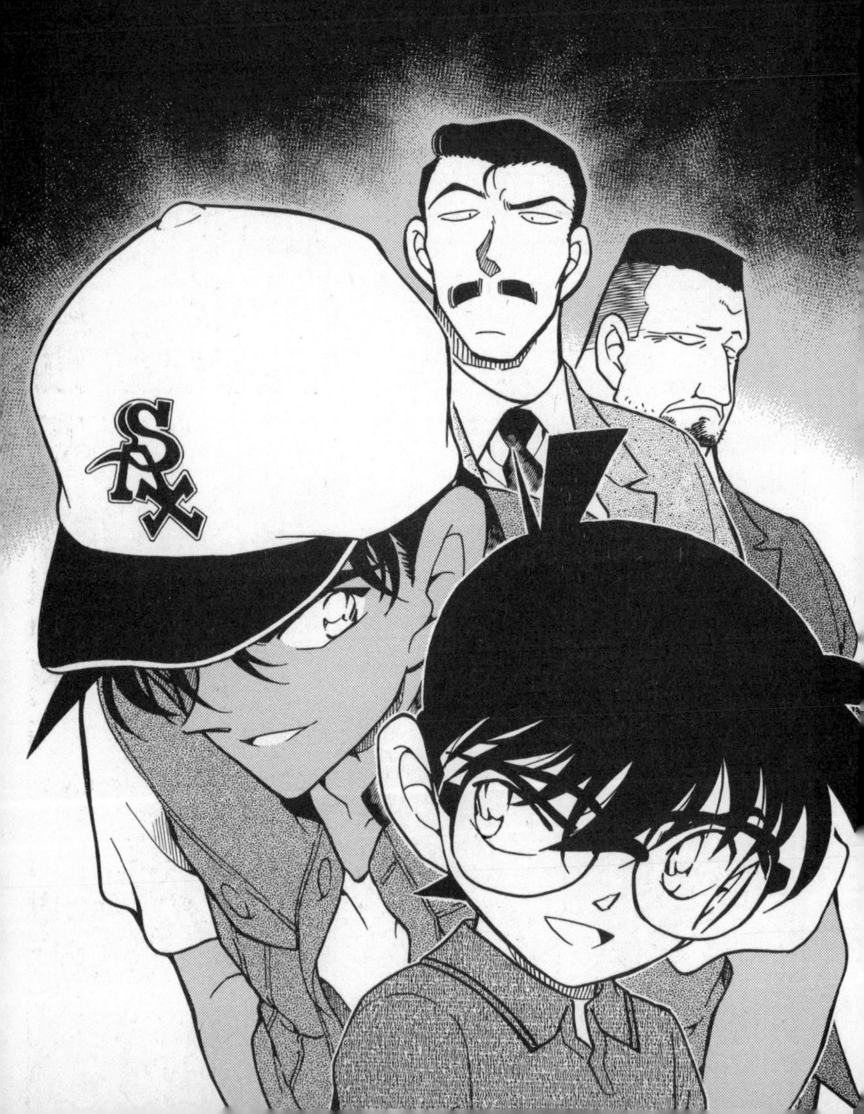

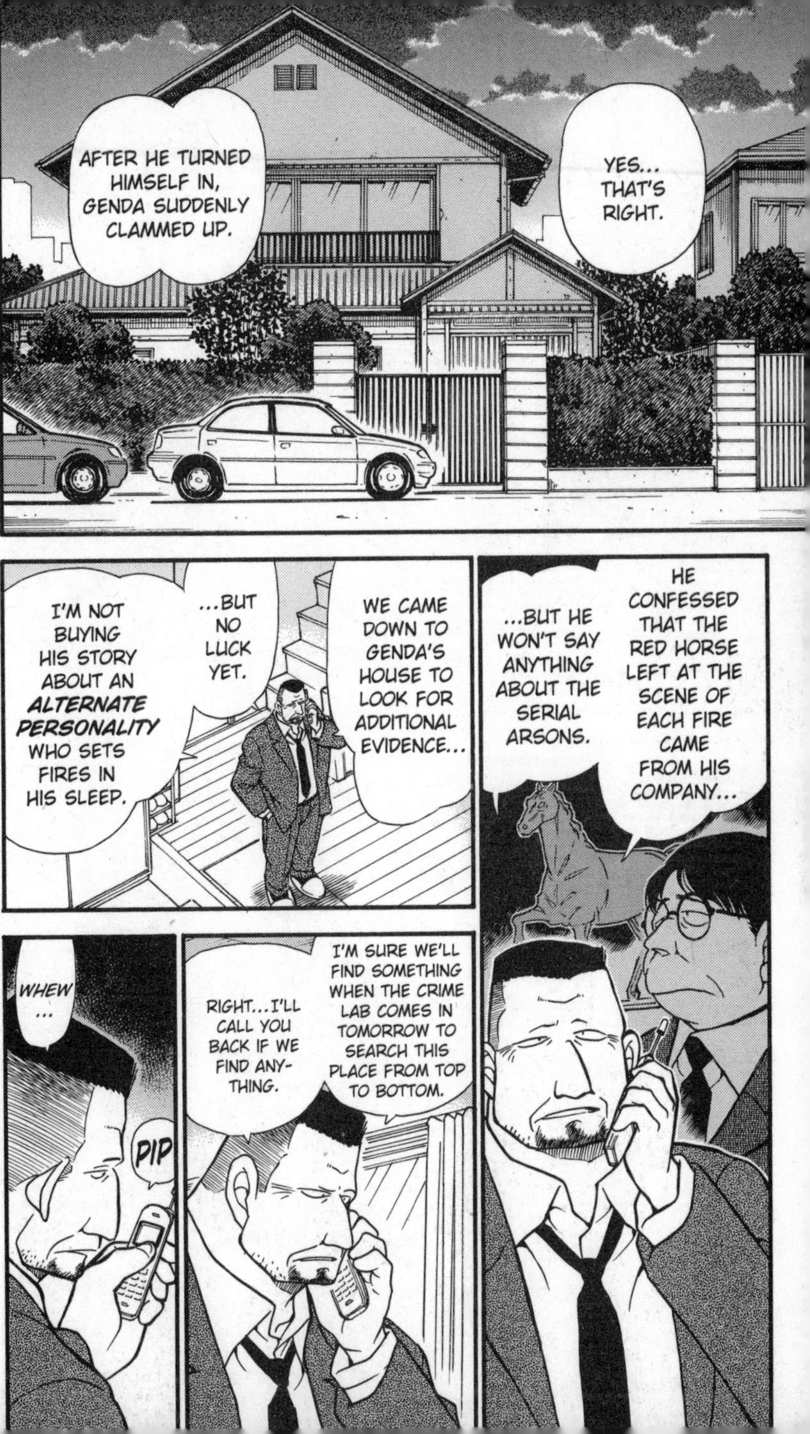
YES... THAT'S RIGHT.
AFTER HE TURNED HIMSELF IN, GENDA SUDDENLY CLAMMED UP.
HE CONFESSED THAT THE RED HORSE LEFT AT THE SCENE OF EACH FIRE CAME FROM HIS COMPANY...
...BUT HE WON'T SAY ANYTHING ABOUT THE SERIAL ARSONS.
WE CAME DOWN TO GENDA'S HOUSE TO LOOK FOR ADDITIONAL EVIDENCE...
...BUT NO LUCK YET.
I'M NOT BUYING HIS STORY ABOUT AN ALTERNATE PERSONALITY WHO SETS FIRES IN HIS SLEEP.
I'M SURE WE'LL FIND SOMETHING WHEN THE CRIME LAB COMES IN TOMORROW TO SEARCH THIS PLACE FROM TOP TO BOTTOM.
RIGHT...I'LL CALL YOU BACK IF WE FIND ANY-THING.
WHEW...
PIP

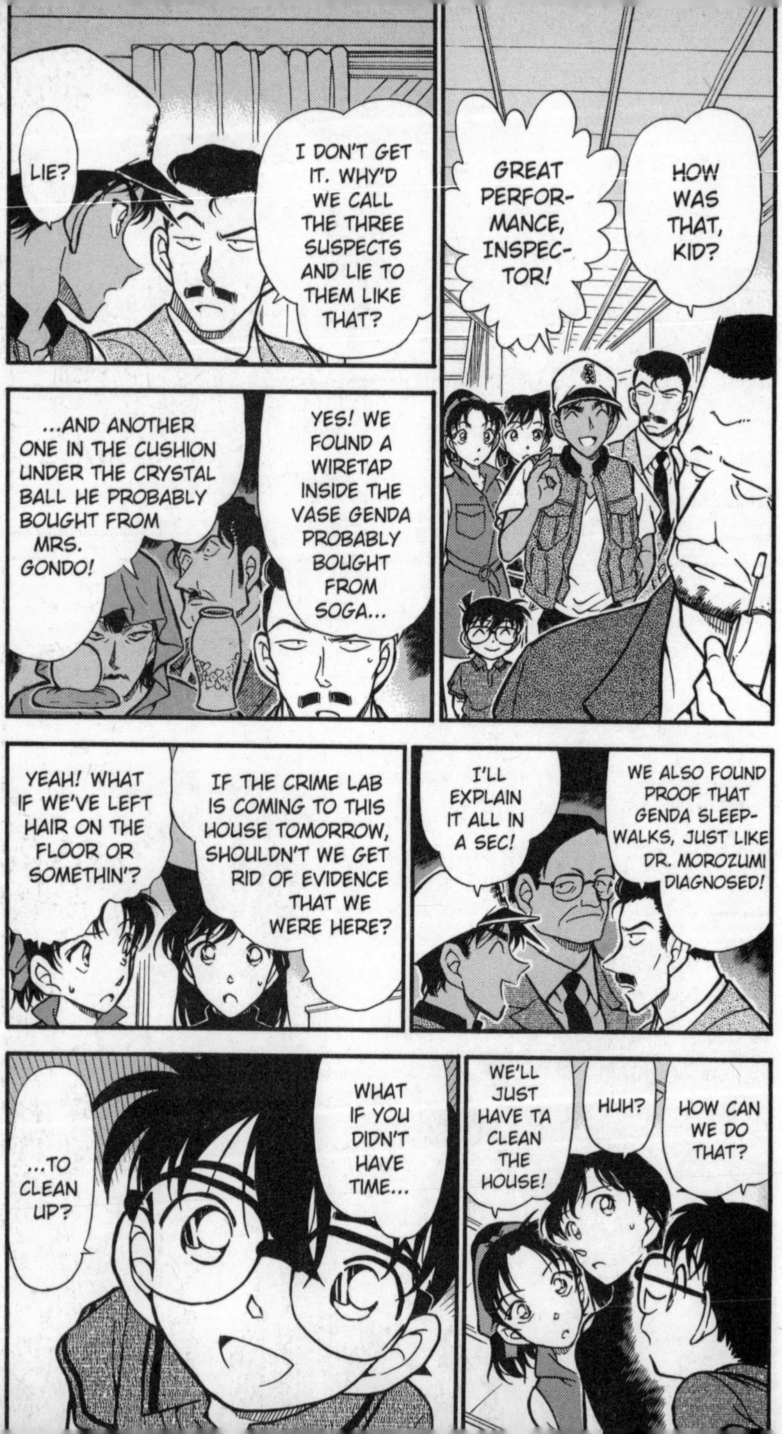
HOW WAS THAT, KID?
GREAT PERFORMANCE, INSPECTOR!
I DON'T GET IT. WHY'D WE CALL THE THREE SUSPECTS AND LIE TO THEM LIKE THAT?
LIE?
YES! WE FOUND A WIRETAP INSIDE THE VASE GENDA PROBABLY BOUGHT FROM SOGA...
...AND ANOTHER ONE IN THE CUSHION UNDER THE CRYSTAL BALL HE PROBABLY BOUGHT FROM MRS. GONDO!
WE ALSO FOUND PROOF THAT GENDA SLEEP-WALKS, JUST LIKE DR. MOROZUMI DIAGNOSED!
I'LL EXPLAIN IT ALL IN A SEC!
IF THE CRIME LAB IS COMING TO THIS HOUSE TOMORROW, SHOULDN'T WE GET RID OF EVIDENCE THAT WE WERE HERE?
YEAH! WHAT IF WE'VE LEFT HAIR ON THE FLOOR OR SOMETHIN'?
HOW CAN WE DO THAT?
HUH?
WE'LL JUST HAVE TA CLEAN THE HOUSE!
WHAT IF YOU DIDN'T HAVE TIME...
...TO CLEAN UP?

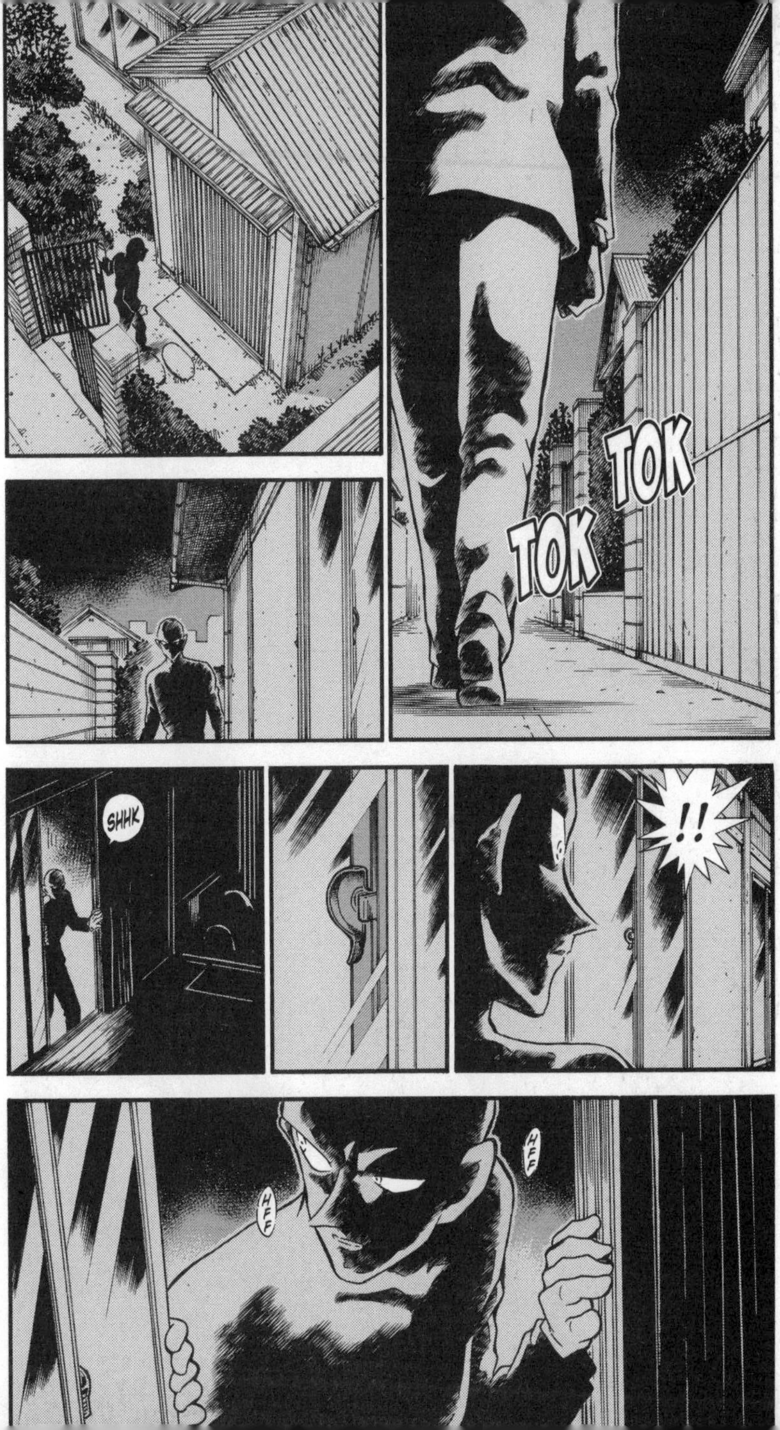
TOK
TOK
SHHK
!!
HFF
HFF

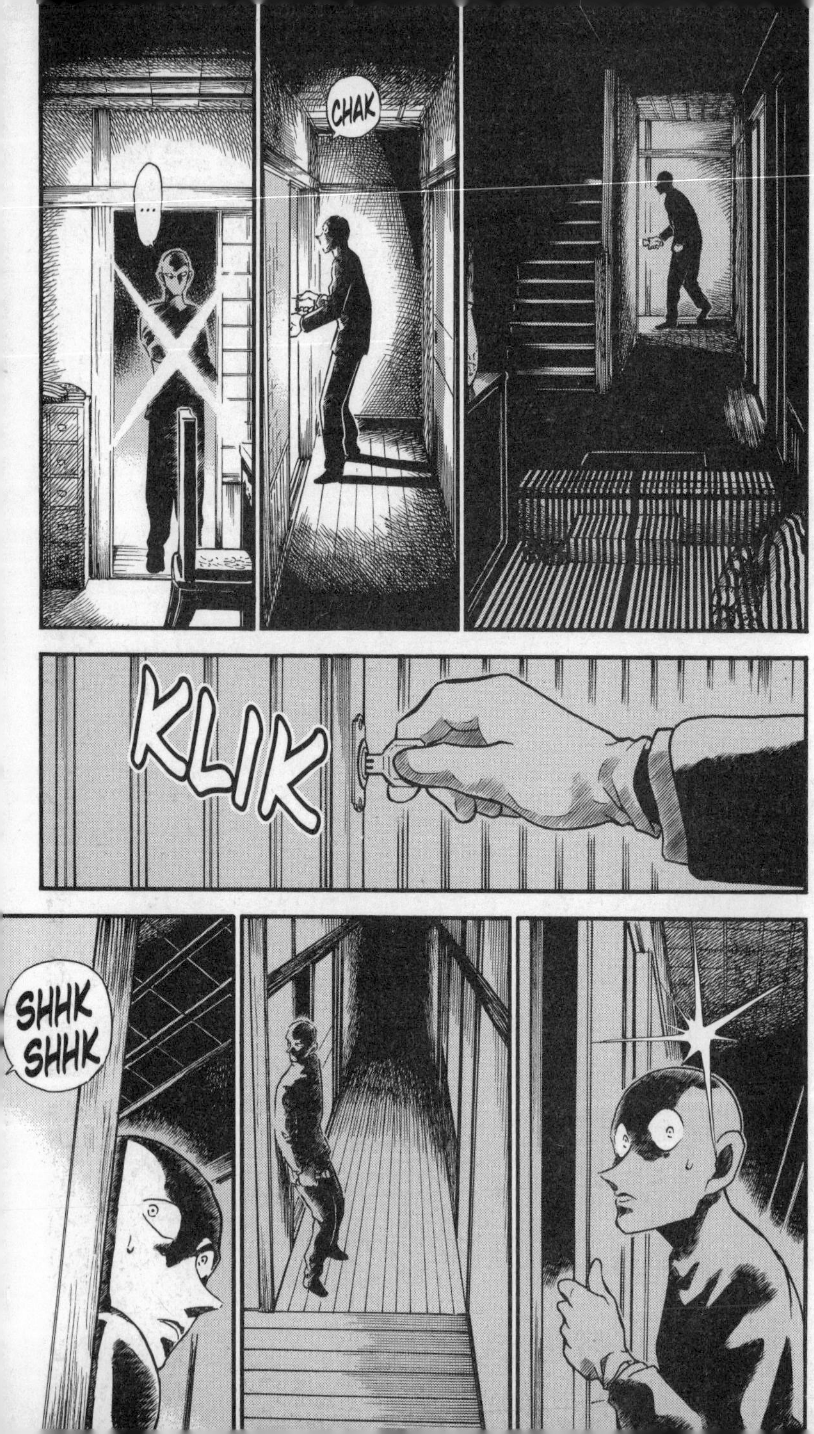
CHAK
...
KLIK
SHHK SHHK

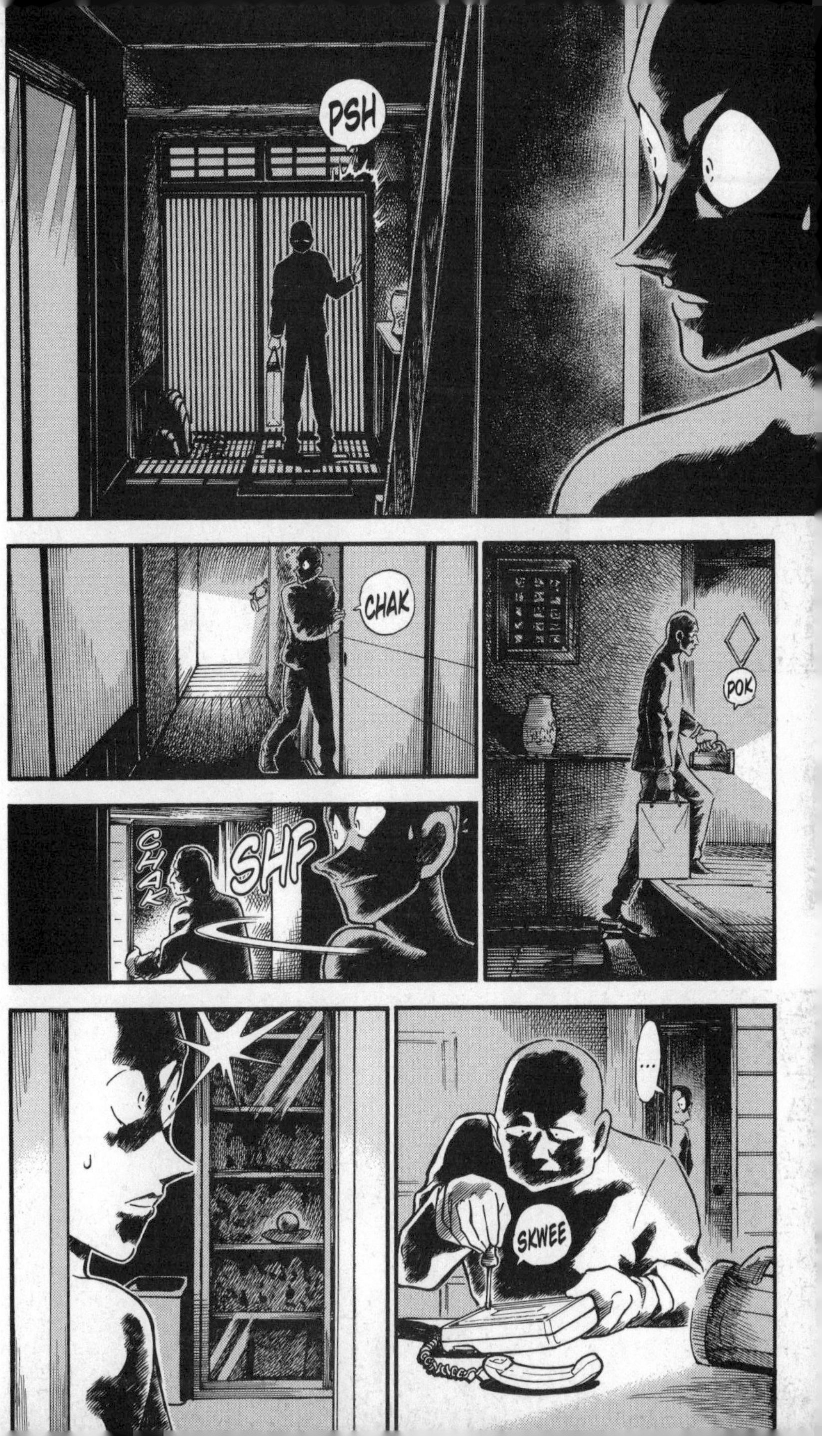
PSH
POK
CHAK
SHF
CHAK
...
SKWEE

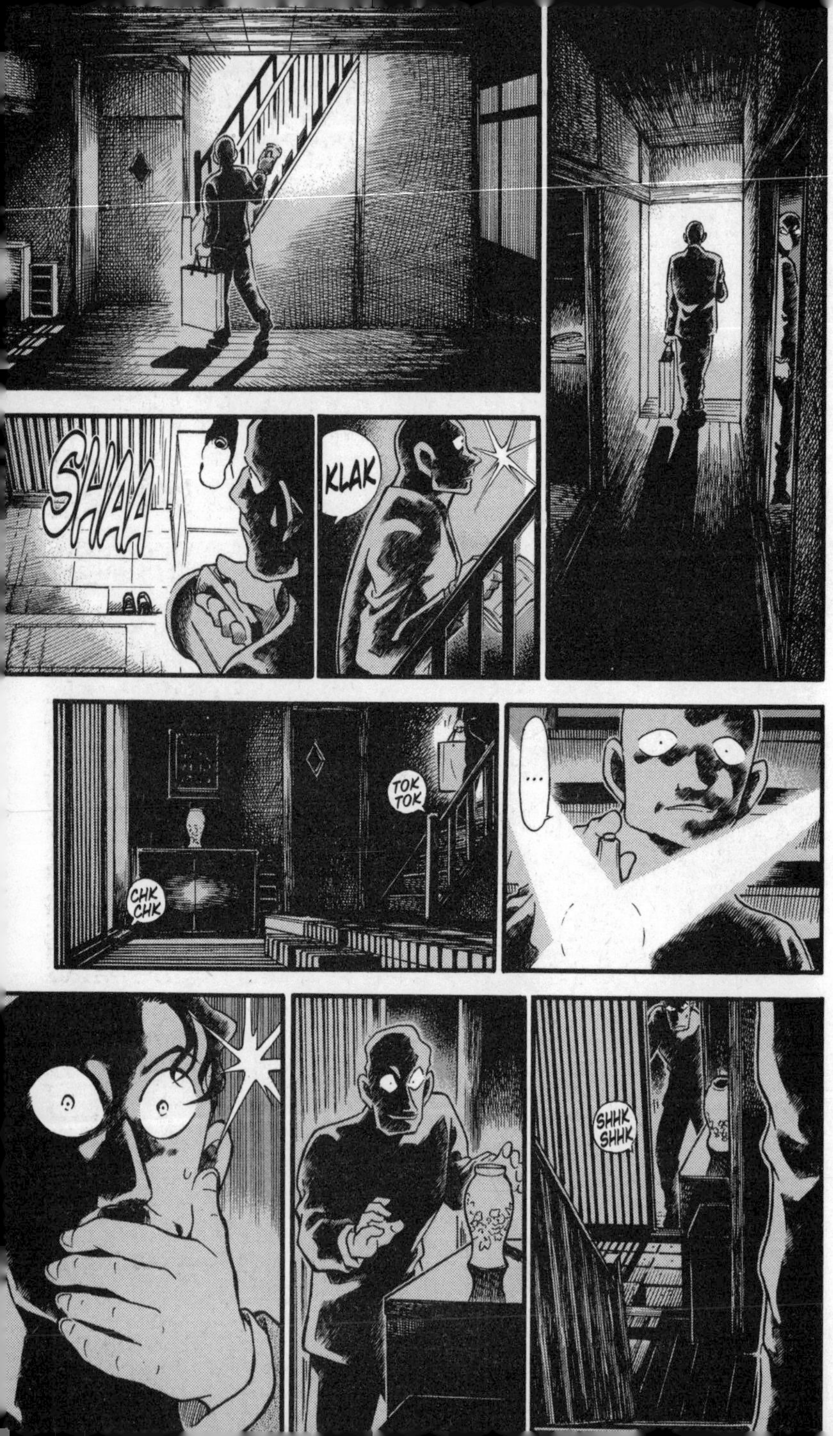
KLAK
SHAA
...
TOK TOK
CHK CHK
SHHK SHHK

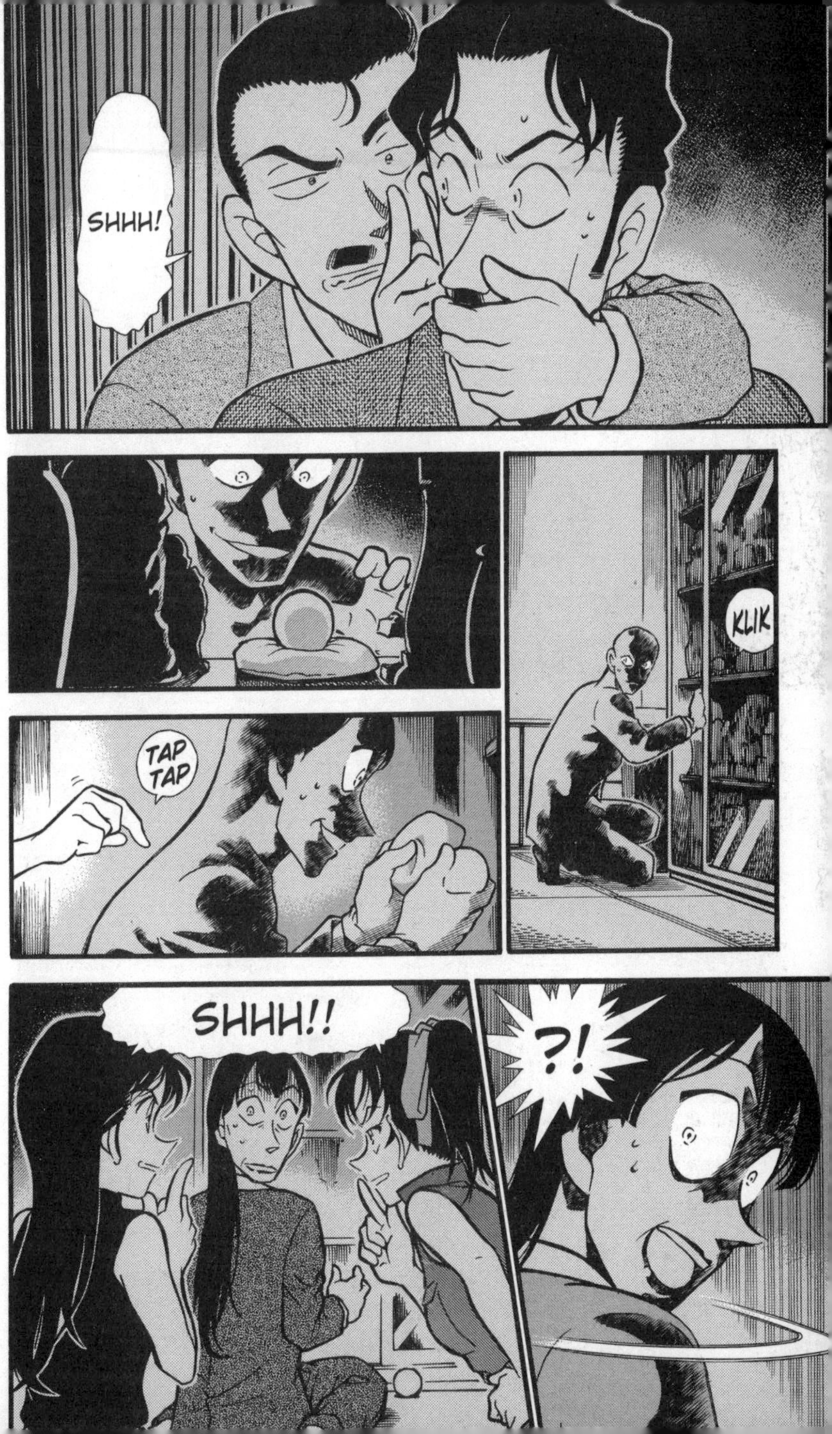
SHHH!
KLIK
TAP TAP
?!
SHHH!!

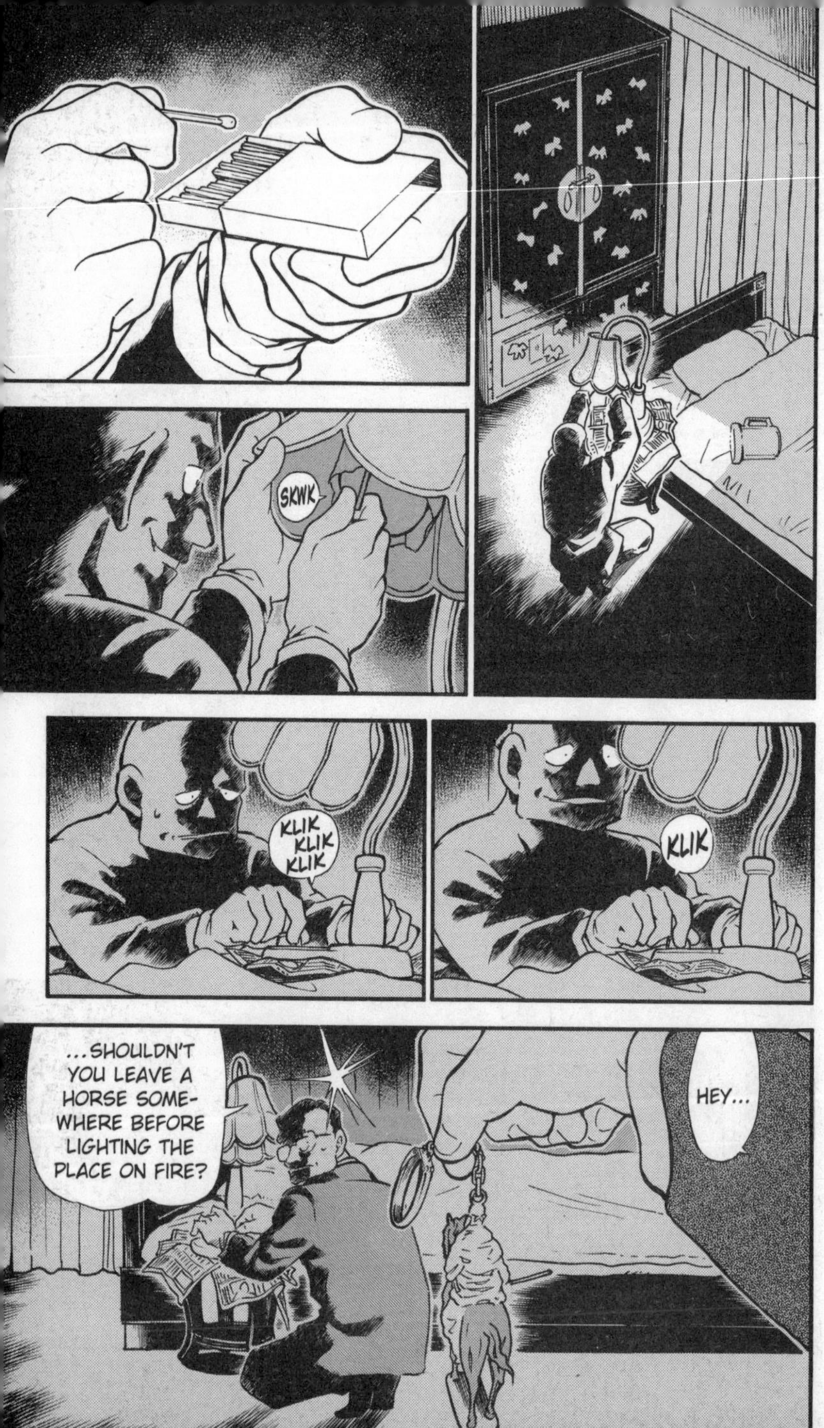
SKWK
KLIK
KLIK KLIK KLIK
HEY...
...SHOULDN'T YOU LEAVE A HORSE SOME-WHERE BEFORE LIGHTING THE PLACE ON FIRE?

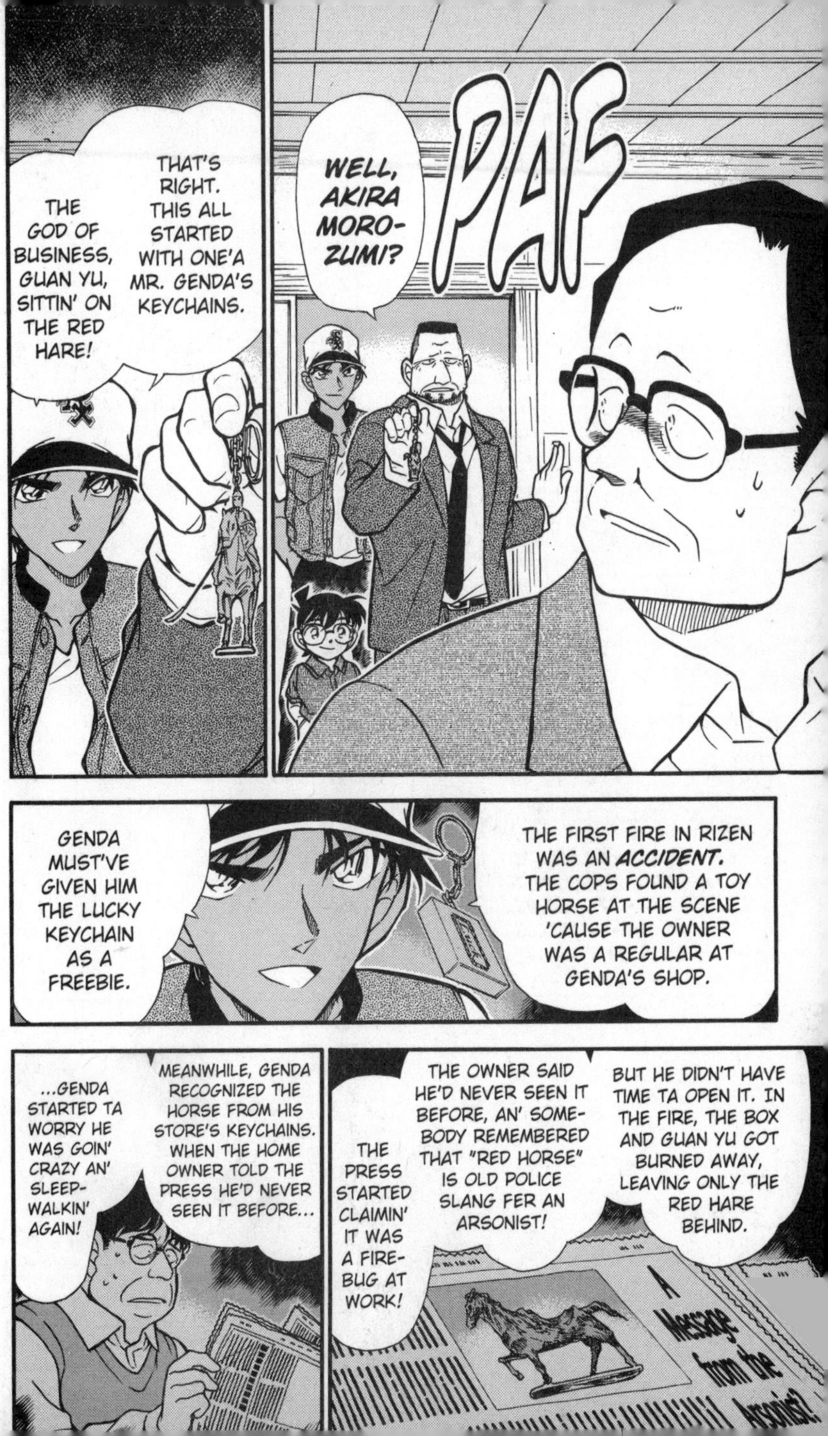
PAF
WELL, AKIRA MORO-ZUMI?
THAT'S RIGHT. THIS ALL STARTED WITH ONE'A MR. GENDA'S KEYCHAINS.
THE GOD OF BUSINESS, GUAN YU, SITTIN' ON THE RED HARE!
THE FIRST FIRE IN RIZEN WAS AN ACCIDENT. THE COPS FOUND A TOY HORSE AT THE SCENE 'CAUSE THE OWNER WAS A REGULAR AT GENDA'S SHOP.
GENDA MUST'VE GIVEN HIM THE LUCKY KEYCHAIN AS A FREEBIE.
BUT HE DIDN'T HAVE TIME TA OPEN IT. IN THE FIRE, THE BOX AND GUAN YU GOT BURNED AWAY, LEAVING ONLY THE RED HARE BEHIND.
THE OWNER SAID HE'D NEVER SEEN IT BEFORE, AN' SOME-BODY REMEMBERED THAT "RED HORSE" IS OLD POLICE SLANG FER AN ARSONIST!
THE PRESS STARTED CLAIMIN' IT WAS A FIRE-BUG AT WORK!
A Message from the Arsonist?
MEANWHILE, GENDA RECOGNIZED THE HORSE FROM HIS STORE'S KEYCHAINS. WHEN THE HOME OWNER TOLD THE PRESS HE'D NEVER SEEN IT BEFORE...
...GENDA STARTED TA WORRY HE WAS GOIN' CRAZY AN' SLEEP-WALKIN' AGAIN!

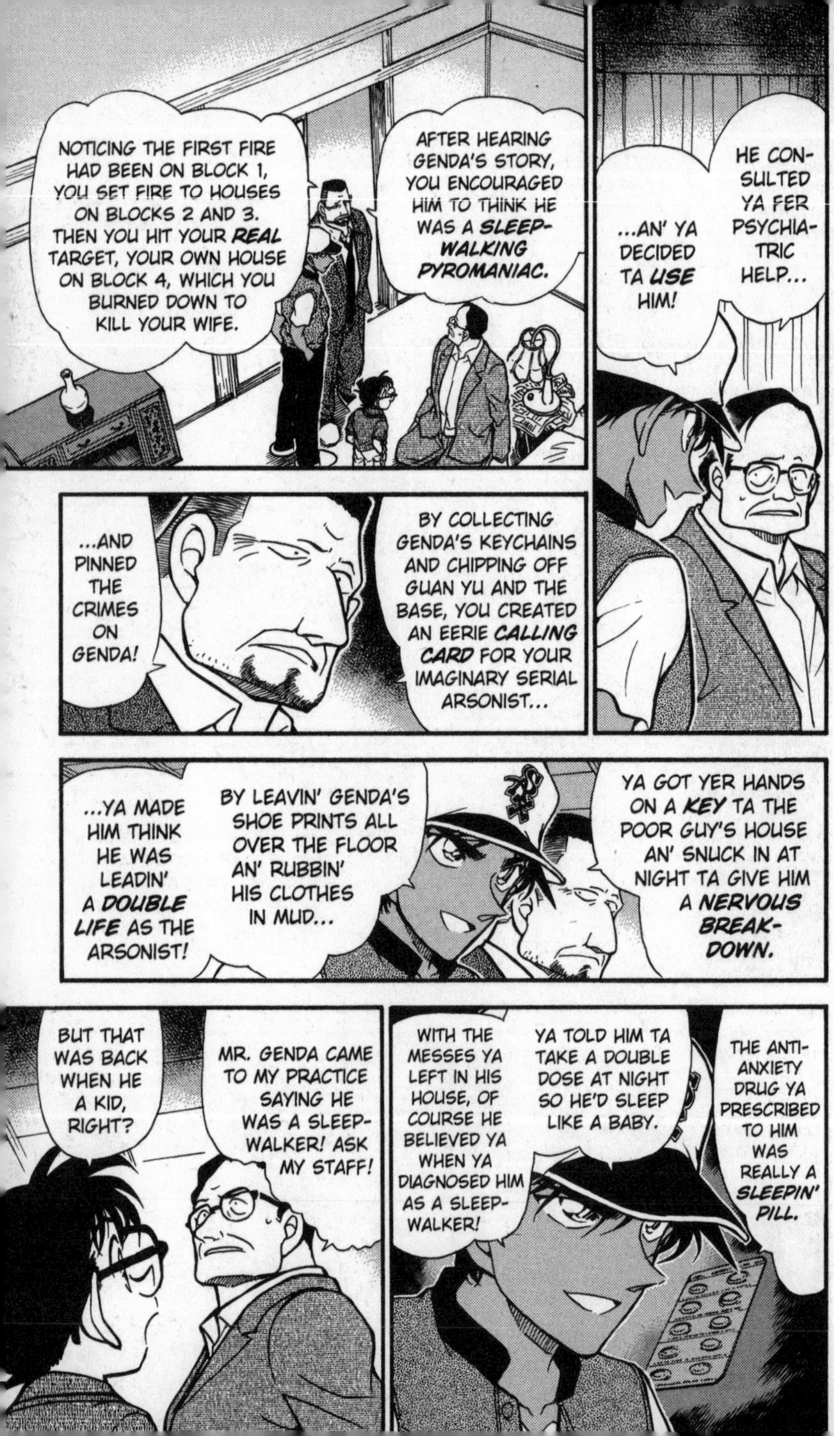
HE CONSULTED YA FER PSYCHIATRIC HELP...
...AN' YA DECIDED TA USE HIM!
AFTER HEARING GENDA'S STORY, YOU ENCOURAGED HIM TO THINK HE WAS A SLEEPWALKING PYROMANIAC.
NOTICING THE FIRST FIRE HAD BEEN ON BLOCK 1, YOU SET FIRE TO HOUSES ON BLOCKS 2 AND 3. THEN YOU HIT YOUR REAL TARGET, YOUR OWN HOUSE ON BLOCK 4, WHICH YOU BURNED DOWN TO KILL YOUR WIFE.
BY COLLECTING GENDA'S KEYCHAINS AND CHIPPING OFF GUAN YU AND THE BASE, YOU CREATED AN EERIE CALLING CARD FOR YOUR IMAGINARY SERIAL ARSONIST...
...AND PINNED THE CRIMES ON GENDA!
YA GOT YER HANDS ON A KEY TA THE POOR GUY'S HOUSE AN' SNUCK IN AT NIGHT TA GIVE HIM A NERVOUS BREAKDOWN.
BY LEAVIN' GENDA'S SHOE PRINTS ALL OVER THE FLOOR AN' RUBBIN' HIS CLOTHES IN MUD...
...YA MADE HIM THINK HE WAS LEADIN' A DOUBLE LIFE AS THE ARSONIST!
THE ANTI-ANXIETY DRUG YA PRESCRIBED TO HIM WAS REALLY A SLEEPIN' PILL.
YA TOLD HIM TA TAKE A DOUBLE DOSE AT NIGHT SO HE'D SLEEP LIKE A BABY.
WITH THE MESSES YA LEFT IN HIS HOUSE, OF COURSE HE BELIEVED YA WHEN YA DIAGNOSED HIM AS A SLEEPWALKER!
MR. GENDA CAME TO MY PRACTICE SAYING HE WAS A SLEEPWALKER! ASK MY STAFF!
BUT THAT WAS BACK WHEN HE A KID, RIGHT?

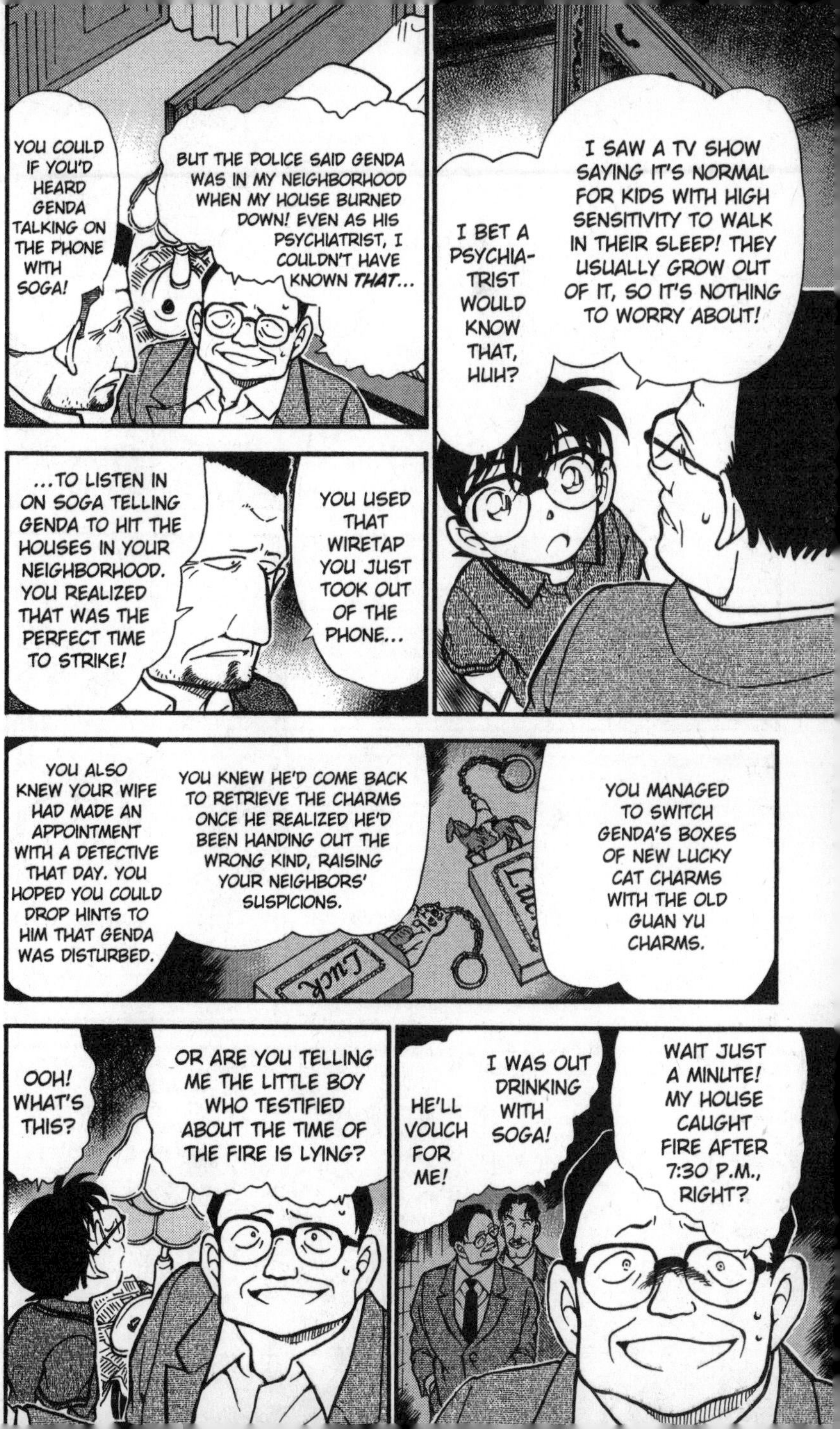
I SAW A TV SHOW SAYING IT'S NORMAL FOR KIDS WITH HIGH SENSITIVITY TO WALK IN THEIR SLEEP! THEY USUALLY GROW OUT OF IT, SO IT'S NOTHING TO WORRY ABOUT!
I BET A PSYCHIA-TRIST WOULD KNOW THAT, HUH?
BUT THE POLICE SAID GENDA WAS IN MY NEIGHBORHOOD WHEN MY HOUSE BURNED DOWN! EVEN AS HIS PSYCHIATRIST, I COULDN'T HAVE KNOWN *THAT*...
YOU COULD IF YOU'D HEARD GENDA TALKING ON THE PHONE WITH SOGA!
YOU USED THAT WIRETAP YOU JUST TOOK OUT OF THE PHONE...
...TO LISTEN IN ON SOGA TELLING GENDA TO HIT THE HOUSES IN YOUR NEIGHBORHOOD. YOU REALIZED THAT WAS THE PERFECT TIME TO STRIKE!
YOU MANAGED TO SWITCH GENDA'S BOXES OF NEW LUCKY CAT CHARMS WITH THE OLD GUAN YU CHARMS.
YOU KNEW HE'D COME BACK TO RETRIEVE THE CHARMS ONCE HE REALIZED HE'D BEEN HANDING OUT THE WRONG KIND, RAISING YOUR NEIGHBORS' SUSPICIONS.
YOU ALSO KNEW YOUR WIFE HAD MADE AN APPOINTMENT WITH A DETECTIVE THAT DAY. YOU HOPED YOU COULD DROP HINTS TO HIM THAT GENDA WAS DISTURBED.
WAIT JUST A MINUTE! MY HOUSE CAUGHT FIRE AFTER 7:30 P.M., RIGHT?
I WAS OUT DRINKING WITH SOGA!
HE'LL VOUCH FOR ME!
OR ARE YOU TELLING ME THE LITTLE BOY WHO TESTIFIED ABOUT THE TIME OF THE FIRE IS LYING?
OOH! WHAT'S THIS?

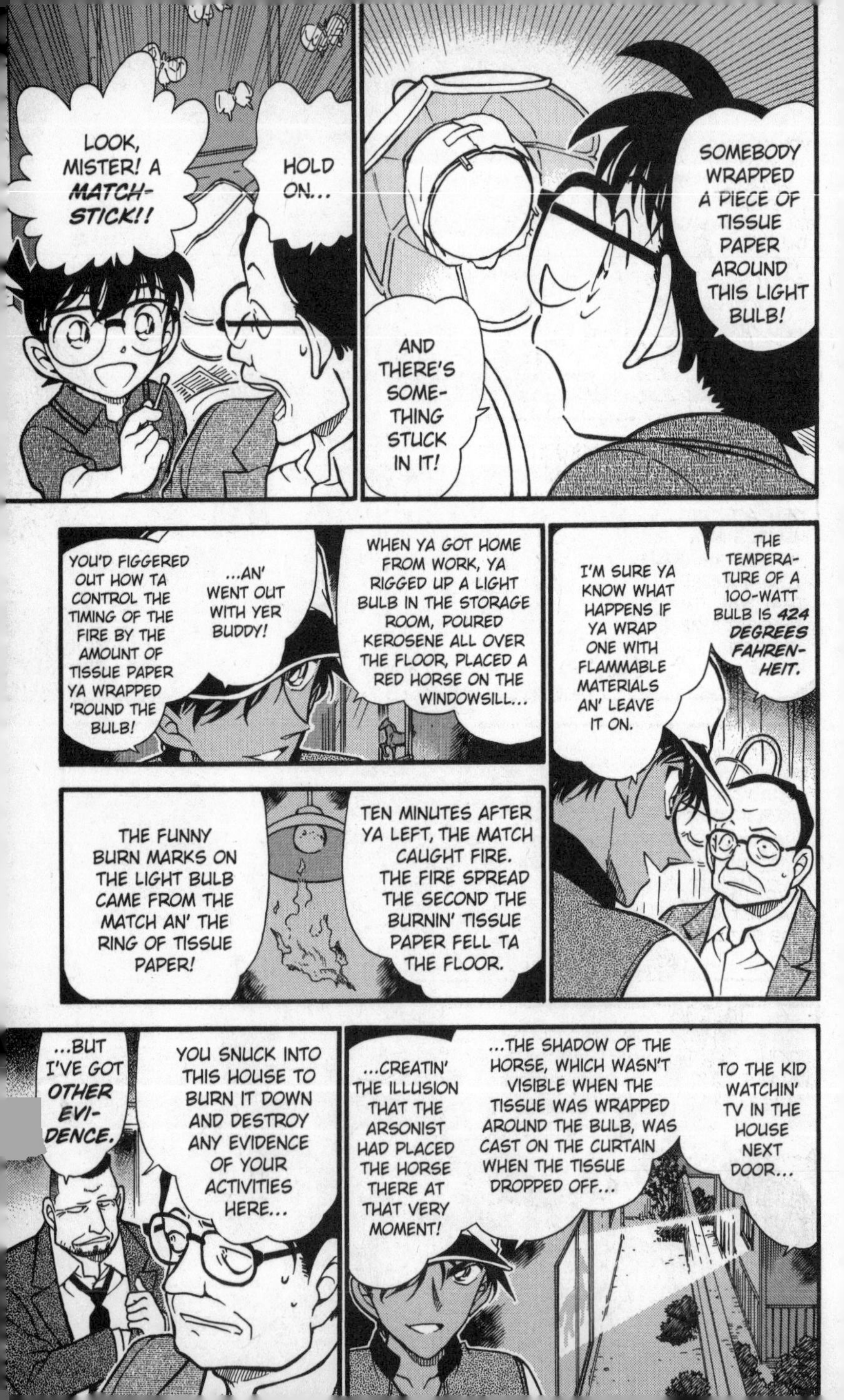
SOMEBODY WRAPPED A PIECE OF TISSUE PAPER AROUND THIS LIGHT BULB!
AND THERE'S SOME-THING STUCK IN IT!
HOLD ON...
LOOK, MISTER! A *MATCH-STICK!!*
THE TEMPERA-TURE OF A 100-WATT BULB IS **424 *DEGREES FAHREN-HEIT.***
I'M SURE YA KNOW WHAT HAPPENS IF YA WRAP ONE WITH FLAMMABLE MATERIALS AN' LEAVE IT ON.
WHEN YA GOT HOME FROM WORK, YA RIGGED UP A LIGHT BULB IN THE STORAGE ROOM, POURED KEROSENE ALL OVER THE FLOOR, PLACED A RED HORSE ON THE WINDOWSILL...
...AN' WENT OUT WITH YER BUDDY!
YOU'D FIGGERED OUT HOW TA CONTROL THE TIMING OF THE FIRE BY THE AMOUNT OF TISSUE PAPER YA WRAPPED 'ROUND THE BULB!
TEN MINUTES AFTER YA LEFT, THE MATCH CAUGHT FIRE. THE FIRE SPREAD THE SECOND THE BURNIN' TISSUE PAPER FELL TA THE FLOOR.
THE FUNNY BURN MARKS ON THE LIGHT BULB CAME FROM THE MATCH AN' THE RING OF TISSUE PAPER!
TO THE KID WATCHIN' TV IN THE HOUSE NEXT DOOR...
...THE SHADOW OF THE HORSE, WHICH WASN'T VISIBLE WHEN THE TISSUE WAS WRAPPED AROUND THE BULB, WAS CAST ON THE CURTAIN WHEN THE TISSUE DROPPED OFF...
...CREATIN' THE ILLUSION THAT THE ARSONIST HAD PLACED THE HORSE THERE AT THAT VERY MOMENT!
YOU SNUCK INTO THIS HOUSE TO BURN IT DOWN AND DESTROY ANY EVIDENCE OF YOUR ACTIVITIES HERE...
...BUT I'VE GOT ***OTHER EVI-DENCE.***

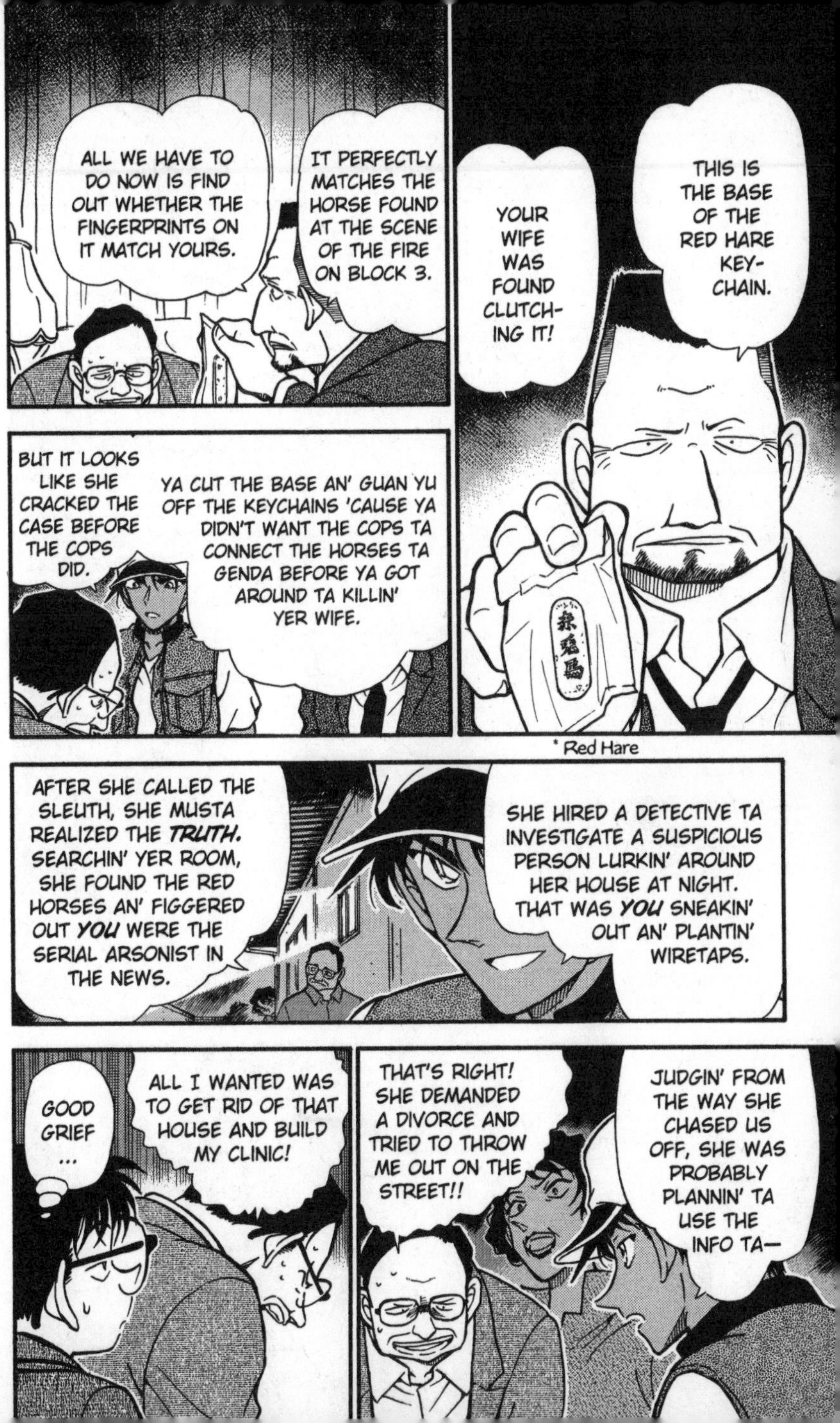
THIS IS THE BASE OF THE RED HARE KEY-CHAIN.
YOUR WIFE WAS FOUND CLUTCHING IT!
赤兎馬
* Red Hare
IT PERFECTLY MATCHES THE HORSE FOUND AT THE SCENE OF THE FIRE ON BLOCK 3.
ALL WE HAVE TO DO NOW IS FIND OUT WHETHER THE FINGERPRINTS ON IT MATCH YOURS.
YA CUT THE BASE AN' GUAN YU OFF THE KEYCHAINS 'CAUSE YA DIDN'T WANT THE COPS TA CONNECT THE HORSES TA GENDA BEFORE YA GOT AROUND TA KILLIN' YER WIFE.
BUT IT LOOKS LIKE SHE CRACKED THE CASE BEFORE THE COPS DID.
SHE HIRED A DETECTIVE TA INVESTIGATE A SUSPICIOUS PERSON LURKIN' AROUND HER HOUSE AT NIGHT. THAT WAS *YOU* SNEAKIN' OUT AN' PLANTIN' WIRETAPS.
AFTER SHE CALLED THE SLEUTH, SHE MUSTA REALIZED THE *TRUTH.* SEARCHIN' YER ROOM, SHE FOUND THE RED HORSES AN' FIGGERED OUT *YOU* WERE THE SERIAL ARSONIST IN THE NEWS.
JUDGIN' FROM THE WAY SHE CHASED US OFF, SHE WAS PROBABLY PLANNIN' TA USE THE INFO TA—
THAT'S RIGHT! SHE DEMANDED A DIVORCE AND TRIED TO THROW ME OUT ON THE STREET!!
ALL I WANTED WAS TO GET RID OF THAT HOUSE AND BUILD MY CLINIC!
GOOD GRIEF ...

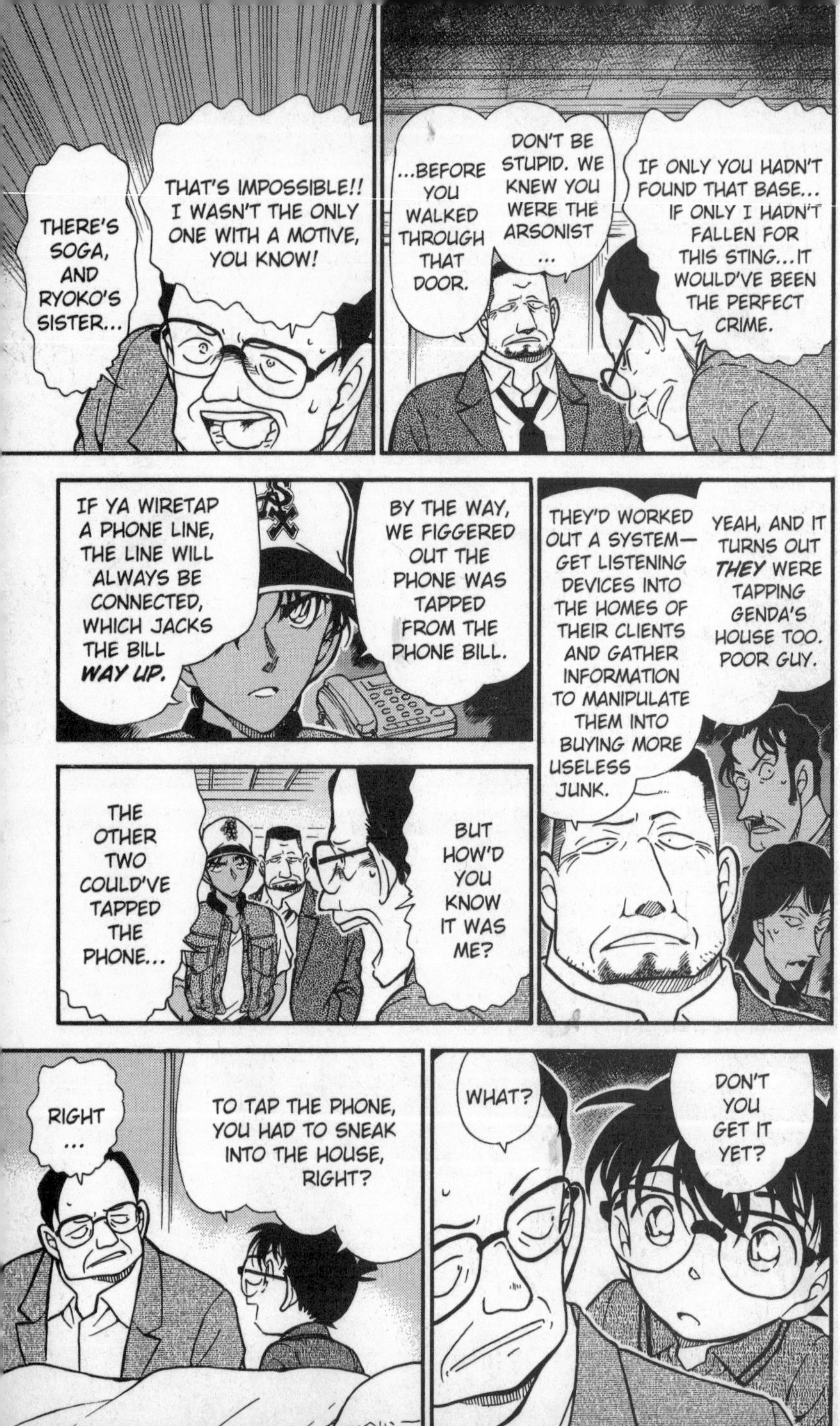
IF ONLY YOU HADN'T FOUND THAT BASE... IF ONLY I HADN'T FALLEN FOR THIS STING...IT WOULD'VE BEEN THE PERFECT CRIME.
DON'T BE STUPID. WE KNEW YOU WERE THE ARSONIST ...
...BEFORE YOU WALKED THROUGH THAT DOOR.
THAT'S IMPOSSIBLE!! I WASN'T THE ONLY ONE WITH A MOTIVE, YOU KNOW!
THERE'S SOGA, AND RYOKO'S SISTER...
YEAH, AND IT TURNS OUT *THEY* WERE TAPPING GENDA'S HOUSE TOO. POOR GUY.
THEY'D WORKED OUT A SYSTEM— GET LISTENING DEVICES INTO THE HOMES OF THEIR CLIENTS AND GATHER INFORMATION TO MANIPULATE THEM INTO BUYING MORE USELESS JUNK.
BY THE WAY, WE FIGGERED OUT THE PHONE WAS TAPPED FROM THE PHONE BILL.
IF YA WIRETAP A PHONE LINE, THE LINE WILL ALWAYS BE CONNECTED, WHICH JACKS THE BILL ***WAY UP.***
BUT HOW'D YOU KNOW IT WAS ME?
THE OTHER TWO COULD'VE TAPPED THE PHONE...
DON'T YOU GET IT YET?
WHAT?
TO TAP THE PHONE, YOU HAD TO SNEAK INTO THE HOUSE, RIGHT?
RIGHT ...

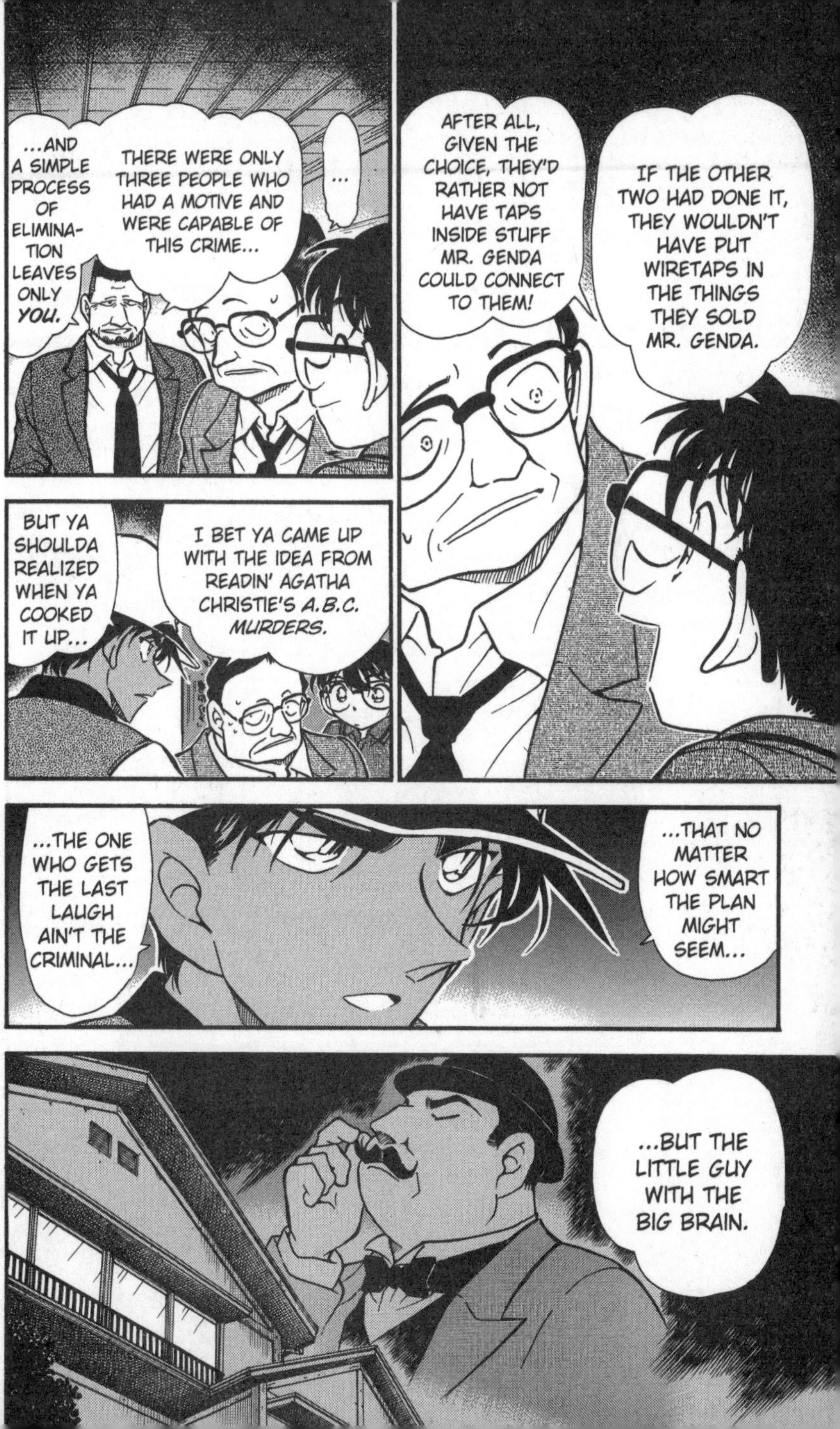
IF THE OTHER TWO HAD DONE IT, THEY WOULDN'T HAVE PUT WIRETAPS IN THE THINGS THEY SOLD MR. GENDA.
AFTER ALL, GIVEN THE CHOICE, THEY'D RATHER NOT HAVE TAPS INSIDE STUFF MR. GENDA COULD CONNECT TO THEM!
...
THERE WERE ONLY THREE PEOPLE WHO HAD A MOTIVE AND WERE CAPABLE OF THIS CRIME...
...AND A SIMPLE PROCESS OF ELIMINATION LEAVES ONLY *YOU.*
I BET YA CAME UP WITH THE IDEA FROM READIN' AGATHA CHRISTIE'S *A.B.C. MURDERS.*
BUT YA SHOULDA REALIZED WHEN YA COOKED IT UP...
...THAT NO MATTER HOW SMART THE PLAN MIGHT SEEM...
...THE ONE WHO GETS THE LAST LAUGH AIN'T THE CRIMINAL...
...BUT THE LITTLE GUY WITH THE BIG BRAIN.

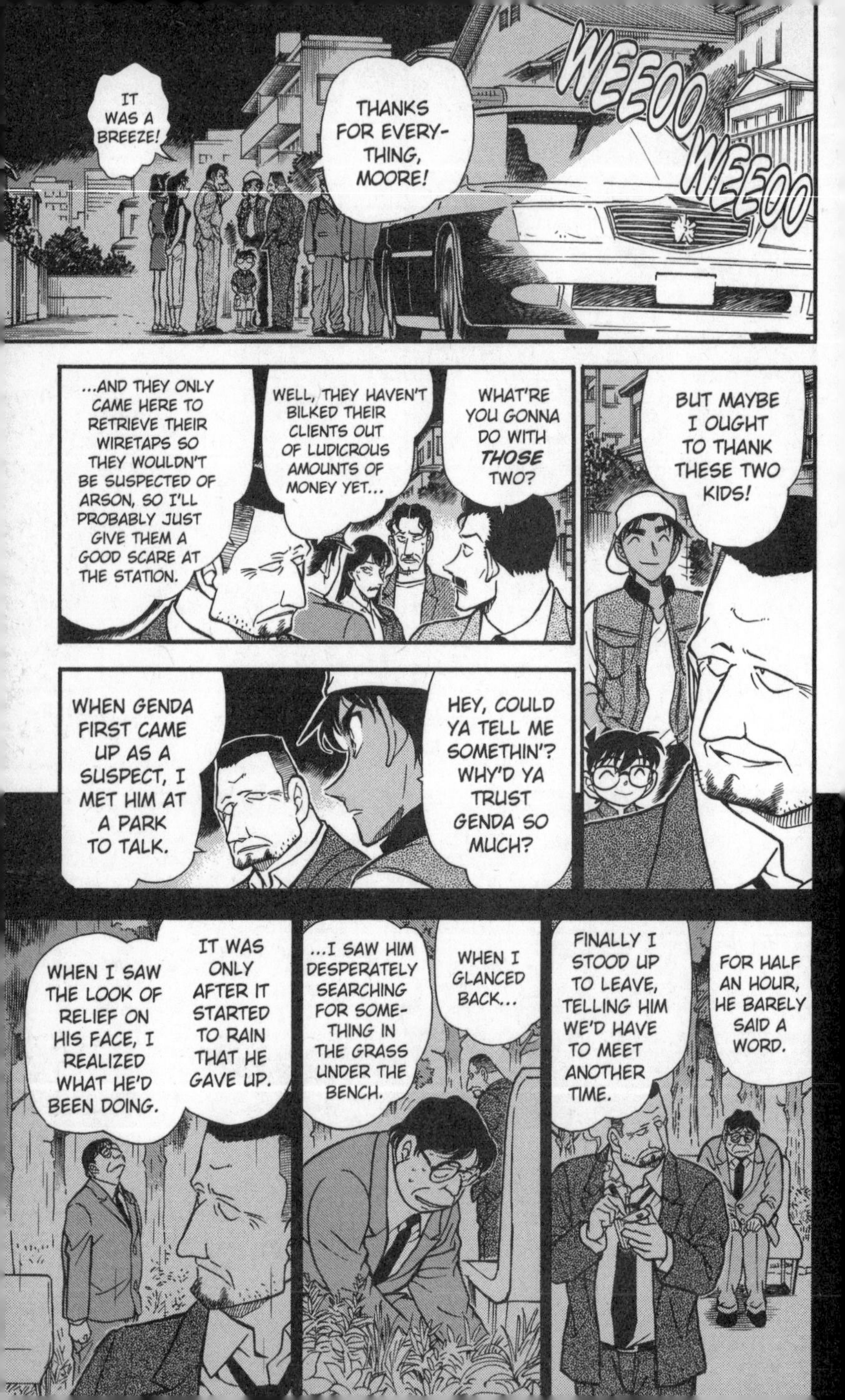
WEEOO WEEOO
THANKS FOR EVERYTHING, MOORE!
IT WAS A BREEZE!
BUT MAYBE I OUGHT TO THANK THESE TWO KIDS!
WHAT'RE YOU GONNA DO WITH THOSE TWO?
WELL, THEY HAVEN'T BILKED THEIR CLIENTS OUT OF LUDICROUS AMOUNTS OF MONEY YET...
...AND THEY ONLY CAME HERE TO RETRIEVE THEIR WIRETAPS SO THEY WOULDN'T BE SUSPECTED OF ARSON, SO I'LL PROBABLY JUST GIVE THEM A GOOD SCARE AT THE STATION.
HEY, COULD YA TELL ME SOMETHIN'? WHY'D YA TRUST GENDA SO MUCH?
WHEN GENDA FIRST CAME UP AS A SUSPECT, I MET HIM AT A PARK TO TALK.
FOR HALF AN HOUR, HE BARELY SAID A WORD.
FINALLY I STOOD UP TO LEAVE, TELLING HIM WE'D HAVE TO MEET ANOTHER TIME.
WHEN I GLANCED BACK...
...I SAW HIM DESPERATELY SEARCHING FOR SOMETHING IN THE GRASS UNDER THE BENCH.
IT WAS ONLY AFTER IT STARTED TO RAIN THAT HE GAVE UP.
WHEN I SAW THE LOOK OF RELIEF ON HIS FACE, I REALIZED WHAT HE'D BEEN DOING.

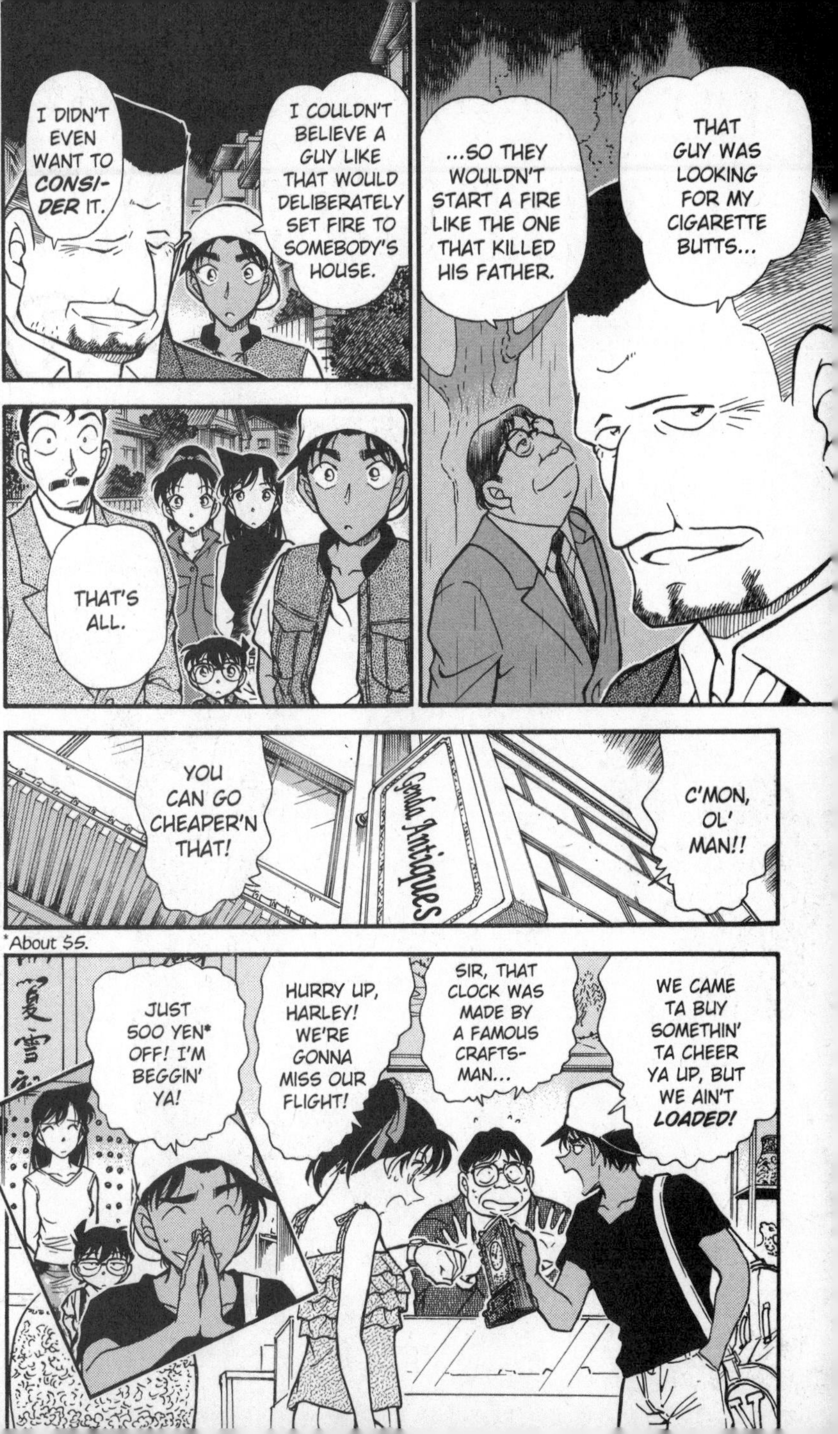
THAT GUY WAS LOOKING FOR MY CIGARETTE BUTTS...
...SO THEY WOULDN'T START A FIRE LIKE THE ONE THAT KILLED HIS FATHER.
I COULDN'T BELIEVE A GUY LIKE THAT WOULD DELIBERATELY SET FIRE TO SOMEBODY'S HOUSE.
I DIDN'T EVEN WANT TO *CONSIDER* IT.
THAT'S ALL.
C'MON, OL' MAN!!
YOU CAN GO CHEAPER'N THAT!
Gonda Antiques
WE CAME TA BUY SOMETHIN' TA CHEER YA UP, BUT WE AIN'T ***LOADED!***
SIR, THAT CLOCK WAS MADE BY A FAMOUS CRAFTSMAN...
HURRY UP, HARLEY! WE'RE GONNA MISS OUR FLIGHT!
JUST 500 YEN* OFF! I'M BEGGIN' YA!

*About $5.

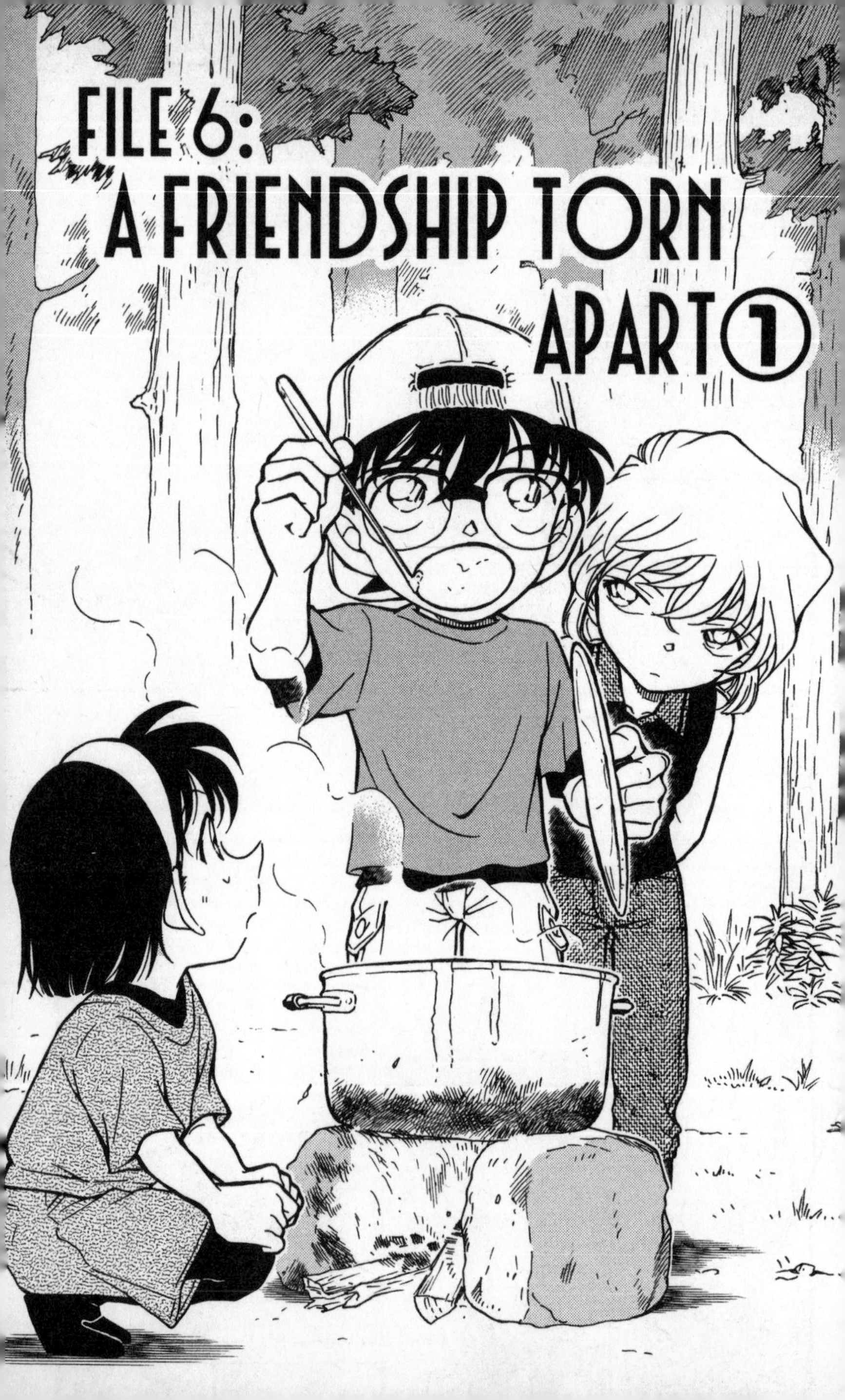
FILE 6:
A FRIENDSHIP TORN APART ①

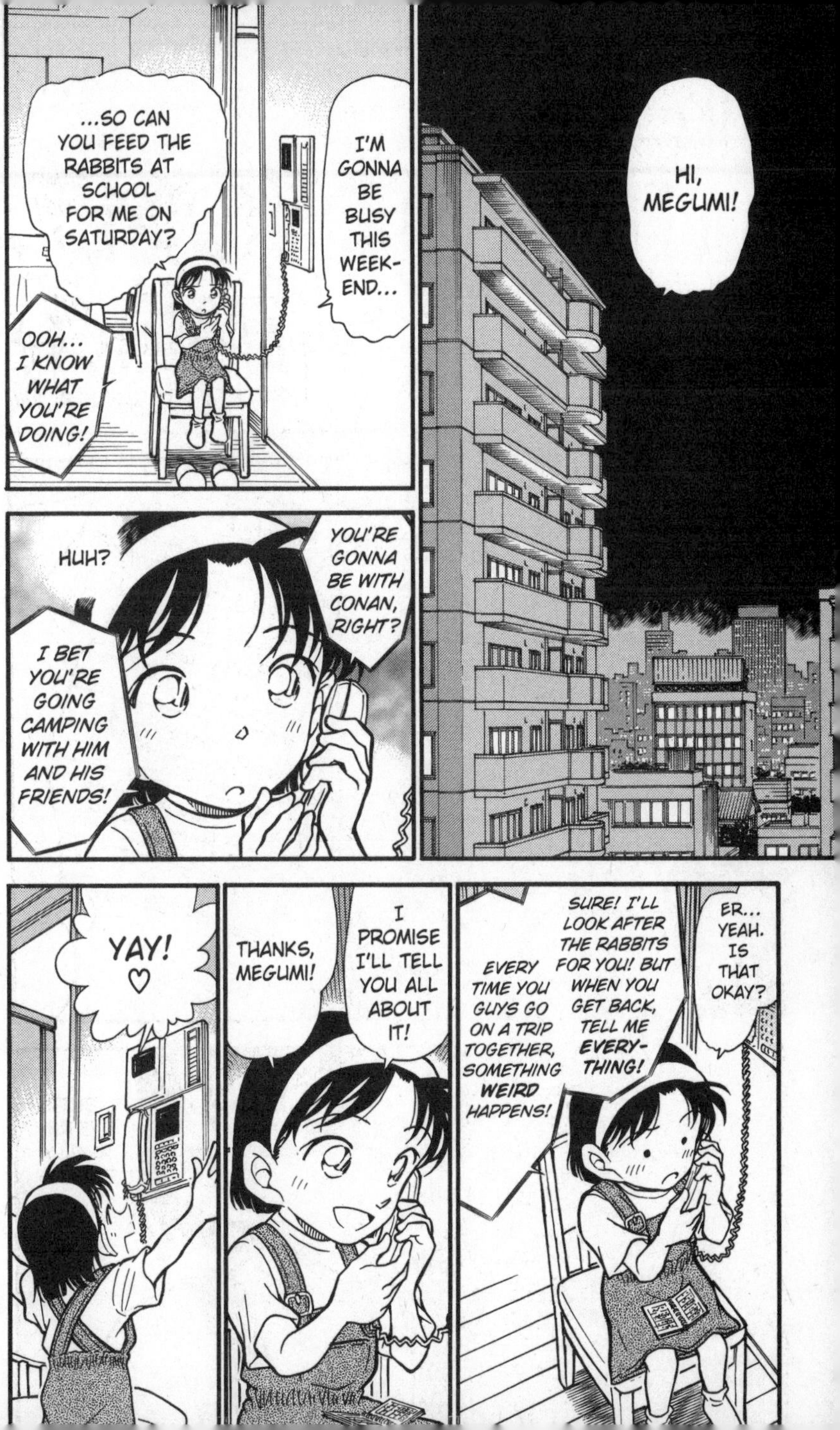
HI, MEGUMI!
I'M GONNA BE BUSY THIS WEEKEND...
...SO CAN YOU FEED THE RABBITS AT SCHOOL FOR ME ON SATURDAY?
OOH... I KNOW WHAT YOU'RE DOING!
YOU'RE GONNA BE WITH CONAN, RIGHT?
HUH?
I BET YOU'RE GOING CAMPING WITH HIM AND HIS FRIENDS!
ER... YEAH. IS THAT OKAY?
SURE! I'LL LOOK AFTER THE RABBITS FOR YOU! BUT WHEN YOU GET BACK, TELL ME EVERYTHING!
EVERY TIME YOU GUYS GO ON A TRIP TOGETHER, SOMETHING WEIRD HAPPENS!
I PROMISE I'LL TELL YOU ALL ABOUT IT!
THANKS, MEGUMI!
YAY! ♡

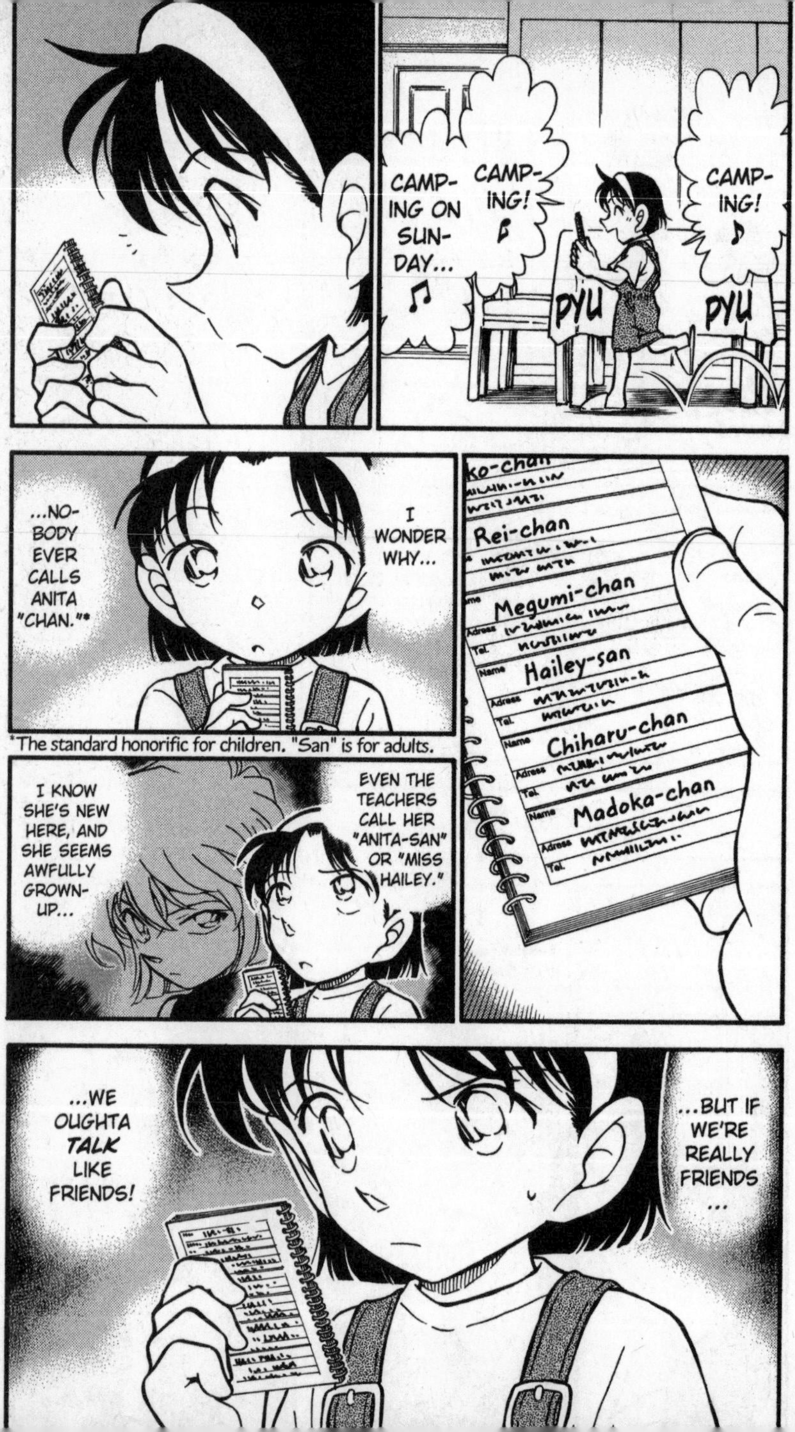
CAMP-ING! ♪
CAMP-ING! ♪
CAMP-ING ON SUN-DAY... ♪
PYU
PYU
ko-chan
Rei-chan
Megumi-chan
Hailey-san
Chiharu-chan
Madoka-chan
I WONDER WHY...
...NO-BODY EVER CALLS ANITA "CHAN."*
EVEN THE TEACHERS CALL HER "ANITA-SAN" OR "MISS HAILEY."
I KNOW SHE'S NEW HERE, AND SHE SEEMS AWFULLY GROWN-UP...
...BUT IF WE'RE REALLY FRIENDS...
...WE OUGHTA *TALK* LIKE FRIENDS!
*The standard honorific for children. "San" is for adults.

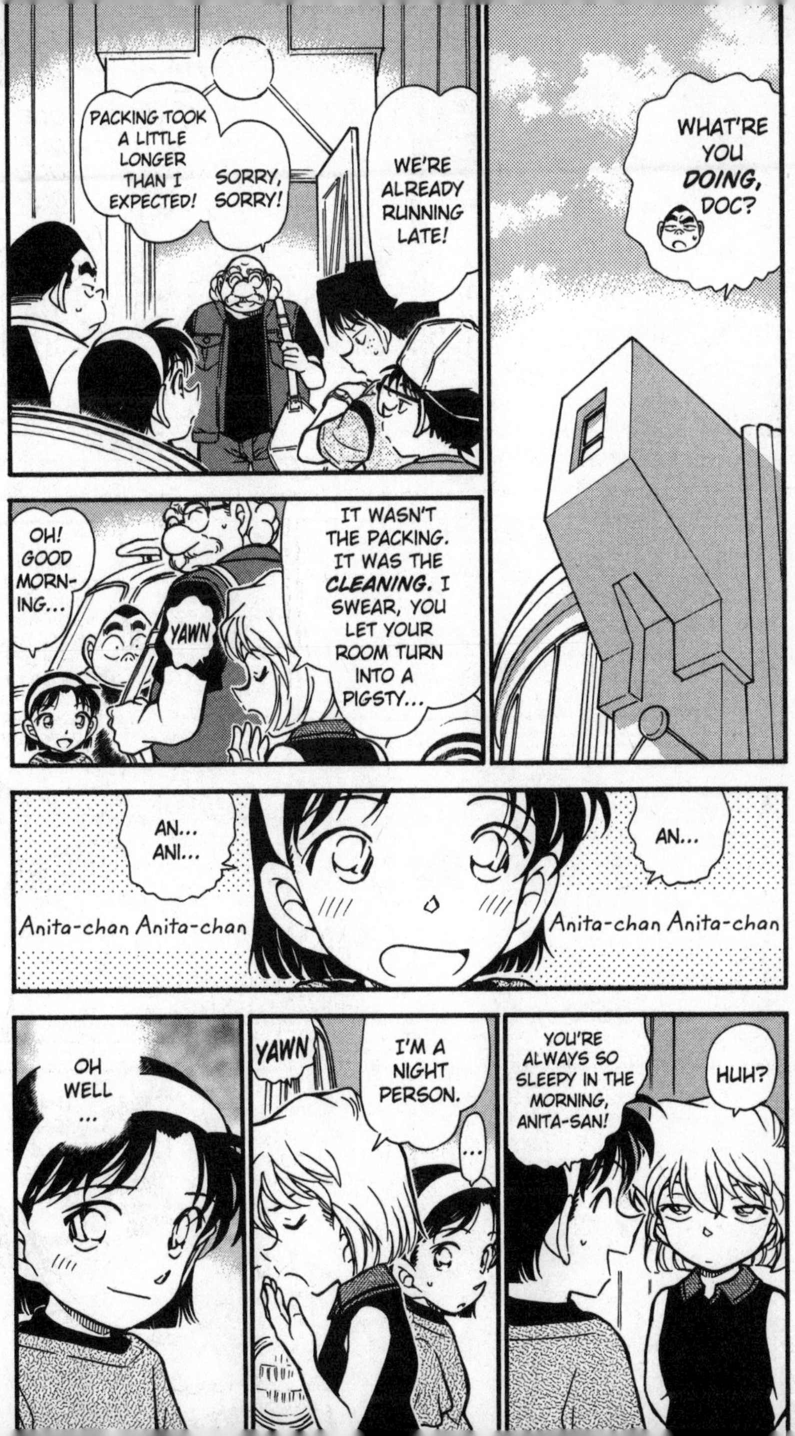
WHAT'RE YOU DOING, DOC?
WE'RE ALREADY RUNNING LATE!
SORRY, SORRY!
PACKING TOOK A LITTLE LONGER THAN I EXPECTED!
IT WASN'T THE PACKING. IT WAS THE CLEANING. I SWEAR, YOU LET YOUR ROOM TURN INTO A PIGSTY...
YAWN
OH! GOOD MORNING...
AN...
Anita-chan Anita-chan
AN... ANI...
Anita-chan Anita-chan
HUH?
YOU'RE ALWAYS SO SLEEPY IN THE MORNING, ANITA-SAN!
I'M A NIGHT PERSON.
...
YAWN
OH WELL ...

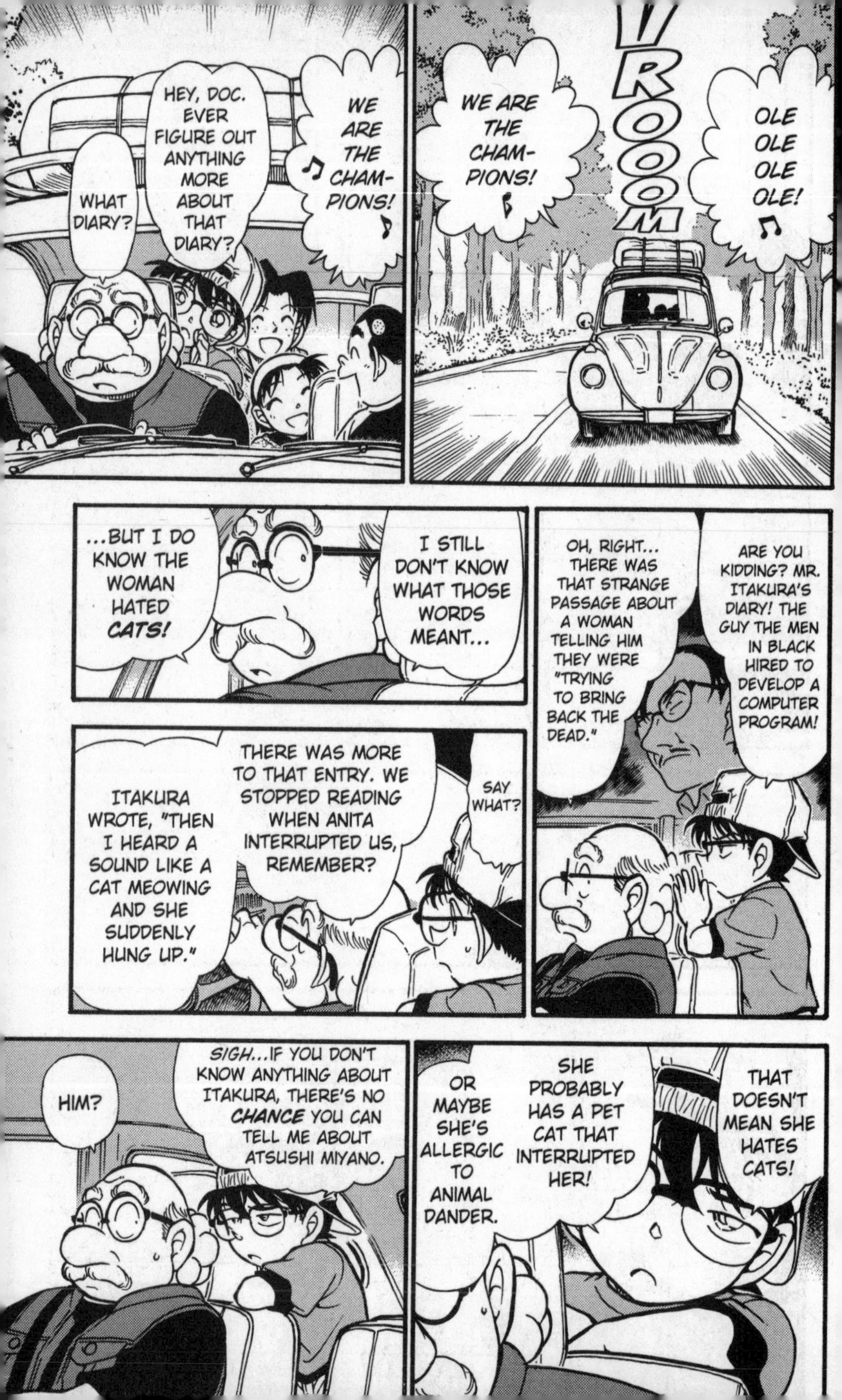

OLE OLE OLE OLE!
VROOOM
WE ARE THE CHAMPIONS!
WE ARE THE CHAMPIONS!
HEY, DOC. EVER FIGURE OUT ANYTHING MORE ABOUT THAT DIARY?
WHAT DIARY?
ARE YOU KIDDING? MR. ITAKURA'S DIARY! THE GUY THE MEN IN BLACK HIRED TO DEVELOP A COMPUTER PROGRAM!
OH, RIGHT... THERE WAS THAT STRANGE PASSAGE ABOUT A WOMAN TELLING HIM THEY WERE "TRYING TO BRING BACK THE DEAD."
I STILL DON'T KNOW WHAT THOSE WORDS MEANT...
...BUT I DO KNOW THE WOMAN HATED ***CATS!***
SAY WHAT?
THERE WAS MORE TO THAT ENTRY. WE STOPPED READING WHEN ANITA INTERRUPTED US, REMEMBER?
ITAKURA WROTE, "THEN I HEARD A SOUND LIKE A CAT MEOWING AND SHE SUDDENLY HUNG UP."
THAT DOESN'T MEAN SHE HATES CATS!
SHE PROBABLY HAS A PET CAT THAT INTERRUPTED HER!
OR MAYBE SHE'S ALLERGIC TO ANIMAL DANDER.
SIGH...IF YOU DON'T KNOW ANYTHING ABOUT ITAKURA, THERE'S NO ***CHANCE*** YOU CAN TELL ME ABOUT ATSUSHI MIYANO.
HIM?

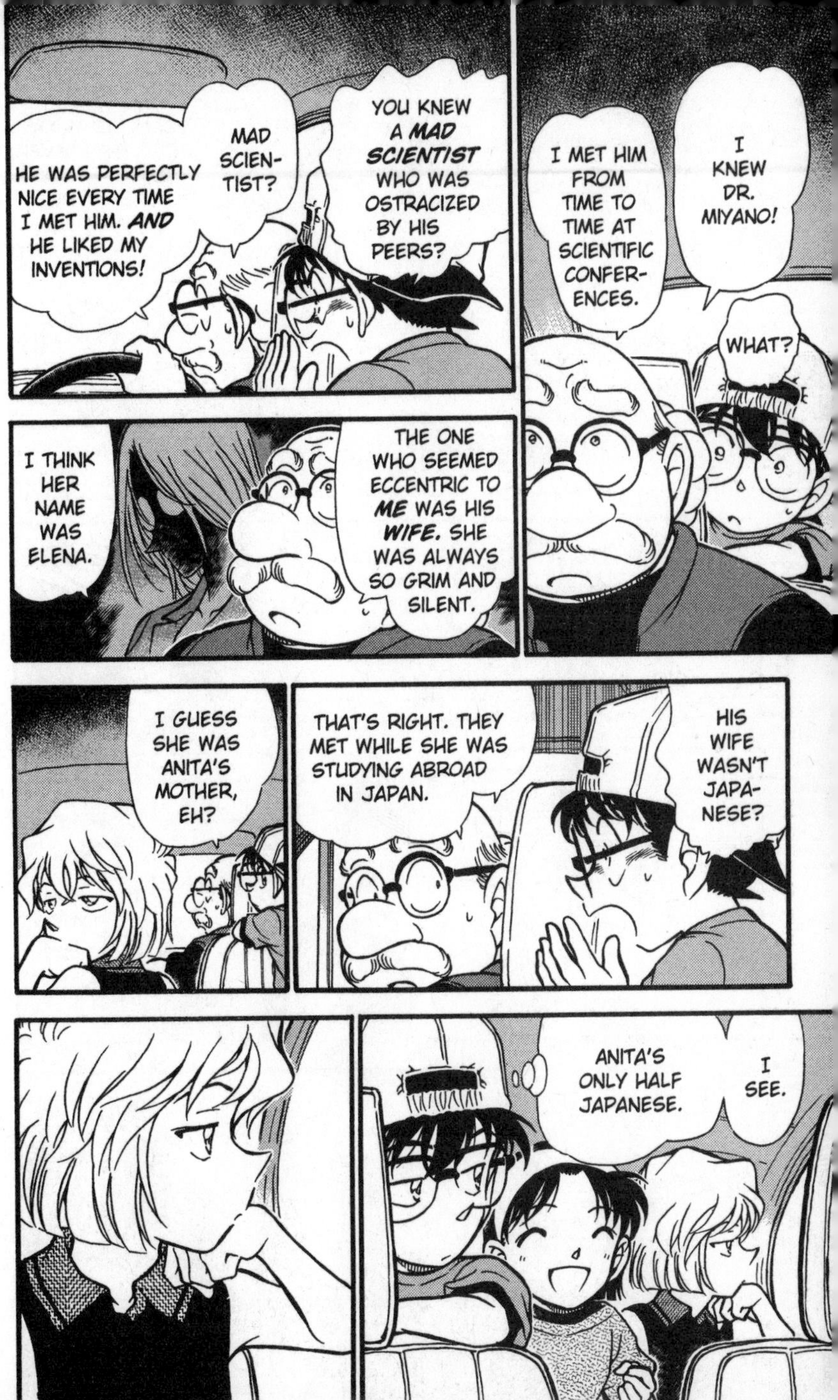
I KNEW DR. MIYANO!
WHAT?
I MET HIM FROM TIME TO TIME AT SCIENTIFIC CONFERENCES.
YOU KNEW A **MAD SCIENTIST** WHO WAS OSTRACIZED BY HIS PEERS?
MAD SCIENTIST?
HE WAS PERFECTLY NICE EVERY TIME I MET HIM. **AND** HE LIKED MY INVENTIONS!
THE ONE WHO SEEMED ECCENTRIC TO **ME** WAS HIS **WIFE.** SHE WAS ALWAYS SO GRIM AND SILENT.
I THINK HER NAME WAS ELENA.
HIS WIFE WASN'T JAPANESE?
THAT'S RIGHT. THEY MET WHILE SHE WAS STUDYING ABROAD IN JAPAN.
I GUESS SHE WAS ANITA'S MOTHER, EH?
I SEE.
ANITA'S ONLY HALF JAPANESE.

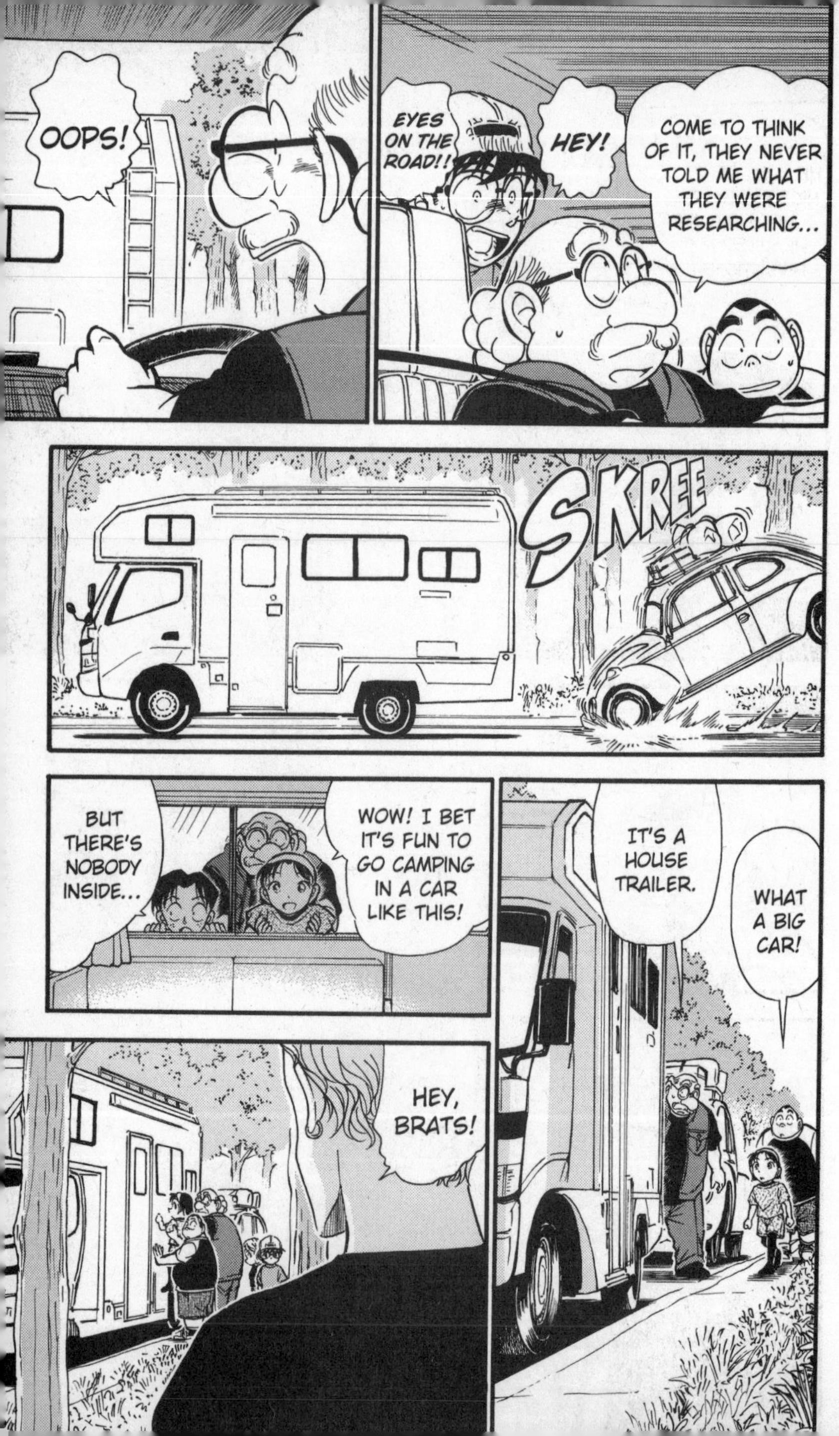
COME TO THINK OF IT, THEY NEVER TOLD ME WHAT THEY WERE RESEARCHING...
HEY!
EYES ON THE ROAD!!
OOPS!
SKREE
WHAT A BIG CAR!
IT'S A HOUSE TRAILER.
WOW! I BET IT'S FUN TO GO CAMPING IN A CAR LIKE THIS!
BUT THERE'S NOBODY INSIDE...
HEY, BRATS!

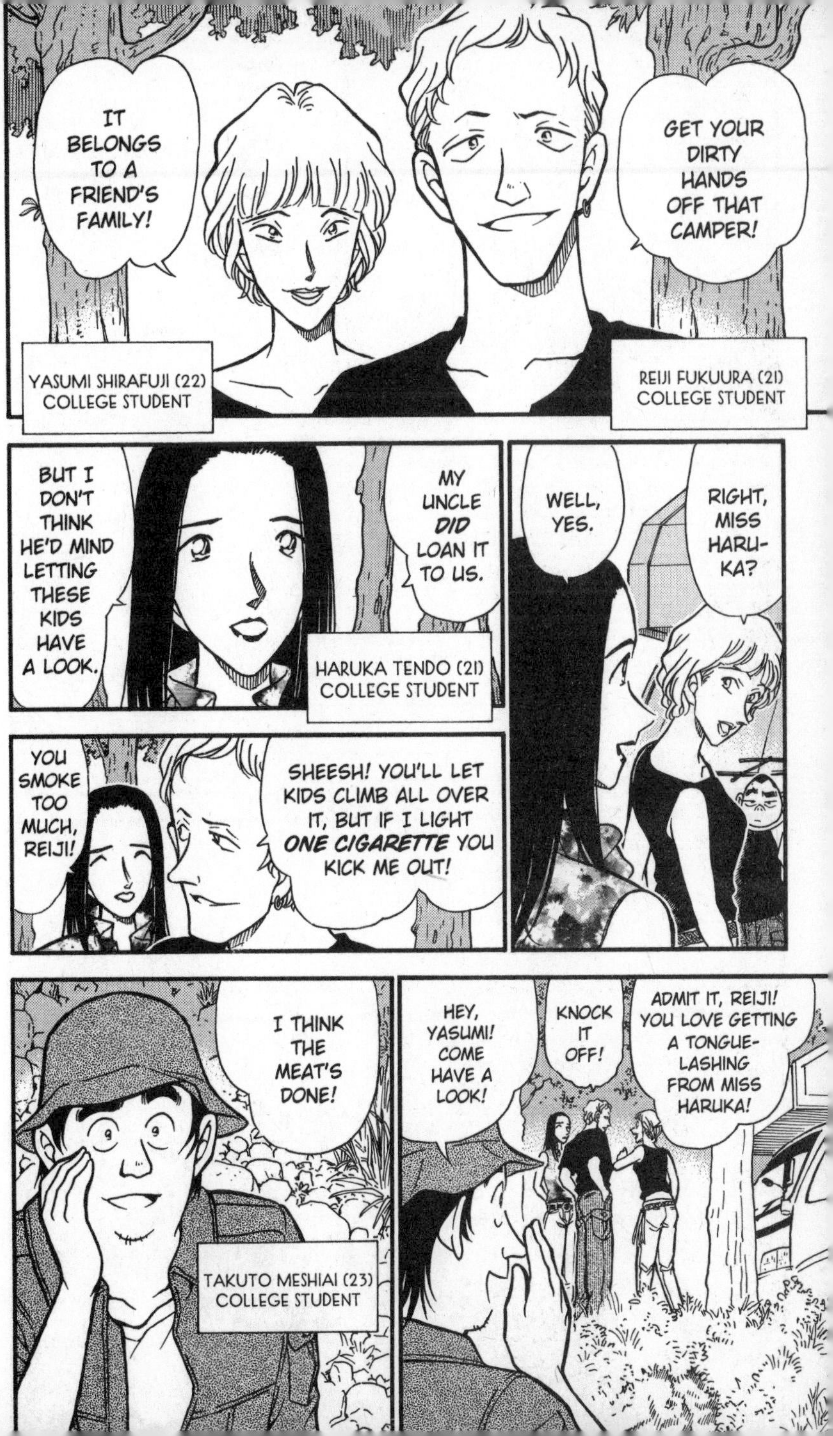
GET YOUR DIRTY HANDS OFF THAT CAMPER!
IT BELONGS TO A FRIEND'S FAMILY!
REIJI FUKUURA (21) COLLEGE STUDENT
YASUMI SHIRAFUJI (22) COLLEGE STUDENT
RIGHT, MISS HARU-KA?
WELL, YES.
MY UNCLE *DID* LOAN IT TO US.
BUT I DON'T THINK HE'D MIND LETTING THESE KIDS HAVE A LOOK.
HARUKA TENDO (21) COLLEGE STUDENT
SHEESH! YOU'LL LET KIDS CLIMB ALL OVER IT, BUT IF I LIGHT *ONE CIGARETTE* YOU KICK ME OUT!
YOU SMOKE TOO MUCH, REIJI!
ADMIT IT, REIJI! YOU LOVE GETTING A TONGUE-LASHING FROM MISS HARUKA!
KNOCK IT OFF!
HEY, YASUMI! COME HAVE A LOOK!
I THINK THE MEAT'S DONE!
TAKUTO MESHIAI (23) COLLEGE STUDENT

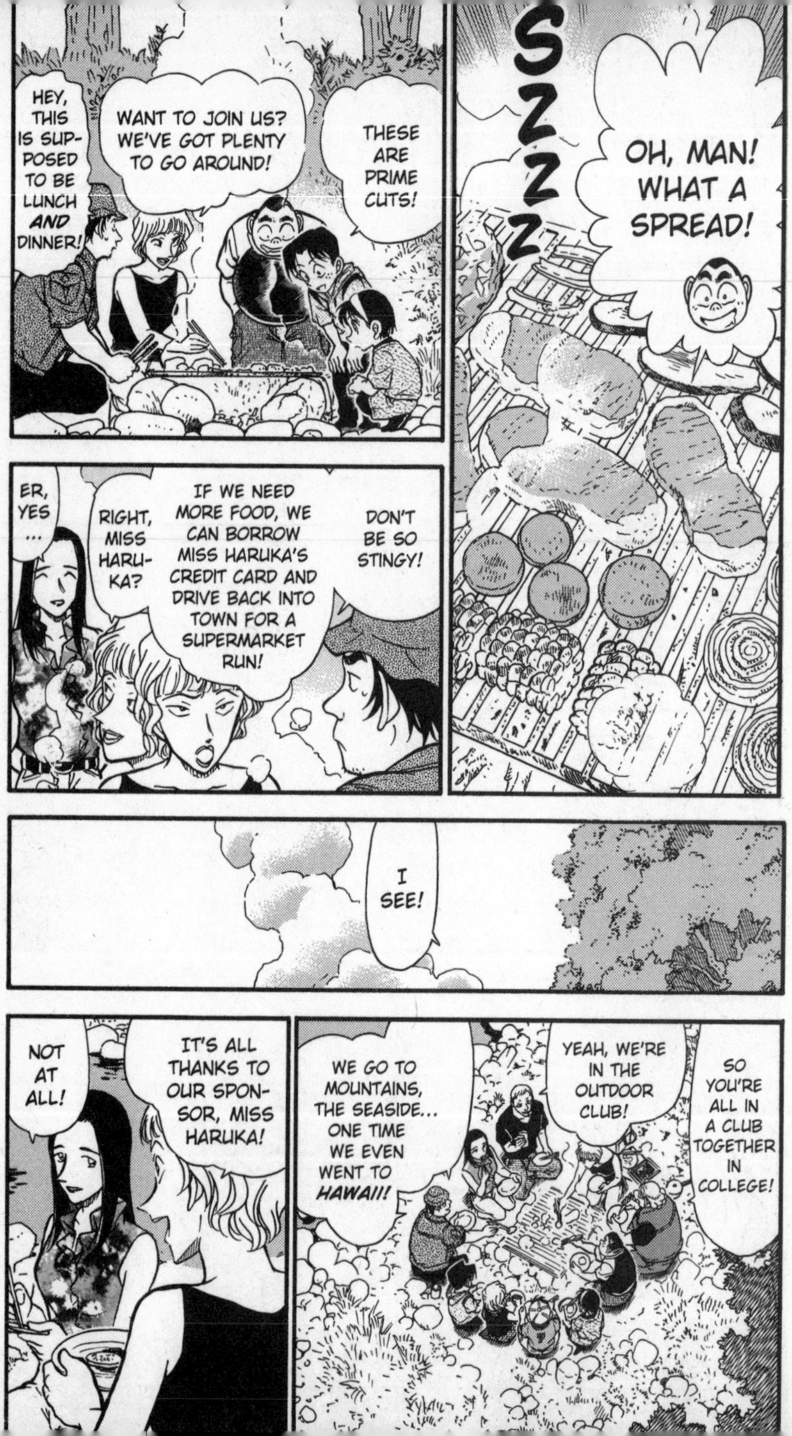
SZZZ
OH, MAN! WHAT A SPREAD!
THESE ARE PRIME CUTS!
WANT TO JOIN US? WE'VE GOT PLENTY TO GO AROUND!
HEY, THIS IS SUP-POSED TO BE LUNCH AND DINNER!
DON'T BE SO STINGY!
IF WE NEED MORE FOOD, WE CAN BORROW MISS HARUKA'S CREDIT CARD AND DRIVE BACK INTO TOWN FOR A SUPERMARKET RUN!
RIGHT, MISS HARU-KA?
ER, YES ...
I SEE!
SO YOU'RE ALL IN A CLUB TOGETHER IN COLLEGE!
YEAH, WE'RE IN THE OUTDOOR CLUB!
WE GO TO MOUNTAINS, THE SEASIDE... ONE TIME WE EVEN WENT TO HAWAII!
IT'S ALL THANKS TO OUR SPON-SOR, MISS HARUKA!
NOT AT ALL!

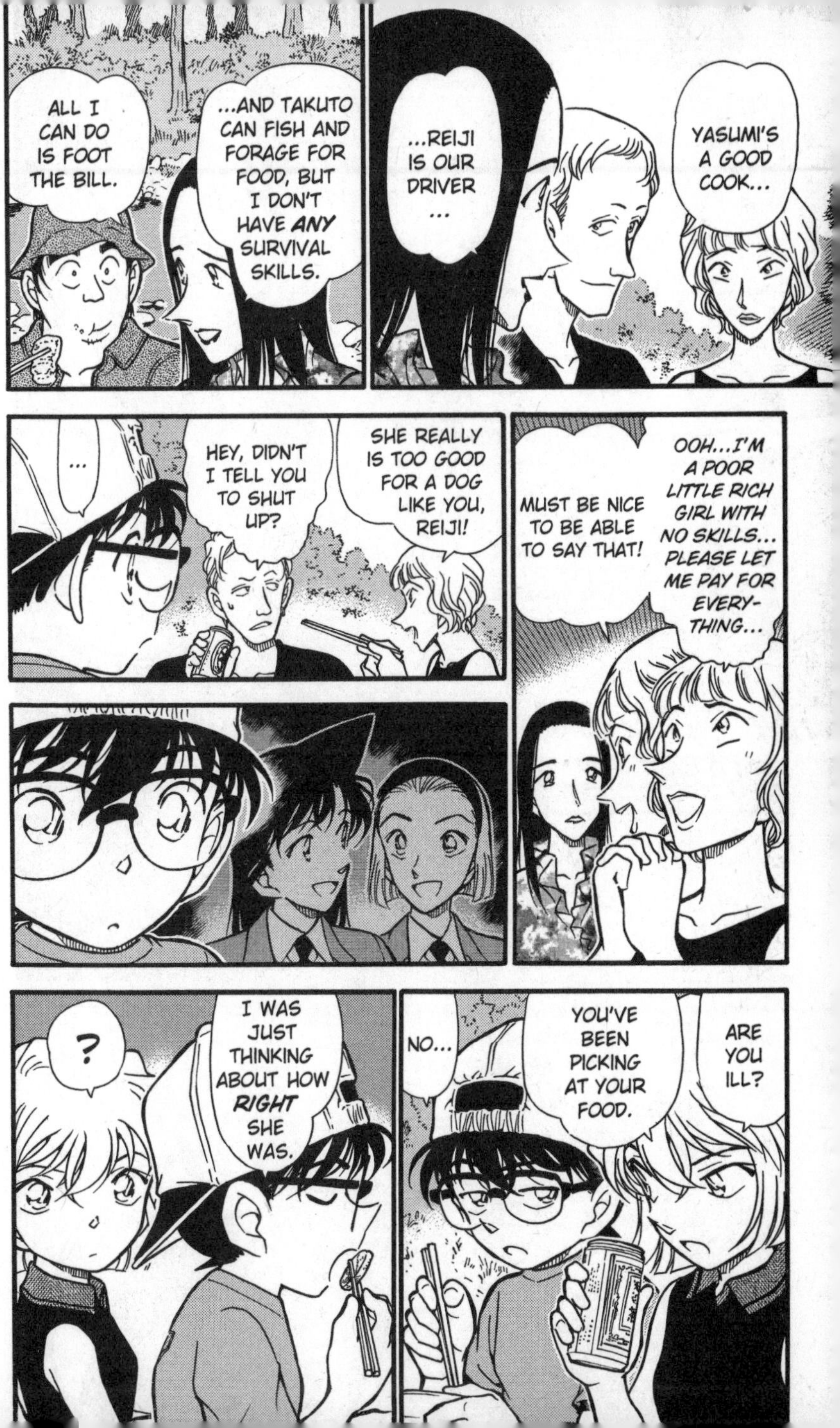
YASUMI'S A GOOD COOK...
...REIJI IS OUR DRIVER ...
...AND TAKUTO CAN FISH AND FORAGE FOR FOOD, BUT I DON'T HAVE *ANY* SURVIVAL SKILLS.
ALL I CAN DO IS FOOT THE BILL.
OOH...I'M A POOR LITTLE RICH GIRL WITH NO SKILLS... PLEASE LET ME PAY FOR EVERY-THING...
MUST BE NICE TO BE ABLE TO SAY THAT!
SHE REALLY IS TOO GOOD FOR A DOG LIKE YOU, REIJI!
HEY, DIDN'T I TELL YOU TO SHUT UP?
...
ARE YOU ILL?
YOU'VE BEEN PICKING AT YOUR FOOD.
NO...
I WAS JUST THINKING ABOUT HOW *RIGHT* SHE WAS.
?

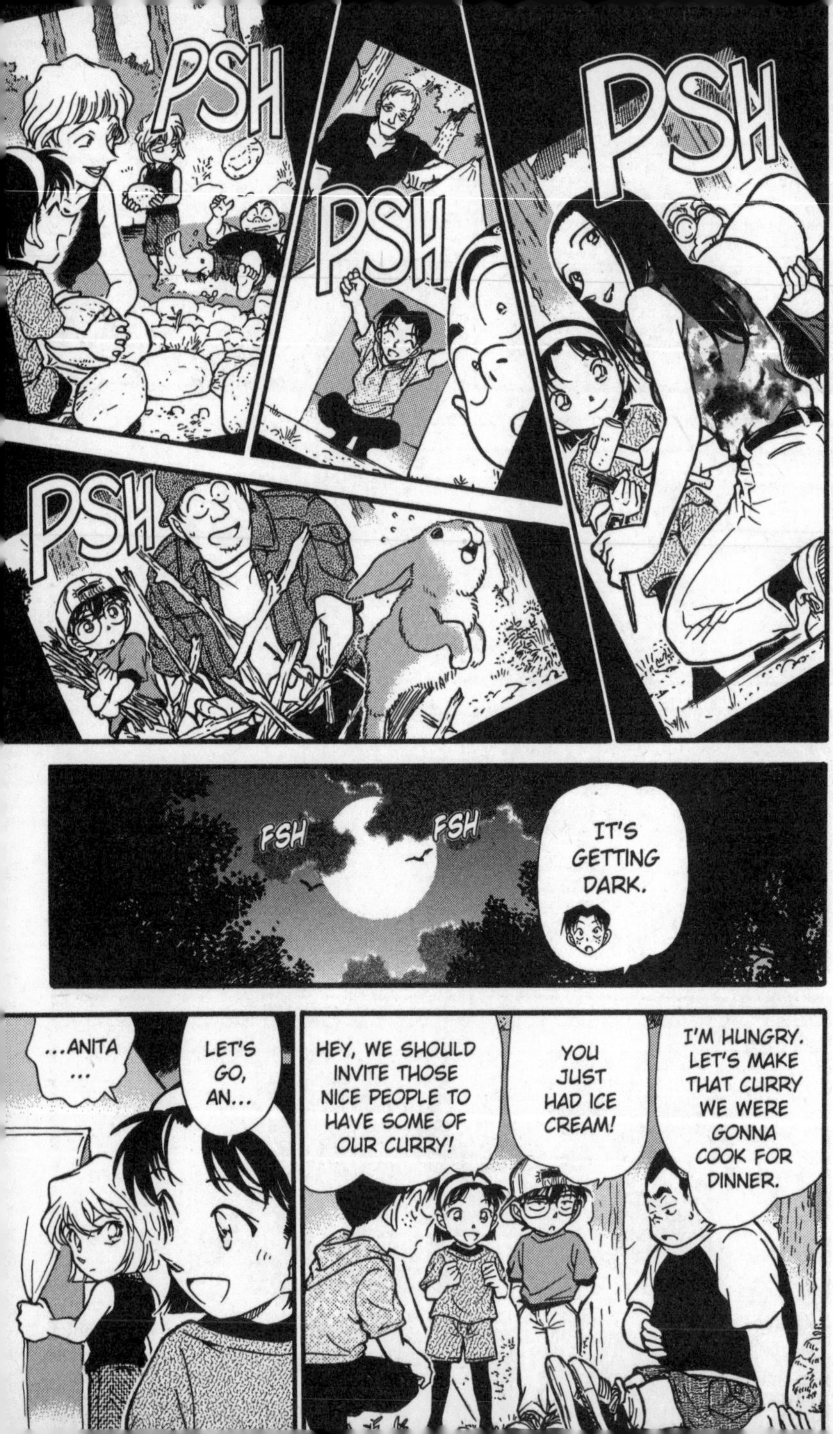
PSH
PSH
PSH
PSH
FSH
FSH
IT'S GETTING DARK.
I'M HUNGRY. LET'S MAKE THAT CURRY WE WERE GONNA COOK FOR DINNER.
YOU JUST HAD ICE CREAM!
HEY, WE SHOULD INVITE THOSE NICE PEOPLE TO HAVE SOME OF OUR CURRY!
LET'S GO, AN...
...ANITA ...

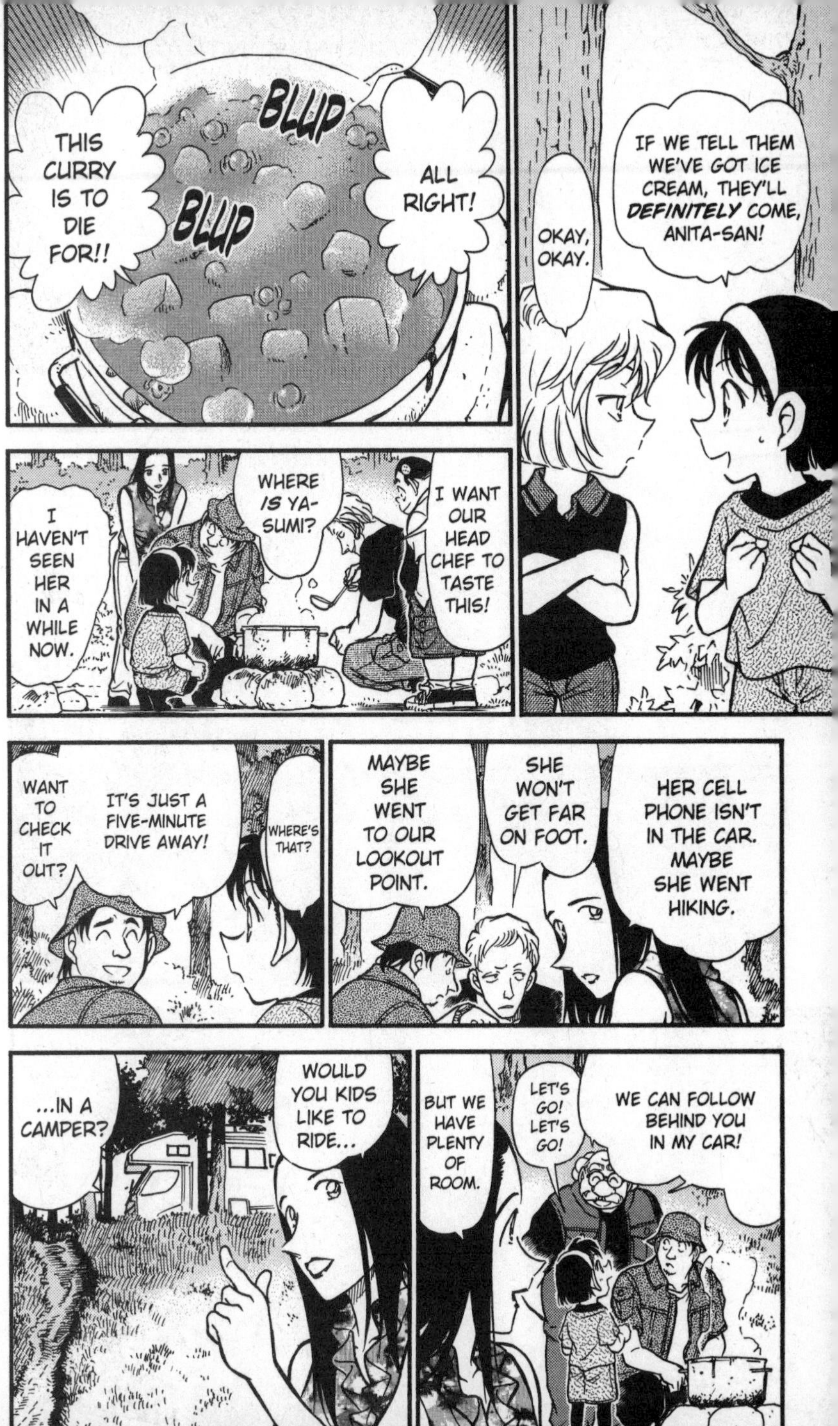
IF WE TELL THEM WE'VE GOT ICE CREAM, THEY'LL *DEFINITELY* COME, ANITA-SAN!
OKAY, OKAY.
ALL RIGHT!
BLUP
BLUP
THIS CURRY IS TO DIE FOR!!
I WANT OUR HEAD CHEF TO TASTE THIS!
WHERE *IS* YA-SUMI?
I HAVEN'T SEEN HER IN A WHILE NOW.
HER CELL PHONE ISN'T IN THE CAR. MAYBE SHE WENT HIKING.
SHE WON'T GET FAR ON FOOT.
MAYBE SHE WENT TO OUR LOOKOUT POINT.
WHERE'S THAT?
IT'S JUST A FIVE-MINUTE DRIVE AWAY!
WANT TO CHECK IT OUT?
WE CAN FOLLOW BEHIND YOU IN MY CAR!
LET'S GO! LET'S GO!
BUT WE HAVE PLENTY OF ROOM.
WOULD YOU KIDS LIKE TO RIDE...
...IN A CAMPER?

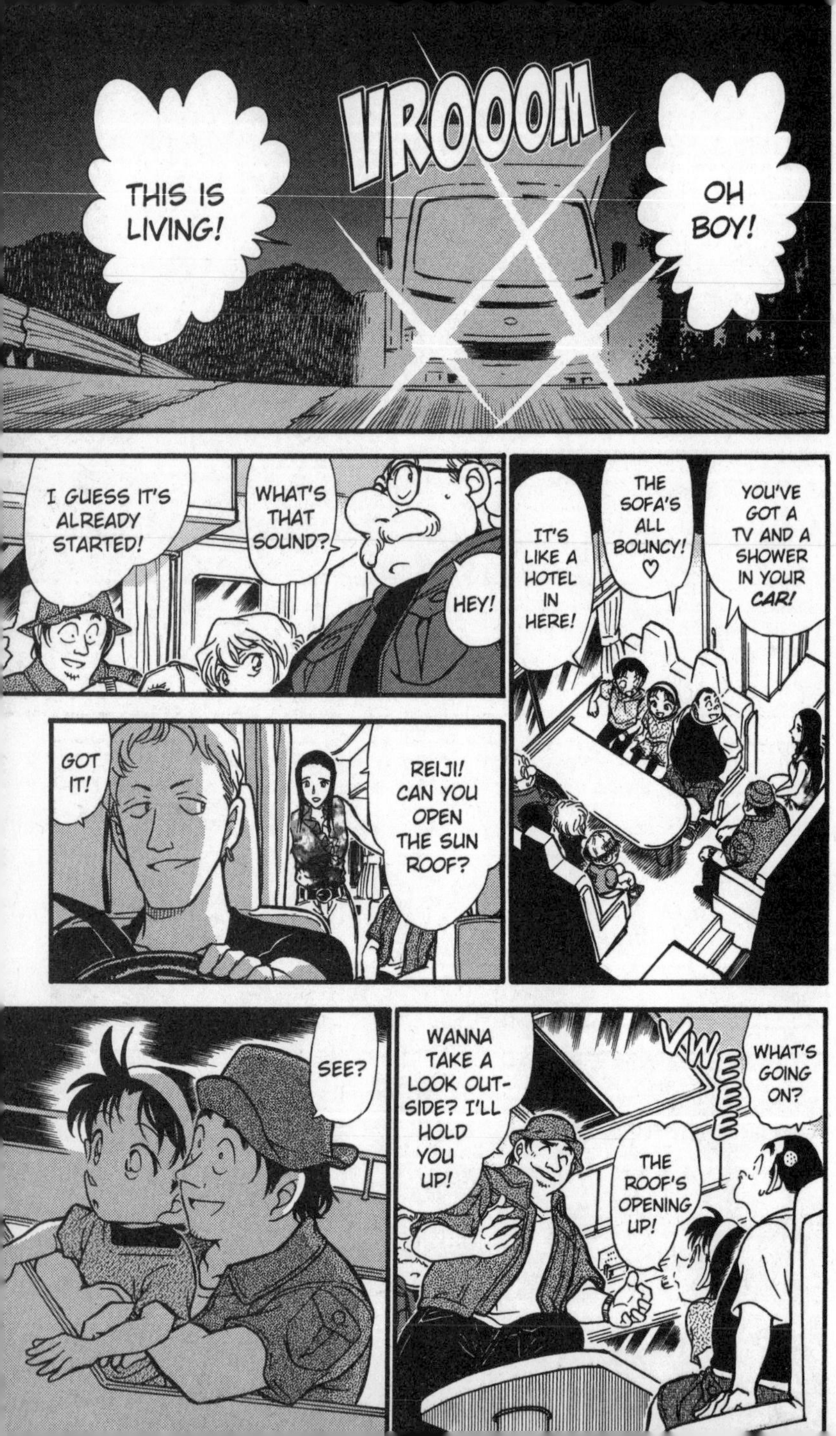
VROOOM
OH BOY!
THIS IS LIVING!
YOU'VE GOT A TV AND A SHOWER IN YOUR CAR!
THE SOFA'S ALL BOUNCY! ♡
IT'S LIKE A HOTEL IN HERE!
HEY!
WHAT'S THAT SOUND?
I GUESS IT'S ALREADY STARTED!
REIJI! CAN YOU OPEN THE SUN ROOF?
GOT IT!
WHAT'S GOING ON?
VWEEE
WANNA TAKE A LOOK OUT-SIDE? I'LL HOLD YOU UP!
THE ROOF'S OPENING UP!
SEE?

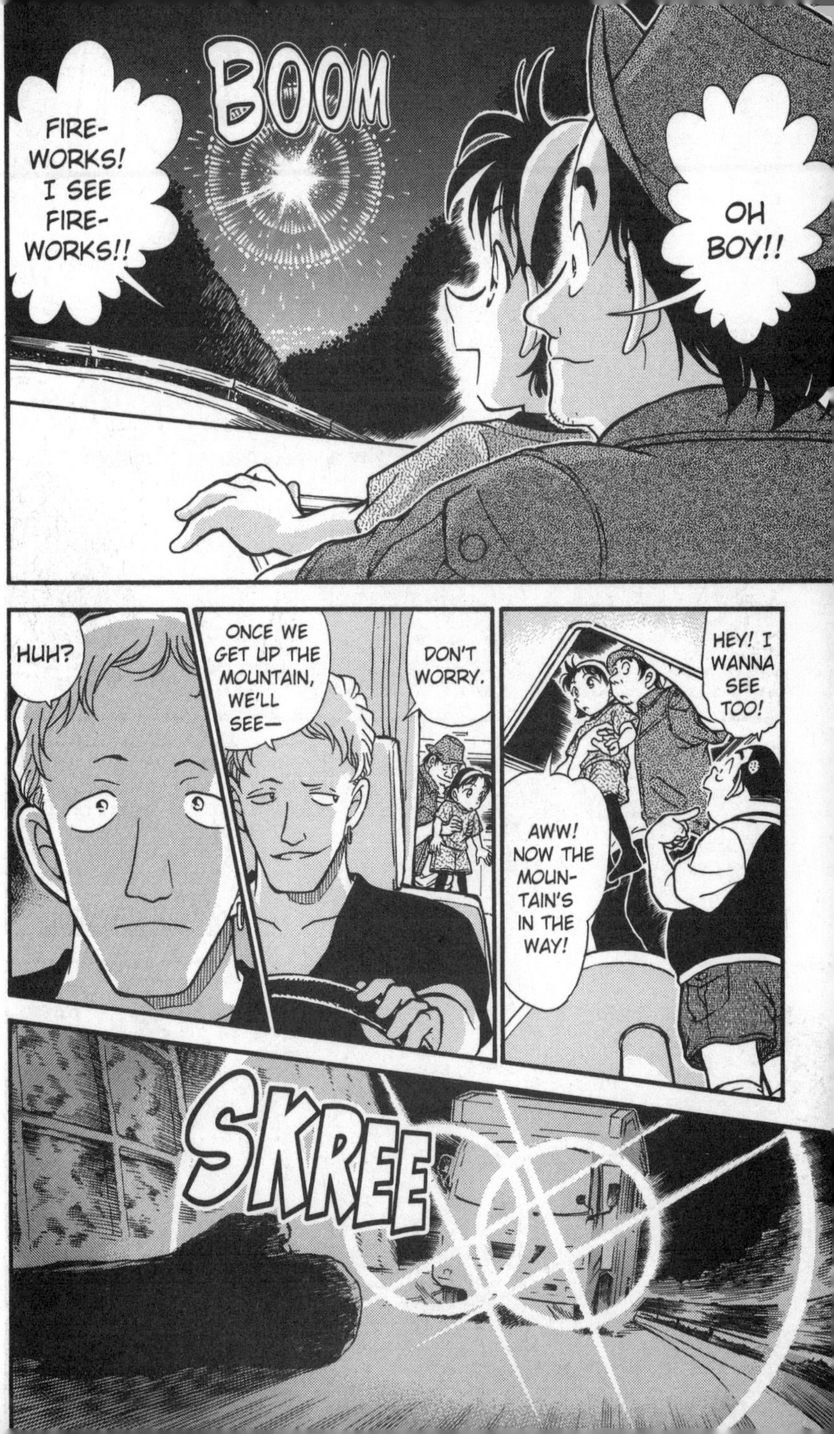
OH BOY!!
BOOM
FIRE-WORKS! I SEE FIRE-WORKS!!
HEY! I WANNA SEE TOO!
AWW! NOW THE MOUN-TAIN'S IN THE WAY!
DON'T WORRY.
ONCE WE GET UP THE MOUNTAIN, WE'LL SEE—
HUH?
SKREE

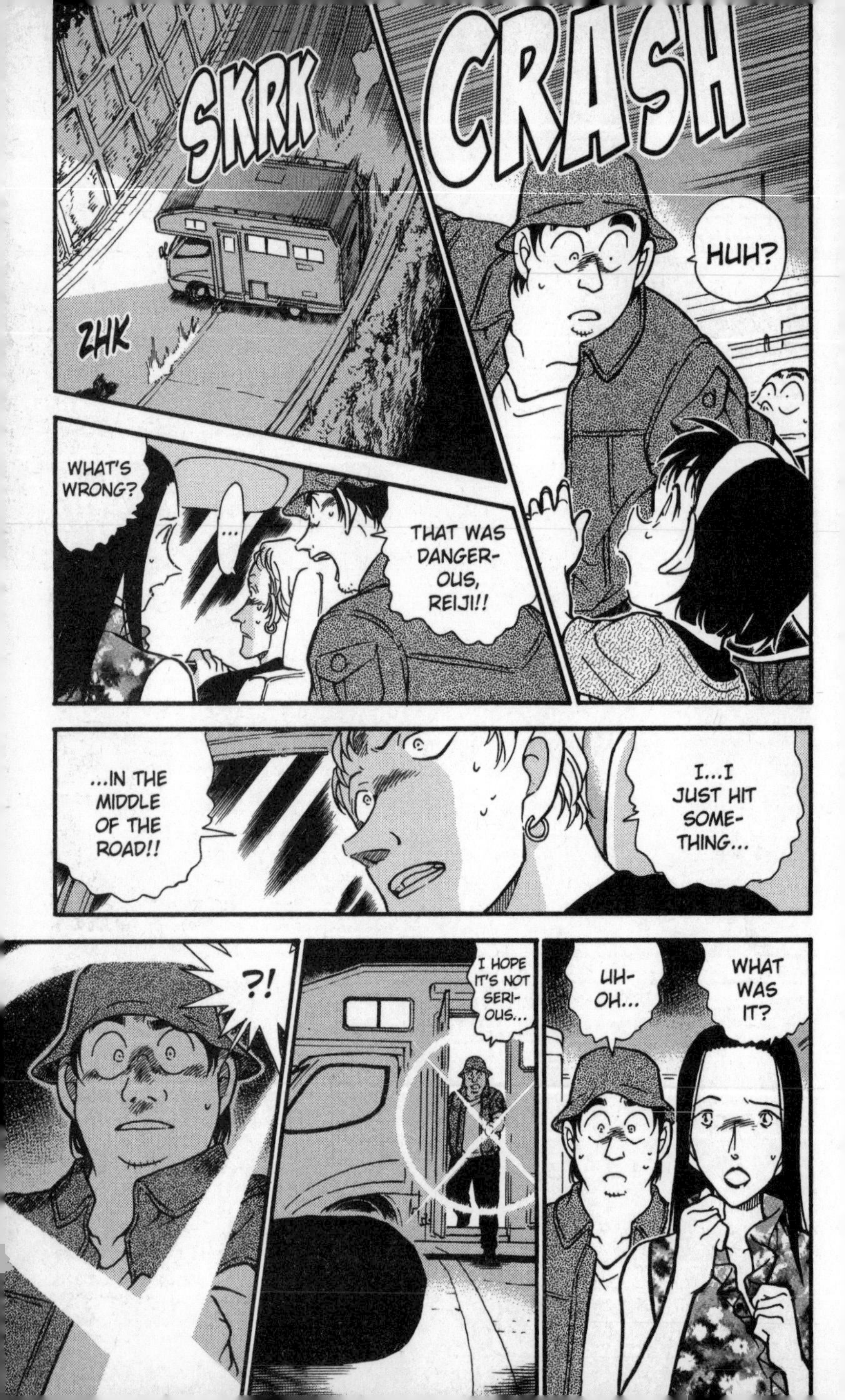
CRASH
HUH?
SKRK
ZHK
THAT WAS DANGER-OUS, REIJI!!
...
WHAT'S WRONG?
I...I JUST HIT SOME-THING...
...IN THE MIDDLE OF THE ROAD!!
WHAT WAS IT?
UH-OH...
I HOPE IT'S NOT SERI-OUS...
?!

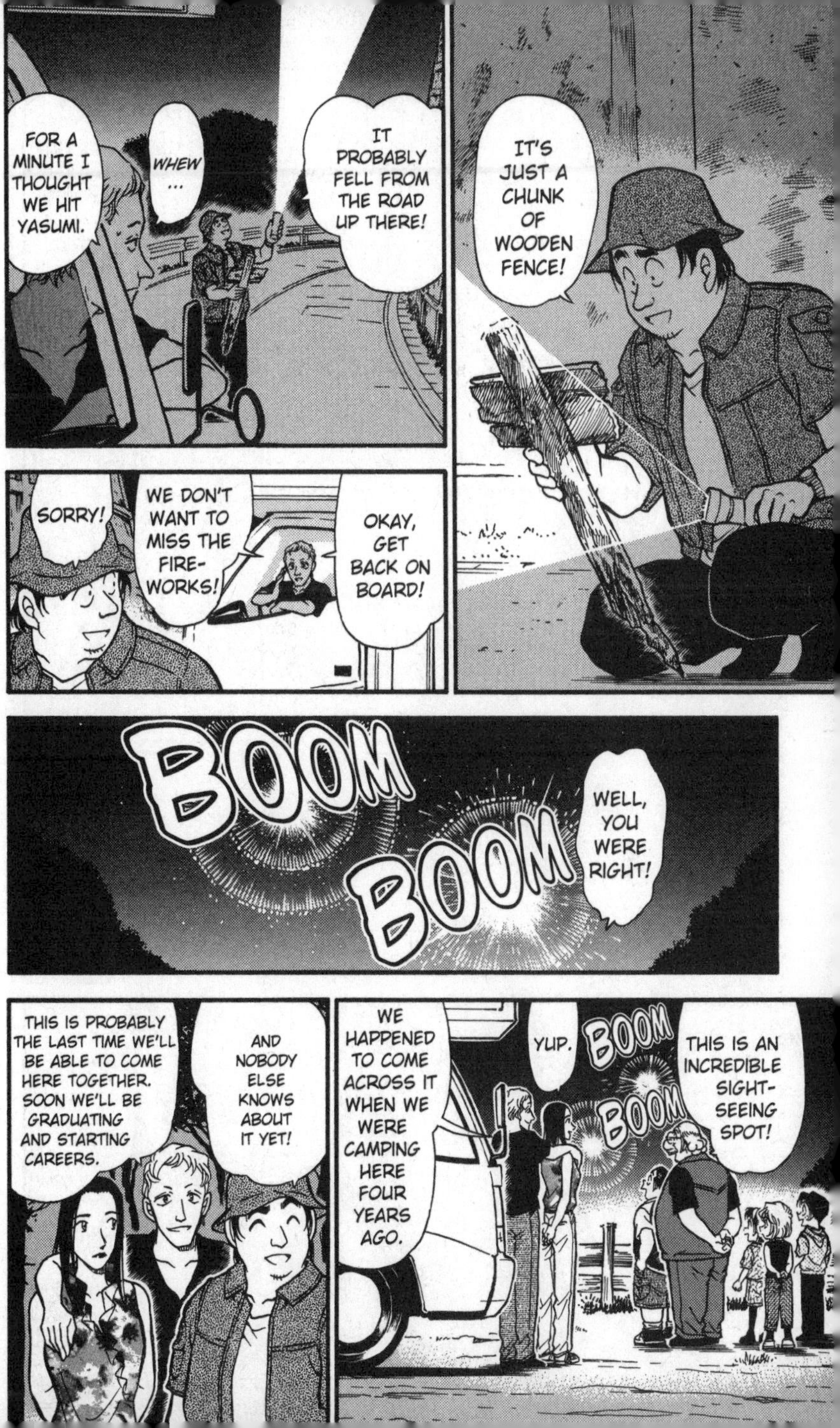
IT'S JUST A CHUNK OF WOODEN FENCE!
IT PROBABLY FELL FROM THE ROAD UP THERE!
WHEW ...
FOR A MINUTE I THOUGHT WE HIT YASUMI.
OKAY, GET BACK ON BOARD!
WE DON'T WANT TO MISS THE FIRE-WORKS!
SORRY!
WELL, YOU WERE RIGHT!
BOOM
BOOM
THIS IS AN INCREDIBLE SIGHT-SEEING SPOT!
BOOM
BOOM
YUP.
WE HAPPENED TO COME ACROSS IT WHEN WE WERE CAMPING HERE FOUR YEARS AGO.
AND NOBODY ELSE KNOWS ABOUT IT YET!
THIS IS PROBABLY THE LAST TIME WE'LL BE ABLE TO COME HERE TOGETHER. SOON WE'LL BE GRADUATING AND STARTING CAREERS.

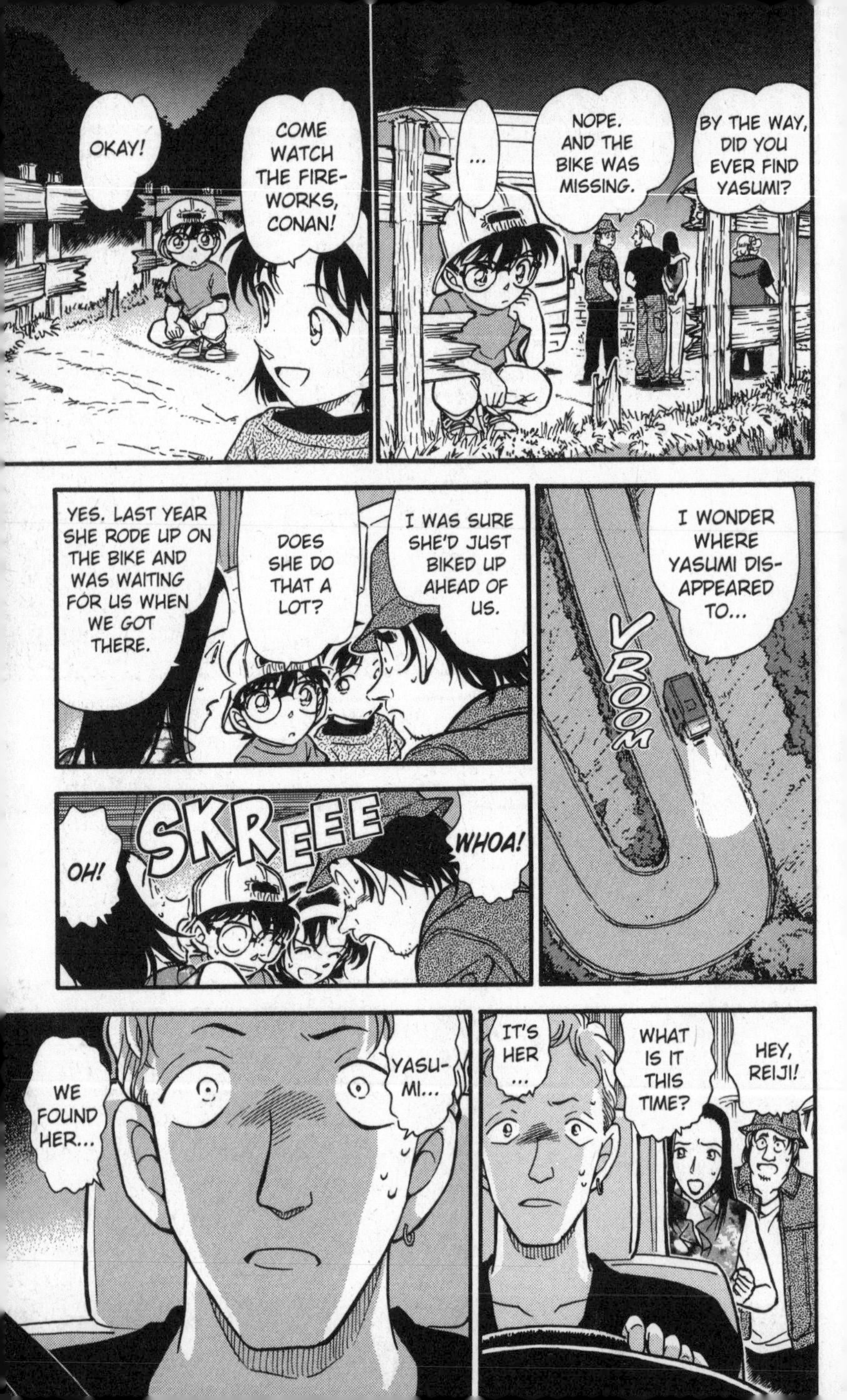

BY THE WAY, DID YOU EVER FIND YASUMI?
NOPE. AND THE BIKE WAS MISSING.
...
COME WATCH THE FIRE-WORKS, CONAN!
OKAY!
I WONDER WHERE YASUMI DIS-APPEARED TO...
VROOM
I WAS SURE SHE'D JUST BIKED UP AHEAD OF US.
DOES SHE DO THAT A LOT?
YES. LAST YEAR SHE RODE UP ON THE BIKE AND WAS WAITING FOR US WHEN WE GOT THERE.
WHOA!
SKREEE
OH!
HEY, REIJI!
WHAT IS IT THIS TIME?
IT'S HER ...
YASU-MI...
WE FOUND HER...

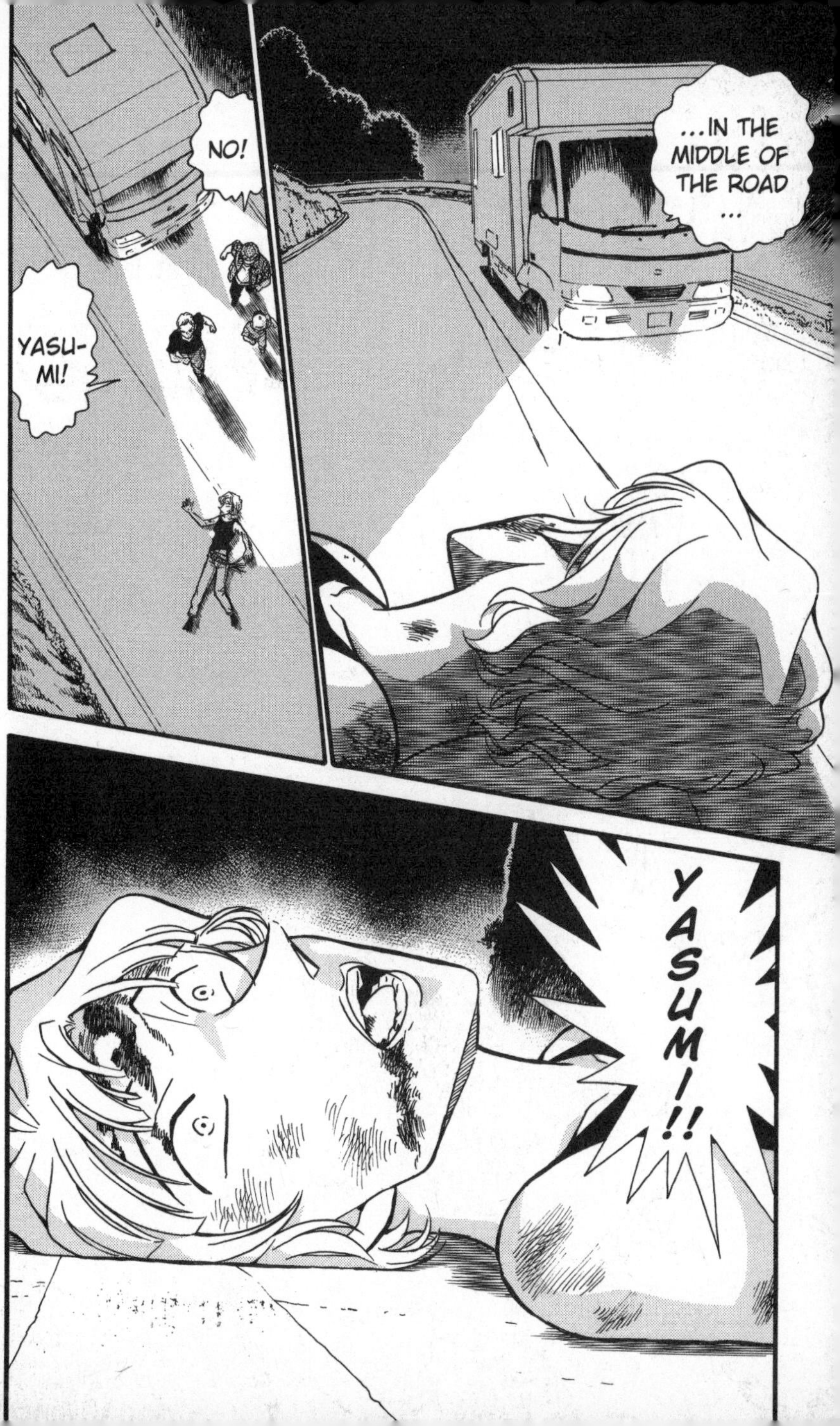
...IN THE MIDDLE OF THE ROAD ...
NO!
YASU-MI!
YASUMI!!

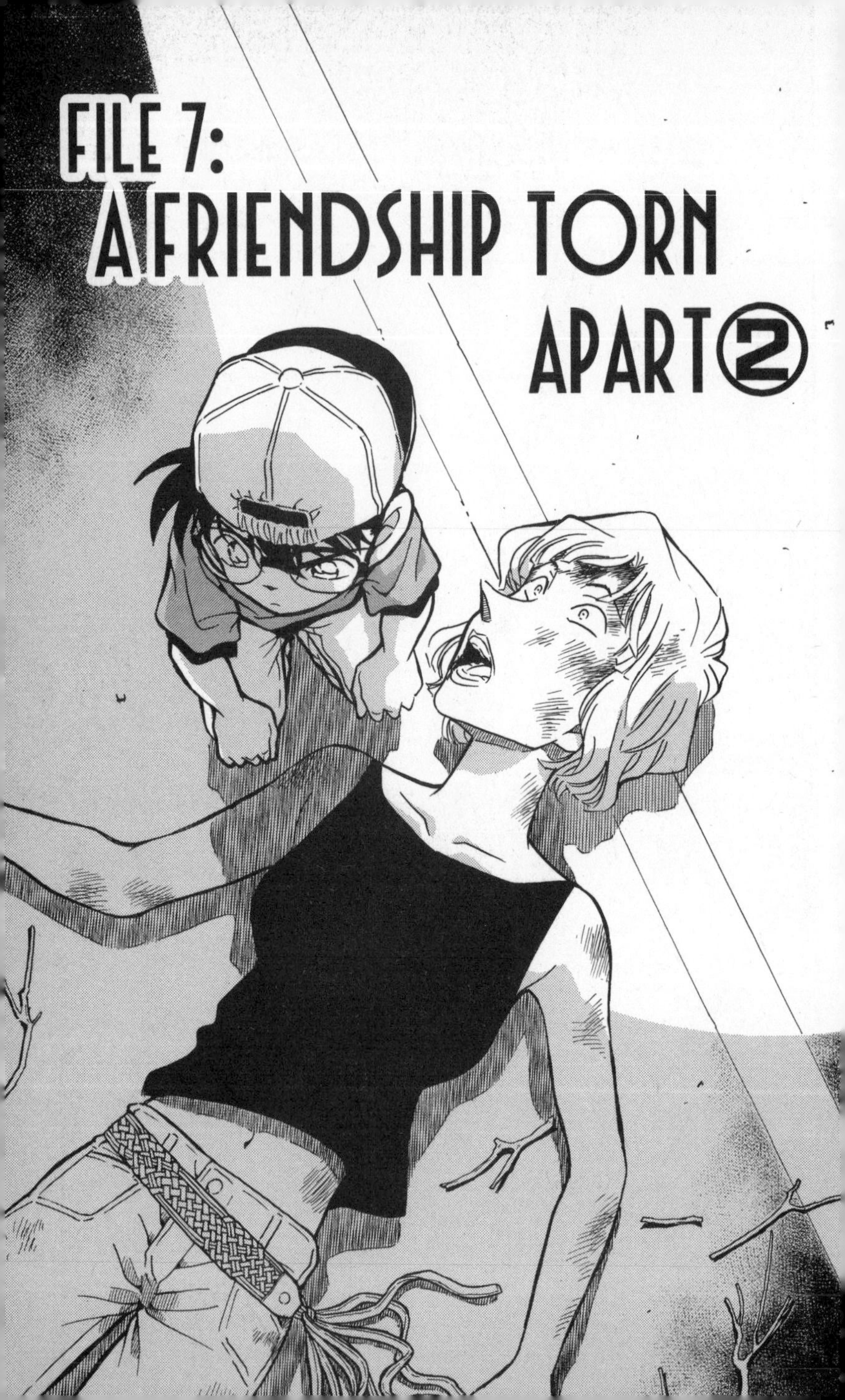
FILE 7:
A FRIENDSHIP TORN APART②

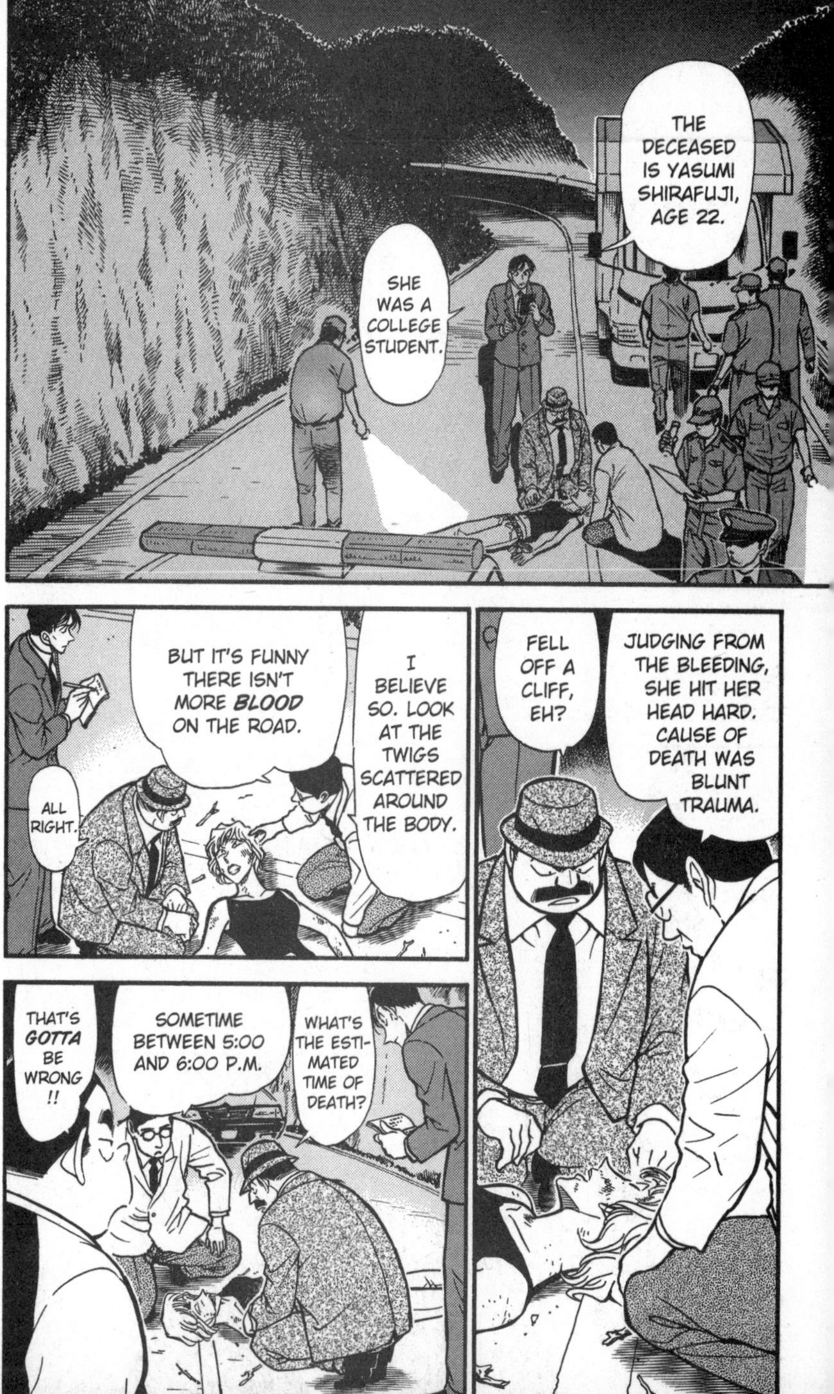
THE DECEASED IS YASUMI SHIRAFUJI, AGE 22.
SHE WAS A COLLEGE STUDENT.
JUDGING FROM THE BLEEDING, SHE HIT HER HEAD HARD. CAUSE OF DEATH WAS BLUNT TRAUMA.
FELL OFF A CLIFF, EH?
I BELIEVE SO. LOOK AT THE TWIGS SCATTERED AROUND THE BODY.
BUT IT'S FUNNY THERE ISN'T MORE ***BLOOD*** ON THE ROAD.
ALL RIGHT.
WHAT'S THE ESTIMATED TIME OF DEATH?
SOMETIME BETWEEN 5:00 AND 6:00 P.M.
THAT'S ***GOTTA*** BE WRONG!!

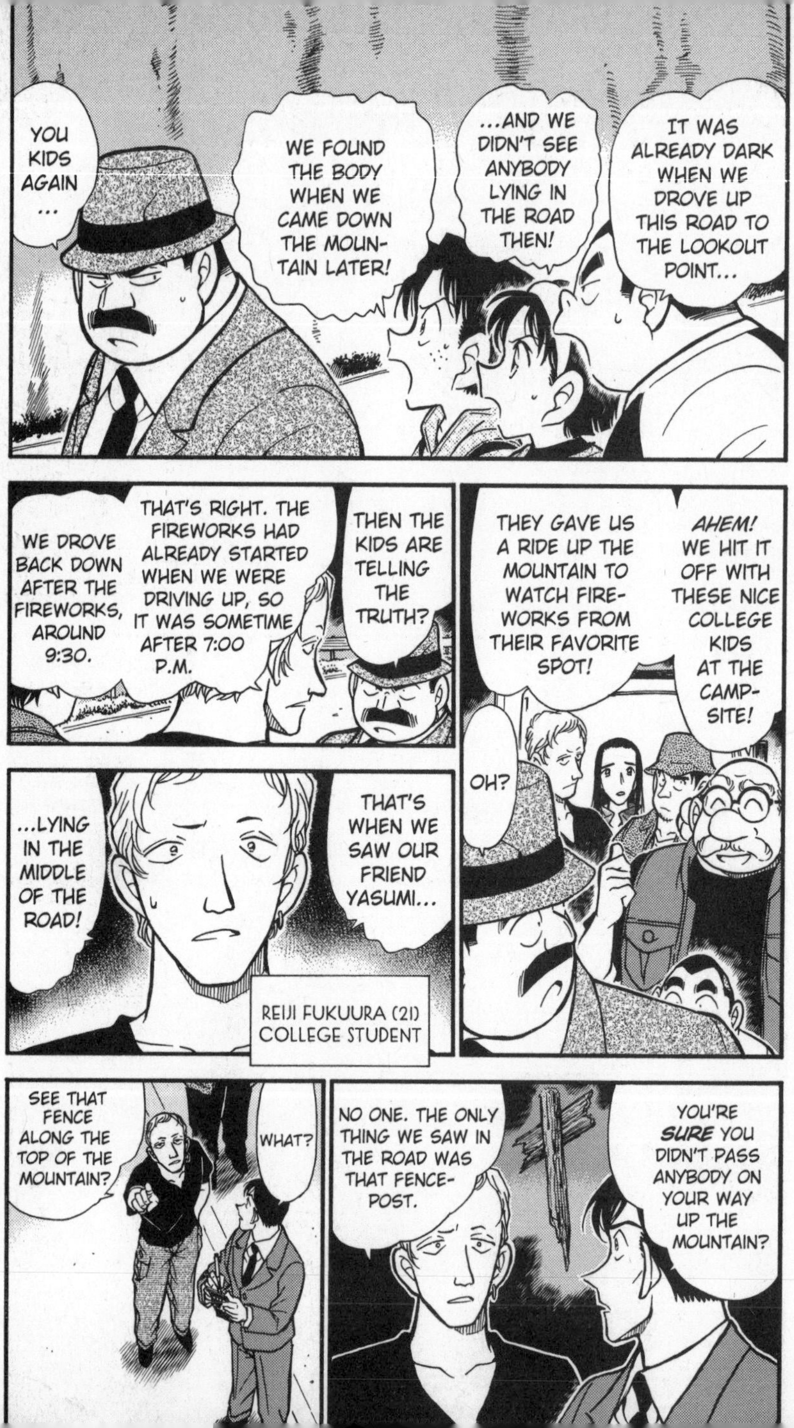

IT WAS ALREADY DARK WHEN WE DROVE UP THIS ROAD TO THE LOOKOUT POINT...
...AND WE DIDN'T SEE ANYBODY LYING IN THE ROAD THEN!
WE FOUND THE BODY WHEN WE CAME DOWN THE MOUN-TAIN LATER!
YOU KIDS AGAIN...
AHEM! WE HIT IT OFF WITH THESE NICE COLLEGE KIDS AT THE CAMP-SITE!
THEY GAVE US A RIDE UP THE MOUNTAIN TO WATCH FIRE-WORKS FROM THEIR FAVORITE SPOT!
OH?
THEN THE KIDS ARE TELLING THE TRUTH?
THAT'S RIGHT. THE FIREWORKS HAD ALREADY STARTED WHEN WE WERE DRIVING UP, SO IT WAS SOMETIME AFTER 7:00 P.M.
WE DROVE BACK DOWN AFTER THE FIREWORKS, AROUND 9:30.
THAT'S WHEN WE SAW OUR FRIEND YASUMI...
...LYING IN THE MIDDLE OF THE ROAD!
REIJI FUKUURA (21) COLLEGE STUDENT
YOU'RE ***SURE*** YOU DIDN'T PASS ANYBODY ON YOUR WAY UP THE MOUNTAIN?
NO ONE. THE ONLY THING WE SAW IN THE ROAD WAS THAT FENCE-POST.
WHAT?
SEE THAT FENCE ALONG THE TOP OF THE MOUNTAIN?

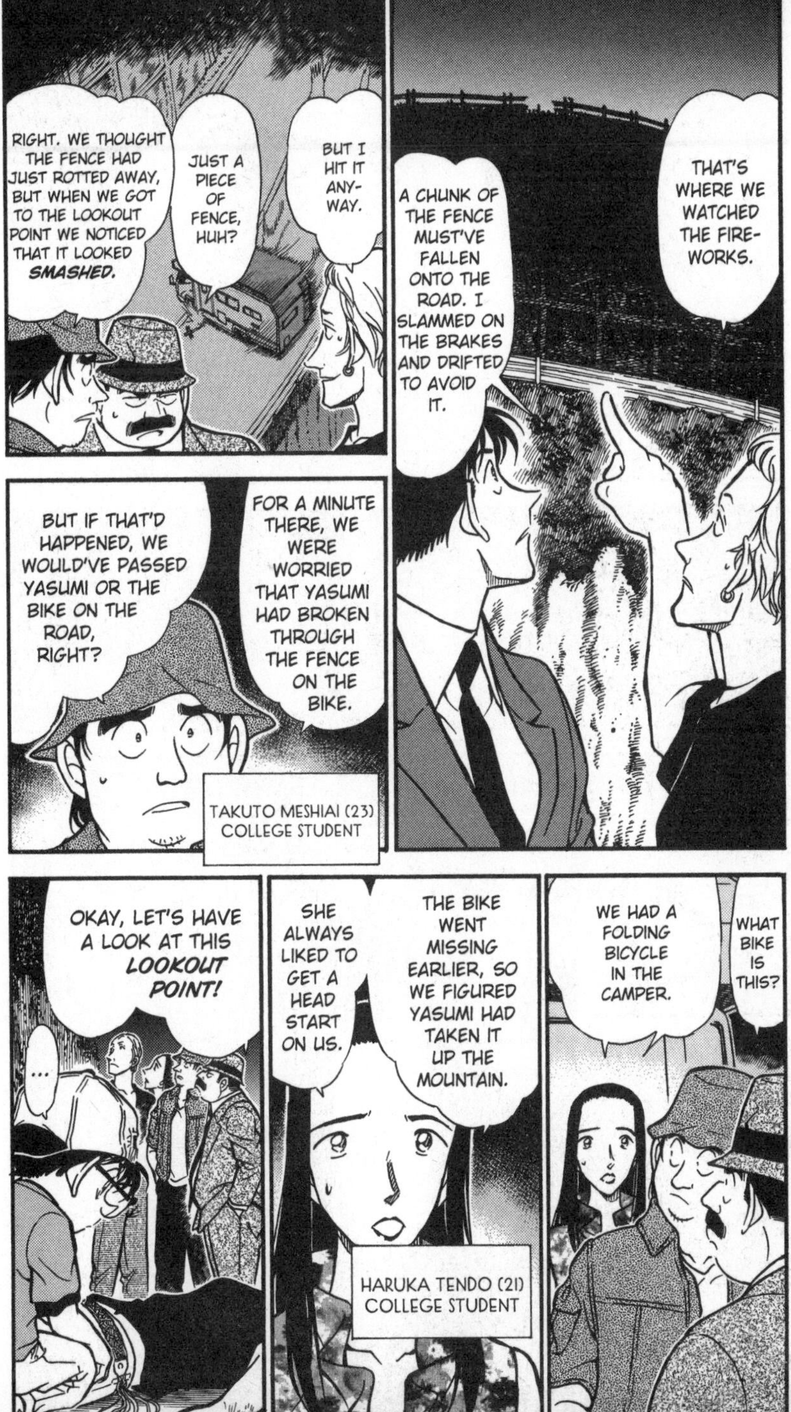
THAT'S WHERE WE WATCHED THE FIRE-WORKS.
A CHUNK OF THE FENCE MUST'VE FALLEN ONTO THE ROAD. I SLAMMED ON THE BRAKES AND DRIFTED TO AVOID IT.
BUT I HIT IT ANY-WAY.
JUST A PIECE OF FENCE, HUH?
RIGHT. WE THOUGHT THE FENCE HAD JUST ROTTED AWAY, BUT WHEN WE GOT TO THE LOOKOUT POINT WE NOTICED THAT IT LOOKED ***SMASHED.***
FOR A MINUTE THERE, WE WERE WORRIED THAT YASUMI HAD BROKEN THROUGH THE FENCE ON THE BIKE.
BUT IF THAT'D HAPPENED, WE WOULD'VE PASSED YASUMI OR THE BIKE ON THE ROAD, RIGHT?
TAKUTO MESHIAI (23) COLLEGE STUDENT
WHAT BIKE IS THIS?
WE HAD A FOLDING BICYCLE IN THE CAMPER.
THE BIKE WENT MISSING EARLIER, SO WE FIGURED YASUMI HAD TAKEN IT UP THE MOUNTAIN.
SHE ALWAYS LIKED TO GET A HEAD START ON US.
HARUKA TENDO (21) COLLEGE STUDENT
OKAY, LET'S HAVE A LOOK AT THIS ***LOOKOUT POINT!***
...

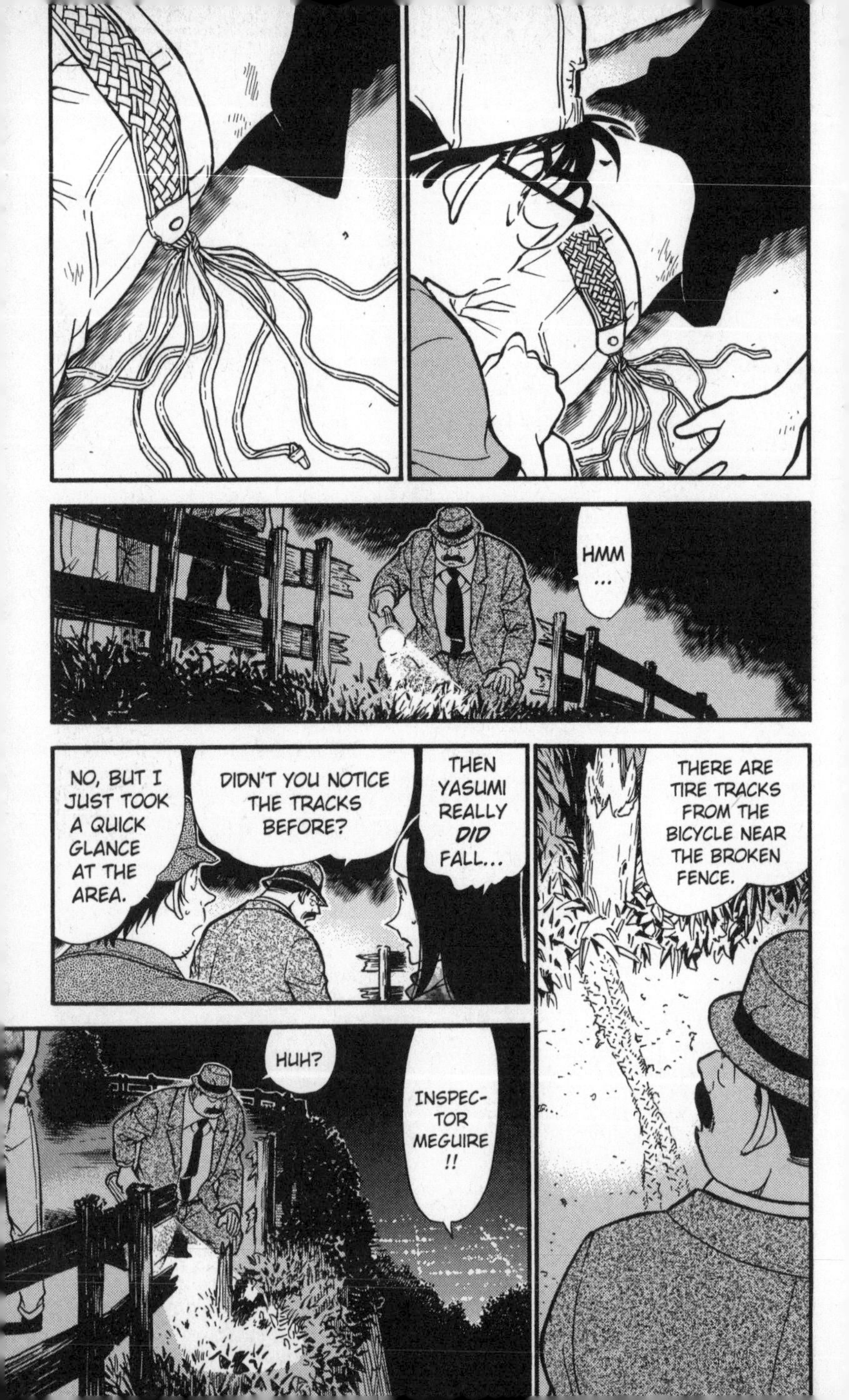
HMM ...
THERE ARE TIRE TRACKS FROM THE BICYCLE NEAR THE BROKEN FENCE.
THEN YASUMI REALLY DID FALL...
DIDN'T YOU NOTICE THE TRACKS BEFORE?
NO, BUT I JUST TOOK A QUICK GLANCE AT THE AREA.
INSPECTOR MEGUIRE !!
HUH?

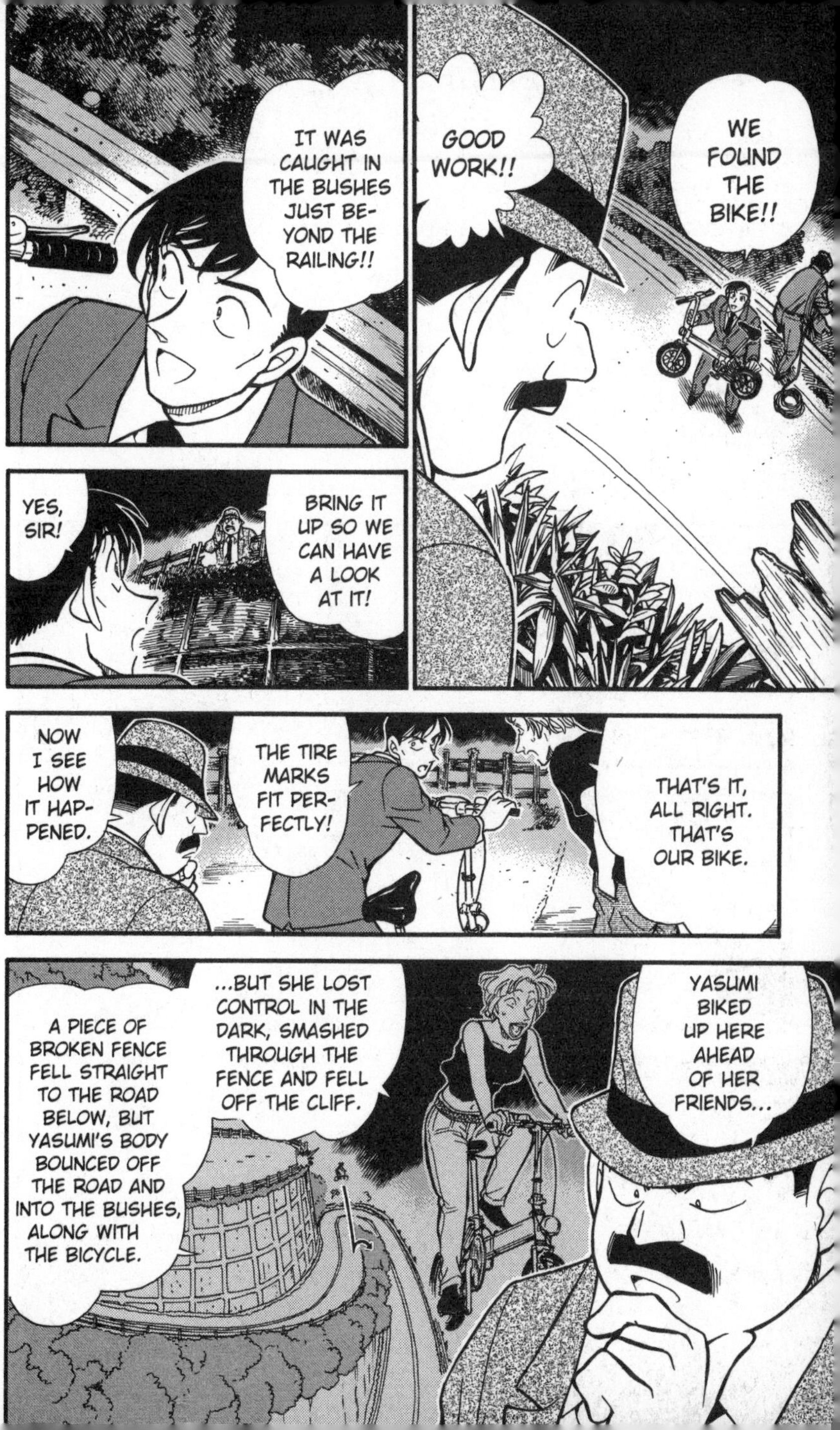
WE FOUND THE BIKE!!
GOOD WORK!!
IT WAS CAUGHT IN THE BUSHES JUST BE-YOND THE RAILING!!
BRING IT UP SO WE CAN HAVE A LOOK AT IT!
YES, SIR!
THAT'S IT, ALL RIGHT. THAT'S OUR BIKE.
THE TIRE MARKS FIT PER-FECTLY!
NOW I SEE HOW IT HAP-PENED.
YASUMI BIKED UP HERE AHEAD OF HER FRIENDS...
...BUT SHE LOST CONTROL IN THE DARK, SMASHED THROUGH THE FENCE AND FELL OFF THE CLIFF.
A PIECE OF BROKEN FENCE FELL STRAIGHT TO THE ROAD BELOW, BUT YASUMI'S BODY BOUNCED OFF THE ROAD AND INTO THE BUSHES, ALONG WITH THE BICYCLE.

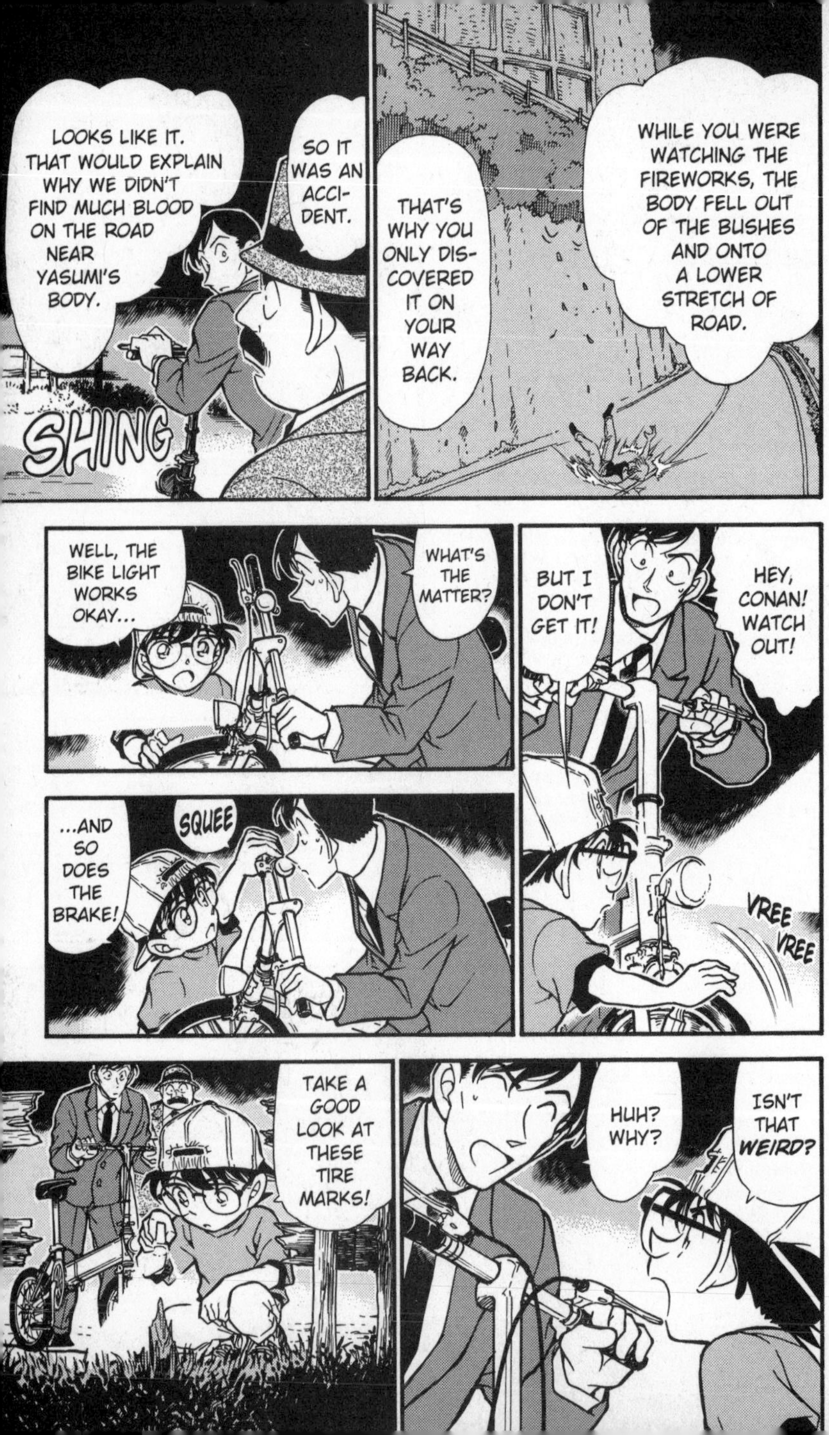
WHILE YOU WERE WATCHING THE FIREWORKS, THE BODY FELL OUT OF THE BUSHES AND ONTO A LOWER STRETCH OF ROAD.
THAT'S WHY YOU ONLY DISCOVERED IT ON YOUR WAY BACK.
SO IT WAS AN ACCIDENT.
LOOKS LIKE IT. THAT WOULD EXPLAIN WHY WE DIDN'T FIND MUCH BLOOD ON THE ROAD NEAR YASUMI'S BODY.
SHING
HEY, CONAN! WATCH OUT!
BUT I DON'T GET IT!
VREE VREE
WHAT'S THE MATTER?
WELL, THE BIKE LIGHT WORKS OKAY...
SQUEE
...AND SO DOES THE BRAKE!
ISN'T THAT *WEIRD?*
HUH? WHY?
TAKE A GOOD LOOK AT THESE TIRE MARKS!

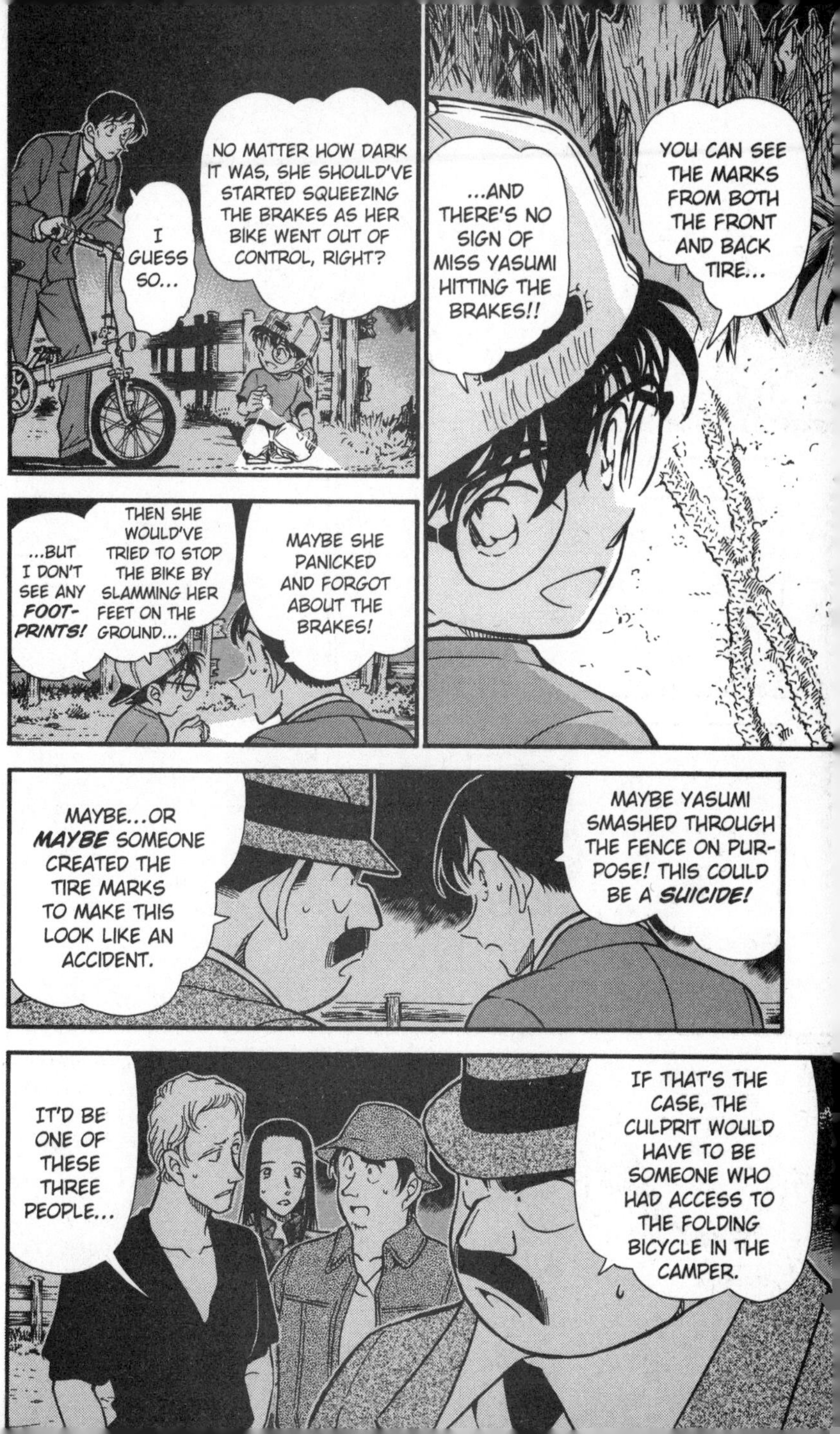
YOU CAN SEE THE MARKS FROM BOTH THE FRONT AND BACK TIRE...
...AND THERE'S NO SIGN OF MISS YASUMI HITTING THE BRAKES!!
NO MATTER HOW DARK IT WAS, SHE SHOULD'VE STARTED SQUEEZING THE BRAKES AS HER BIKE WENT OUT OF CONTROL, RIGHT?
I GUESS SO...
MAYBE SHE PANICKED AND FORGOT ABOUT THE BRAKES!
THEN SHE WOULD'VE TRIED TO STOP THE BIKE BY SLAMMING HER FEET ON THE GROUND...
...BUT I DON'T SEE ANY *FOOT-PRINTS!*
MAYBE YASUMI SMASHED THROUGH THE FENCE ON PUR-POSE! THIS COULD BE A *SUICIDE!*
MAYBE...OR *MAYBE* SOMEONE CREATED THE TIRE MARKS TO MAKE THIS LOOK LIKE AN ACCIDENT.
IF THAT'S THE CASE, THE CULPRIT WOULD HAVE TO BE SOMEONE WHO HAD ACCESS TO THE FOLDING BICYCLE IN THE CAMPER.
IT'D BE ONE OF THESE THREE PEOPLE...

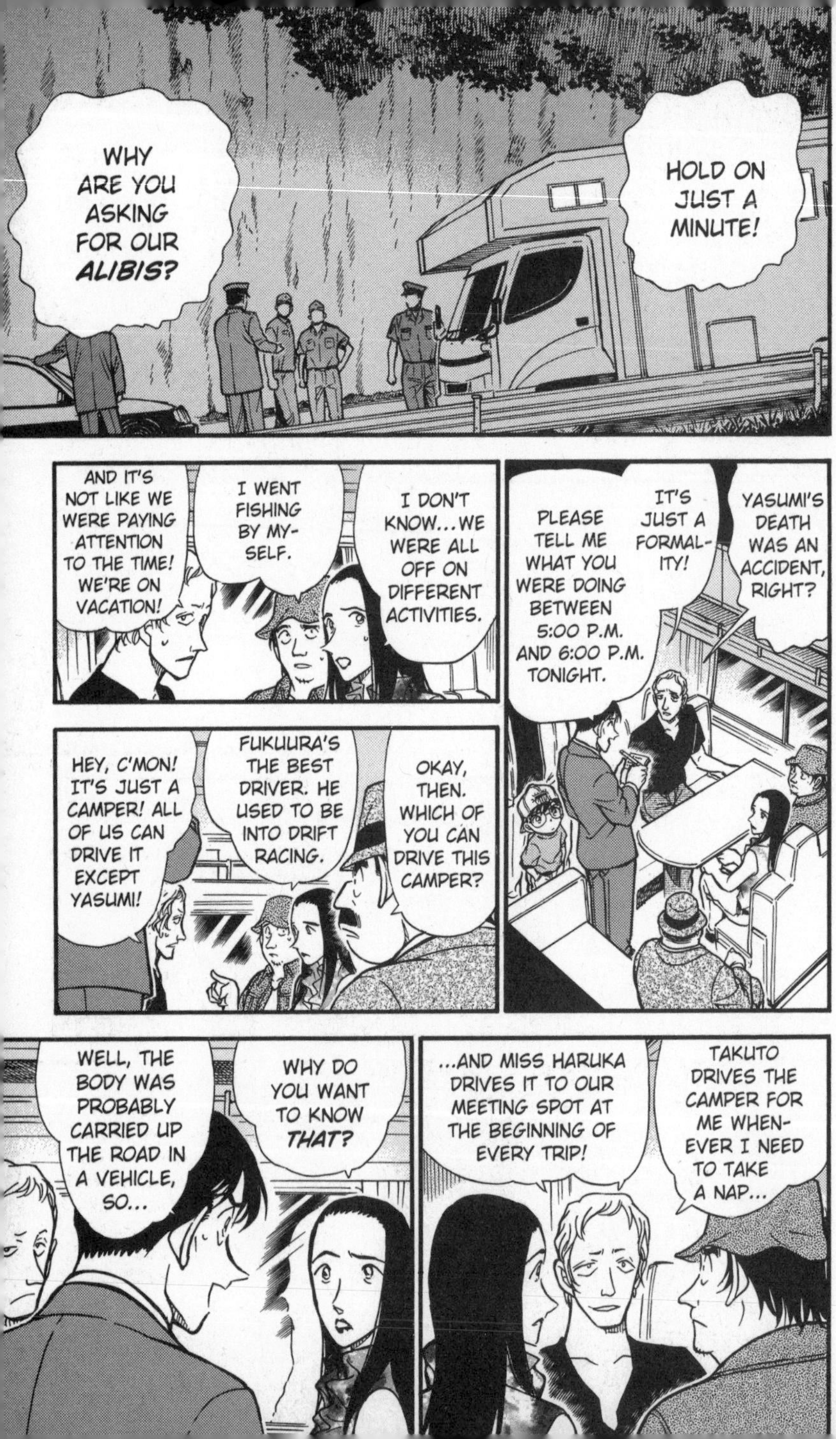
HOLD ON JUST A MINUTE!
WHY ARE YOU ASKING FOR OUR *ALIBIS?*
YASUMI'S DEATH WAS AN ACCIDENT, RIGHT?
IT'S JUST A FORMALITY!
PLEASE TELL ME WHAT YOU WERE DOING BETWEEN 5:00 P.M. AND 6:00 P.M. TONIGHT.
I DON'T KNOW... WE WERE ALL OFF ON DIFFERENT ACTIVITIES.
I WENT FISHING BY MYSELF.
AND IT'S NOT LIKE WE WERE PAYING ATTENTION TO THE TIME! WE'RE ON VACATION!
OKAY, THEN. WHICH OF YOU CAN DRIVE THIS CAMPER?
FUKUURA'S THE BEST DRIVER. HE USED TO BE INTO DRIFT RACING.
HEY, C'MON! IT'S JUST A CAMPER! ALL OF US CAN DRIVE IT EXCEPT YASUMI!
TAKUTO DRIVES THE CAMPER FOR ME WHENEVER I NEED TO TAKE A NAP...
...AND MISS HARUKA DRIVES IT TO OUR MEETING SPOT AT THE BEGINNING OF EVERY TRIP!
WHY DO YOU WANT TO KNOW *THAT?*
WELL, THE BODY WAS PROBABLY CARRIED UP THE ROAD IN A VEHICLE, SO...

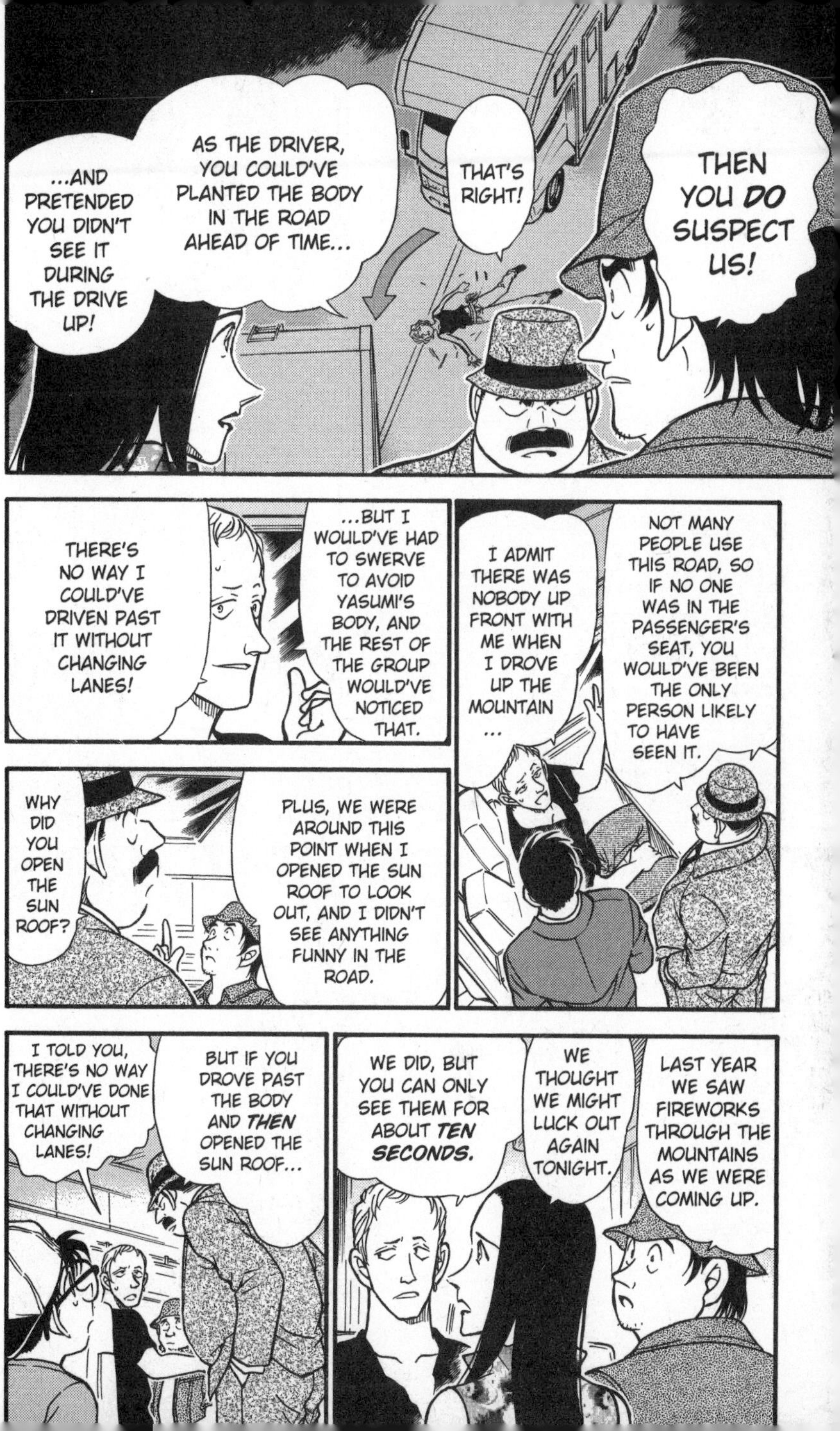
THEN YOU *DO* SUSPECT US!
THAT'S RIGHT!
AS THE DRIVER, YOU COULD'VE PLANTED THE BODY IN THE ROAD AHEAD OF TIME...
...AND PRETENDED YOU DIDN'T SEE IT DURING THE DRIVE UP!
NOT MANY PEOPLE USE THIS ROAD, SO IF NO ONE WAS IN THE PASSENGER'S SEAT, YOU WOULD'VE BEEN THE ONLY PERSON LIKELY TO HAVE SEEN IT.
I ADMIT THERE WAS NOBODY UP FRONT WITH ME WHEN I DROVE UP THE MOUNTAIN ...
...BUT I WOULD'VE HAD TO SWERVE TO AVOID YASUMI'S BODY, AND THE REST OF THE GROUP WOULD'VE NOTICED THAT.
THERE'S NO WAY I COULD'VE DRIVEN PAST IT WITHOUT CHANGING LANES!
PLUS, WE WERE AROUND THIS POINT WHEN I OPENED THE SUN ROOF TO LOOK OUT, AND I DIDN'T SEE ANYTHING FUNNY IN THE ROAD.
WHY DID YOU OPEN THE SUN ROOF?
LAST YEAR WE SAW FIREWORKS THROUGH THE MOUNTAINS AS WE WERE COMING UP.
WE THOUGHT WE MIGHT LUCK OUT AGAIN TONIGHT.
WE DID, BUT YOU CAN ONLY SEE THEM FOR ABOUT ***TEN SECONDS.***
BUT IF YOU DROVE PAST THE BODY AND ***THEN*** OPENED THE SUN ROOF...
I TOLD YOU, THERE'S NO WAY I COULD'VE DONE THAT WITHOUT CHANGING LANES!

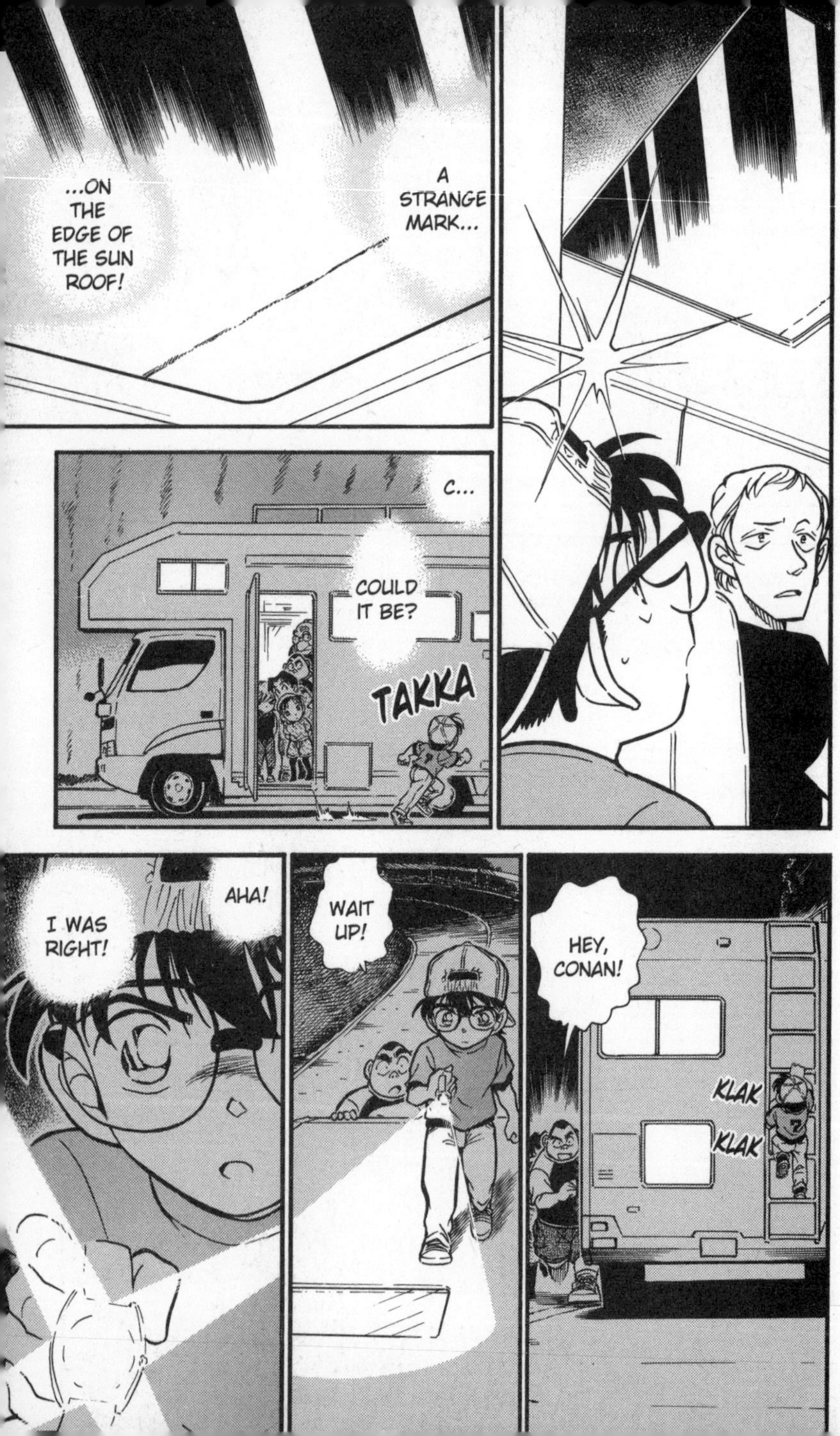
A STRANGE MARK...
...ON THE EDGE OF THE SUN ROOF!
C...
COULD IT BE?
TAKKA
HEY, CONAN!
KLAK
KLAK
WAIT UP!
AHA!
I WAS RIGHT!

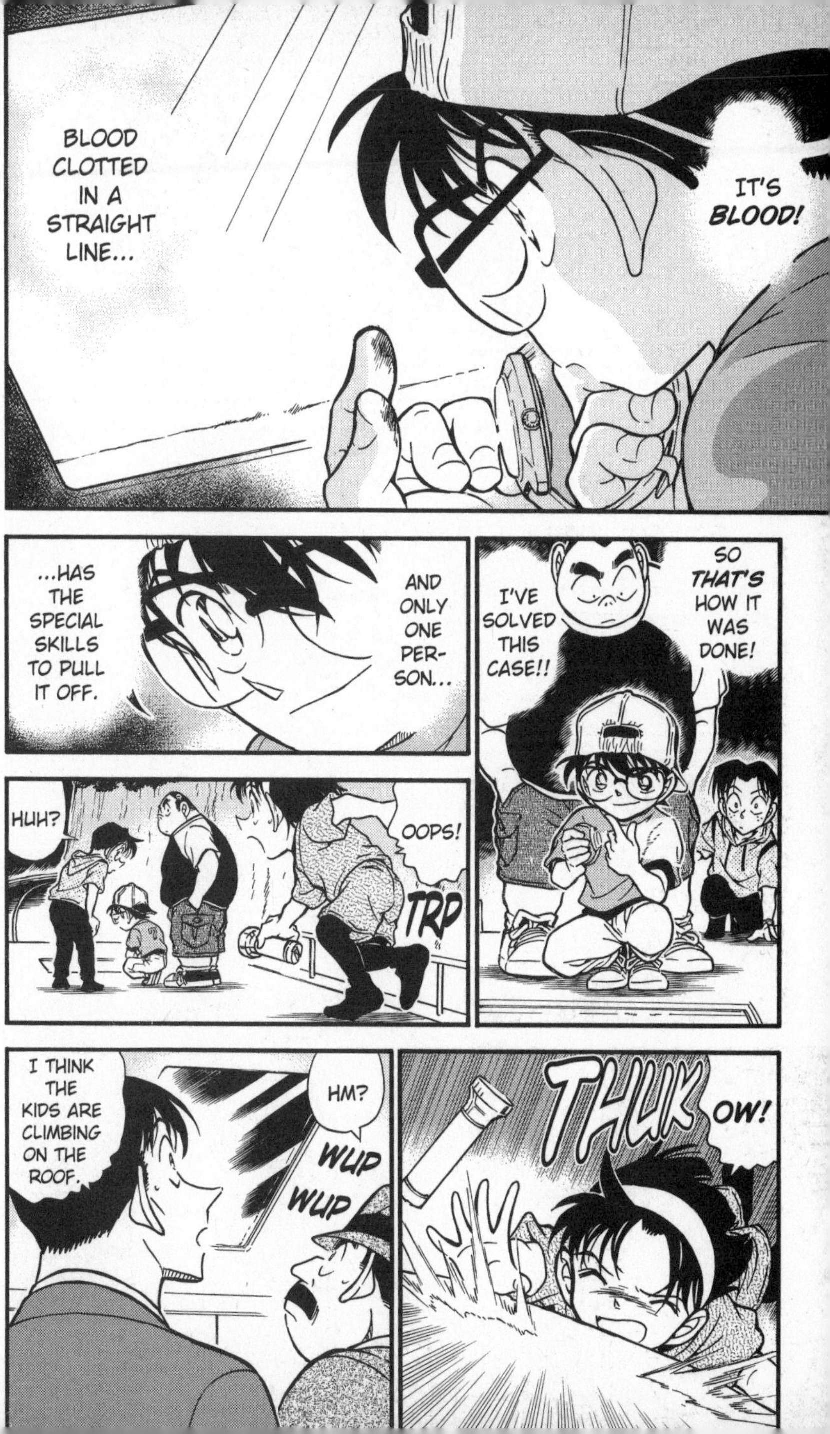
IT'S BLOOD!
BLOOD CLOTTED IN A STRAIGHT LINE...
SO THAT'S HOW IT WAS DONE!
I'VE SOLVED THIS CASE!!
AND ONLY ONE PERSON...
...HAS THE SPECIAL SKILLS TO PULL IT OFF.
OOPS!
TRP
HUH?
OW!
THUK
HM?
WUP WUP
I THINK THE KIDS ARE CLIMBING ON THE ROOF.

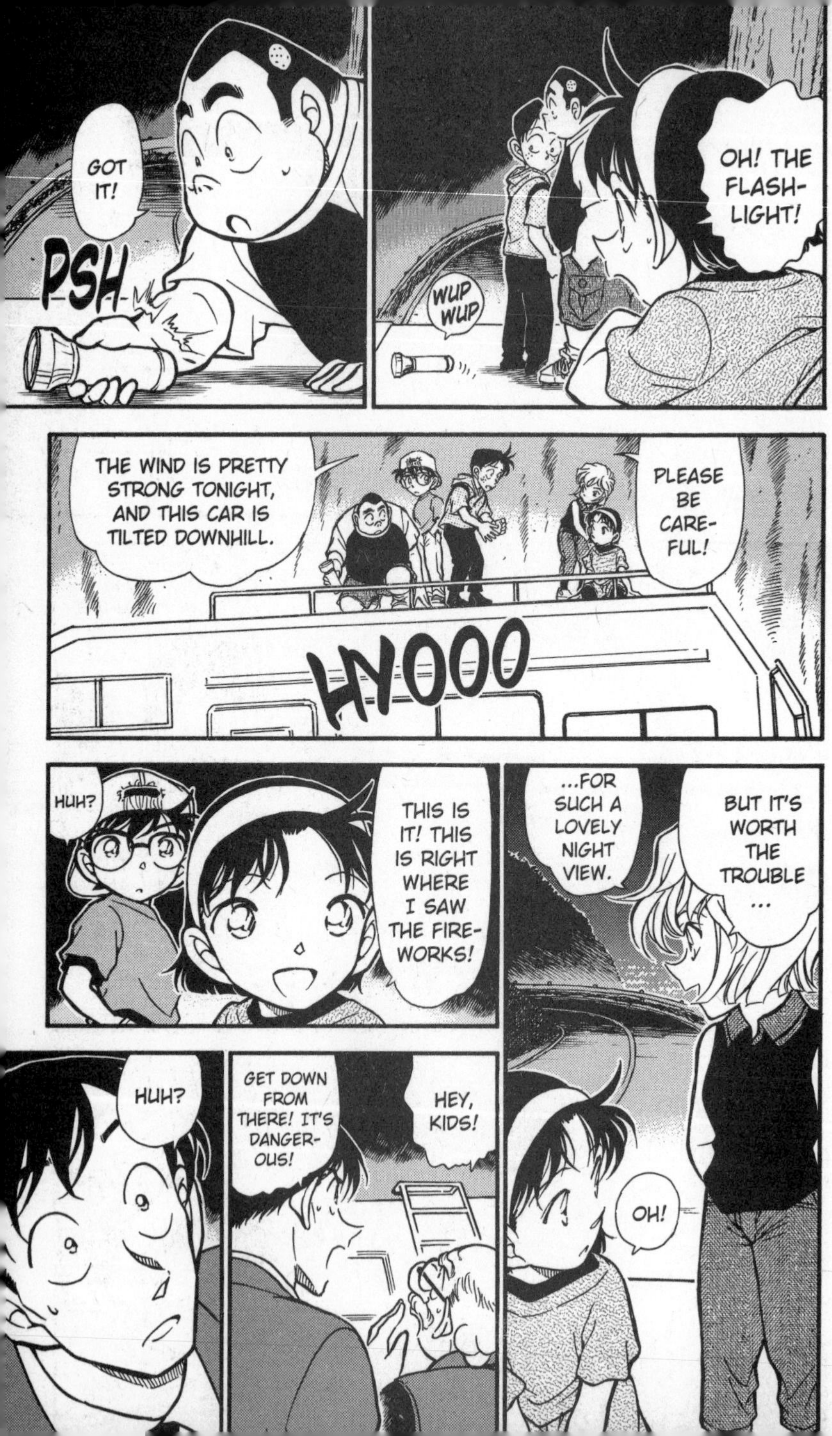
OH! THE FLASH-LIGHT!
WUP WUP
GOT IT!
PSH
PLEASE BE CARE-FUL!
THE WIND IS PRETTY STRONG TONIGHT, AND THIS CAR IS TILTED DOWNHILL.
HYOOO
BUT IT'S WORTH THE TROUBLE ...
...FOR SUCH A LOVELY NIGHT VIEW.
OH!
THIS IS IT! THIS IS RIGHT WHERE I SAW THE FIRE-WORKS!
HUH?
HEY, KIDS!
GET DOWN FROM THERE! IT'S DANGER-OUS!
HUH?

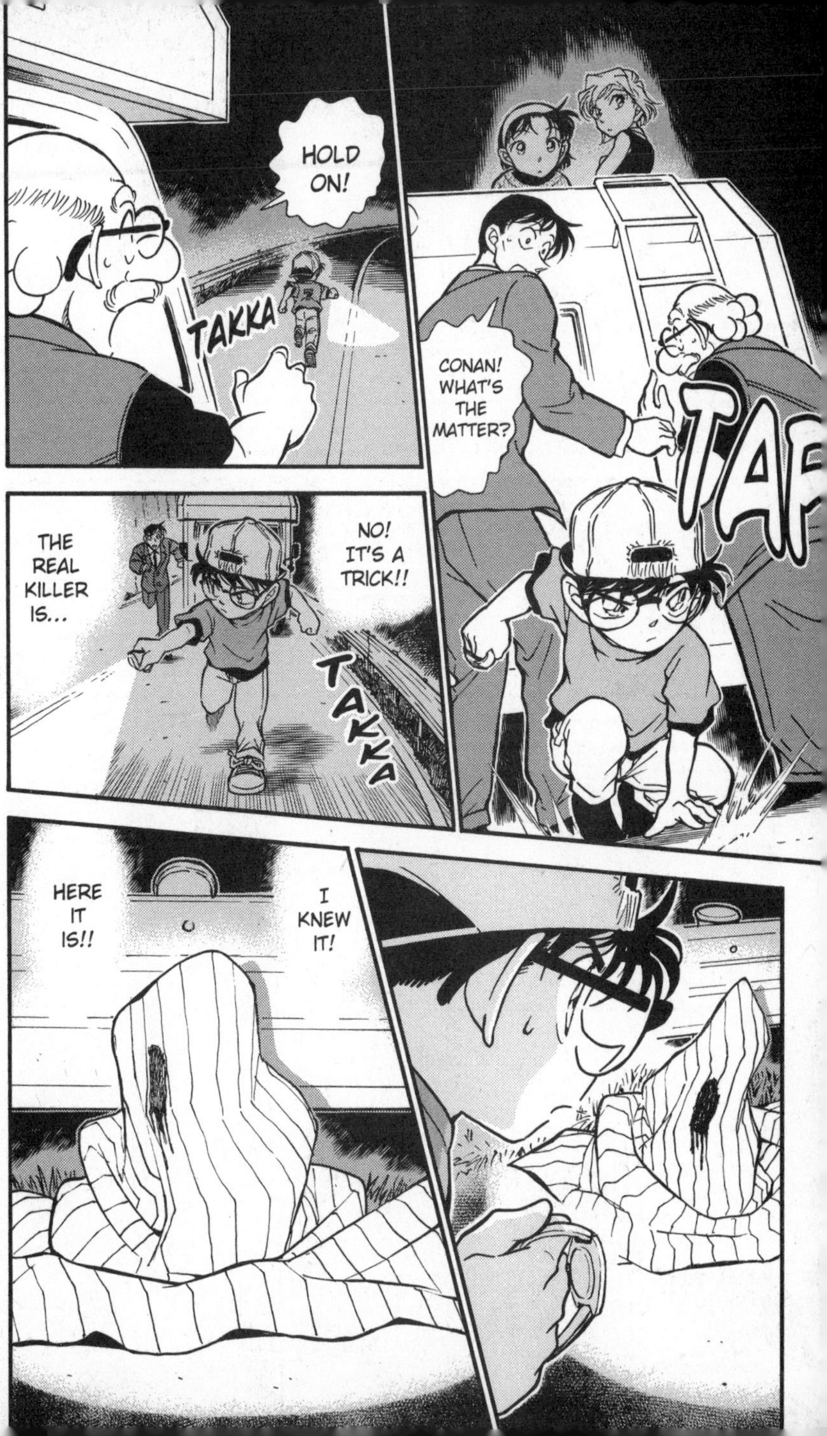
CONAN! WHAT'S THE MATTER?
TAP
HOLD ON!
TAKKA
NO! IT'S A TRICK!!
THE REAL KILLER IS...
TAKKA
I KNEW IT!
HERE IT IS!!

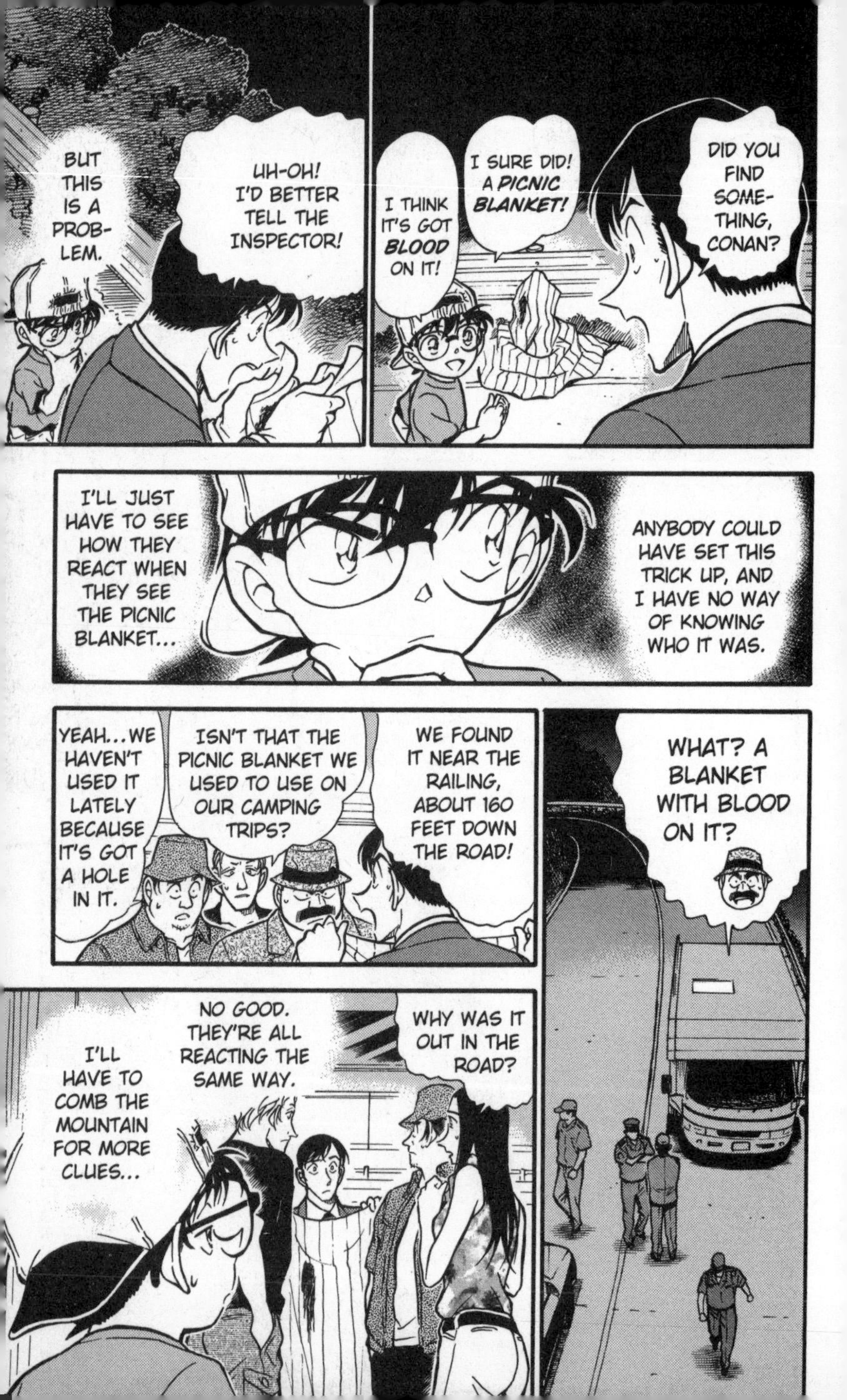
DID YOU FIND SOME-THING, CONAN?
I SURE DID! A *PICNIC BLANKET!*
I THINK IT'S GOT *BLOOD* ON IT!
UH-OH! I'D BETTER TELL THE INSPECTOR!
BUT THIS IS A PROB-LEM.
ANYBODY COULD HAVE SET THIS TRICK UP, AND I HAVE NO WAY OF KNOWING WHO IT WAS.
I'LL JUST HAVE TO SEE HOW THEY REACT WHEN THEY SEE THE PICNIC BLANKET...
WHAT? A BLANKET WITH BLOOD ON IT?
WE FOUND IT NEAR THE RAILING, ABOUT 160 FEET DOWN THE ROAD!
ISN'T THAT THE PICNIC BLANKET WE USED TO USE ON OUR CAMPING TRIPS?
YEAH...WE HAVEN'T USED IT LATELY BECAUSE IT'S GOT A HOLE IN IT.
WHY WAS IT OUT IN THE ROAD?
NO GOOD. THEY'RE ALL REACTING THE SAME WAY.
I'LL HAVE TO COMB THE MOUNTAIN FOR MORE CLUES...

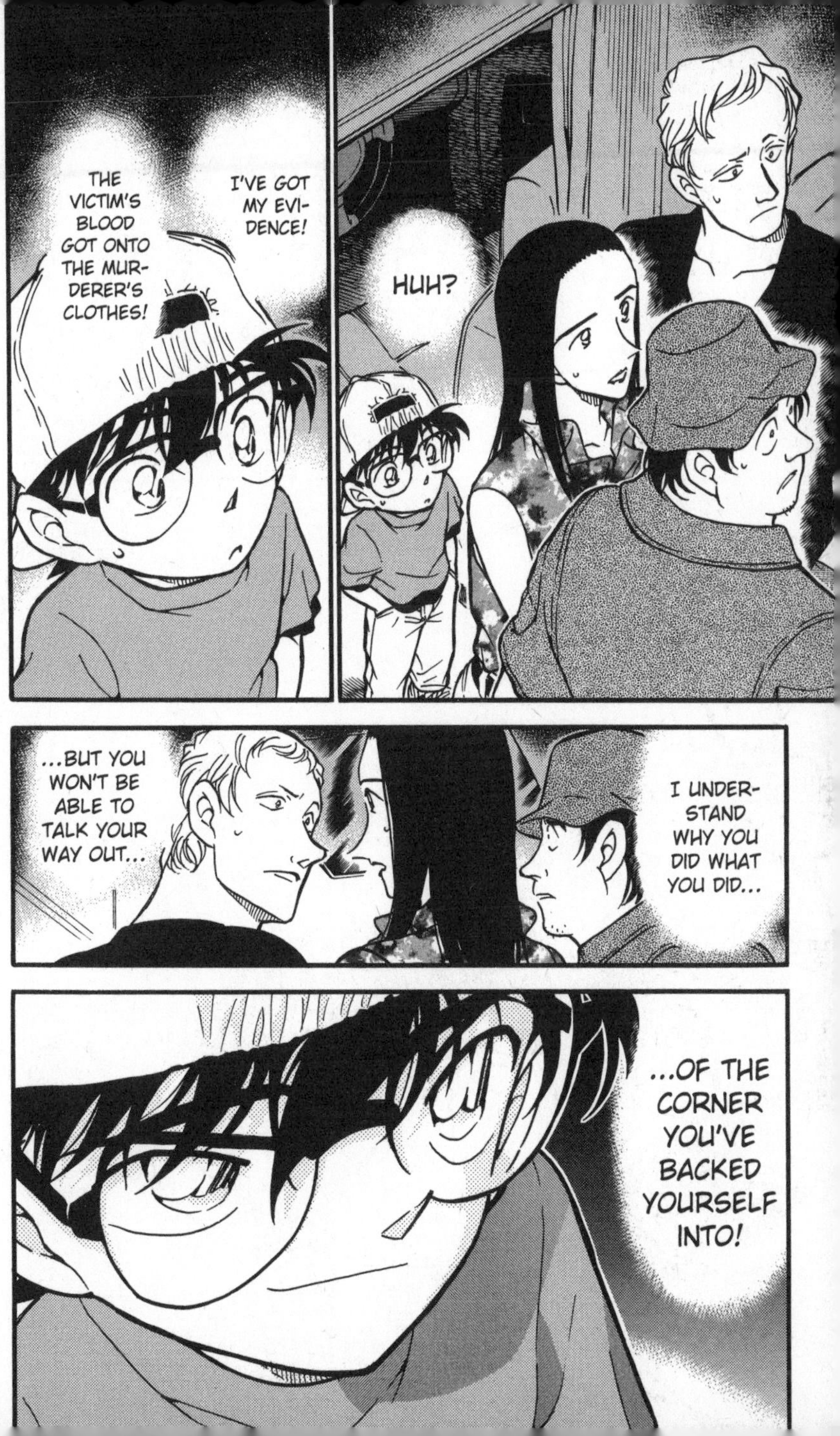
HUH?
I'VE GOT MY EVIDENCE!
THE VICTIM'S BLOOD GOT ONTO THE MURDERER'S CLOTHES!
I UNDERSTAND WHY YOU DID WHAT YOU DID...
...BUT YOU WON'T BE ABLE TO TALK YOUR WAY OUT...
...OF THE CORNER YOU'VE BACKED YOURSELF INTO!

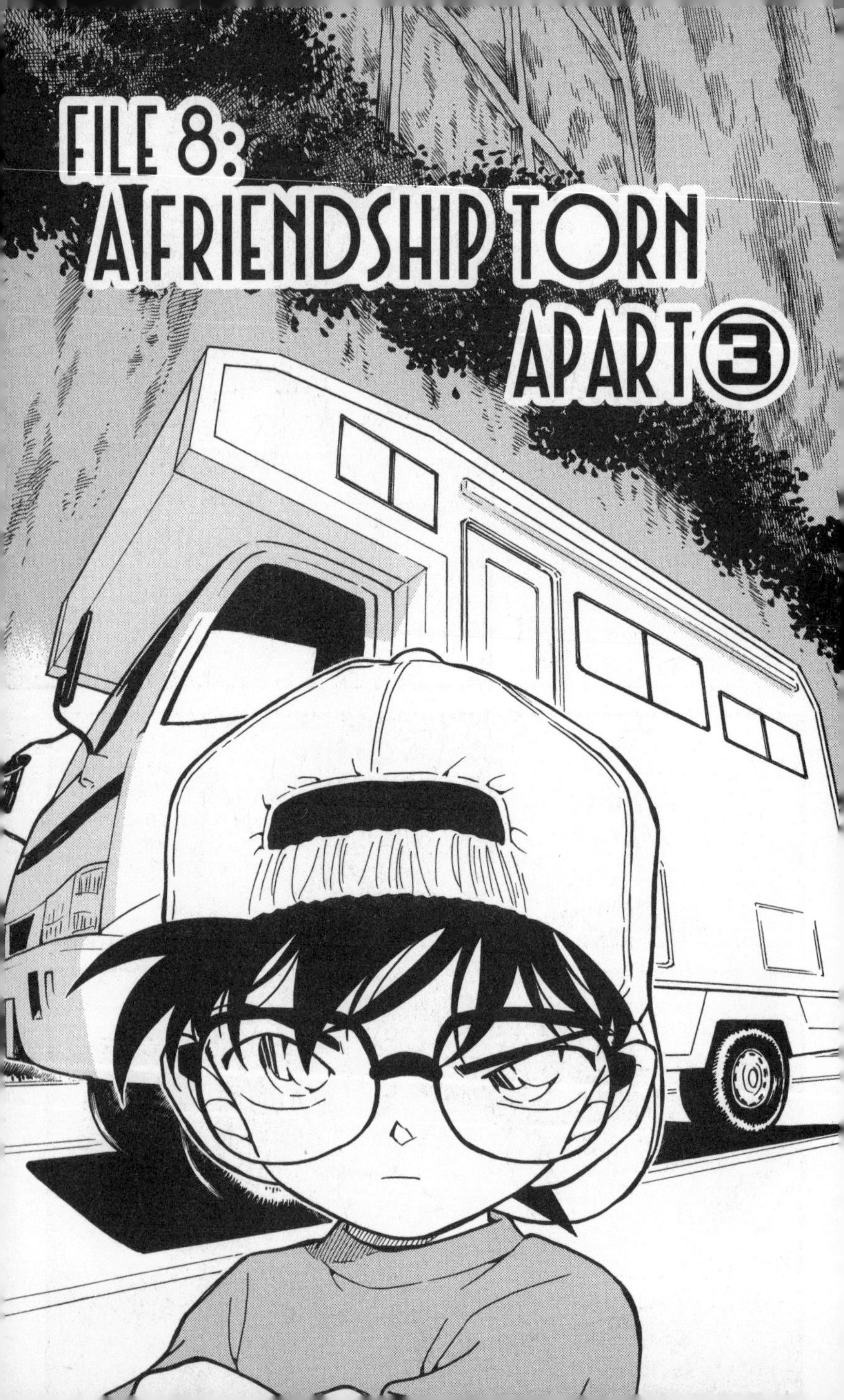
FILE 8:
A FRIENDSHIP TORN APART ③

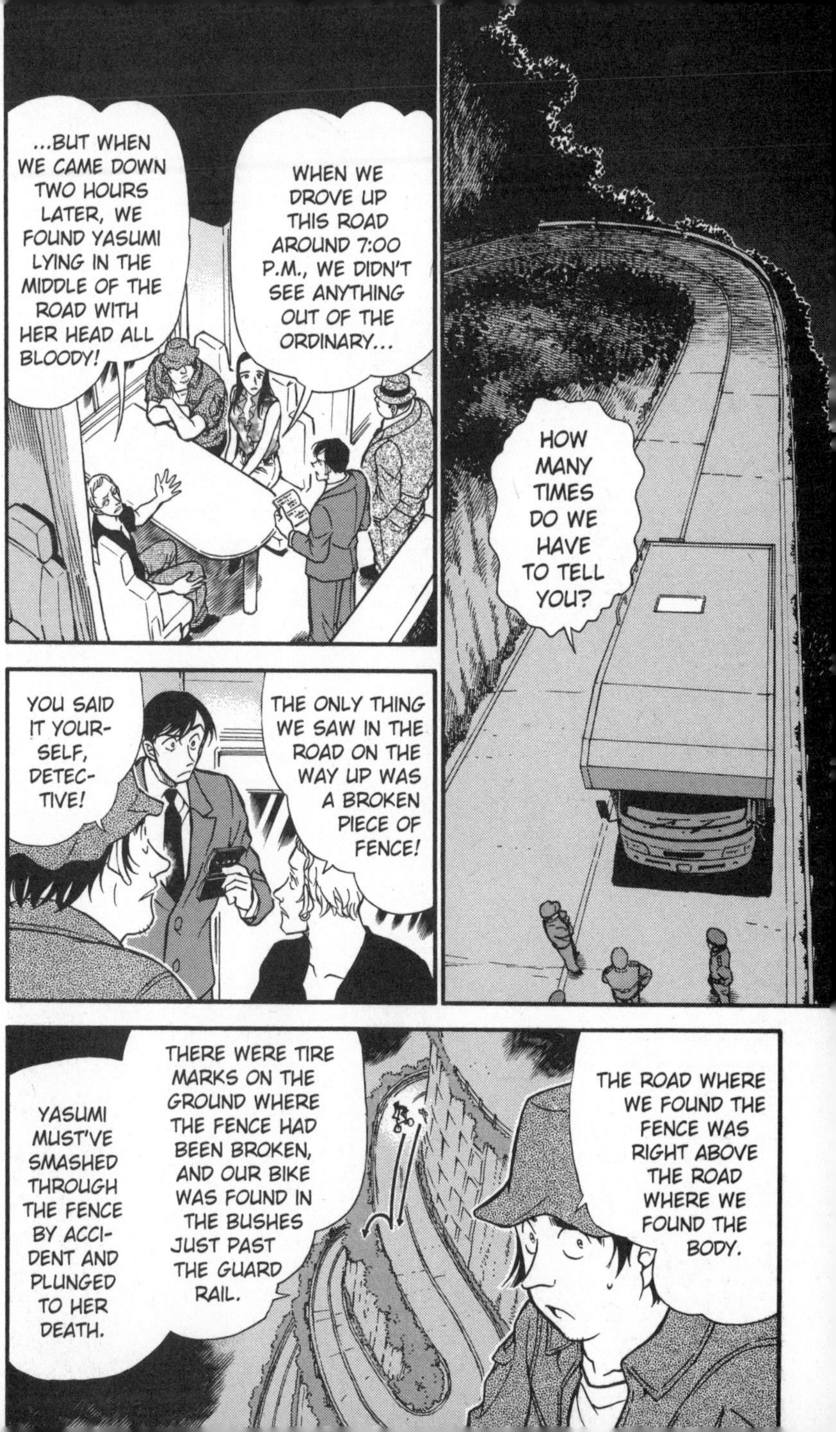
HOW MANY TIMES DO WE HAVE TO TELL YOU?
WHEN WE DROVE UP THIS ROAD AROUND 7:00 P.M., WE DIDN'T SEE ANYTHING OUT OF THE ORDINARY...
...BUT WHEN WE CAME DOWN TWO HOURS LATER, WE FOUND YASUMI LYING IN THE MIDDLE OF THE ROAD WITH HER HEAD ALL BLOODY!
THE ONLY THING WE SAW IN THE ROAD ON THE WAY UP WAS A BROKEN PIECE OF FENCE!
YOU SAID IT YOURSELF, DETECTIVE!
THE ROAD WHERE WE FOUND THE FENCE WAS RIGHT ABOVE THE ROAD WHERE WE FOUND THE BODY.
THERE WERE TIRE MARKS ON THE GROUND WHERE THE FENCE HAD BEEN BROKEN, AND OUR BIKE WAS FOUND IN THE BUSHES JUST PAST THE GUARD RAIL.
YASUMI MUST'VE SMASHED THROUGH THE FENCE BY ACCIDENT AND PLUNGED TO HER DEATH.

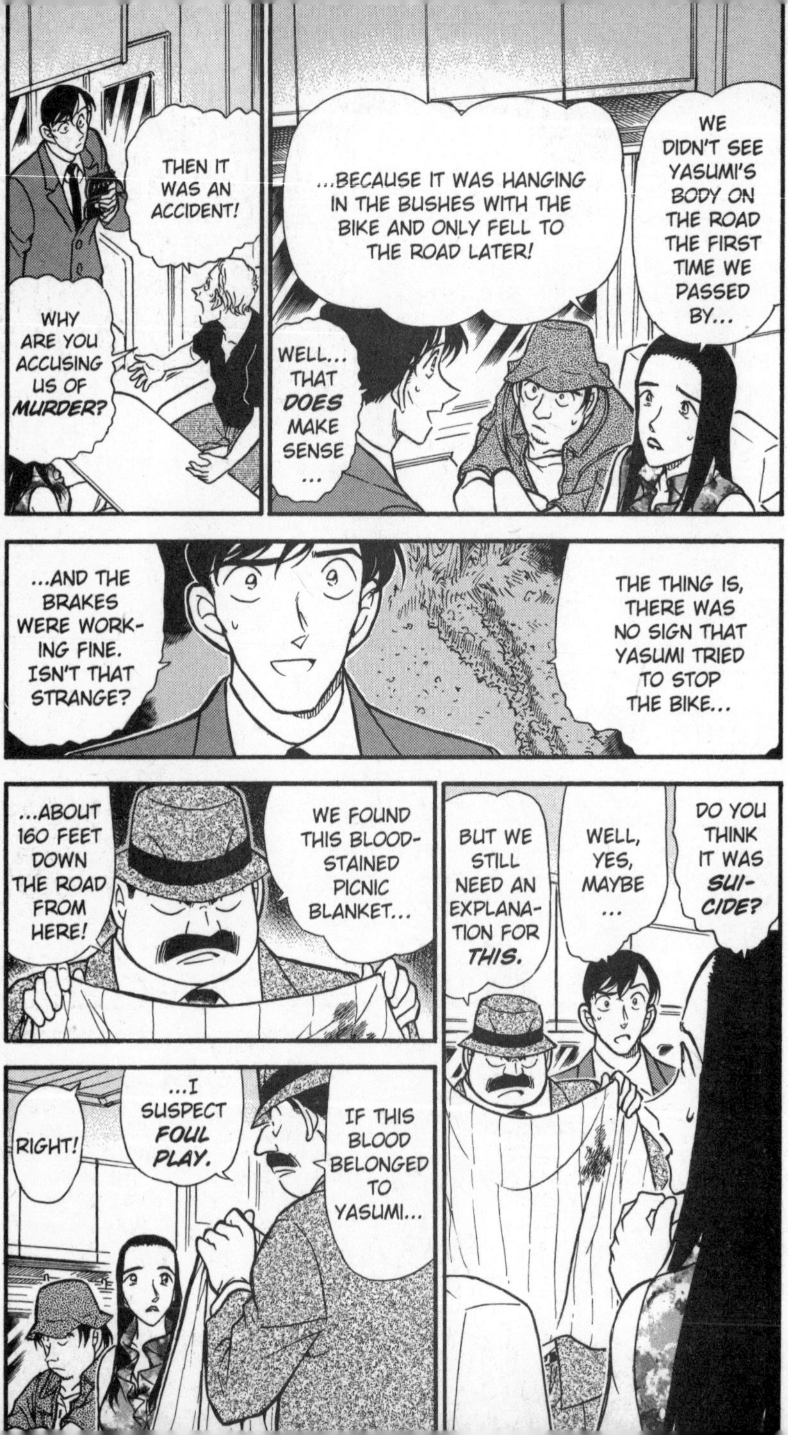
WE DIDN'T SEE YASUMI'S BODY ON THE ROAD THE FIRST TIME WE PASSED BY...
...BECAUSE IT WAS HANGING IN THE BUSHES WITH THE BIKE AND ONLY FELL TO THE ROAD LATER!
WELL... THAT *DOES* MAKE SENSE...
THEN IT WAS AN ACCIDENT!
WHY ARE YOU ACCUSING US OF *MURDER?*
THE THING IS, THERE WAS NO SIGN THAT YASUMI TRIED TO STOP THE BIKE...
...AND THE BRAKES WERE WORKING FINE. ISN'T THAT STRANGE?
DO YOU THINK IT WAS *SUICIDE?*
WELL, YES, MAYBE...
BUT WE STILL NEED AN EXPLANATION FOR *THIS.*
WE FOUND THIS BLOOD-STAINED PICNIC BLANKET...
...ABOUT 160 FEET DOWN THE ROAD FROM HERE!
IF THIS BLOOD BELONGED TO YASUMI...
...I SUSPECT *FOUL PLAY.*
RIGHT!

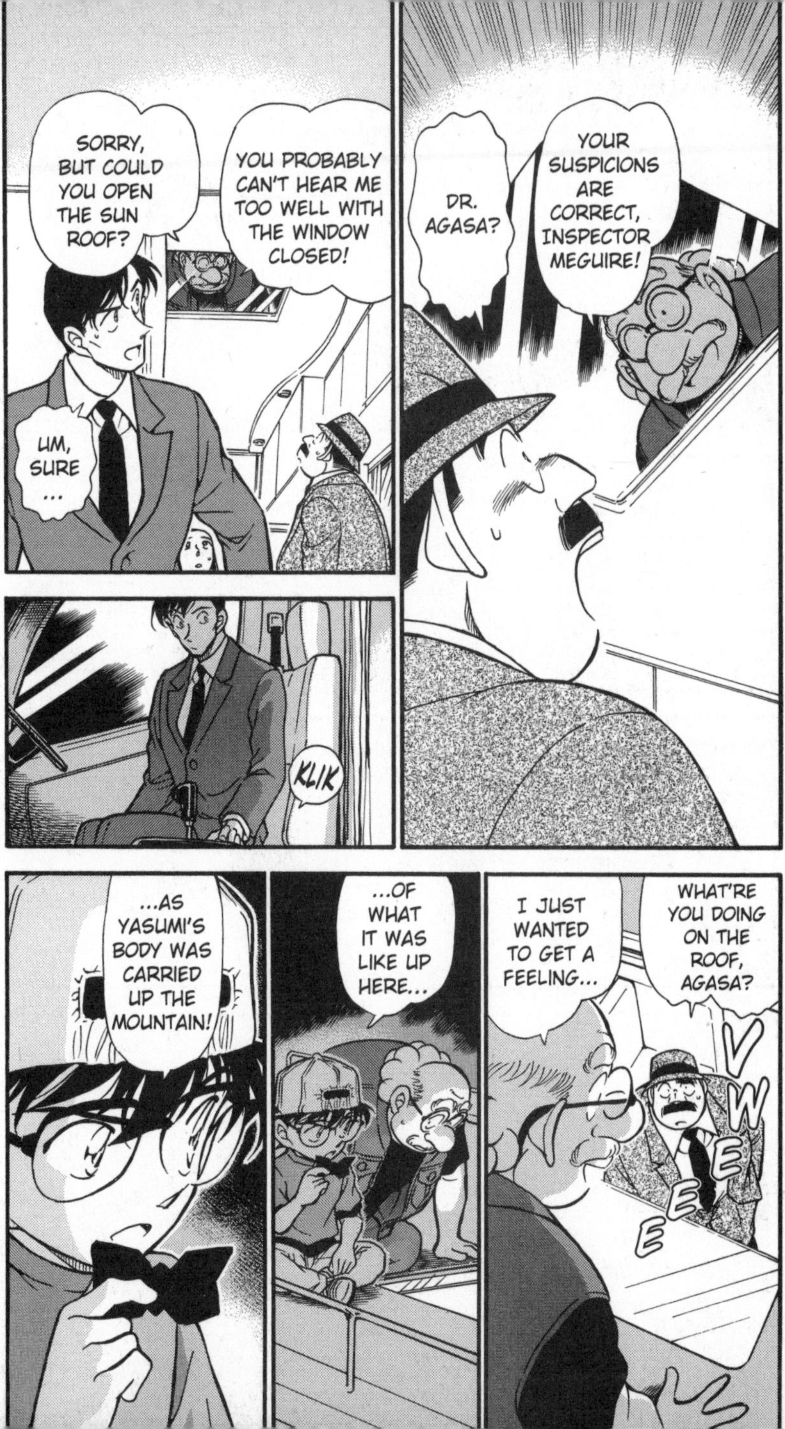
YOUR SUSPICIONS ARE CORRECT, INSPECTOR MEGUIRE!
DR. AGASA?
YOU PROBABLY CAN'T HEAR ME TOO WELL WITH THE WINDOW CLOSED!
SORRY, BUT COULD YOU OPEN THE SUN ROOF?
UM, SURE ...
KLIK
WHAT'RE YOU DOING ON THE ROOF, AGASA?
I JUST WANTED TO GET A FEELING...
VWEEE
...OF WHAT IT WAS LIKE UP HERE...
...AS YASUMI'S BODY WAS CARRIED UP THE MOUNTAIN!

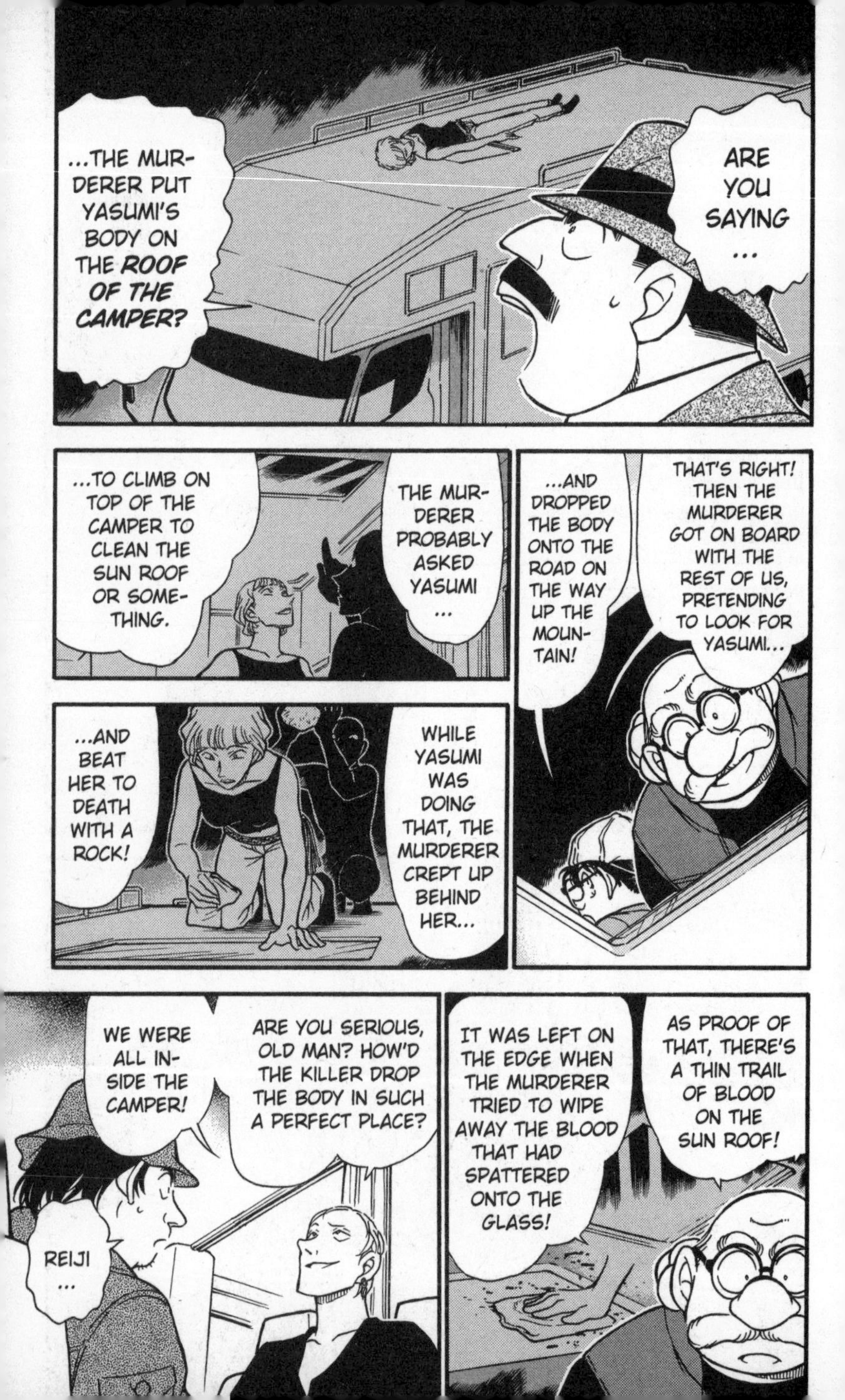
ARE YOU SAYING ...
...THE MURDERER PUT YASUMI'S BODY ON THE *ROOF OF THE CAMPER?*
THAT'S RIGHT! THEN THE MURDERER GOT ON BOARD WITH THE REST OF US, PRETENDING TO LOOK FOR YASUMI...
...AND DROPPED THE BODY ONTO THE ROAD ON THE WAY UP THE MOUNTAIN!
THE MURDERER PROBABLY ASKED YASUMI ...
...TO CLIMB ON TOP OF THE CAMPER TO CLEAN THE SUN ROOF OR SOMETHING.
WHILE YASUMI WAS DOING THAT, THE MURDERER CREPT UP BEHIND HER...
...AND BEAT HER TO DEATH WITH A ROCK!
AS PROOF OF THAT, THERE'S A THIN TRAIL OF BLOOD ON THE SUN ROOF!
IT WAS LEFT ON THE EDGE WHEN THE MURDERER TRIED TO WIPE AWAY THE BLOOD THAT HAD SPATTERED ONTO THE GLASS!
ARE YOU SERIOUS, OLD MAN? HOW'D THE KILLER DROP THE BODY IN SUCH A PERFECT PLACE?
WE WERE ALL INSIDE THE CAMPER!
REIJI ...

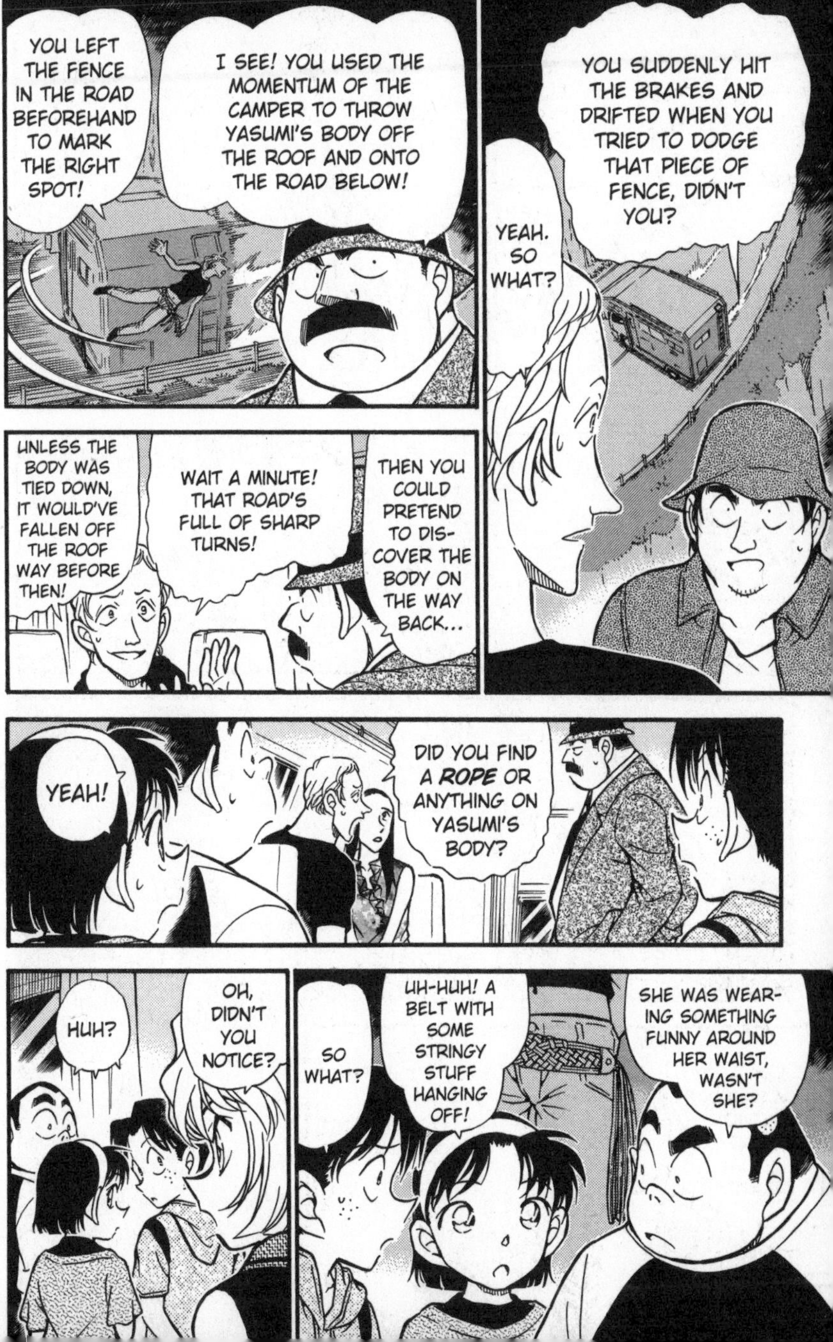
YOU SUDDENLY HIT THE BRAKES AND DRIFTED WHEN YOU TRIED TO DODGE THAT PIECE OF FENCE, DIDN'T YOU?
YEAH. SO WHAT?
I SEE! YOU USED THE MOMENTUM OF THE CAMPER TO THROW YASUMI'S BODY OFF THE ROOF AND ONTO THE ROAD BELOW!
YOU LEFT THE FENCE IN THE ROAD BEFOREHAND TO MARK THE RIGHT SPOT!
THEN YOU COULD PRETEND TO DIS-COVER THE BODY ON THE WAY BACK...
WAIT A MINUTE! THAT ROAD'S FULL OF SHARP TURNS!
UNLESS THE BODY WAS TIED DOWN, IT WOULD'VE FALLEN OFF THE ROOF WAY BEFORE THEN!
DID YOU FIND A *ROPE* OR ANYTHING ON YASUMI'S BODY?
YEAH!
SHE WAS WEAR-ING SOMETHING FUNNY AROUND HER WAIST, WASN'T SHE?
UH-HUH! A BELT WITH SOME STRINGY STUFF HANGING OFF!
SO WHAT?
OH, DIDN'T YOU NOTICE?
HUH?

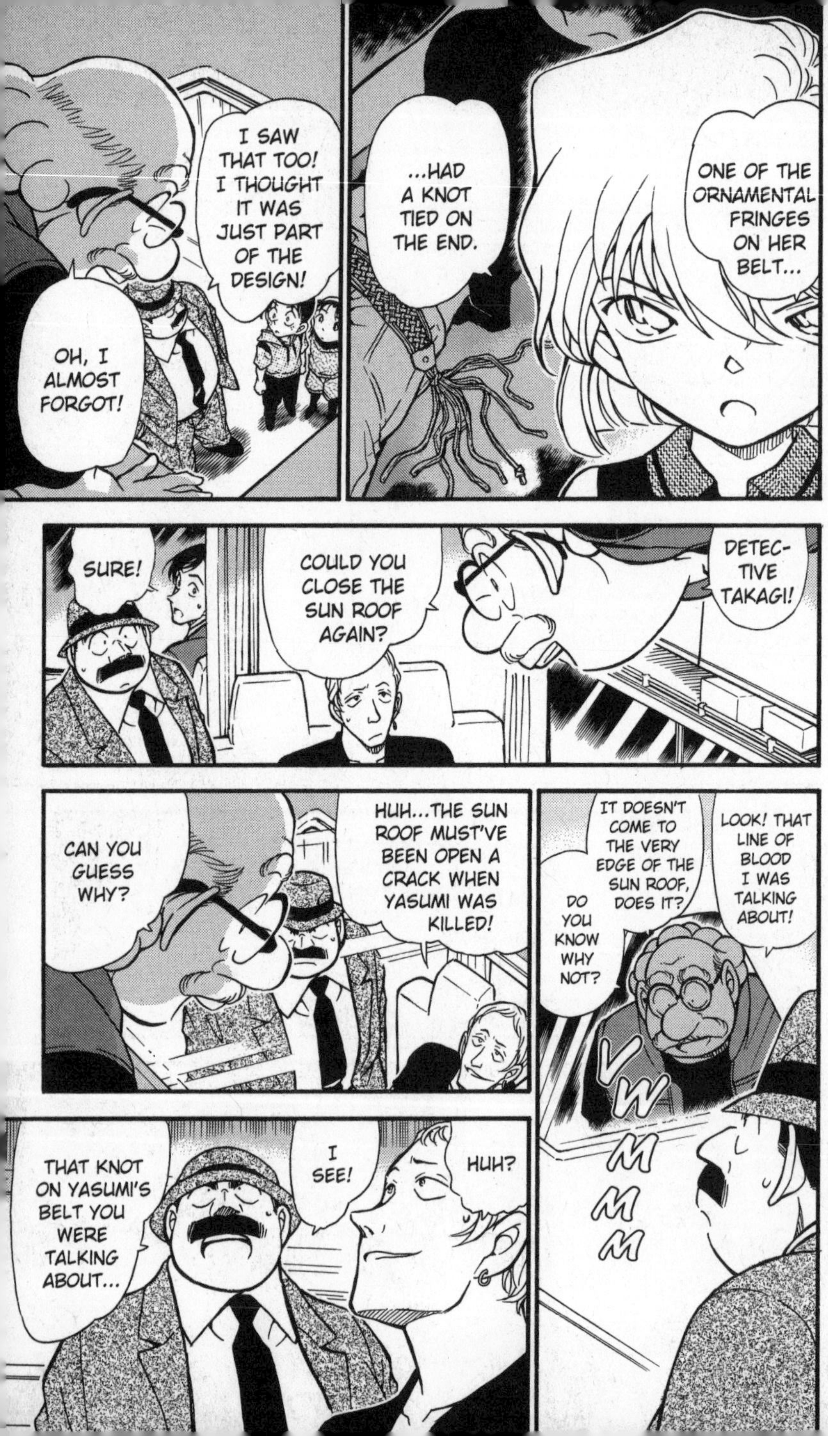
ONE OF THE ORNAMENTAL FRINGES ON HER BELT...
...HAD A KNOT TIED ON THE END.
I SAW THAT TOO! I THOUGHT IT WAS JUST PART OF THE DESIGN!
OH, I ALMOST FORGOT!
DETEC-TIVE TAKAGI!
COULD YOU CLOSE THE SUN ROOF AGAIN?
SURE!
LOOK! THAT LINE OF BLOOD I WAS TALKING ABOUT!
IT DOESN'T COME TO THE VERY EDGE OF THE SUN ROOF, DOES IT?
DO YOU KNOW WHY NOT?
VWMMMM
HUH...THE SUN ROOF MUST'VE BEEN OPEN A CRACK WHEN YASUMI WAS KILLED!
CAN YOU GUESS WHY?
HUH?
I SEE!
THAT KNOT ON YASUMI'S BELT YOU WERE TALKING ABOUT...

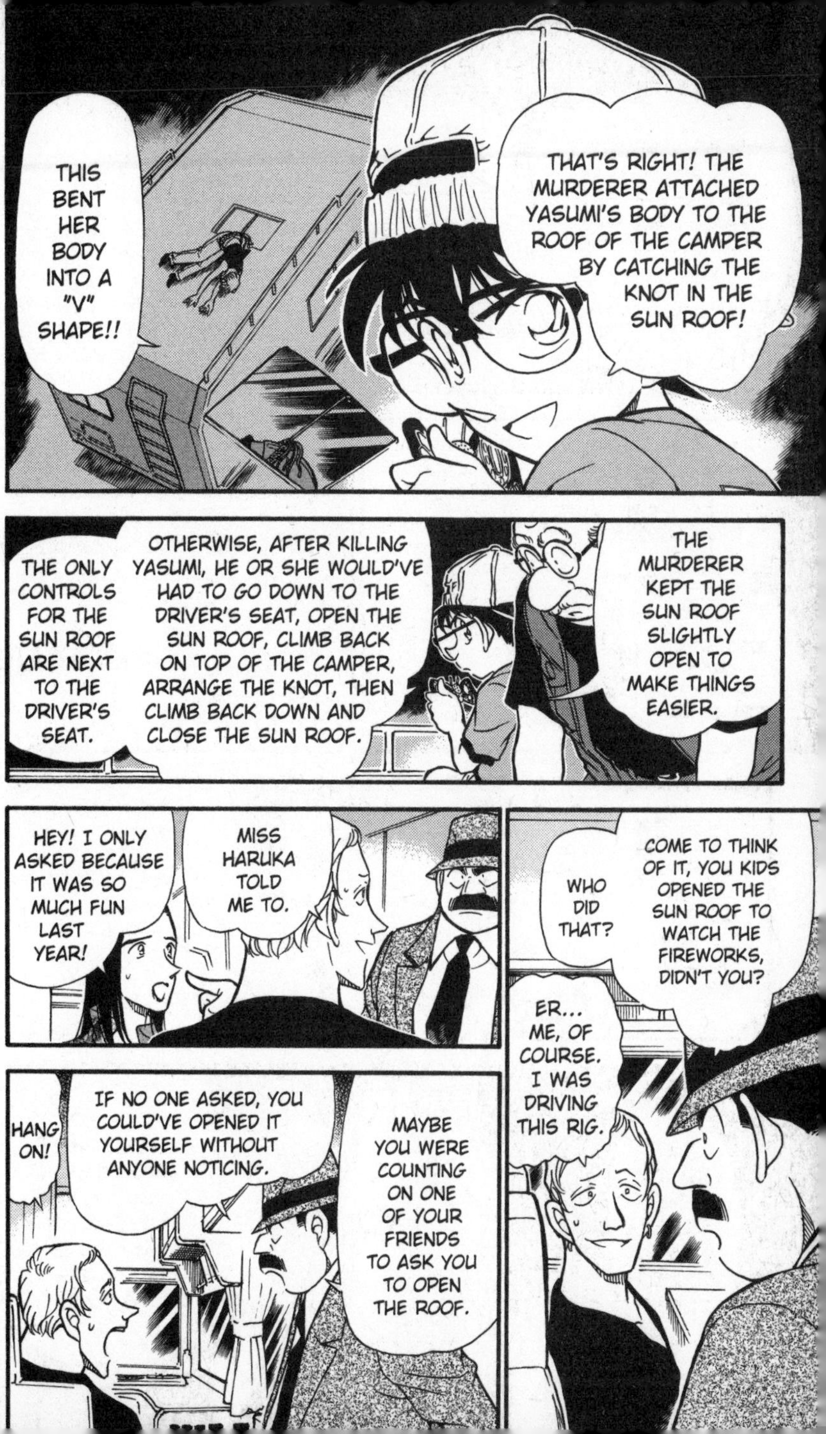
THAT'S RIGHT! THE MURDERER ATTACHED YASUMI'S BODY TO THE ROOF OF THE CAMPER BY CATCHING THE KNOT IN THE SUN ROOF!
THIS BENT HER BODY INTO A "V" SHAPE!!
THE MURDERER KEPT THE SUN ROOF SLIGHTLY OPEN TO MAKE THINGS EASIER.
OTHERWISE, AFTER KILLING YASUMI, HE OR SHE WOULD'VE HAD TO GO DOWN TO THE DRIVER'S SEAT, OPEN THE SUN ROOF, CLIMB BACK ON TOP OF THE CAMPER, ARRANGE THE KNOT, THEN CLIMB BACK DOWN AND CLOSE THE SUN ROOF.
THE ONLY CONTROLS FOR THE SUN ROOF ARE NEXT TO THE DRIVER'S SEAT.
COME TO THINK OF IT, YOU KIDS OPENED THE SUN ROOF TO WATCH THE FIREWORKS, DIDN'T YOU?
WHO DID THAT?
ER... ME, OF COURSE. I WAS DRIVING THIS RIG.
MISS HARUKA TOLD ME TO.
HEY! I ONLY ASKED BECAUSE IT WAS SO MUCH FUN LAST YEAR!
MAYBE YOU WERE COUNTING ON ONE OF YOUR FRIENDS TO ASK YOU TO OPEN THE ROOF.
IF NO ONE ASKED, YOU COULD'VE OPENED IT YOURSELF WITHOUT ANYONE NOTICING.
HANG ON!

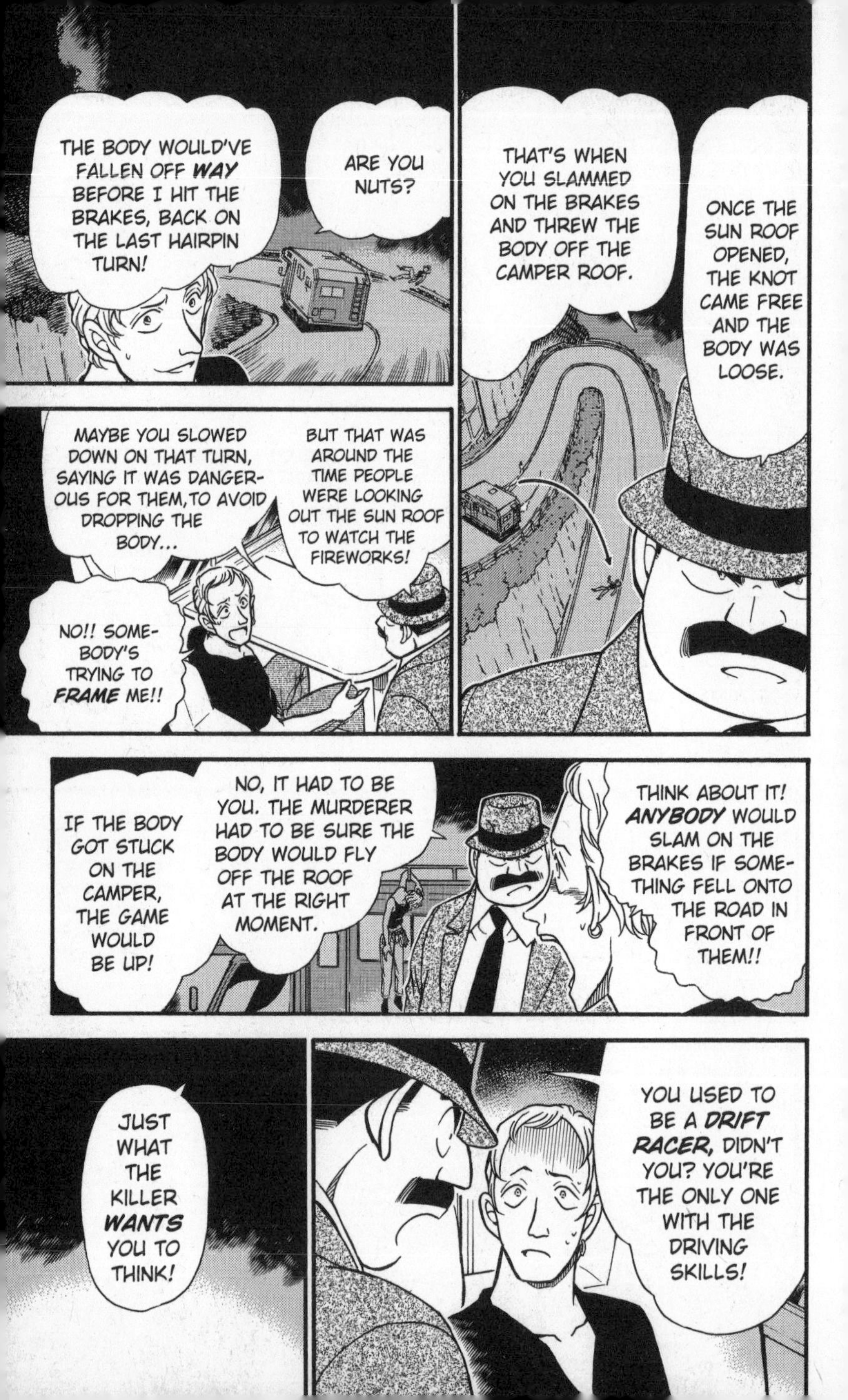
ONCE THE SUN ROOF OPENED, THE KNOT CAME FREE AND THE BODY WAS LOOSE.
THAT'S WHEN YOU SLAMMED ON THE BRAKES AND THREW THE BODY OFF THE CAMPER ROOF.
ARE YOU NUTS?
THE BODY WOULD'VE FALLEN OFF ***WAY*** BEFORE I HIT THE BRAKES, BACK ON THE LAST HAIRPIN TURN!
BUT THAT WAS AROUND THE TIME PEOPLE WERE LOOKING OUT THE SUN ROOF TO WATCH THE FIREWORKS!
MAYBE YOU SLOWED DOWN ON THAT TURN, SAYING IT WAS DANGEROUS FOR THEM, TO AVOID DROPPING THE BODY...
NO!! SOMEBODY'S TRYING TO ***FRAME*** ME!!
THINK ABOUT IT! ***ANYBODY*** WOULD SLAM ON THE BRAKES IF SOMETHING FELL ONTO THE ROAD IN FRONT OF THEM!!
NO, IT HAD TO BE YOU. THE MURDERER HAD TO BE SURE THE BODY WOULD FLY OFF THE ROOF AT THE RIGHT MOMENT.
IF THE BODY GOT STUCK ON THE CAMPER, THE GAME WOULD BE UP!
YOU USED TO BE A ***DRIFT RACER,*** DIDN'T YOU? YOU'RE THE ONLY ONE WITH THE DRIVING SKILLS!
JUST WHAT THE KILLER ***WANTS*** YOU TO THINK!

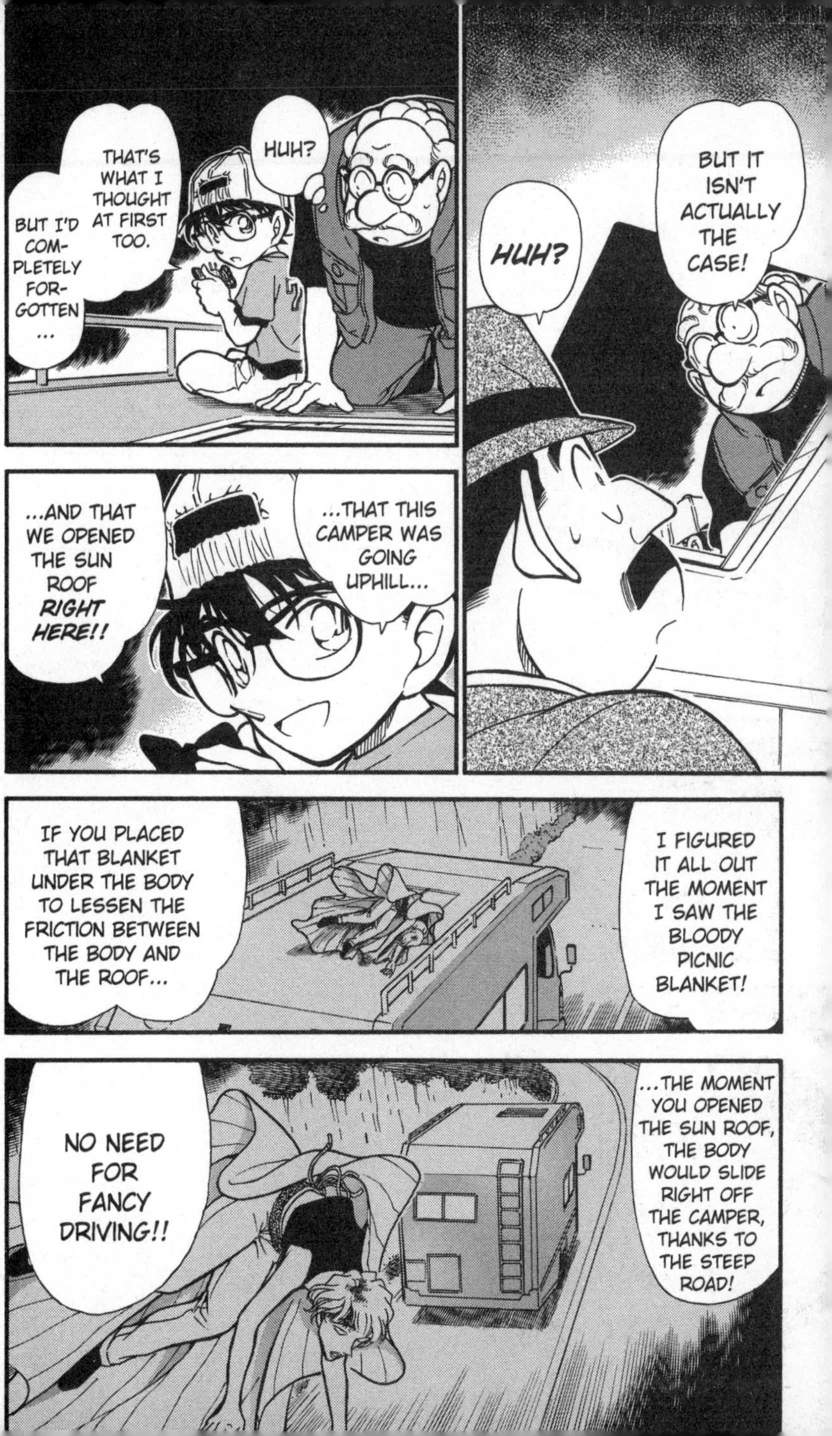
BUT IT ISN'T ACTUALLY THE CASE!
HUH?
HUH?
THAT'S WHAT I THOUGHT AT FIRST TOO.
BUT I'D COM-PLETELY FOR-GOTTEN ...
...THAT THIS CAMPER WAS GOING UPHILL...
...AND THAT WE OPENED THE SUN ROOF RIGHT HERE!!
I FIGURED IT ALL OUT THE MOMENT I SAW THE BLOODY PICNIC BLANKET!
IF YOU PLACED THAT BLANKET UNDER THE BODY TO LESSEN THE FRICTION BETWEEN THE BODY AND THE ROOF...
...THE MOMENT YOU OPENED THE SUN ROOF, THE BODY WOULD SLIDE RIGHT OFF THE CAMPER, THANKS TO THE STEEP ROAD!
NO NEED FOR FANCY DRIVING!!

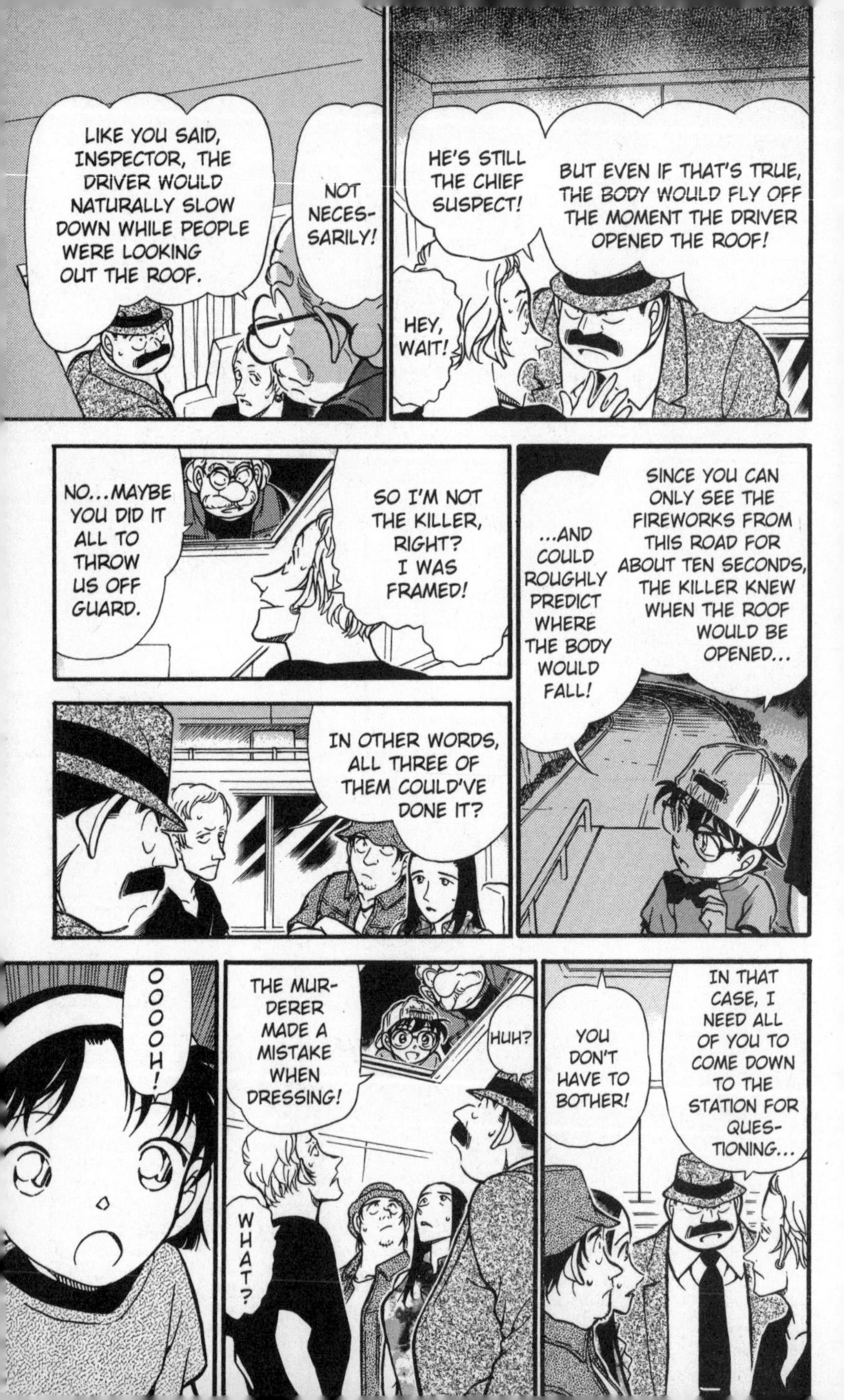

BUT EVEN IF THAT'S TRUE, THE BODY WOULD FLY OFF THE MOMENT THE DRIVER OPENED THE ROOF!
HE'S STILL THE CHIEF SUSPECT!
HEY, WAIT!
NOT NECES-SARILY!
LIKE YOU SAID, INSPECTOR, THE DRIVER WOULD NATURALLY SLOW DOWN WHILE PEOPLE WERE LOOKING OUT THE ROOF.
SINCE YOU CAN ONLY SEE THE FIREWORKS FROM THIS ROAD FOR ABOUT TEN SECONDS, THE KILLER KNEW WHEN THE ROOF WOULD BE OPENED...
...AND COULD ROUGHLY PREDICT WHERE THE BODY WOULD FALL!
SO I'M NOT THE KILLER, RIGHT? I WAS FRAMED!
NO...MAYBE YOU DID IT ALL TO THROW US OFF GUARD.
IN OTHER WORDS, ALL THREE OF THEM COULD'VE DONE IT?
IN THAT CASE, I NEED ALL OF YOU TO COME DOWN TO THE STATION FOR QUES-TIONING...
YOU DON'T HAVE TO BOTHER!
HUH?
THE MUR-DERER MADE A MISTAKE WHEN DRESSING!
WHAT?
OOOOOH!

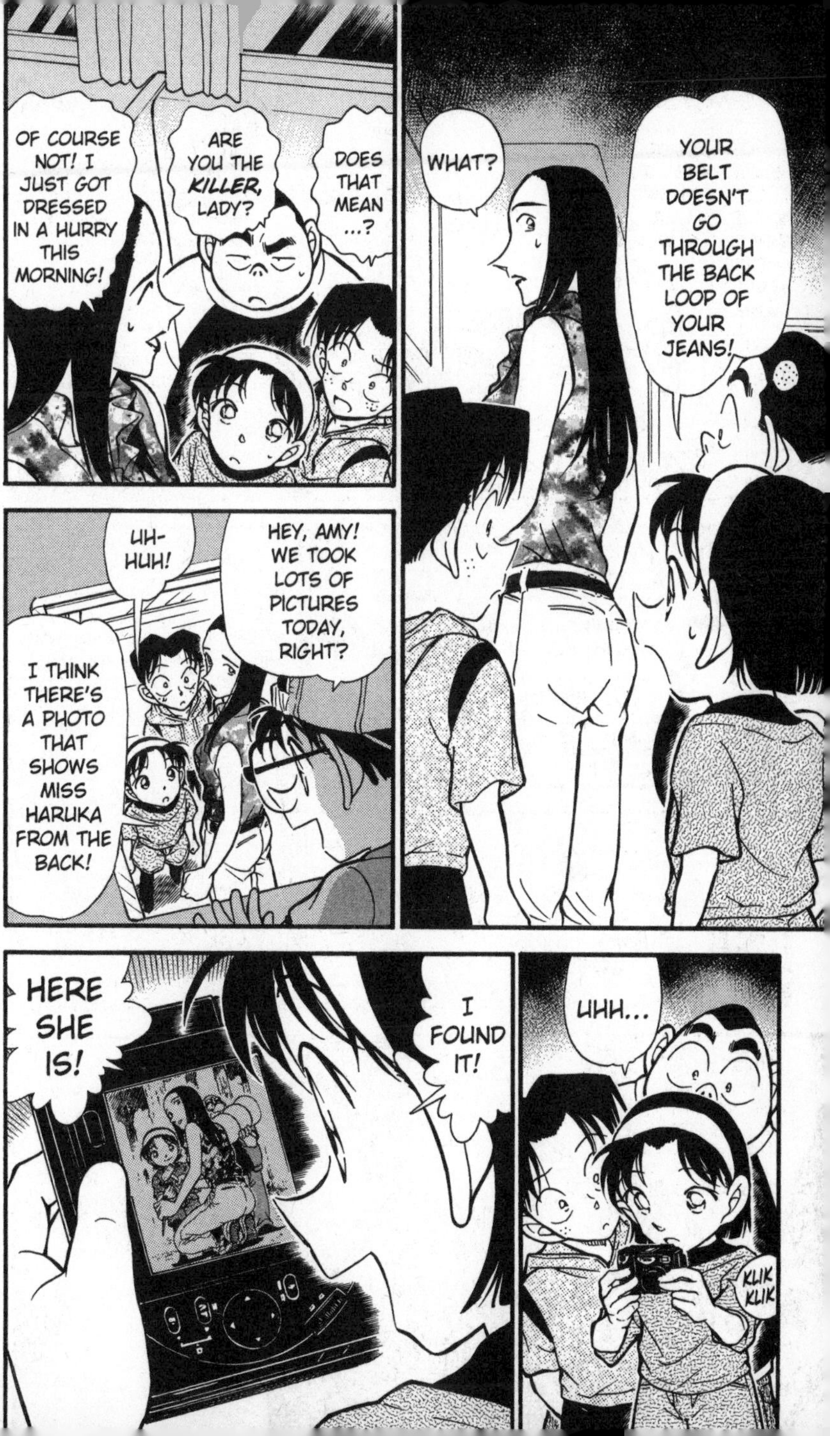

YOUR BELT DOESN'T GO THROUGH THE BACK LOOP OF YOUR JEANS!
WHAT?
DOES THAT MEAN ...?
ARE YOU THE *KILLER*, LADY?
OF COURSE NOT! I JUST GOT DRESSED IN A HURRY THIS MORNING!
HEY, AMY! WE TOOK LOTS OF PICTURES TODAY, RIGHT?
UH-HUH!
I THINK THERE'S A PHOTO THAT SHOWS MISS HARUKA FROM THE BACK!
UHH...
KLIK KLIK
I FOUND IT!
HERE SHE IS!

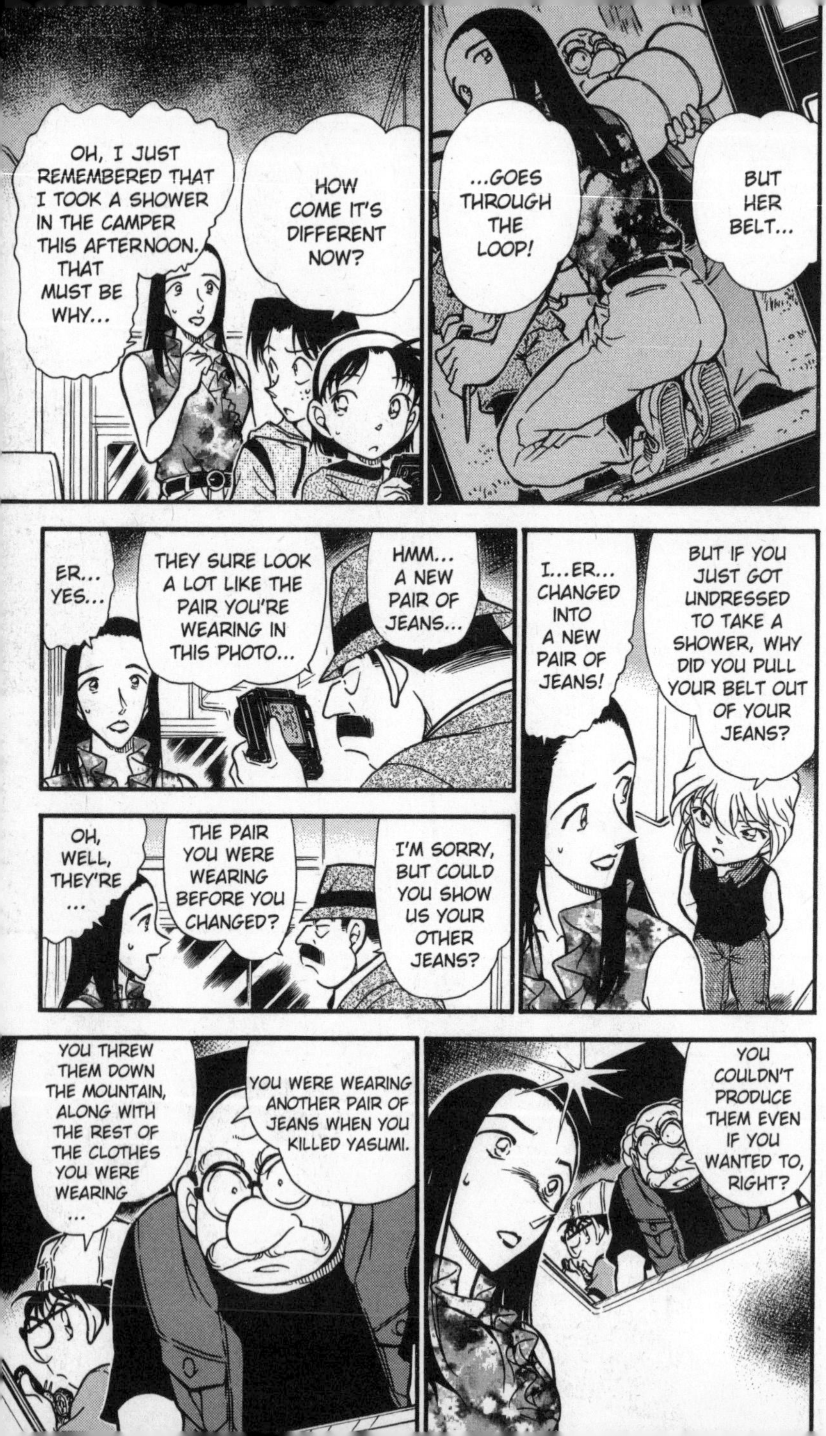
BUT HER BELT...
...GOES THROUGH THE LOOP!
HOW COME IT'S DIFFERENT NOW?
OH, I JUST REMEMBERED THAT I TOOK A SHOWER IN THE CAMPER THIS AFTERNOON. THAT MUST BE WHY...
BUT IF YOU JUST GOT UNDRESSED TO TAKE A SHOWER, WHY DID YOU PULL YOUR BELT OUT OF YOUR JEANS?
I...ER... CHANGED INTO A NEW PAIR OF JEANS!
HMM... A NEW PAIR OF JEANS...
THEY SURE LOOK A LOT LIKE THE PAIR YOU'RE WEARING IN THIS PHOTO...
ER... YES...
I'M SORRY, BUT COULD YOU SHOW US YOUR OTHER JEANS?
THE PAIR YOU WERE WEARING BEFORE YOU CHANGED?
OH, WELL, THEY'RE ...
YOU COULDN'T PRODUCE THEM EVEN IF YOU WANTED TO, RIGHT?
YOU WERE WEARING ANOTHER PAIR OF JEANS WHEN YOU KILLED YASUMI.
YOU THREW THEM DOWN THE MOUNTAIN, ALONG WITH THE REST OF THE CLOTHES YOU WERE WEARING ...

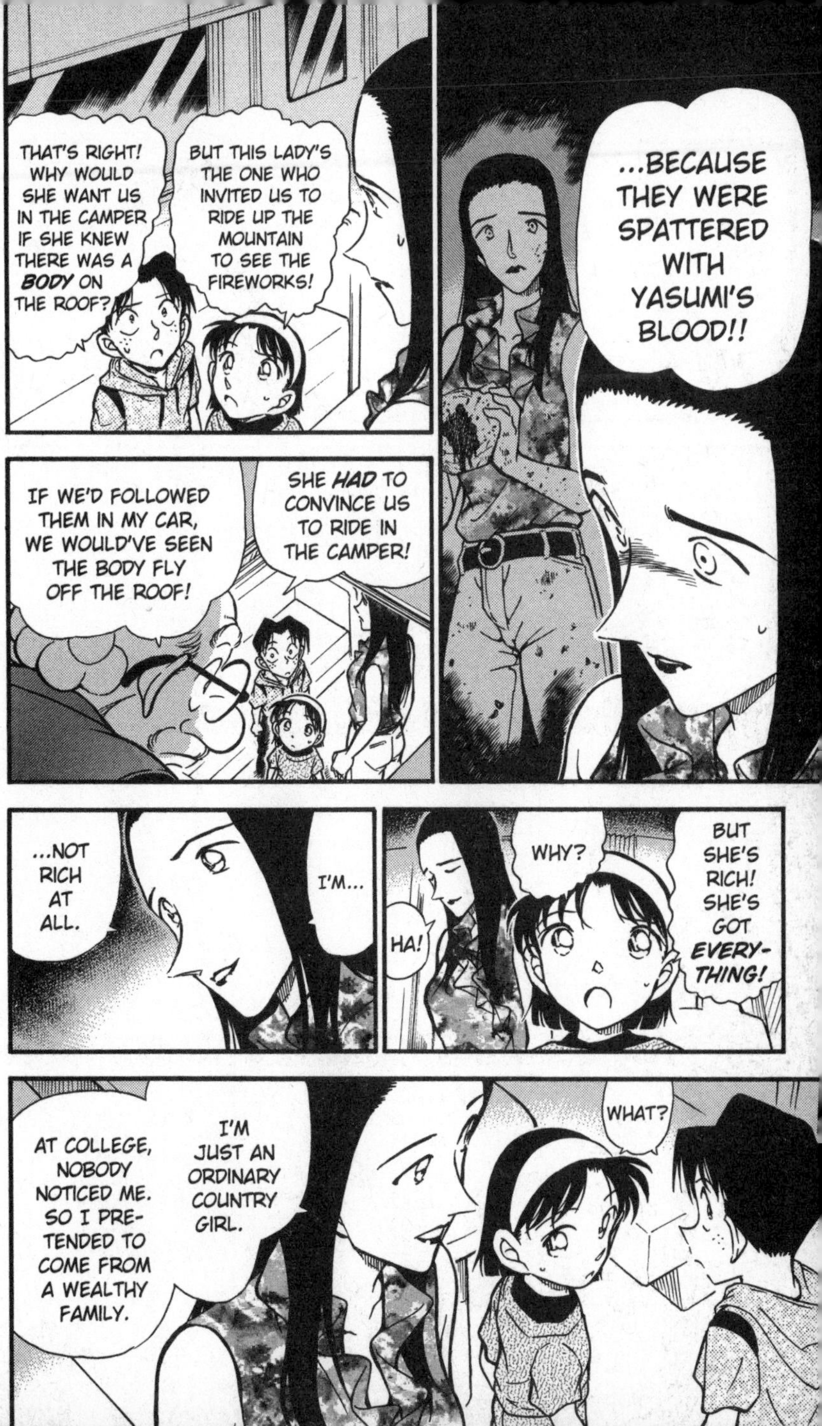
...BECAUSE THEY WERE SPATTERED WITH YASUMI'S BLOOD!!
BUT THIS LADY'S THE ONE WHO INVITED US TO RIDE UP THE MOUNTAIN TO SEE THE FIREWORKS!
THAT'S RIGHT! WHY WOULD SHE WANT US IN THE CAMPER IF SHE KNEW THERE WAS A *BODY* ON THE ROOF?
SHE *HAD* TO CONVINCE US TO RIDE IN THE CAMPER!
IF WE'D FOLLOWED THEM IN MY CAR, WE WOULD'VE SEEN THE BODY FLY OFF THE ROOF!
BUT SHE'S RICH! SHE'S GOT *EVERYTHING!*
WHY?
HA!
I'M...
...NOT RICH AT ALL.
WHAT?
I'M JUST AN ORDINARY COUNTRY GIRL.
AT COLLEGE, NOBODY NOTICED ME. SO I PRETENDED TO COME FROM A WEALTHY FAMILY.

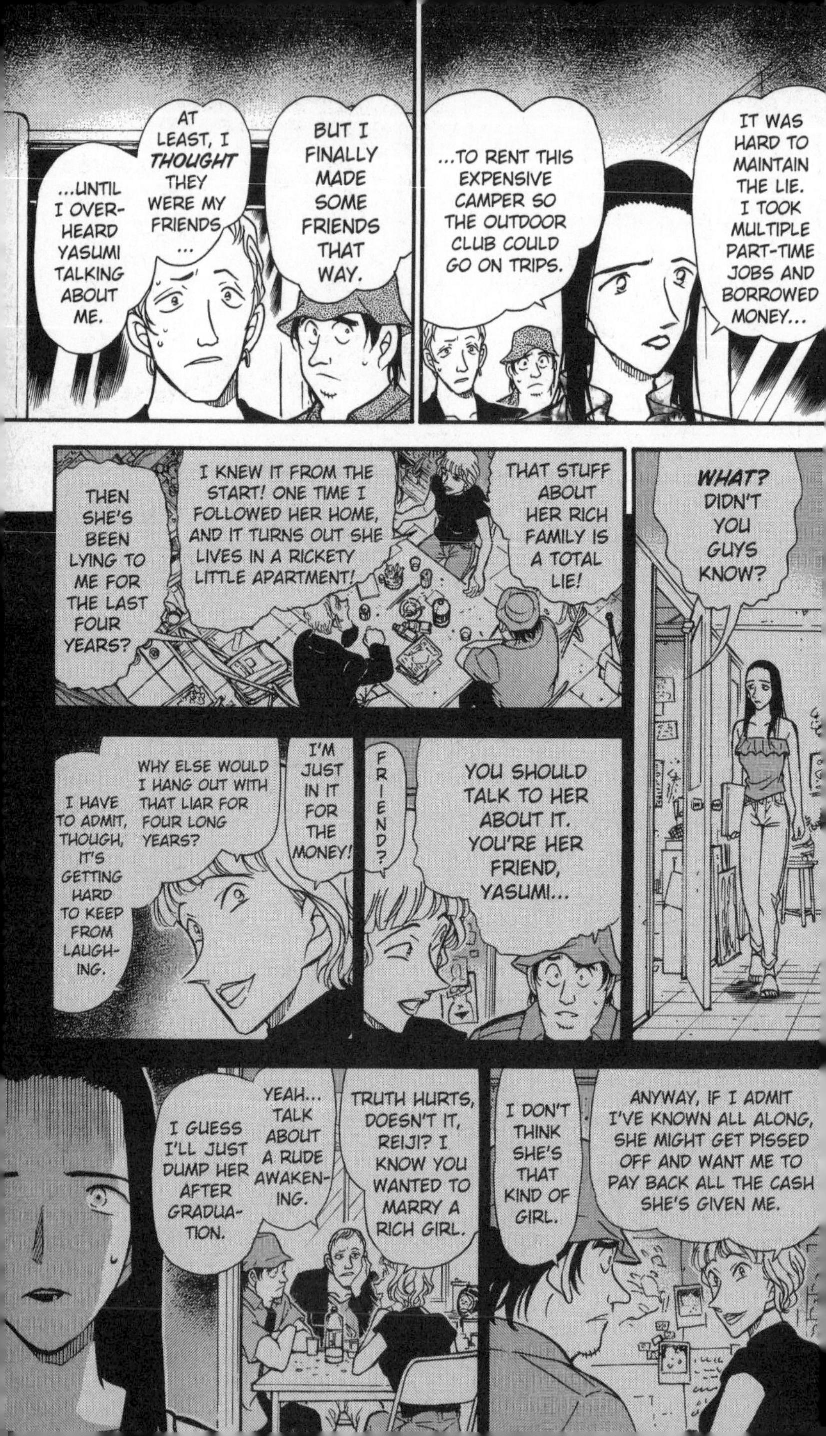
IT WAS HARD TO MAINTAIN THE LIE. I TOOK MULTIPLE PART-TIME JOBS AND BORROWED MONEY...
...TO RENT THIS EXPENSIVE CAMPER SO THE OUTDOOR CLUB COULD GO ON TRIPS.
BUT I FINALLY MADE SOME FRIENDS THAT WAY.
AT LEAST, I *THOUGHT* THEY WERE MY FRIENDS...
...UNTIL I OVERHEARD YASUMI TALKING ABOUT ME.
WHAT? DIDN'T YOU GUYS KNOW?
THAT STUFF ABOUT HER RICH FAMILY IS A TOTAL LIE!
I KNEW IT FROM THE START! ONE TIME I FOLLOWED HER HOME, AND IT TURNS OUT SHE LIVES IN A RICKETY LITTLE APARTMENT!
THEN SHE'S BEEN LYING TO ME FOR THE LAST FOUR YEARS?
YOU SHOULD TALK TO HER ABOUT IT. YOU'RE HER FRIEND, YASUMI...
FRIEND?
I'M JUST IN IT FOR THE MONEY!
WHY ELSE WOULD I HANG OUT WITH THAT LIAR FOR FOUR LONG YEARS?
I HAVE TO ADMIT, THOUGH, IT'S GETTING HARD TO KEEP FROM LAUGHING.
ANYWAY, IF I ADMIT I'VE KNOWN ALL ALONG, SHE MIGHT GET PISSED OFF AND WANT ME TO PAY BACK ALL THE CASH SHE'S GIVEN ME.
I DON'T THINK SHE'S THAT KIND OF GIRL.
TRUTH HURTS, DOESN'T IT, REIJI? I KNOW YOU WANTED TO MARRY A RICH GIRL.
YEAH... TALK ABOUT A RUDE AWAKENING.
I GUESS I'LL JUST DUMP HER AFTER GRADUATION.

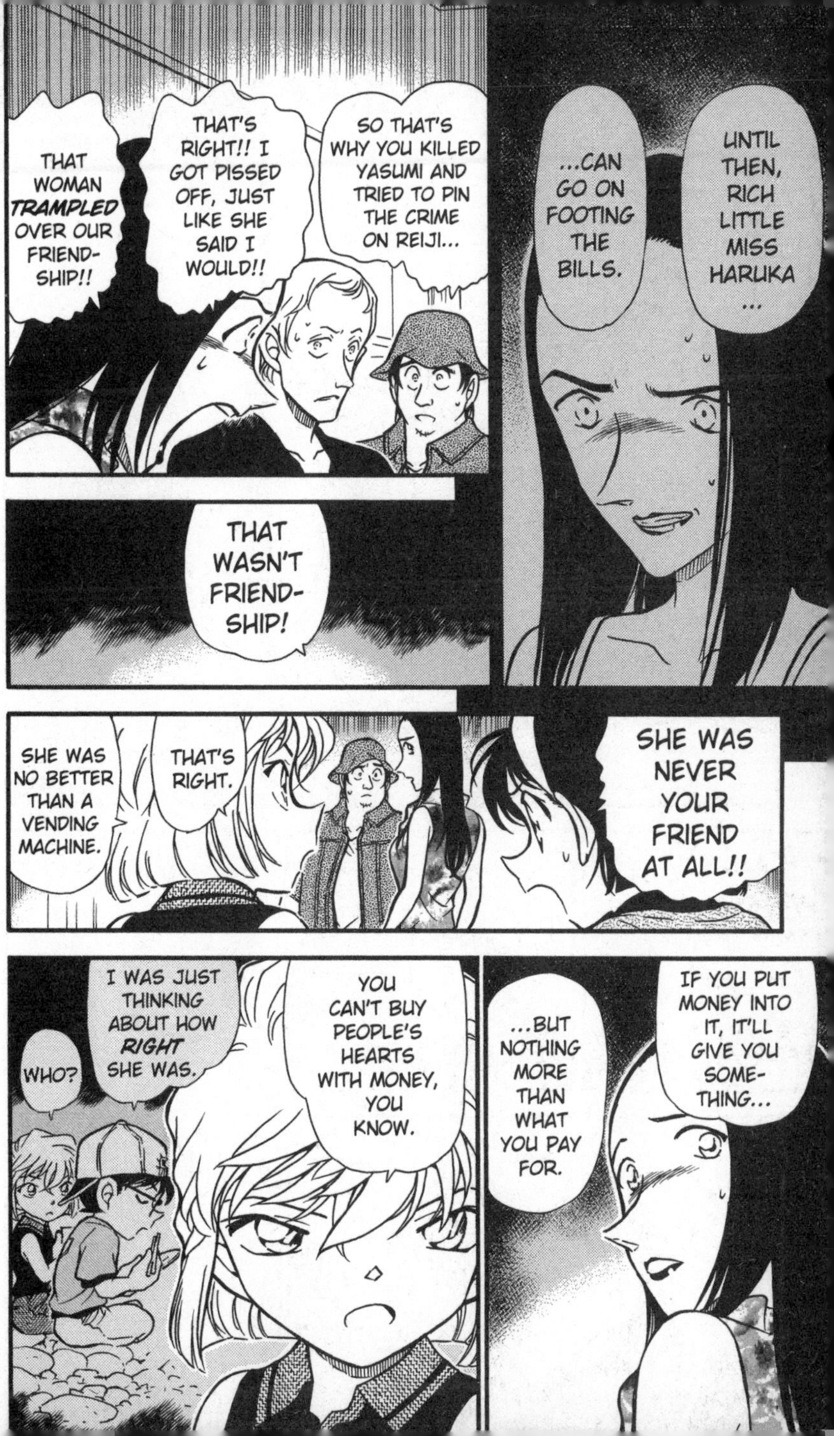
UNTIL THEN, RICH LITTLE MISS HARUKA ...
...CAN GO ON FOOTING THE BILLS.
SO THAT'S WHY YOU KILLED YASUMI AND TRIED TO PIN THE CRIME ON REIJI...
THAT'S RIGHT!! I GOT PISSED OFF, JUST LIKE SHE SAID I WOULD!!
THAT WOMAN *TRAMPLED* OVER OUR FRIEND-SHIP!!
THAT WASN'T FRIEND-SHIP!
SHE WAS NEVER YOUR FRIEND AT ALL!!
THAT'S RIGHT.
SHE WAS NO BETTER THAN A VENDING MACHINE.
IF YOU PUT MONEY INTO IT, IT'LL GIVE YOU SOME-THING...
...BUT NOTHING MORE THAN WHAT YOU PAY FOR.
YOU CAN'T BUY PEOPLE'S HEARTS WITH MONEY, YOU KNOW.
I WAS JUST THINKING ABOUT HOW *RIGHT* SHE WAS.
WHO?

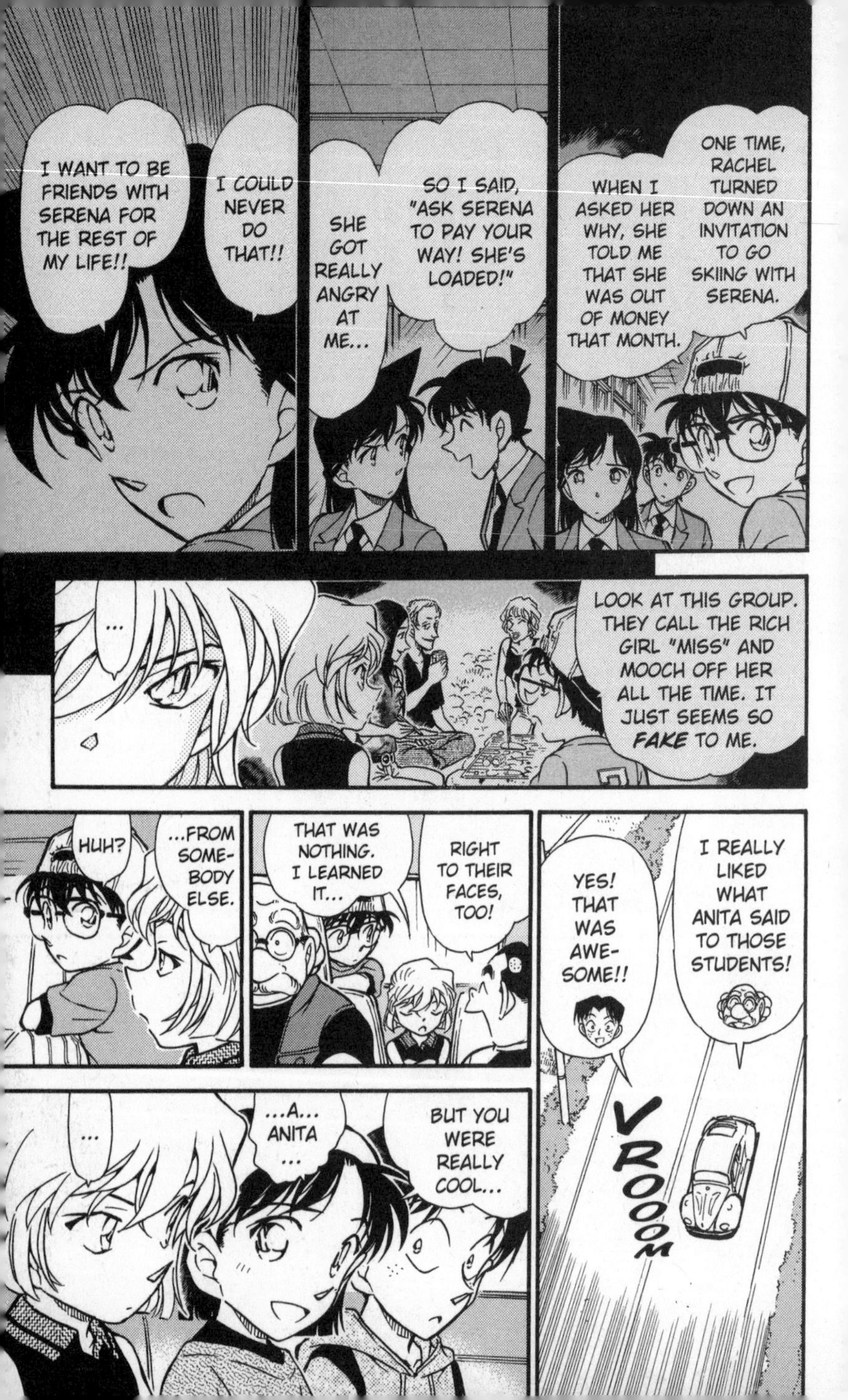
ONE TIME, RACHEL TURNED DOWN AN INVITATION TO GO SKIING WITH SERENA.
WHEN I ASKED HER WHY, SHE TOLD ME THAT SHE WAS OUT OF MONEY THAT MONTH.
SO I SAID, "ASK SERENA TO PAY YOUR WAY! SHE'S LOADED!"
SHE GOT REALLY ANGRY AT ME...
I COULD NEVER DO THAT!!
I WANT TO BE FRIENDS WITH SERENA FOR THE REST OF MY LIFE!!
LOOK AT THIS GROUP. THEY CALL THE RICH GIRL "MISS" AND MOOCH OFF HER ALL THE TIME. IT JUST SEEMS SO *FAKE* TO ME.
...
I REALLY LIKED WHAT ANITA SAID TO THOSE STUDENTS!
YES! THAT WAS AWESOME!!
VROOOOM
RIGHT TO THEIR FACES, TOO!
THAT WAS NOTHING. I LEARNED IT...
...FROM SOMEBODY ELSE.
HUH?
BUT YOU WERE REALLY COOL...
...A... ANITA ...
...

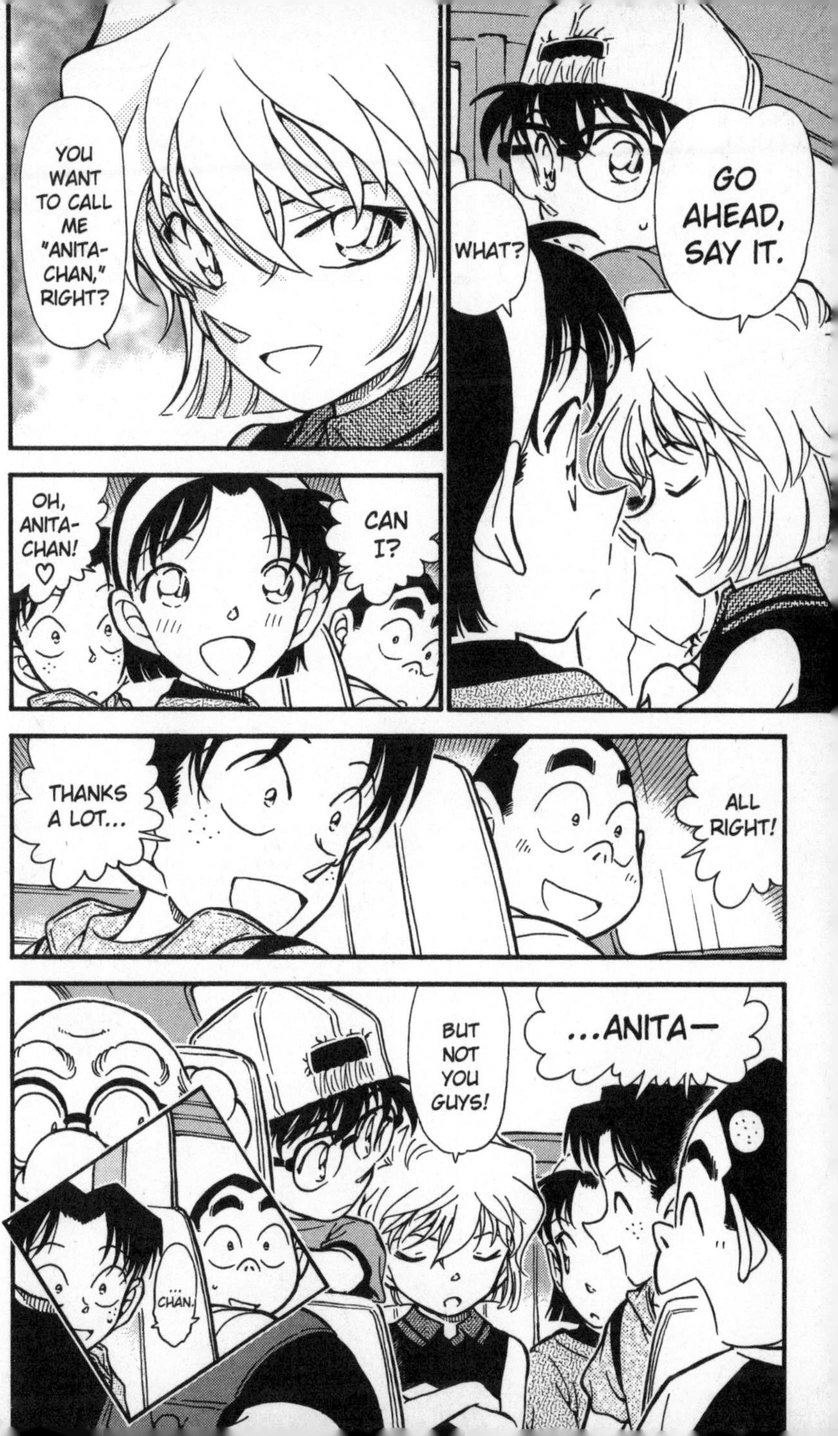
GO AHEAD, SAY IT.
WHAT?
YOU WANT TO CALL ME "ANITA-CHAN," RIGHT?
CAN I?
OH, ANITA-CHAN! ♡
ALL RIGHT!
THANKS A LOT...
...ANITA—
BUT NOT YOU GUYS!
...CHAN.

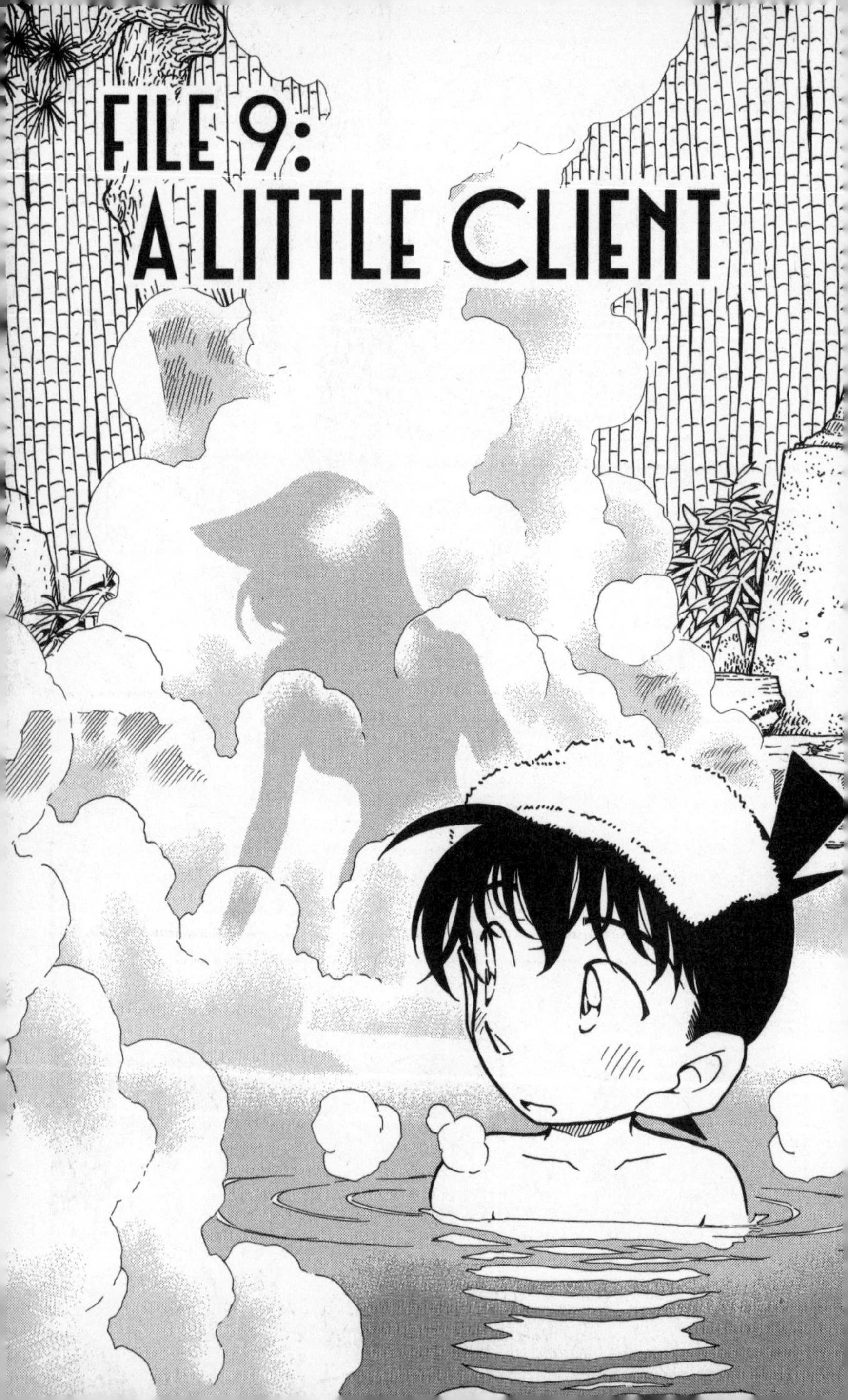
FILE 9:
A LITTLE CLIENT

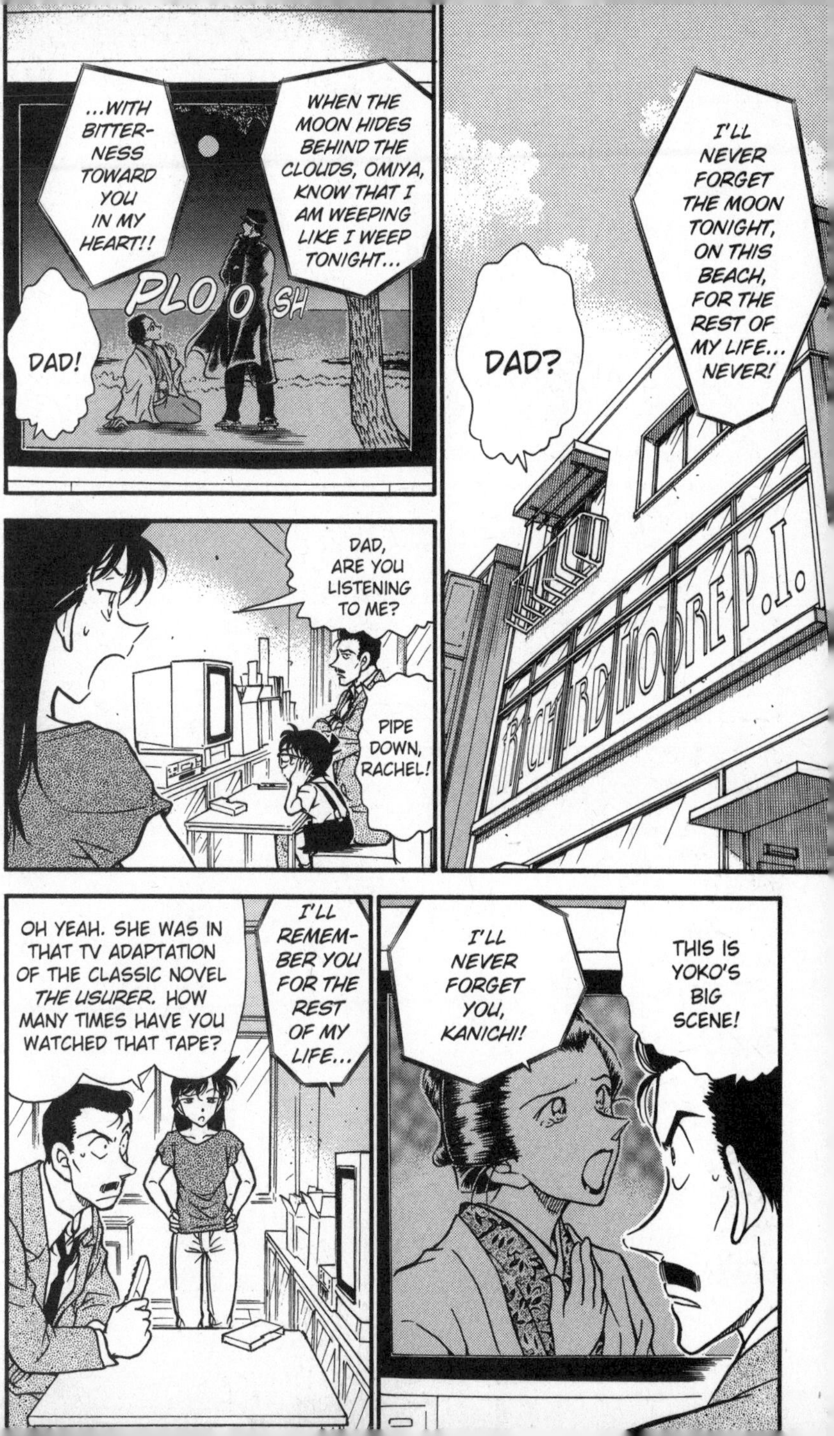
I'LL NEVER FORGET THE MOON TONIGHT, ON THIS BEACH, FOR THE REST OF MY LIFE... NEVER!
DAD?
RICHARD MOORE P.I.
WHEN THE MOON HIDES BEHIND THE CLOUDS, OMIYA, KNOW THAT I AM WEEPING LIKE I WEEP TONIGHT...
...WITH BITTERNESS TOWARD YOU IN MY HEART!!
PLOOSH
DAD!
DAD, ARE YOU LISTENING TO ME?
PIPE DOWN, RACHEL!
THIS IS YOKO'S BIG SCENE!
I'LL NEVER FORGET YOU, KANICHI!
I'LL REMEMBER YOU FOR THE REST OF MY LIFE...
OH YEAH. SHE WAS IN THAT TV ADAPTATION OF THE CLASSIC NOVEL *THE USURER*. HOW MANY TIMES HAVE YOU WATCHED THAT TAPE?

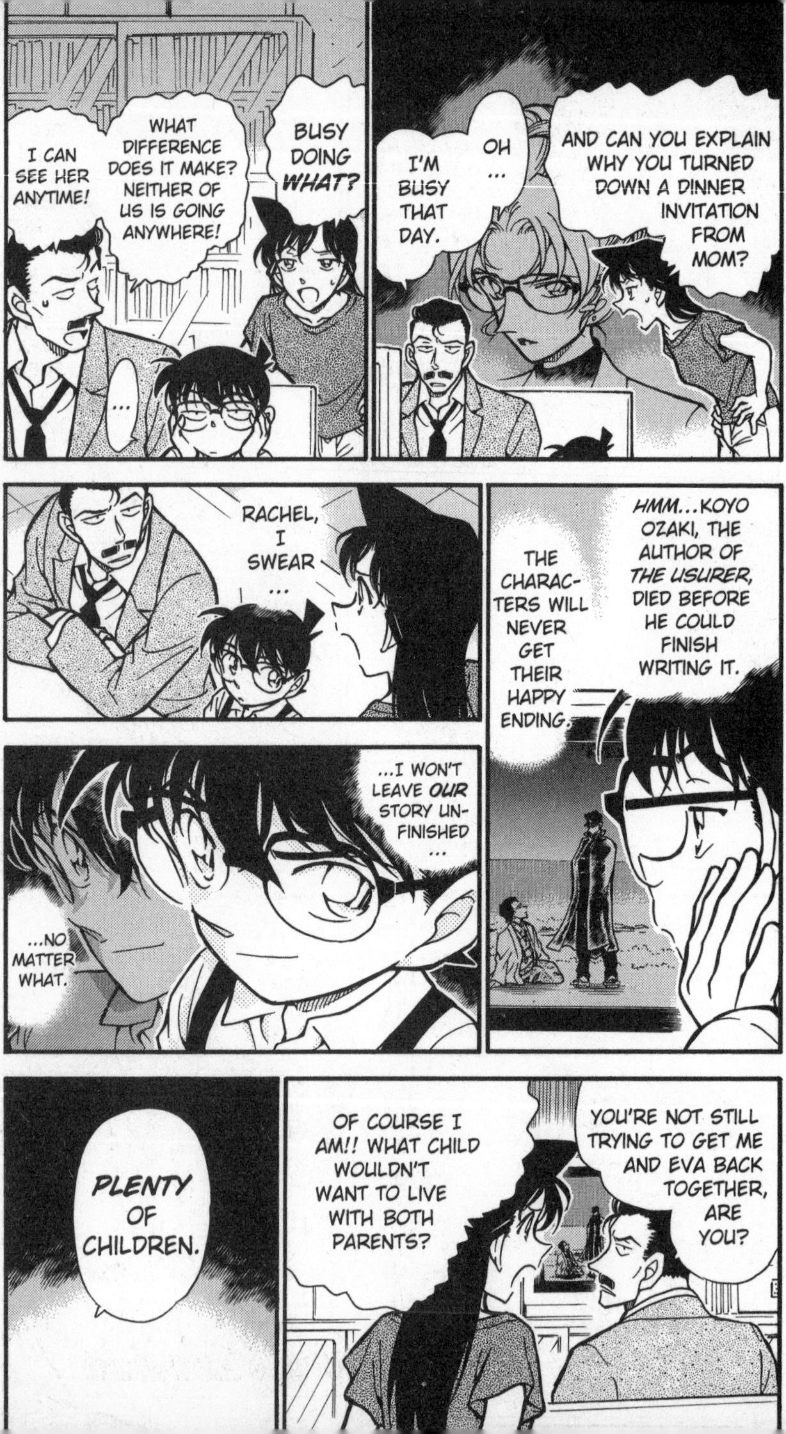
AND CAN YOU EXPLAIN WHY YOU TURNED DOWN A DINNER INVITATION FROM MOM?
OH ...
I'M BUSY THAT DAY.
BUSY DOING *WHAT?*
WHAT DIFFERENCE DOES IT MAKE? NEITHER OF US IS GOING ANYWHERE!
I CAN SEE HER ANYTIME!
...
*HMM...*KOYO OZAKI, THE AUTHOR OF *THE USURER*, DIED BEFORE HE COULD FINISH WRITING IT.
THE CHARAC-TERS WILL NEVER GET THEIR HAPPY ENDING.
RACHEL, I SWEAR ...
...I WON'T LEAVE *OUR* STORY UN-FINISHED ...
...NO MATTER WHAT.
YOU'RE NOT STILL TRYING TO GET ME AND EVA BACK TOGETHER, ARE YOU?
OF COURSE I AM!! WHAT CHILD WOULDN'T WANT TO LIVE WITH BOTH PARENTS?
PLENTY OF CHILDREN.

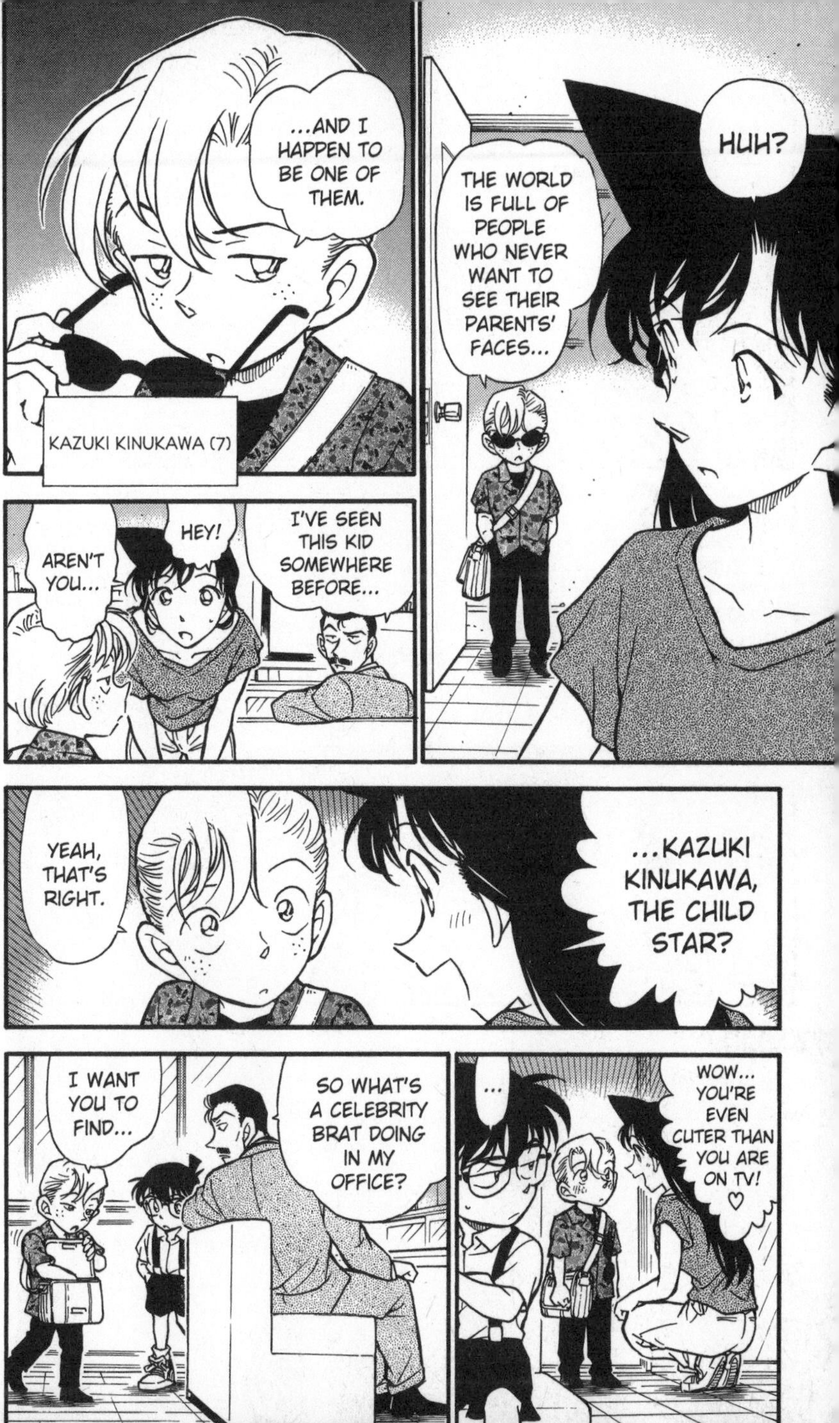
HUH?
THE WORLD IS FULL OF PEOPLE WHO NEVER WANT TO SEE THEIR PARENTS' FACES...
...AND I HAPPEN TO BE ONE OF THEM.
KAZUKI KINUKAWA (7)
I'VE SEEN THIS KID SOMEWHERE BEFORE...
HEY!
AREN'T YOU...
...KAZUKI KINUKAWA, THE CHILD STAR?
YEAH, THAT'S RIGHT.
WOW... YOU'RE EVEN CUTER THAN YOU ARE ON TV! ♡
...
SO WHAT'S A CELEBRITY BRAT DOING IN MY OFFICE?
I WANT YOU TO FIND...

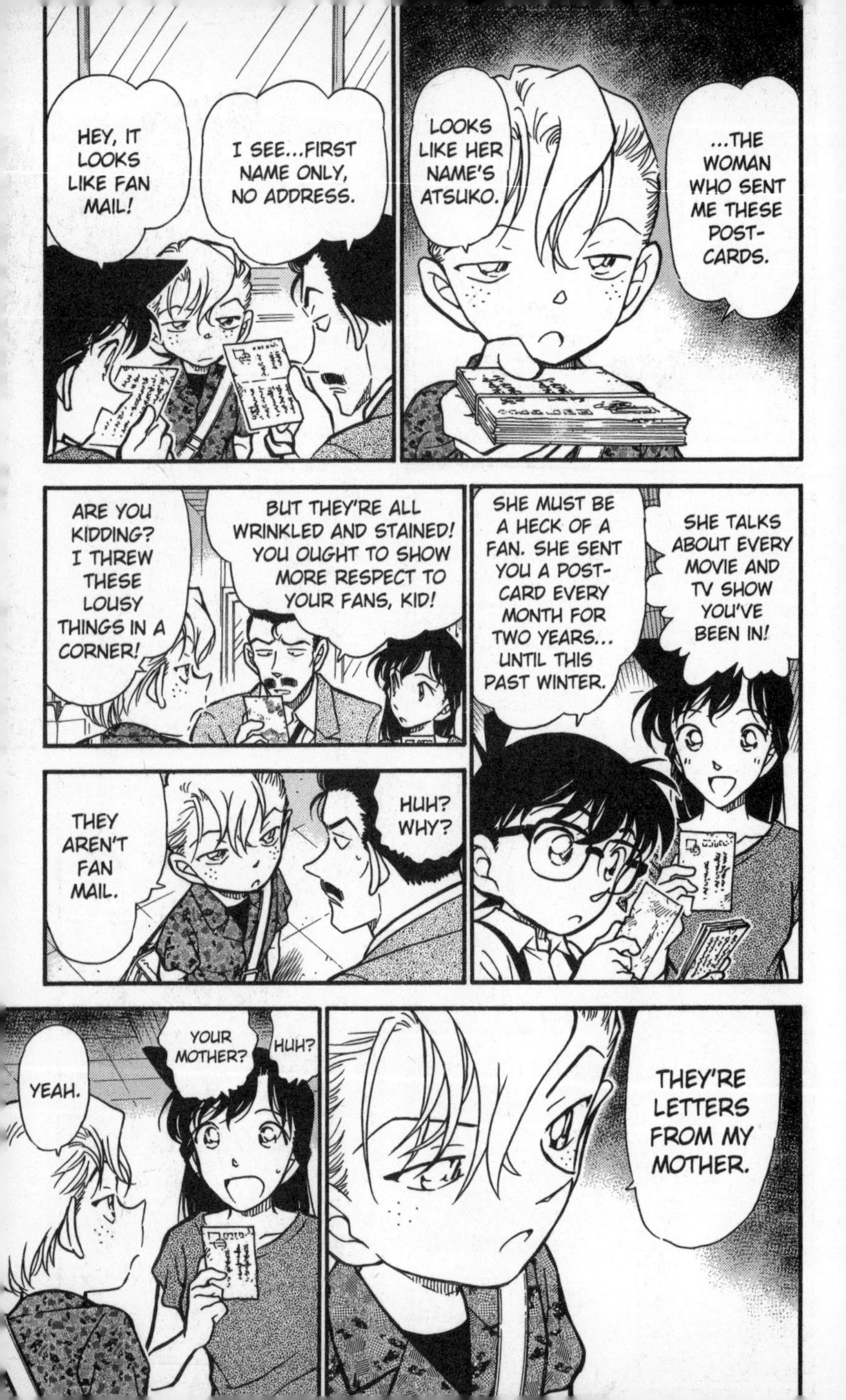
...THE WOMAN WHO SENT ME THESE POST-CARDS.
LOOKS LIKE HER NAME'S ATSUKO.
I SEE...FIRST NAME ONLY, NO ADDRESS.
HEY, IT LOOKS LIKE FAN MAIL!
SHE TALKS ABOUT EVERY MOVIE AND TV SHOW YOU'VE BEEN IN!
SHE MUST BE A HECK OF A FAN. SHE SENT YOU A POST-CARD EVERY MONTH FOR TWO YEARS... UNTIL THIS PAST WINTER.
BUT THEY'RE ALL WRINKLED AND STAINED! YOU OUGHT TO SHOW MORE RESPECT TO YOUR FANS, KID!
ARE YOU KIDDING? I THREW THESE LOUSY THINGS IN A CORNER!
HUH? WHY?
THEY AREN'T FAN MAIL.
THEY'RE LETTERS FROM MY MOTHER.
HUH?
YOUR MOTHER?
YEAH.

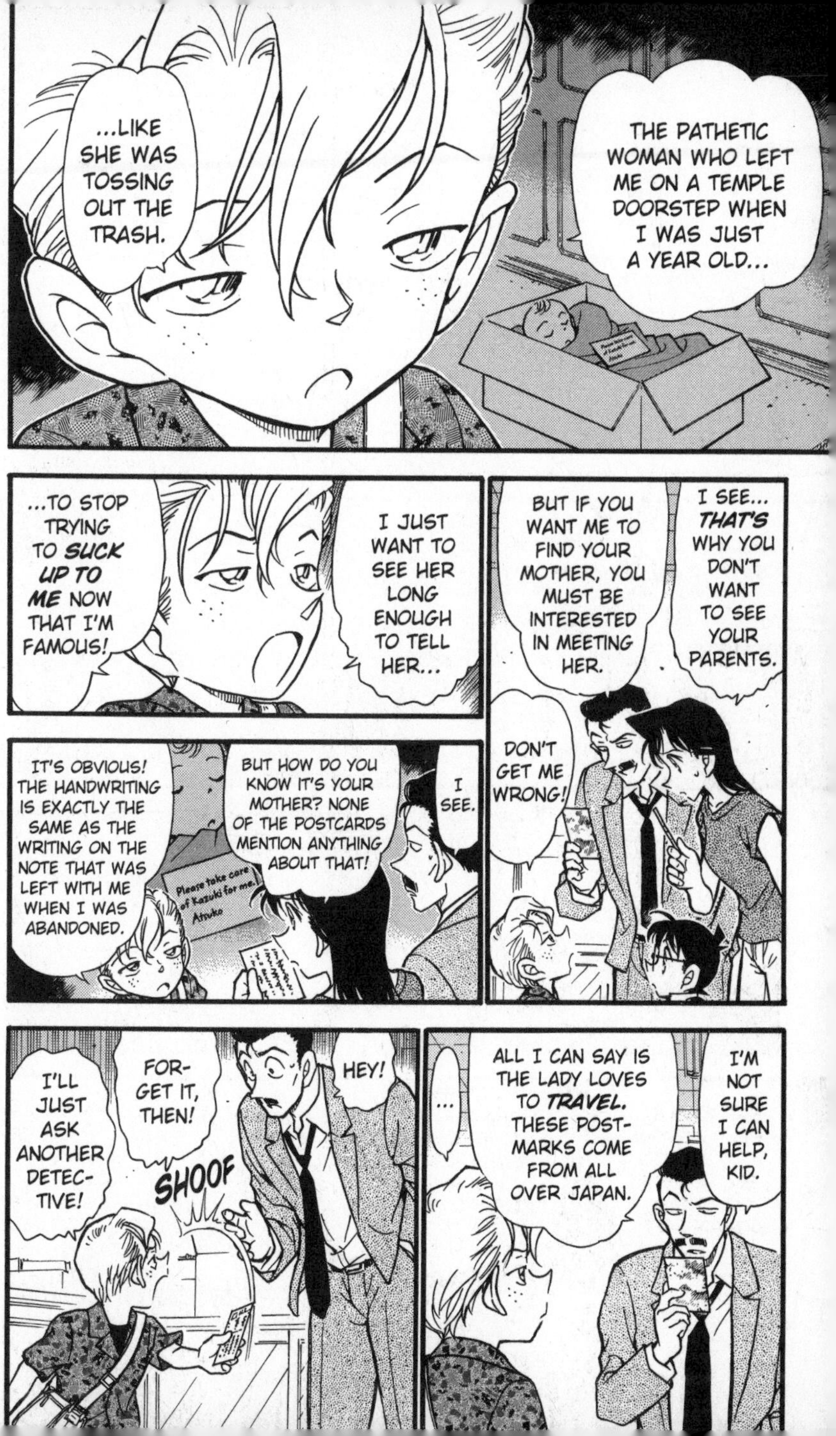
THE PATHETIC WOMAN WHO LEFT ME ON A TEMPLE DOORSTEP WHEN I WAS JUST A YEAR OLD...
...LIKE SHE WAS TOSSING OUT THE TRASH.
I SEE... ***THAT'S*** WHY YOU DON'T WANT TO SEE YOUR PARENTS.
BUT IF YOU WANT ME TO FIND YOUR MOTHER, YOU MUST BE INTERESTED IN MEETING HER.
DON'T GET ME WRONG!
I JUST WANT TO SEE HER LONG ENOUGH TO TELL HER...
...TO STOP TRYING TO ***SUCK UP TO ME*** NOW THAT I'M FAMOUS!
I SEE.
BUT HOW DO YOU KNOW IT'S YOUR MOTHER? NONE OF THE POSTCARDS MENTION ANYTHING ABOUT THAT!
IT'S OBVIOUS! THE HANDWRITING IS EXACTLY THE SAME AS THE WRITING ON THE NOTE THAT WAS LEFT WITH ME WHEN I WAS ABANDONED.
Please take care of Kazuki for me. Atsuko
I'M NOT SURE I CAN HELP, KID.
ALL I CAN SAY IS THE LADY LOVES TO ***TRAVEL.*** THESE POST-MARKS COME FROM ALL OVER JAPAN.
...
HEY!
FOR-GET IT, THEN!
I'LL JUST ASK ANOTHER DETEC-TIVE!
SHOOF

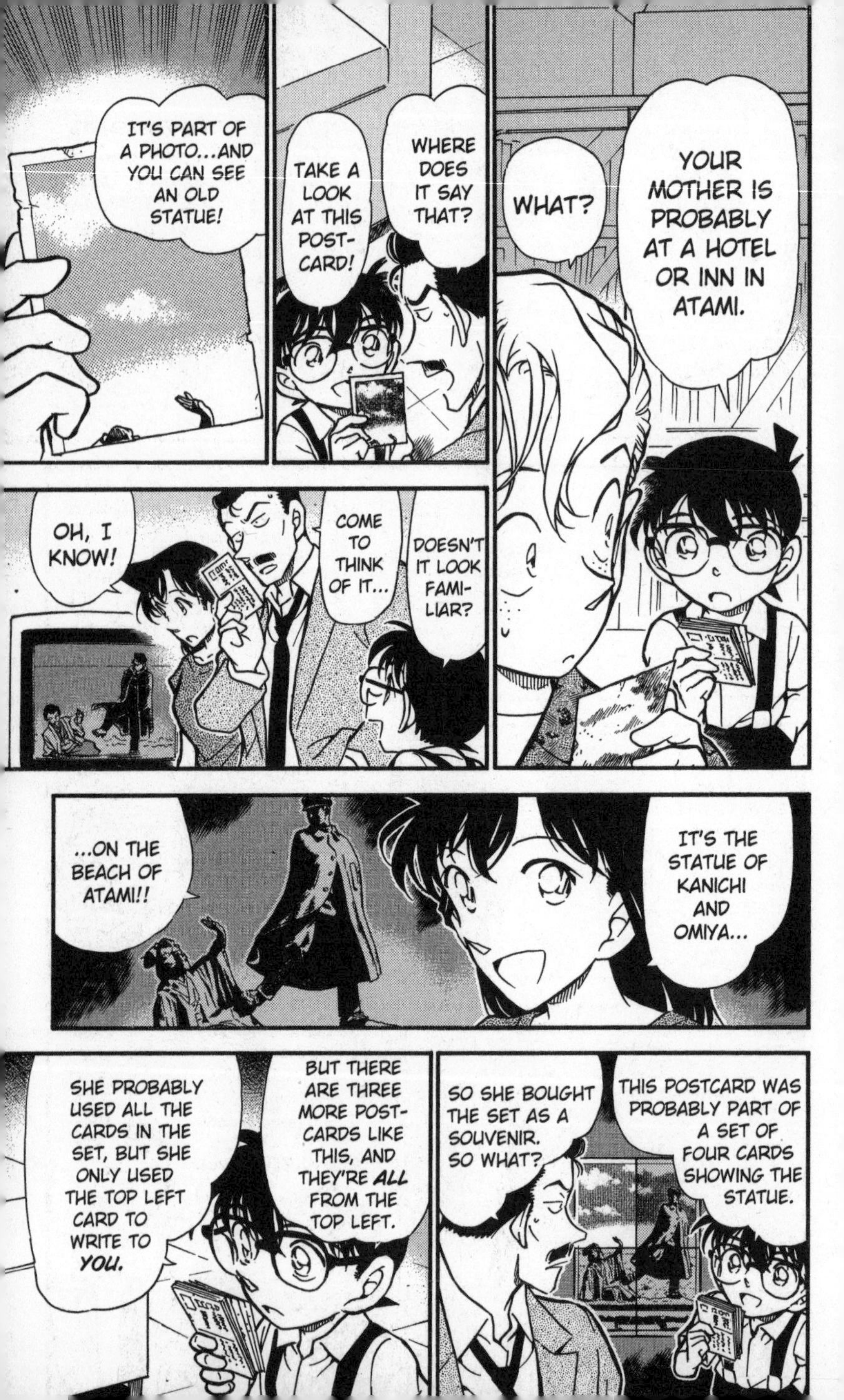
YOUR MOTHER IS PROBABLY AT A HOTEL OR INN IN ATAMI.
WHAT?
WHERE DOES IT SAY THAT?
TAKE A LOOK AT THIS POST-CARD!
IT'S PART OF A PHOTO...AND YOU CAN SEE AN OLD STATUE!
DOESN'T IT LOOK FAMI-LIAR?
COME TO THINK OF IT...
OH, I KNOW!
IT'S THE STATUE OF KANICHI AND OMIYA...
...ON THE BEACH OF ATAMI!!
THIS POSTCARD WAS PROBABLY PART OF A SET OF FOUR CARDS SHOWING THE STATUE.
SO SHE BOUGHT THE SET AS A SOUVENIR. SO WHAT?
BUT THERE ARE THREE MORE POST-CARDS LIKE THIS, AND THEY'RE ALL FROM THE TOP LEFT.
SHE PROBABLY USED ALL THE CARDS IN THE SET, BUT SHE ONLY USED THE TOP LEFT CARD TO WRITE TO YOU.

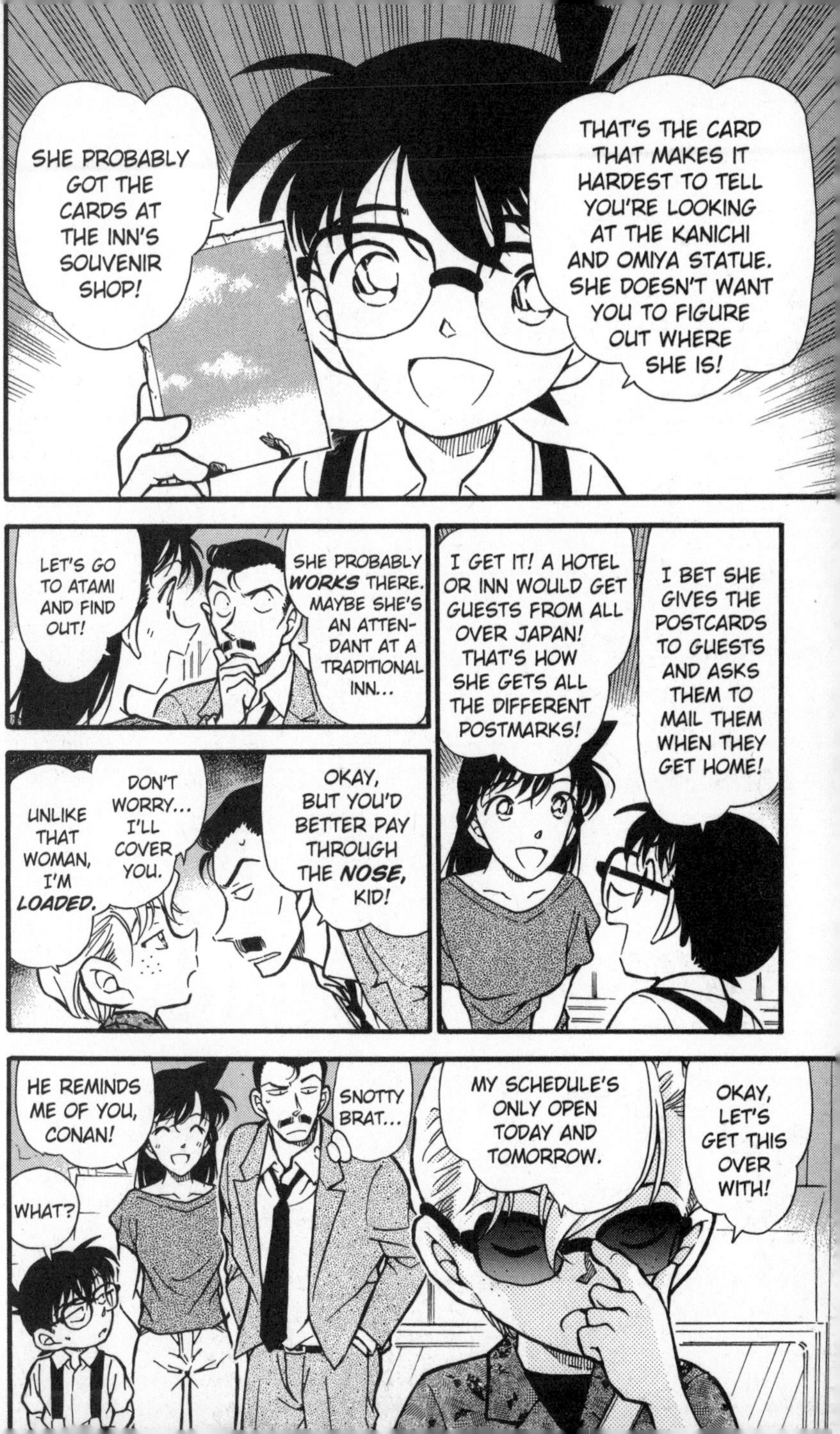
THAT'S THE CARD THAT MAKES IT HARDEST TO TELL YOU'RE LOOKING AT THE KANICHI AND OMIYA STATUE. SHE DOESN'T WANT YOU TO FIGURE OUT WHERE SHE IS!
SHE PROBABLY GOT THE CARDS AT THE INN'S SOUVENIR SHOP!
I BET SHE GIVES THE POSTCARDS TO GUESTS AND ASKS THEM TO MAIL THEM WHEN THEY GET HOME!
I GET IT! A HOTEL OR INN WOULD GET GUESTS FROM ALL OVER JAPAN! THAT'S HOW SHE GETS ALL THE DIFFERENT POSTMARKS!
SHE PROBABLY **WORKS** THERE. MAYBE SHE'S AN ATTEN-DANT AT A TRADITIONAL INN...
LET'S GO TO ATAMI AND FIND OUT!
OKAY, BUT YOU'D BETTER PAY THROUGH THE **NOSE,** KID!
DON'T WORRY... I'LL COVER YOU.
UNLIKE THAT WOMAN, I'M **LOADED.**
OKAY, LET'S GET THIS OVER WITH!
MY SCHEDULE'S ONLY OPEN TODAY AND TOMORROW.
SNOTTY BRAT...
HE REMINDS ME OF YOU, CONAN!
WHAT?

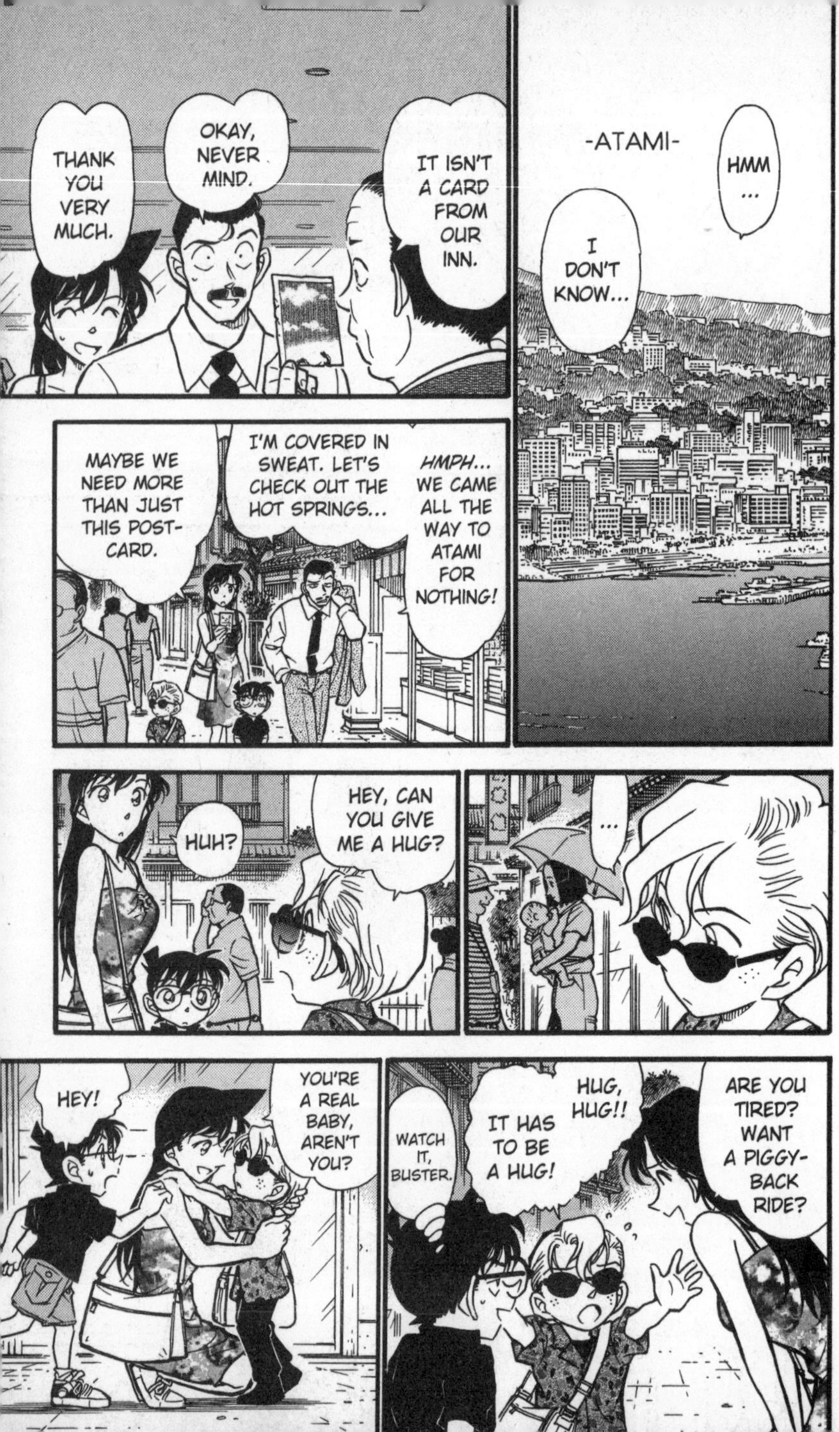
-ATAMI-
HMM...
I DON'T KNOW...
IT ISN'T A CARD FROM OUR INN.
OKAY, NEVER MIND.
THANK YOU VERY MUCH.
HMPH... WE CAME ALL THE WAY TO ATAMI FOR NOTHING!
I'M COVERED IN SWEAT. LET'S CHECK OUT THE HOT SPRINGS...
MAYBE WE NEED MORE THAN JUST THIS POST-CARD.
...
HEY, CAN YOU GIVE ME A HUG?
HUH?
ARE YOU TIRED? WANT A PIGGY-BACK RIDE?
HUG, HUG!!
IT HAS TO BE A HUG!
WATCH IT, BUSTER.
YOU'RE A REAL BABY, AREN'T YOU?
HEY!

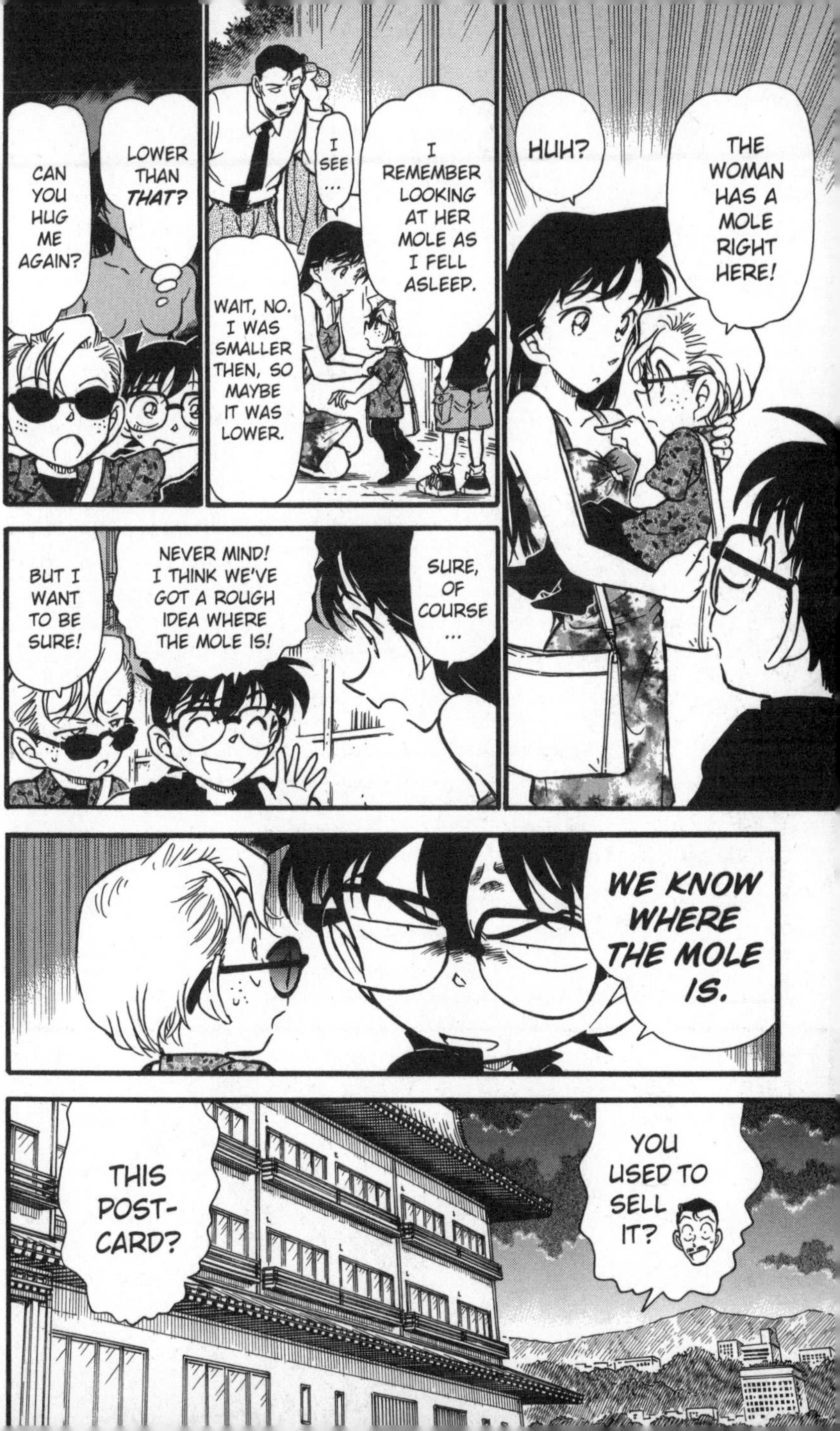
THE WOMAN HAS A MOLE RIGHT HERE!
HUH?
I REMEMBER LOOKING AT HER MOLE AS I FELL ASLEEP.
I SEE...
WAIT, NO. I WAS SMALLER THEN, SO MAYBE IT WAS LOWER.
LOWER THAN *THAT?*
CAN YOU HUG ME AGAIN?
SURE, OF COURSE...
NEVER MIND! I THINK WE'VE GOT A ROUGH IDEA WHERE THE MOLE IS!
BUT I WANT TO BE SURE!
WE KNOW WHERE THE MOLE IS.
YOU USED TO SELL IT?
THIS POST-CARD?

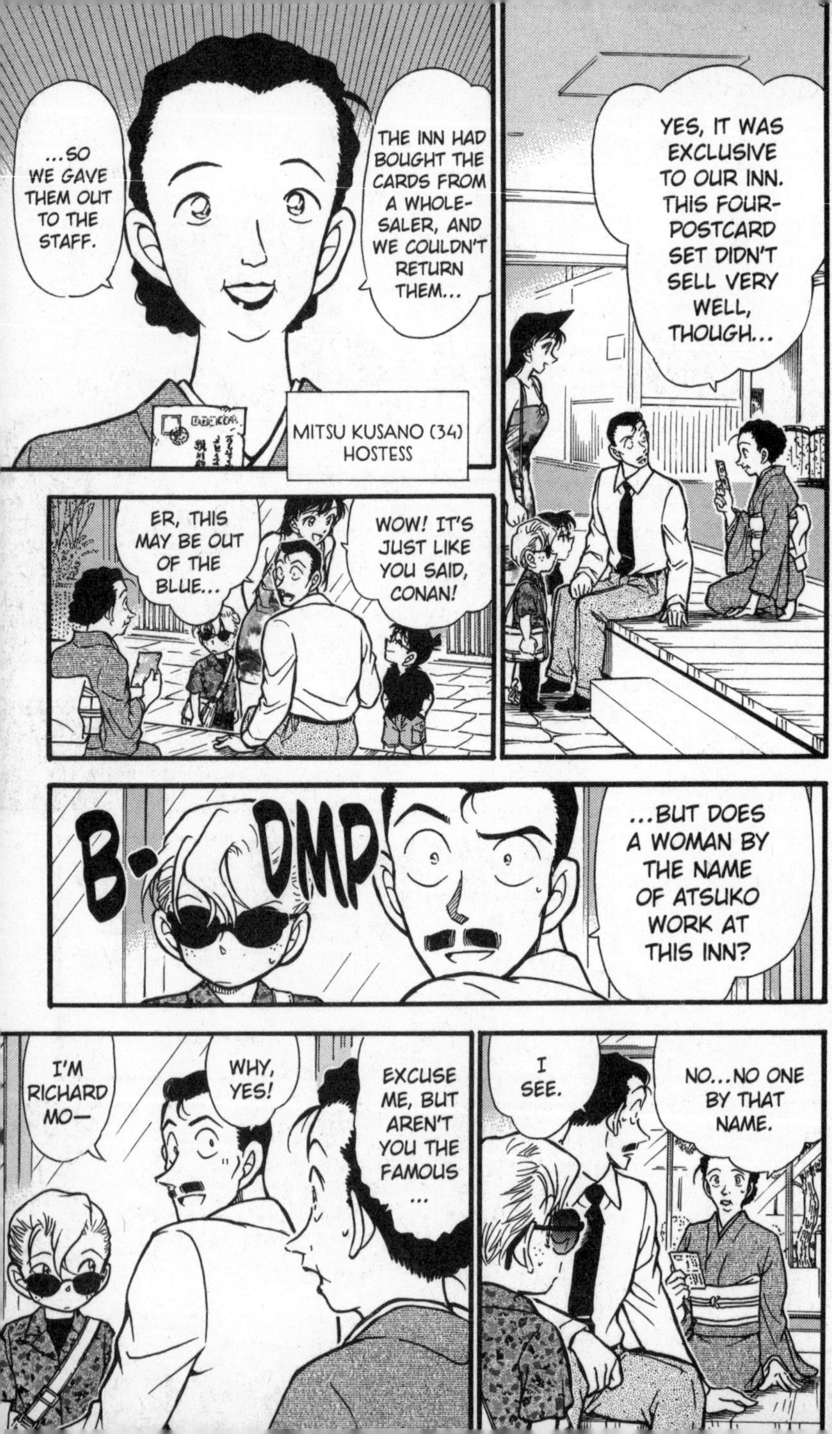
YES, IT WAS EXCLUSIVE TO OUR INN. THIS FOUR-POSTCARD SET DIDN'T SELL VERY WELL, THOUGH...
THE INN HAD BOUGHT THE CARDS FROM A WHOLE-SALER, AND WE COULDN'T RETURN THEM...
...SO WE GAVE THEM OUT TO THE STAFF.
MITSU KUSANO (34) HOSTESS
WOW! IT'S JUST LIKE YOU SAID, CONAN!
ER, THIS MAY BE OUT OF THE BLUE...
...BUT DOES A WOMAN BY THE NAME OF ATSUKO WORK AT THIS INN?
B-DMP
NO...NO ONE BY THAT NAME.
I SEE.
EXCUSE ME, BUT AREN'T YOU THE FAMOUS ...
WHY, YES!
I'M RICHARD MO—

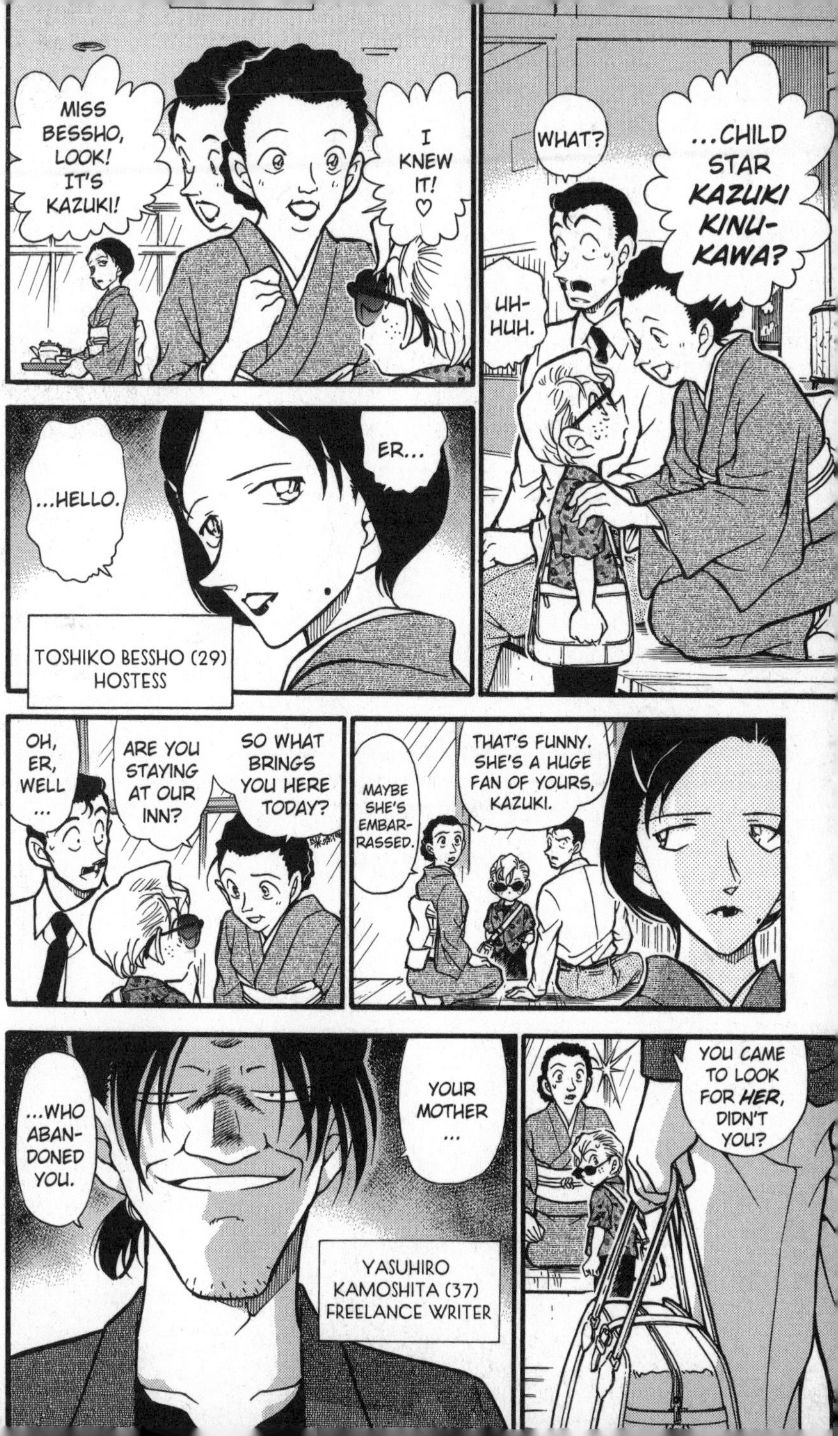
...CHILD STAR KAZUKI KINUKAWA?
WHAT?
UH-HUH.
MISS BESSHO, LOOK! IT'S KAZUKI!
I KNEW IT! ♡
ER...
...HELLO.
TOSHIKO BESSHO (29) HOSTESS
THAT'S FUNNY. SHE'S A HUGE FAN OF YOURS, KAZUKI.
MAYBE SHE'S EMBARRASSED.
SO WHAT BRINGS YOU HERE TODAY?
ARE YOU STAYING AT OUR INN?
OH, ER, WELL ...
YOU CAME TO LOOK FOR *HER*, DIDN'T YOU?
YOUR MOTHER ...
...WHO ABANDONED YOU.
YASUHIRO KAMOSHITA (37) FREELANCE WRITER

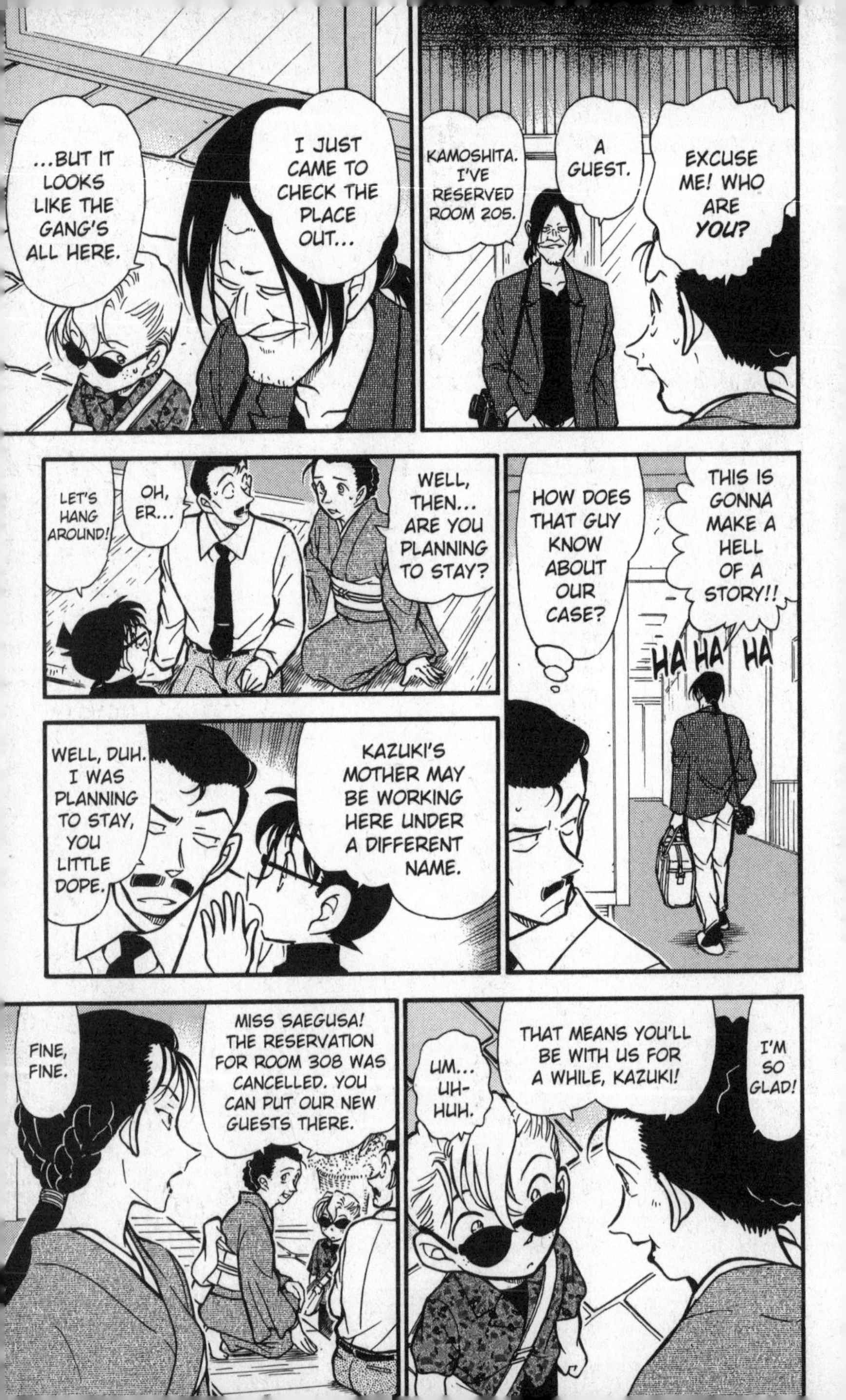
EXCUSE ME! WHO ARE YOU?
A GUEST.
KAMOSHITA. I'VE RESERVED ROOM 205.
I JUST CAME TO CHECK THE PLACE OUT...
...BUT IT LOOKS LIKE THE GANG'S ALL HERE.
THIS IS GONNA MAKE A HELL OF A STORY!!
HA HA HA
HOW DOES THAT GUY KNOW ABOUT OUR CASE?
WELL, THEN... ARE YOU PLANNING TO STAY?
OH, ER...
LET'S HANG AROUND!
KAZUKI'S MOTHER MAY BE WORKING HERE UNDER A DIFFERENT NAME.
WELL, DUH. I WAS PLANNING TO STAY, YOU LITTLE DOPE.
I'M SO GLAD!
THAT MEANS YOU'LL BE WITH US FOR A WHILE, KAZUKI!
UM... UH-HUH.
MISS SAEGUSA! THE RESERVATION FOR ROOM 308 WAS CANCELLED. YOU CAN PUT OUR NEW GUESTS THERE.
FINE, FINE.

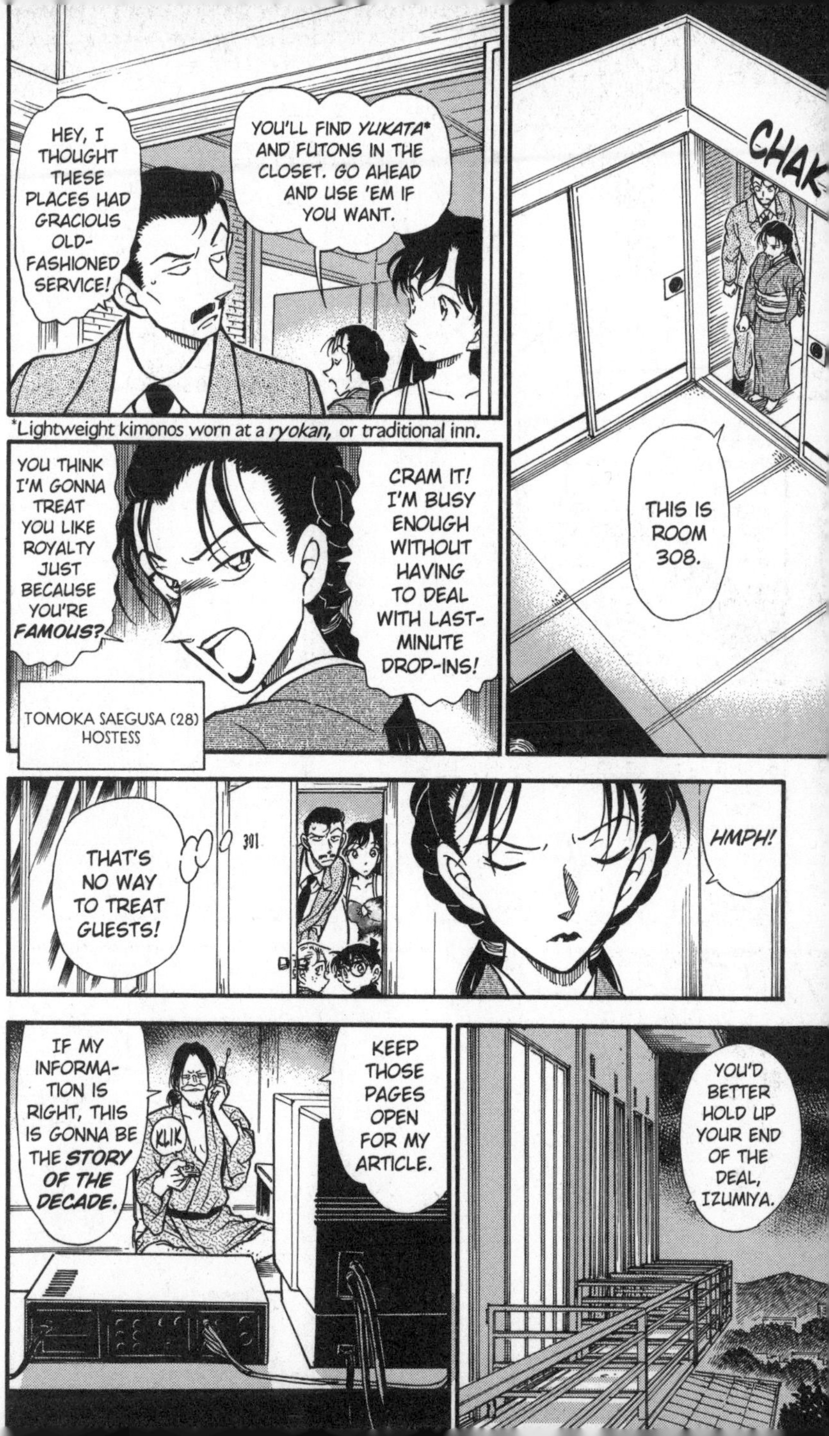
CHAK
THIS IS ROOM 308.
YOU'LL FIND *YUKATA** AND FUTONS IN THE CLOSET. GO AHEAD AND USE 'EM IF YOU WANT.
HEY, I THOUGHT THESE PLACES HAD GRACIOUS OLD-FASHIONED SERVICE!
CRAM IT! I'M BUSY ENOUGH WITHOUT HAVING TO DEAL WITH LAST-MINUTE DROP-INS!
YOU THINK I'M GONNA TREAT YOU LIKE ROYALTY JUST BECAUSE YOU'RE **FAMOUS?**
TOMOKA SAEGUSA (28) HOSTESS
HMPH!
301
THAT'S NO WAY TO TREAT GUESTS!
YOU'D BETTER HOLD UP YOUR END OF THE DEAL, IZUMIYA.
KEEP THOSE PAGES OPEN FOR MY ARTICLE.
IF MY INFORMATION IS RIGHT, THIS IS GONNA BE THE **STORY OF THE DECADE.**
KLIK

*Lightweight kimonos worn at a *ryokan,* or traditional inn.

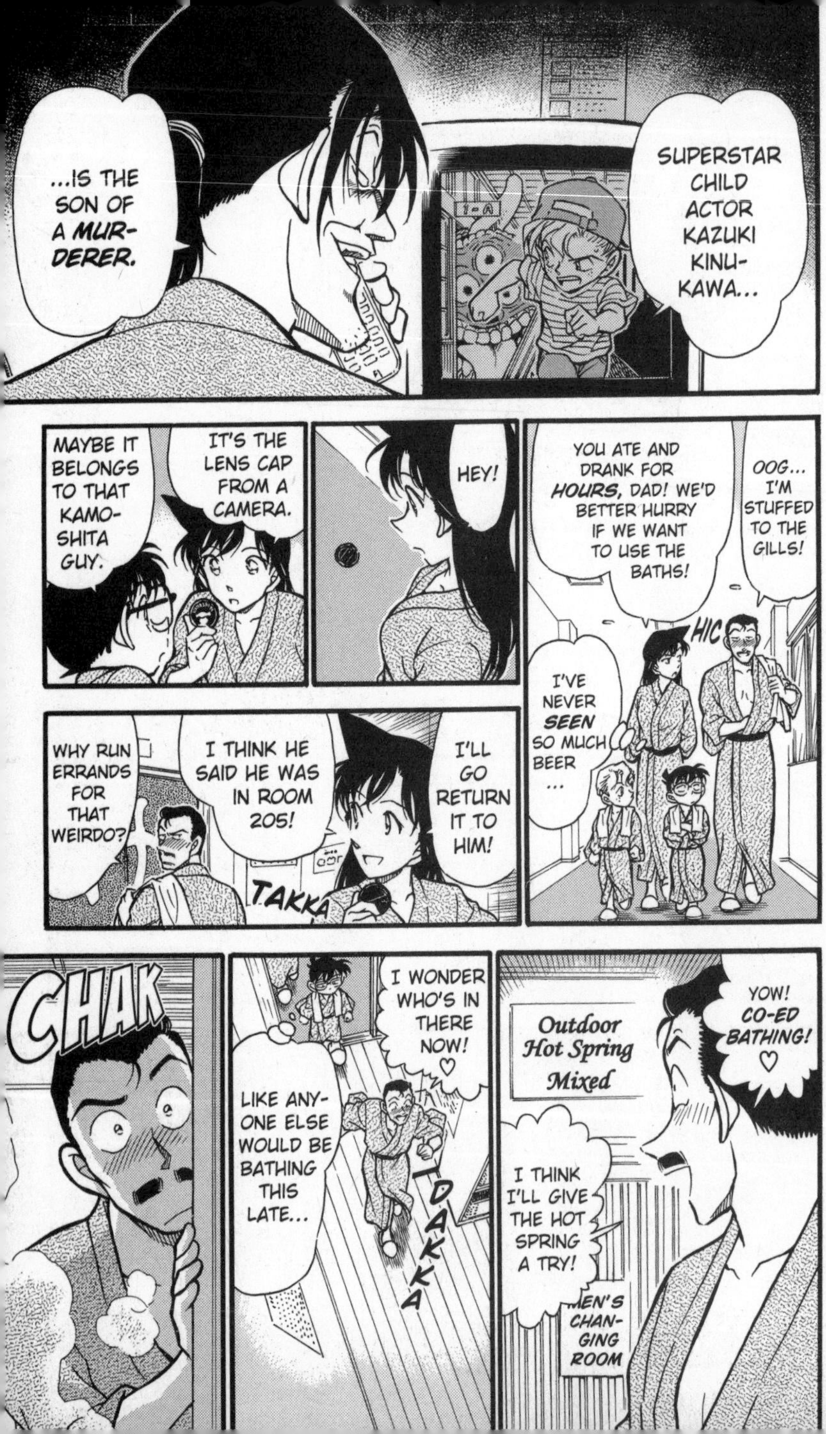
SUPERSTAR CHILD ACTOR KAZUKI KINU-KAWA...
...IS THE SON OF A MUR-DERER.
OOG... I'M STUFFED TO THE GILLS!
YOU ATE AND DRANK FOR HOURS, DAD! WE'D BETTER HURRY IF WE WANT TO USE THE BATHS!
HIC
I'VE NEVER SEEN SO MUCH BEER...
HEY!
IT'S THE LENS CAP FROM A CAMERA.
MAYBE IT BELONGS TO THAT KAMO-SHITA GUY.
I'LL GO RETURN IT TO HIM!
I THINK HE SAID HE WAS IN ROOM 205!
TAKKA
WHY RUN ERRANDS FOR THAT WEIRDO?
YOW! CO-ED BATHING! ♡
Outdoor Hot Spring Mixed
I THINK I'LL GIVE THE HOT SPRING A TRY!
MEN'S CHANG-ING ROOM
I WONDER WHO'S IN THERE NOW! ♡
LIKE ANY-ONE ELSE WOULD BE BATHING THIS LATE...
DAKKA
CHAK

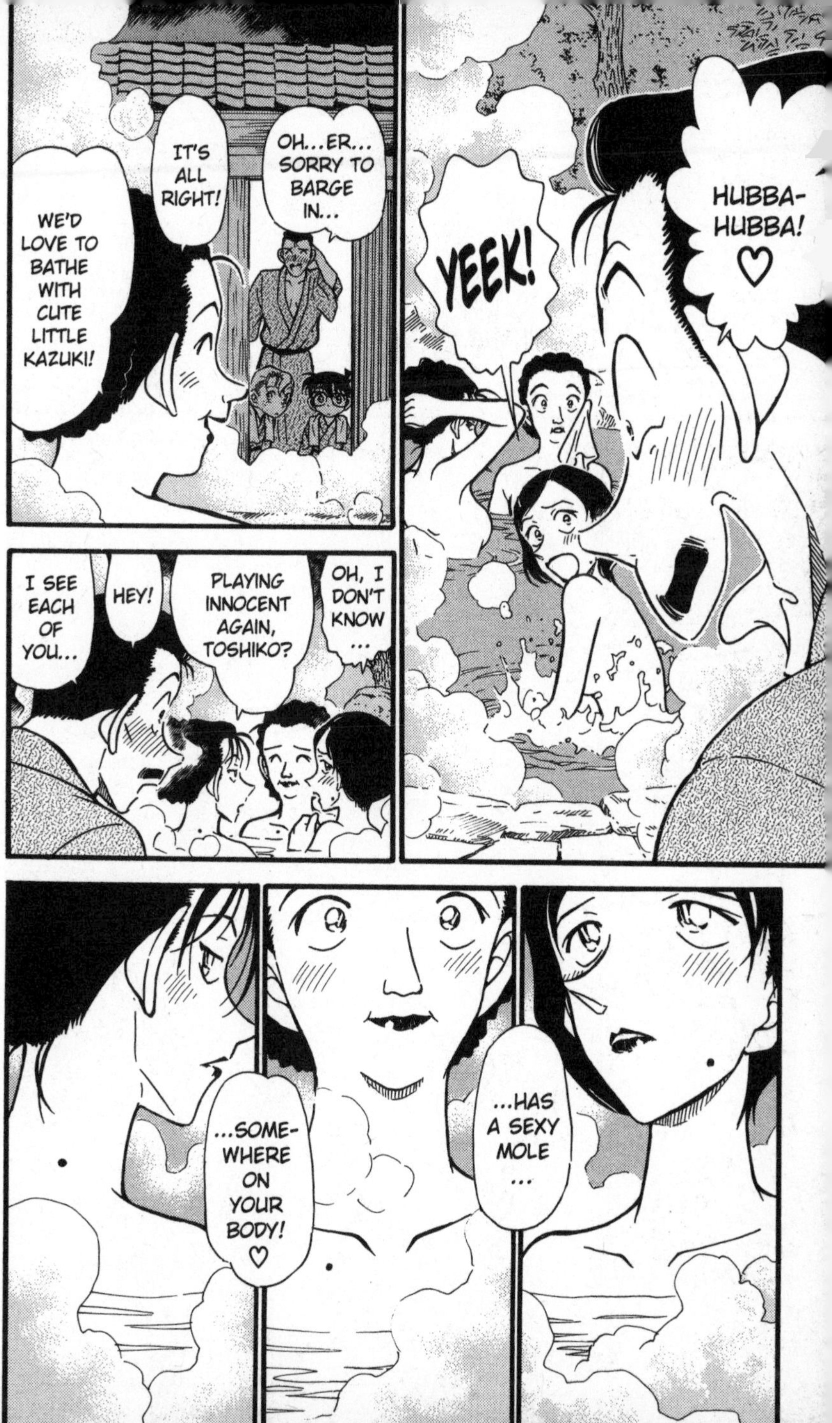
HUBBA-HUBBA! ♡
YEEK!
OH...ER... SORRY TO BARGE IN...
IT'S ALL RIGHT!
WE'D LOVE TO BATHE WITH CUTE LITTLE KAZUKI!
OH, I DON'T KNOW ...
PLAYING INNOCENT AGAIN, TOSHIKO?
HEY!
I SEE EACH OF YOU...
...HAS A SEXY MOLE ...
...SOME-WHERE ON YOUR BODY! ♡

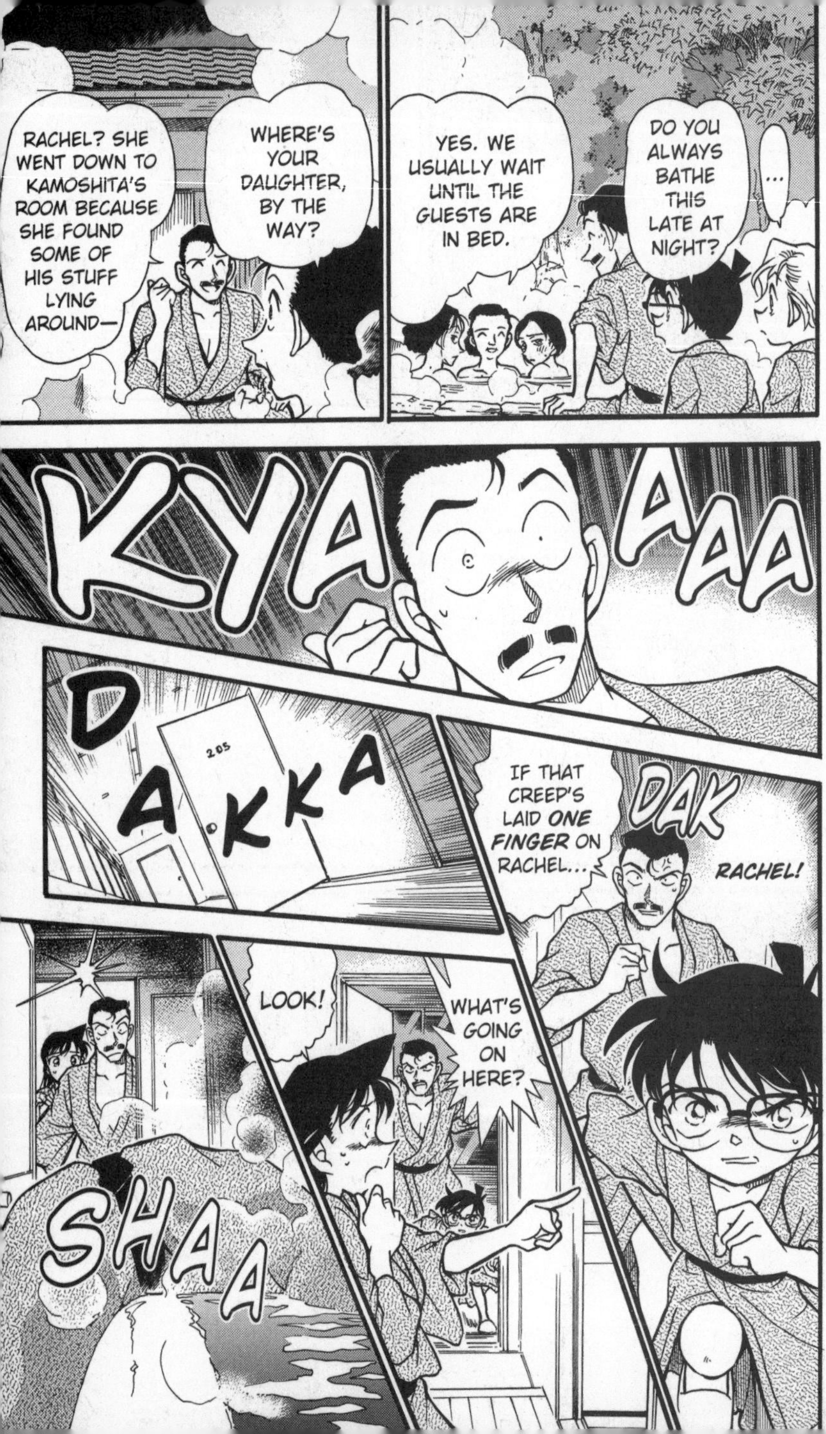
...
DO YOU ALWAYS BATHE THIS LATE AT NIGHT?
YES. WE USUALLY WAIT UNTIL THE GUESTS ARE IN BED.
WHERE'S YOUR DAUGHTER, BY THE WAY?
RACHEL? SHE WENT DOWN TO KAMOSHITA'S ROOM BECAUSE SHE FOUND SOME OF HIS STUFF LYING AROUND—
KYAAAA
DAK
RACHEL!
IF THAT CREEP'S LAID ONE FINGER ON RACHEL...
205
DAKKA
WHAT'S GOING ON HERE?
LOOK!
SHAA

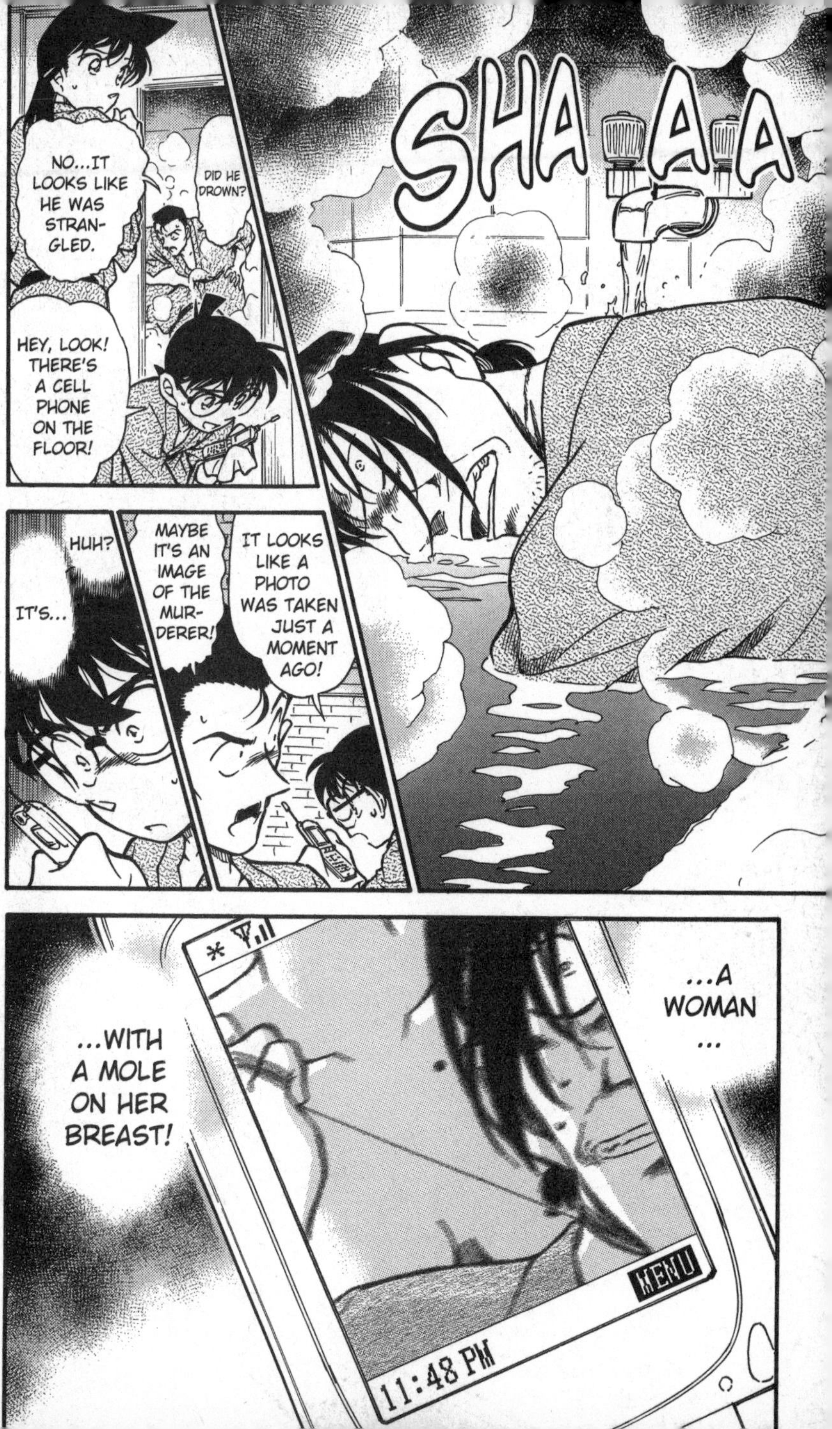
SHA A A
DID HE DROWN?
NO...IT LOOKS LIKE HE WAS STRANGLED.
HEY, LOOK! THERE'S A CELL PHONE ON THE FLOOR!
IT LOOKS LIKE A PHOTO WAS TAKEN JUST A MOMENT AGO!
MAYBE IT'S AN IMAGE OF THE MURDERER!
HUH?
IT'S...
...A WOMAN ...
...WITH A MOLE ON HER BREAST!
MENU
11:48 PM

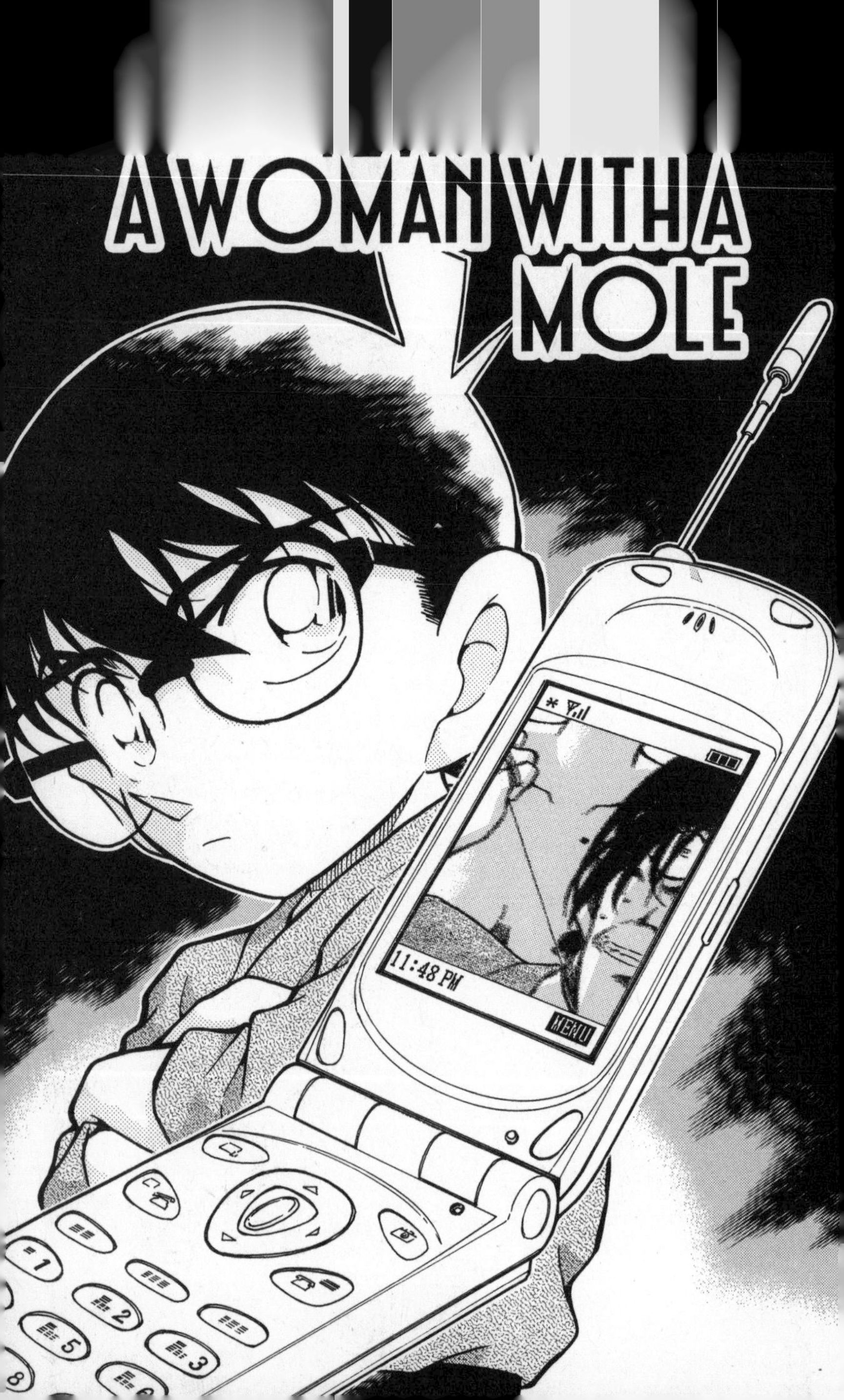
A WOMAN WITH A MOLE
11:48 PM
MENU

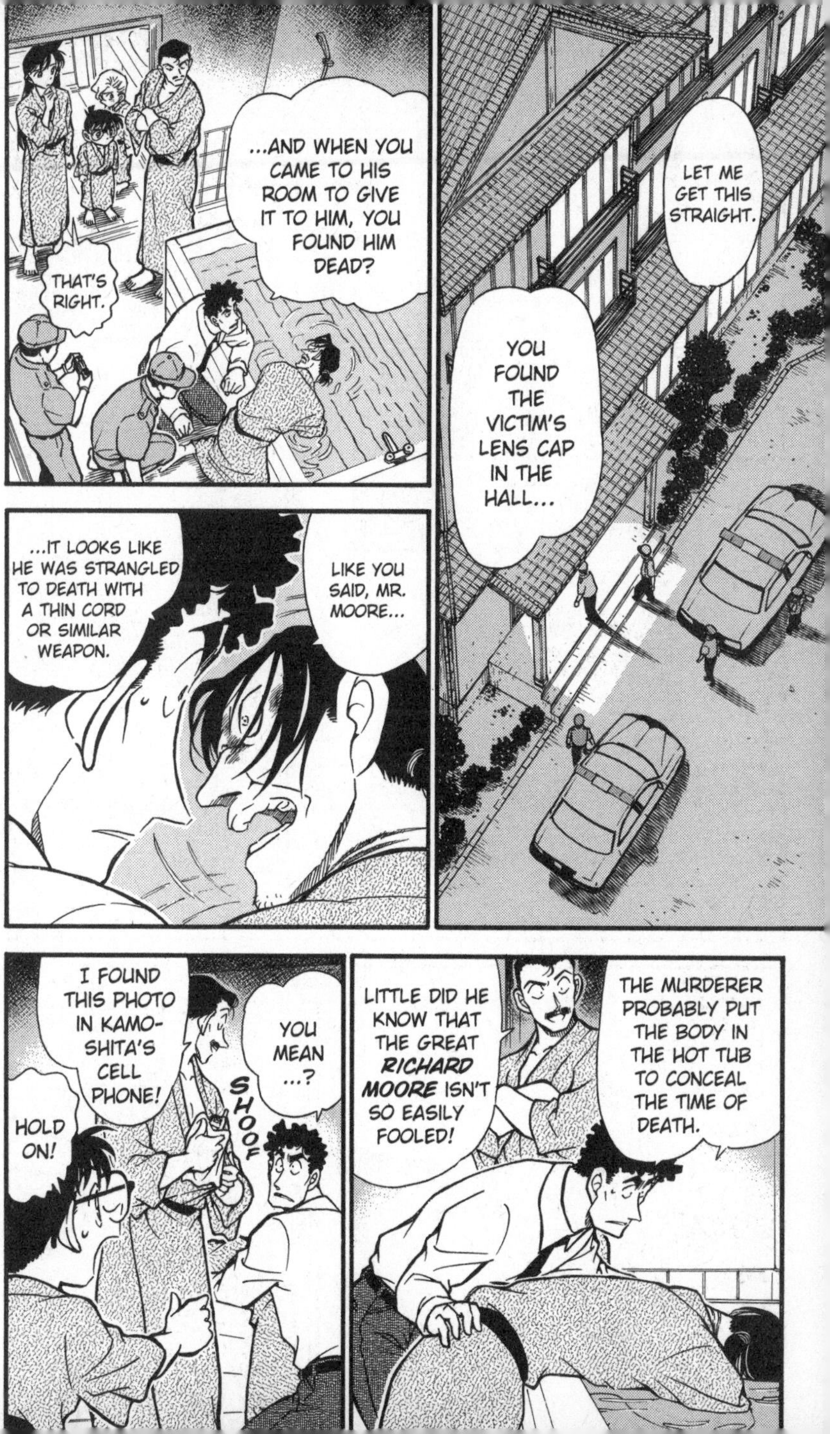
LET ME GET THIS STRAIGHT.
YOU FOUND THE VICTIM'S LENS CAP IN THE HALL...
...AND WHEN YOU CAME TO HIS ROOM TO GIVE IT TO HIM, YOU FOUND HIM DEAD?
THAT'S RIGHT.
LIKE YOU SAID, MR. MOORE...
...IT LOOKS LIKE HE WAS STRANGLED TO DEATH WITH A THIN CORD OR SIMILAR WEAPON.
THE MURDERER PROBABLY PUT THE BODY IN THE HOT TUB TO CONCEAL THE TIME OF DEATH.
LITTLE DID HE KNOW THAT THE GREAT *RICHARD MOORE* ISN'T SO EASILY FOOLED!
YOU MEAN ...?
I FOUND THIS PHOTO IN KAMO-SHITA'S CELL PHONE!
SHOOF
HOLD ON!

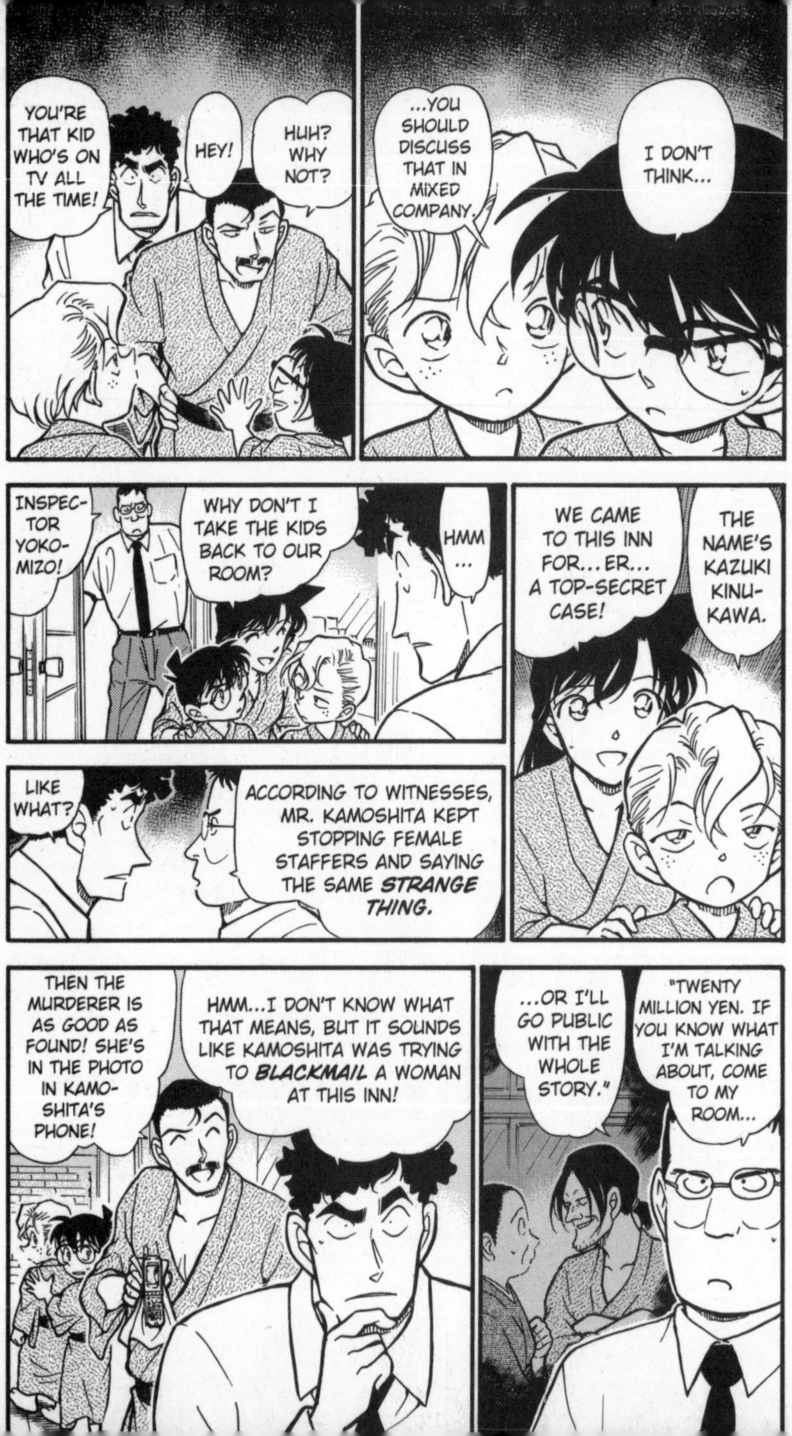
I DON'T THINK...
...YOU SHOULD DISCUSS THAT IN MIXED COMPANY.
HUH? WHY NOT?
HEY!
YOU'RE THAT KID WHO'S ON TV ALL THE TIME!
THE NAME'S KAZUKI KINUKAWA.
WE CAME TO THIS INN FOR... ER... A TOP-SECRET CASE!
HMM ...
WHY DON'T I TAKE THE KIDS BACK TO OUR ROOM?
INSPECTOR YOKOMIZO!
ACCORDING TO WITNESSES, MR. KAMOSHITA KEPT STOPPING FEMALE STAFFERS AND SAYING THE SAME ***STRANGE THING.***
LIKE WHAT?
"TWENTY MILLION YEN. IF YOU KNOW WHAT I'M TALKING ABOUT, COME TO MY ROOM...
...OR I'LL GO PUBLIC WITH THE WHOLE STORY."
HMM...I DON'T KNOW WHAT THAT MEANS, BUT IT SOUNDS LIKE KAMOSHITA WAS TRYING TO ***BLACKMAIL*** A WOMAN AT THIS INN!
THEN THE MURDERER IS AS GOOD AS FOUND! SHE'S IN THE PHOTO IN KAMOSHITA'S PHONE!

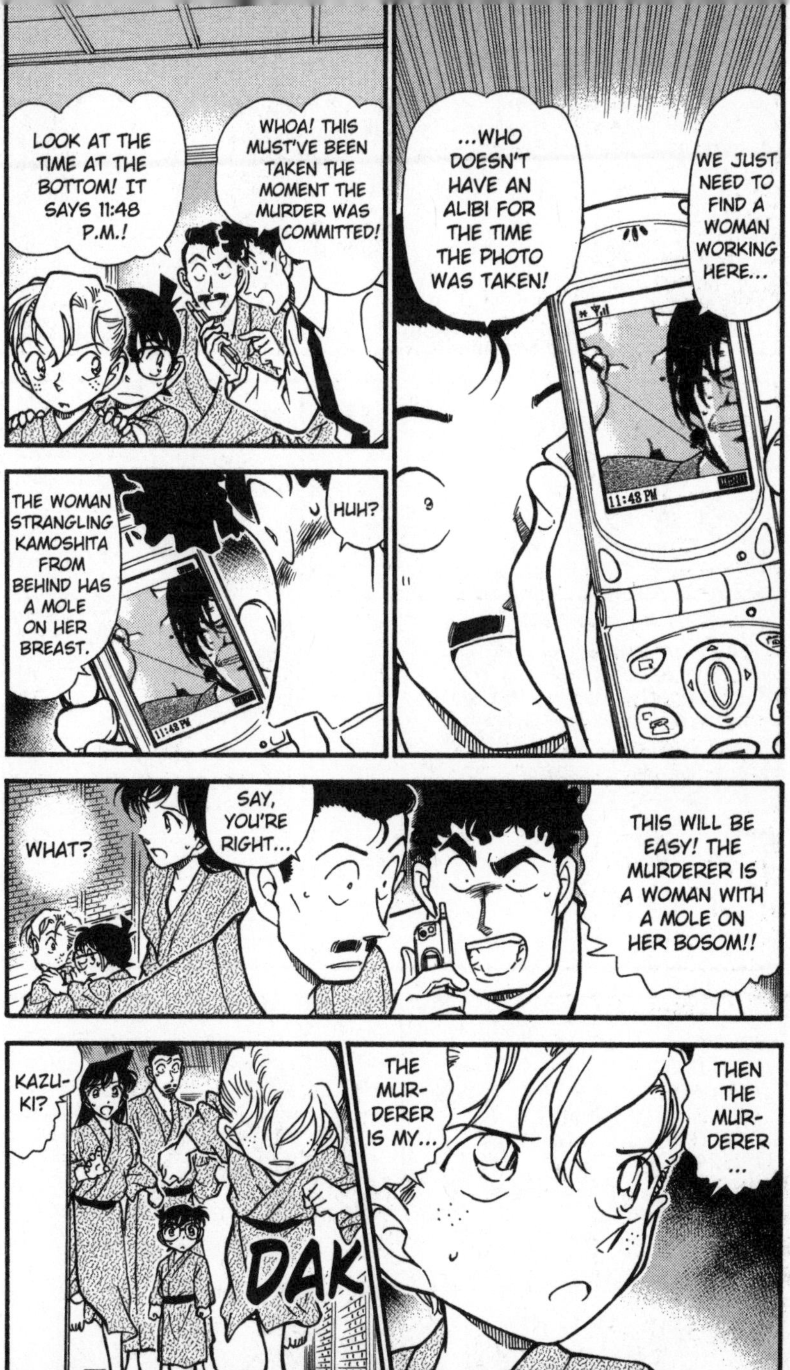

WE JUST NEED TO FIND A WOMAN WORKING HERE...
...WHO DOESN'T HAVE AN ALIBI FOR THE TIME THE PHOTO WAS TAKEN!
11:48 PM
WHOA! THIS MUST'VE BEEN TAKEN THE MOMENT THE MURDER WAS COMMITTED!
LOOK AT THE TIME AT THE BOTTOM! IT SAYS 11:48 P.M.!
HUH?
THE WOMAN STRANGLING KAMOSHITA FROM BEHIND HAS A MOLE ON HER BREAST.
11:48 PM
THIS WILL BE EASY! THE MURDERER IS A WOMAN WITH A MOLE ON HER BOSOM!!
SAY, YOU'RE RIGHT...
WHAT?
THEN THE MUR-DERER ...
THE MUR-DERER IS MY...
DAK
KAZU-KI?

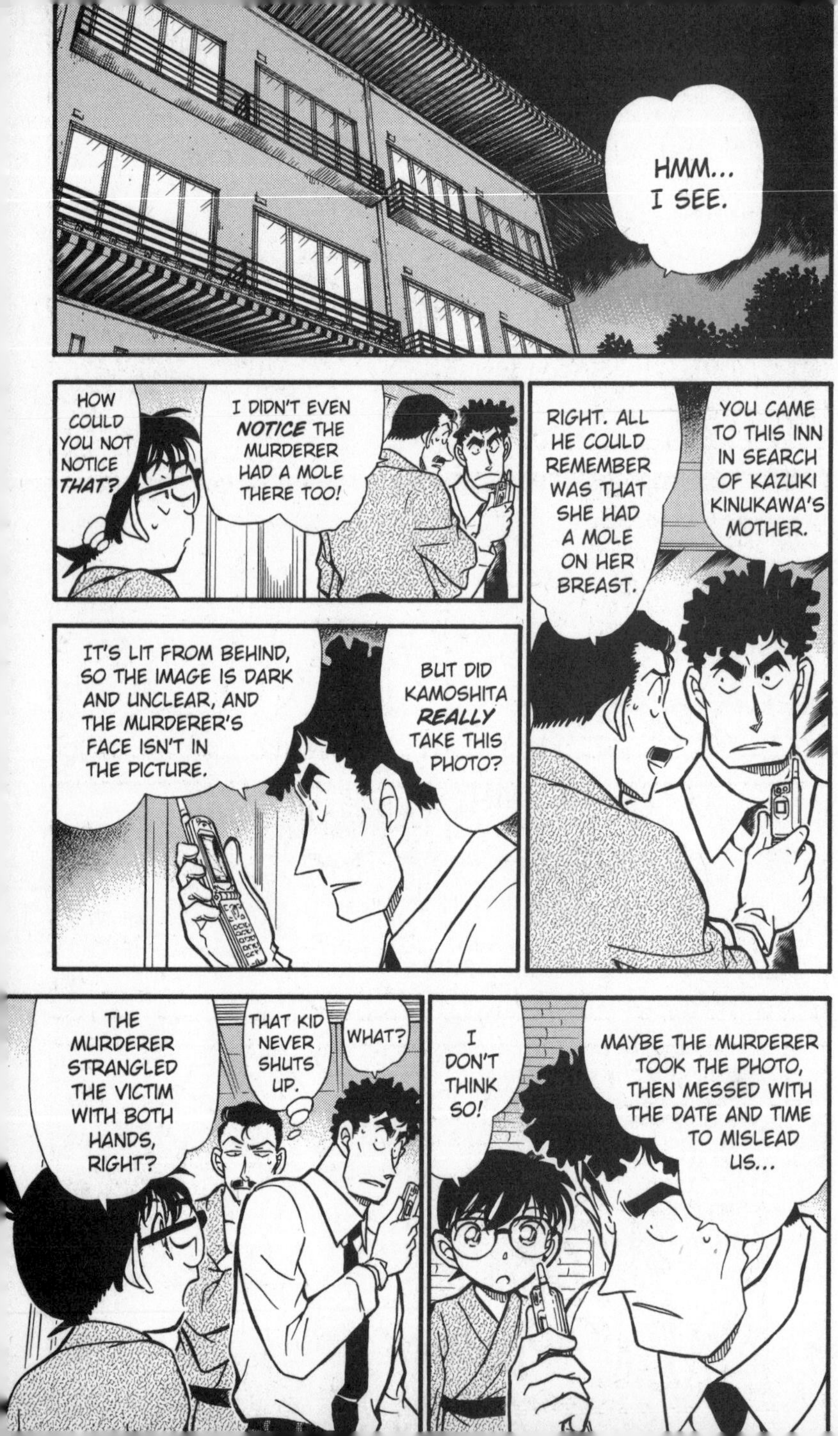
HMM... I SEE.
YOU CAME TO THIS INN IN SEARCH OF KAZUKI KINUKAWA'S MOTHER.
RIGHT. ALL HE COULD REMEMBER WAS THAT SHE HAD A MOLE ON HER BREAST.
I DIDN'T EVEN *NOTICE* THE MURDERER HAD A MOLE THERE TOO!
HOW COULD YOU NOT NOTICE *THAT*?
BUT DID KAMOSHITA *REALLY* TAKE THIS PHOTO?
IT'S LIT FROM BEHIND, SO THE IMAGE IS DARK AND UNCLEAR, AND THE MURDERER'S FACE ISN'T IN THE PICTURE.
MAYBE THE MURDERER TOOK THE PHOTO, THEN MESSED WITH THE DATE AND TIME TO MISLEAD US...
I DON'T THINK SO!
WHAT?
THAT KID NEVER SHUTS UP.
THE MURDERER STRANGLED THE VICTIM WITH BOTH HANDS, RIGHT?

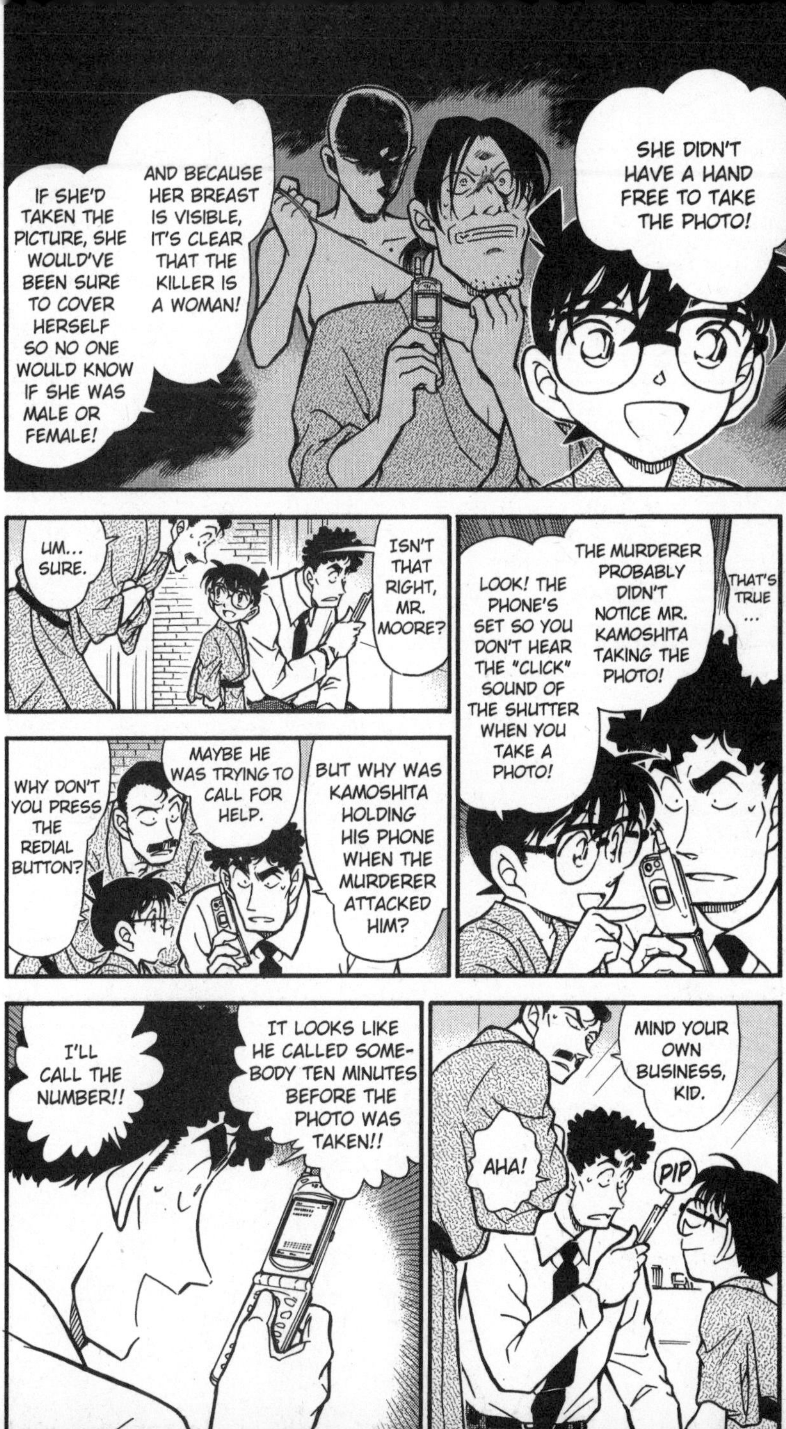
SHE DIDN'T HAVE A HAND FREE TO TAKE THE PHOTO!
AND BECAUSE HER BREAST IS VISIBLE, IT'S CLEAR THAT THE KILLER IS A WOMAN!
IF SHE'D TAKEN THE PICTURE, SHE WOULD'VE BEEN SURE TO COVER HERSELF SO NO ONE WOULD KNOW IF SHE WAS MALE OR FEMALE!
THAT'S TRUE ...
THE MURDERER PROBABLY DIDN'T NOTICE MR. KAMOSHITA TAKING THE PHOTO!
LOOK! THE PHONE'S SET SO YOU DON'T HEAR THE "CLICK" SOUND OF THE SHUTTER WHEN YOU TAKE A PHOTO!
ISN'T THAT RIGHT, MR. MOORE?
UM... SURE.
BUT WHY WAS KAMOSHITA HOLDING HIS PHONE WHEN THE MURDERER ATTACKED HIM?
MAYBE HE WAS TRYING TO CALL FOR HELP.
WHY DON'T YOU PRESS THE REDIAL BUTTON?
MIND YOUR OWN BUSINESS, KID.
PIP
AHA!
IT LOOKS LIKE HE CALLED SOME-BODY TEN MINUTES BEFORE THE PHOTO WAS TAKEN!!
I'LL CALL THE NUMBER!!

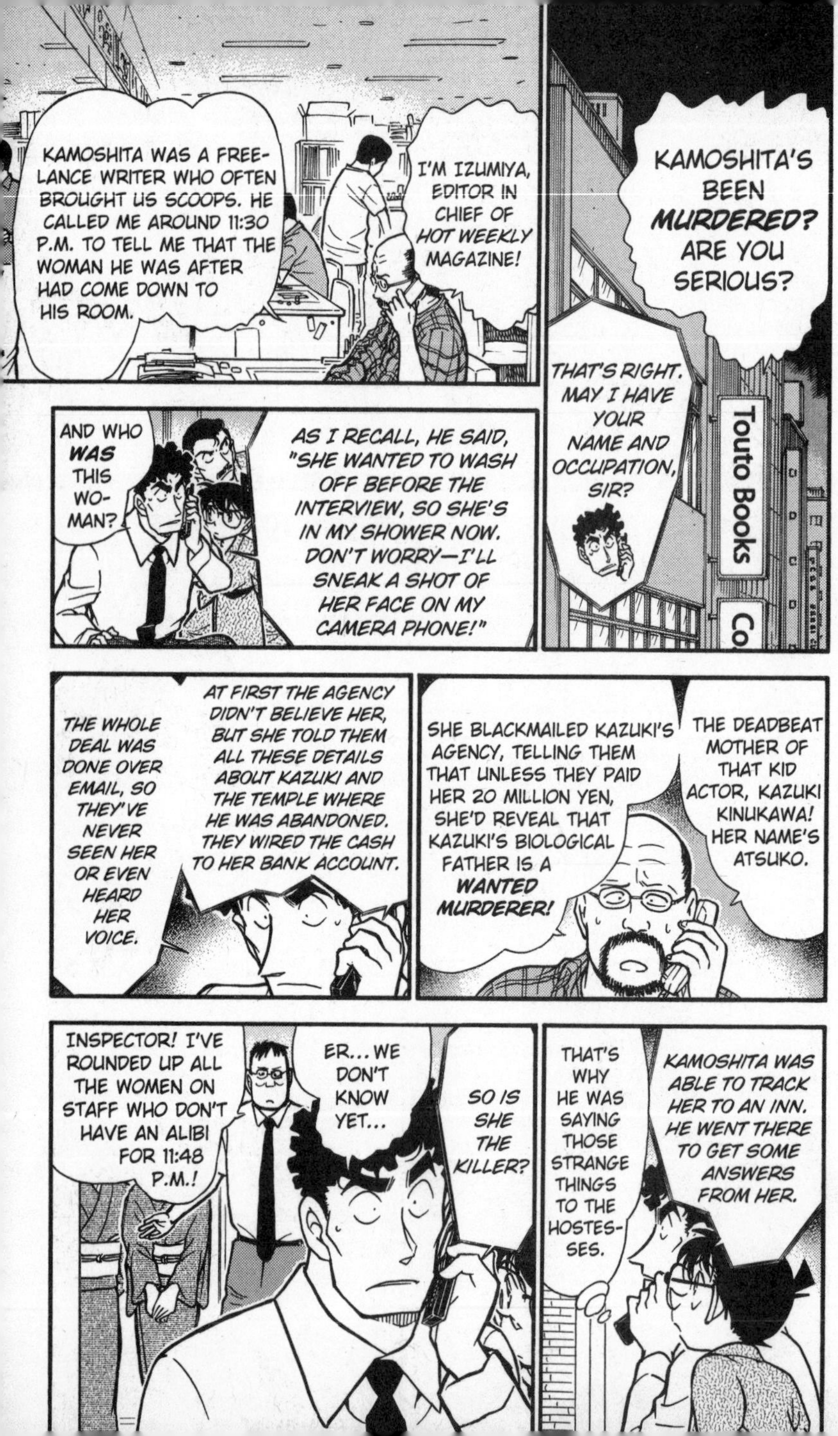

KAMOSHITA'S BEEN MURDERED? ARE YOU SERIOUS?
THAT'S RIGHT. MAY I HAVE YOUR NAME AND OCCUPATION, SIR?
Touto Books
I'M IZUMIYA, EDITOR IN CHIEF OF HOT WEEKLY MAGAZINE!
KAMOSHITA WAS A FREE-LANCE WRITER WHO OFTEN BROUGHT US SCOOPS. HE CALLED ME AROUND 11:30 P.M. TO TELL ME THAT THE WOMAN HE WAS AFTER HAD COME DOWN TO HIS ROOM.
AND WHO WAS THIS WO-MAN?
AS I RECALL, HE SAID, "SHE WANTED TO WASH OFF BEFORE THE INTERVIEW, SO SHE'S IN MY SHOWER NOW. DON'T WORRY—I'LL SNEAK A SHOT OF HER FACE ON MY CAMERA PHONE!"
THE DEADBEAT MOTHER OF THAT KID ACTOR, KAZUKI KINUKAWA! HER NAME'S ATSUKO.
SHE BLACKMAILED KAZUKI'S AGENCY, TELLING THEM THAT UNLESS THEY PAID HER 20 MILLION YEN, SHE'D REVEAL THAT KAZUKI'S BIOLOGICAL FATHER IS A WANTED MURDERER!
AT FIRST THE AGENCY DIDN'T BELIEVE HER, BUT SHE TOLD THEM ALL THESE DETAILS ABOUT KAZUKI AND THE TEMPLE WHERE HE WAS ABANDONED. THEY WIRED THE CASH TO HER BANK ACCOUNT.
THE WHOLE DEAL WAS DONE OVER EMAIL, SO THEY'VE NEVER SEEN HER OR EVEN HEARD HER VOICE.
KAMOSHITA WAS ABLE TO TRACK HER TO AN INN. HE WENT THERE TO GET SOME ANSWERS FROM HER.
THAT'S WHY HE WAS SAYING THOSE STRANGE THINGS TO THE HOSTES-SES.
SO IS SHE THE KILLER?
ER... WE DON'T KNOW YET...
INSPECTOR! I'VE ROUNDED UP ALL THE WOMEN ON STAFF WHO DON'T HAVE AN ALIBI FOR 11:48 P.M.!

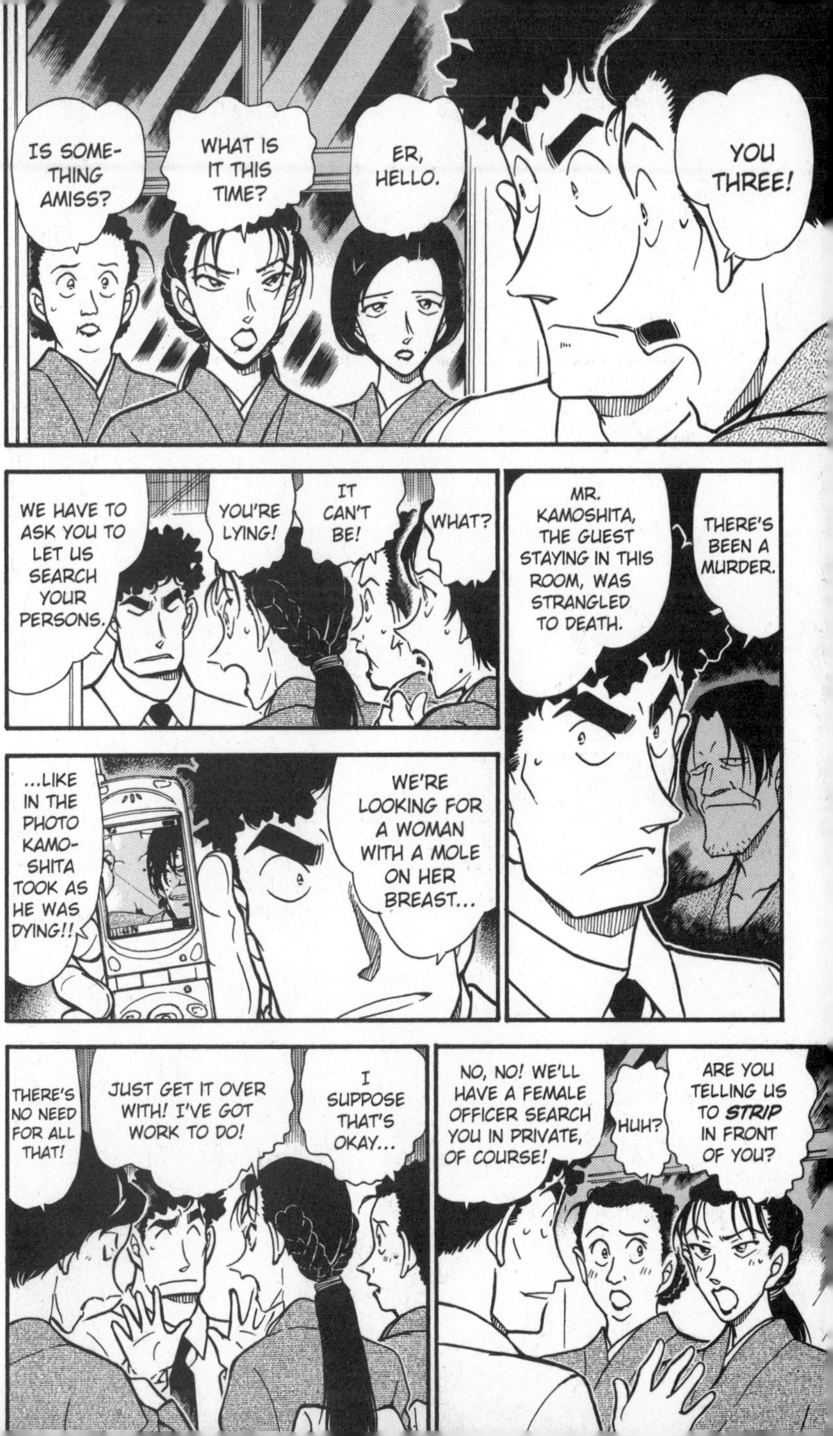
YOU THREE!
ER, HELLO.
WHAT IS IT THIS TIME?
IS SOME-THING AMISS?
THERE'S BEEN A MURDER.
MR. KAMOSHITA, THE GUEST STAYING IN THIS ROOM, WAS STRANGLED TO DEATH.
WHAT?
IT CAN'T BE!
YOU'RE LYING!
WE HAVE TO ASK YOU TO LET US SEARCH YOUR PERSONS.
WE'RE LOOKING FOR A WOMAN WITH A MOLE ON HER BREAST...
...LIKE IN THE PHOTO KAMO-SHITA TOOK AS HE WAS DYING!!
ARE YOU TELLING US TO *STRIP* IN FRONT OF YOU?
HUH?
NO, NO! WE'LL HAVE A FEMALE OFFICER SEARCH YOU IN PRIVATE, OF COURSE!
I SUPPOSE THAT'S OKAY...
JUST GET IT OVER WITH! I'VE GOT WORK TO DO!
THERE'S NO NEED FOR ALL THAT!

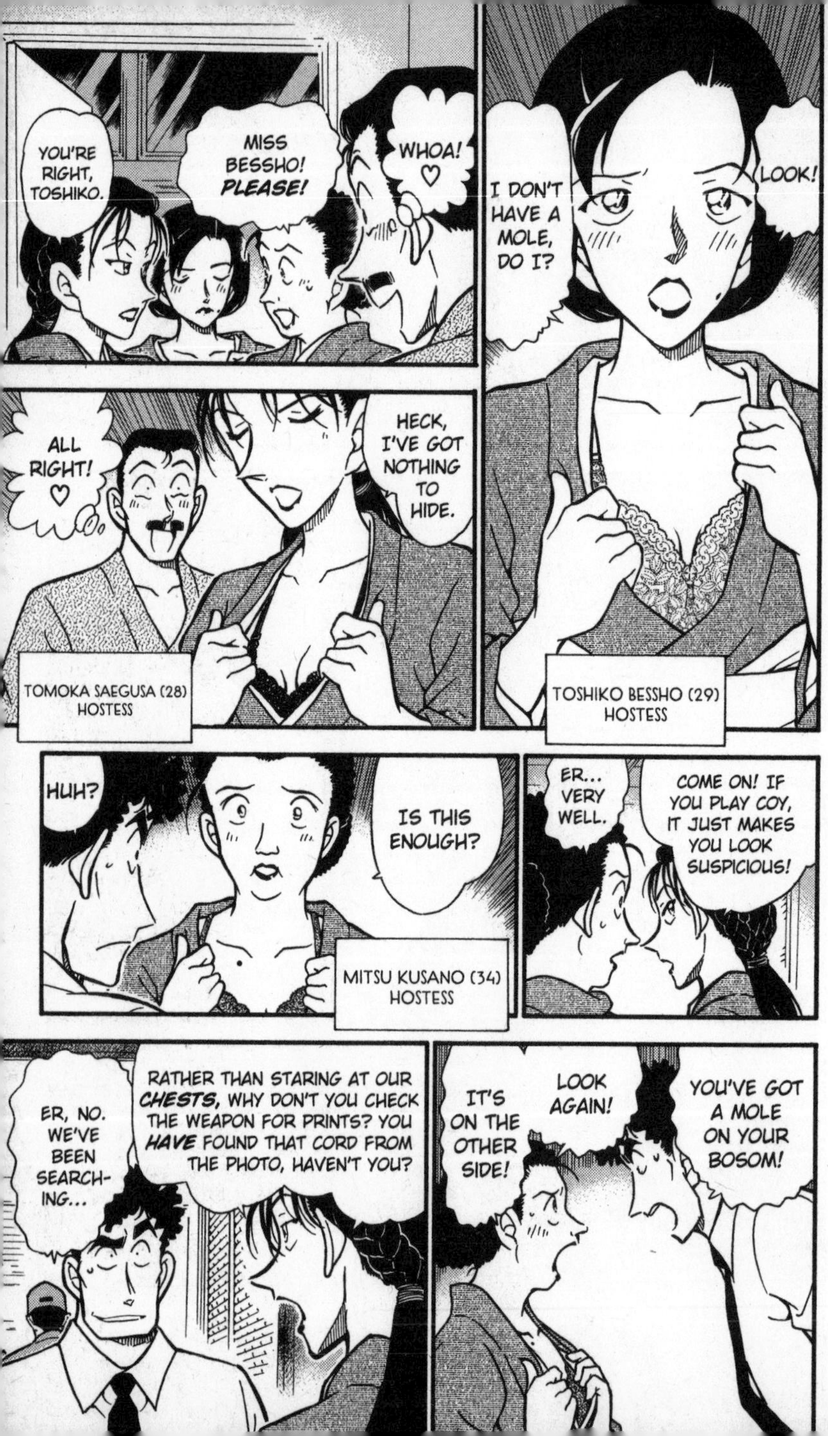
LOOK!
I DON'T HAVE A MOLE, DO I?
TOSHIKO BESSHO (29) HOSTESS
WHOA! ♡
MISS BESSHO! PLEASE!
YOU'RE RIGHT, TOSHIKO.
HECK, I'VE GOT NOTHING TO HIDE.
ALL RIGHT! ♡
TOMOKA SAEGUSA (28) HOSTESS
COME ON! IF YOU PLAY COY, IT JUST MAKES YOU LOOK SUSPICIOUS!
ER... VERY WELL.
IS THIS ENOUGH?
HUH?
MITSU KUSANO (34) HOSTESS
YOU'VE GOT A MOLE ON YOUR BOSOM!
LOOK AGAIN!
IT'S ON THE OTHER SIDE!
RATHER THAN STARING AT OUR CHESTS, WHY DON'T YOU CHECK THE WEAPON FOR PRINTS? YOU HAVE FOUND THAT CORD FROM THE PHOTO, HAVEN'T YOU?
ER, NO. WE'VE BEEN SEARCH-ING...

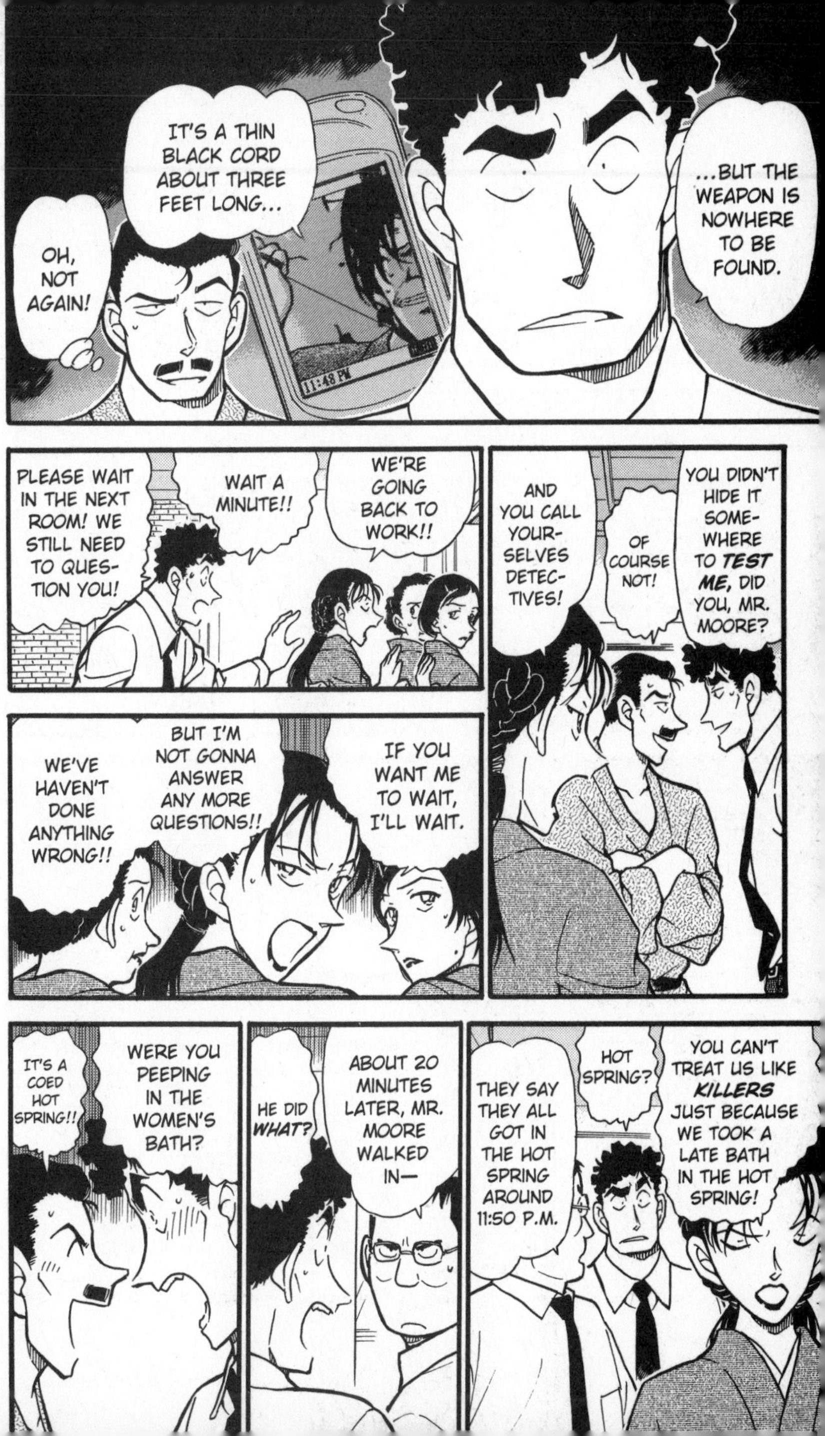
...BUT THE WEAPON IS NOWHERE TO BE FOUND.
IT'S A THIN BLACK CORD ABOUT THREE FEET LONG...
11:48 PM
OH, NOT AGAIN!
YOU DIDN'T HIDE IT SOME-WHERE TO ***TEST ME,*** DID YOU, MR. MOORE?
OF COURSE NOT!
AND YOU CALL YOUR-SELVES DETEC-TIVES!
WE'RE GOING BACK TO WORK!!
WAIT A MINUTE!!
PLEASE WAIT IN THE NEXT ROOM! WE STILL NEED TO QUES-TION YOU!
IF YOU WANT ME TO WAIT, I'LL WAIT.
BUT I'M NOT GONNA ANSWER ANY MORE QUESTIONS!!
WE'VE HAVEN'T DONE ANYTHING WRONG!!
YOU CAN'T TREAT US LIKE ***KILLERS*** JUST BECAUSE WE TOOK A LATE BATH IN THE HOT SPRING!
HOT SPRING?
THEY SAY THEY ALL GOT IN THE HOT SPRING AROUND 11:50 P.M.
ABOUT 20 MINUTES LATER, MR. MOORE WALKED IN—
HE DID ***WHAT?***
WERE YOU PEEPING IN THE WOMEN'S BATH?
IT'S A COED HOT SPRING!!

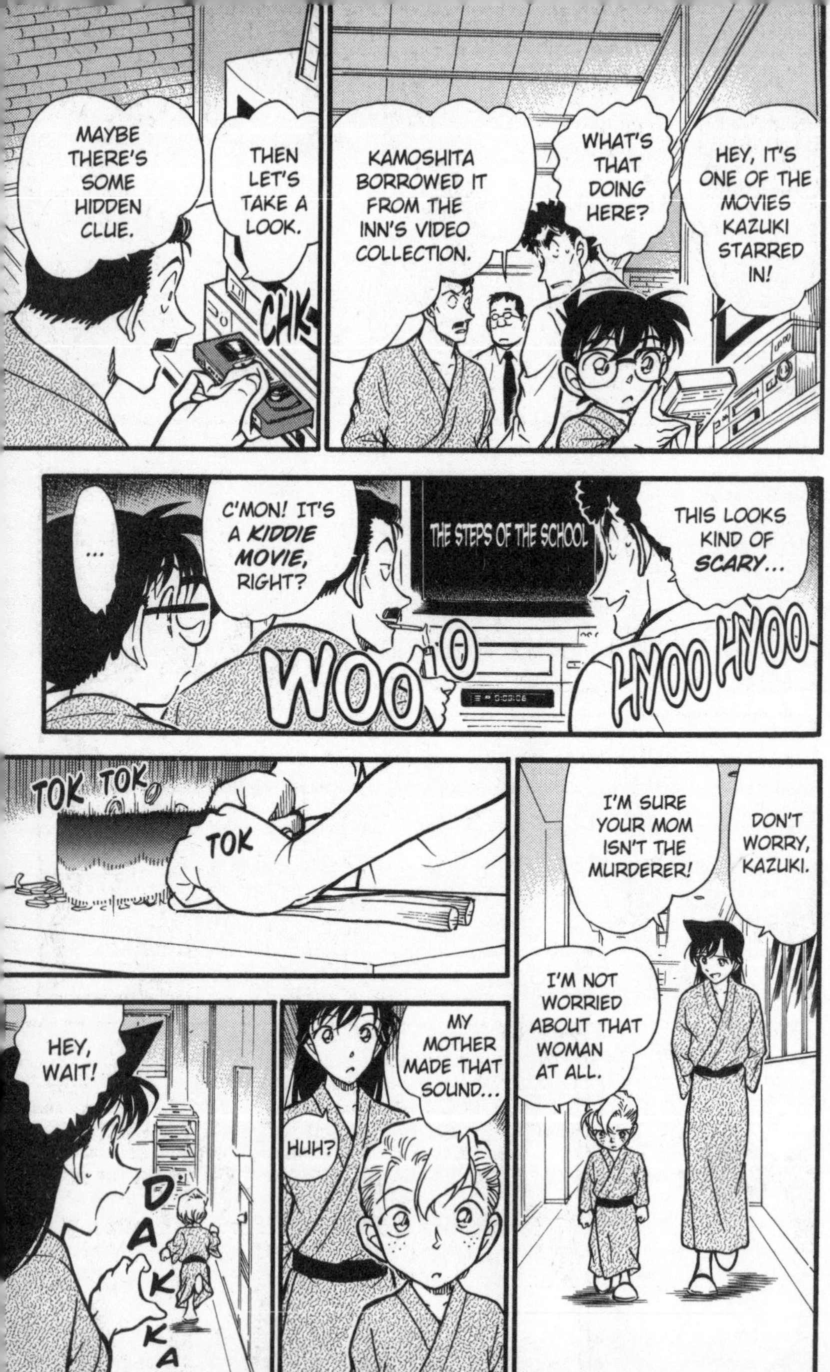
HEY, IT'S ONE OF THE MOVIES KAZUKI STARRED IN!
WHAT'S THAT DOING HERE?
KAMOSHITA BORROWED IT FROM THE INN'S VIDEO COLLECTION.
THEN LET'S TAKE A LOOK.
MAYBE THERE'S SOME HIDDEN CLUE.
CHK
THIS LOOKS KIND OF *SCARY*...
THE STEPS OF THE SCHOOL
C'MON! IT'S A *KIDDIE MOVIE*, RIGHT?
...
HYOO HYOO
WOOO
DON'T WORRY, KAZUKI.
I'M SURE YOUR MOM ISN'T THE MURDERER!
I'M NOT WORRIED ABOUT THAT WOMAN AT ALL.
TOK TOK
TOK
MY MOTHER MADE THAT SOUND...
HUH?
HEY, WAIT!
DAKKA

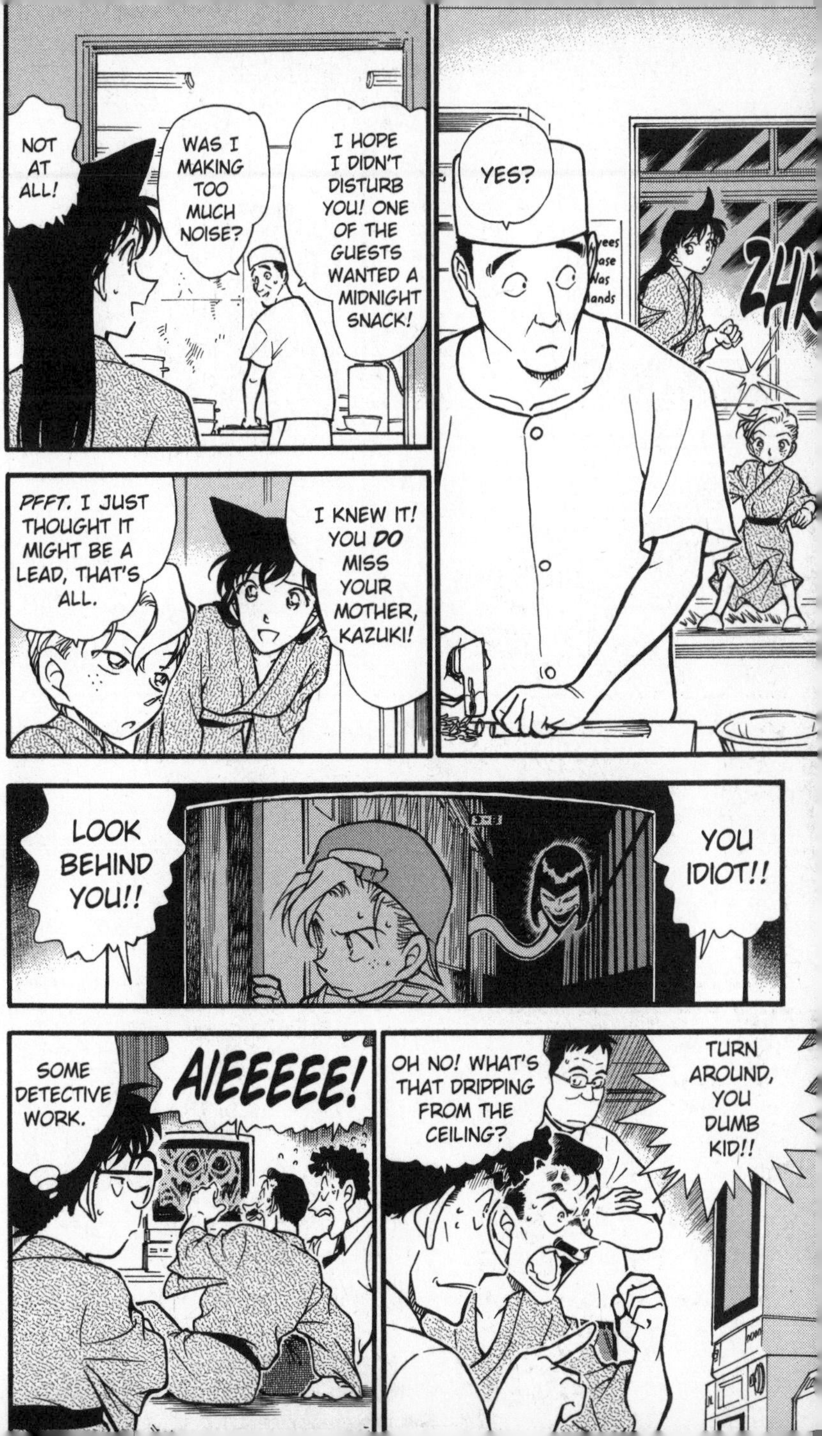
YES?
I HOPE I DIDN'T DISTURB YOU! ONE OF THE GUESTS WANTED A MIDNIGHT SNACK!
WAS I MAKING TOO MUCH NOISE?
NOT AT ALL!
I KNEW IT! YOU *DO* MISS YOUR MOTHER, KAZUKI!
PFFT. I JUST THOUGHT IT MIGHT BE A LEAD, THAT'S ALL.
YOU IDIOT!!
LOOK BEHIND YOU!!
TURN AROUND, YOU DUMB KID!!
OH NO! WHAT'S THAT DRIPPING FROM THE CEILING?
AIEEEEEE!
SOME DETECTIVE WORK.

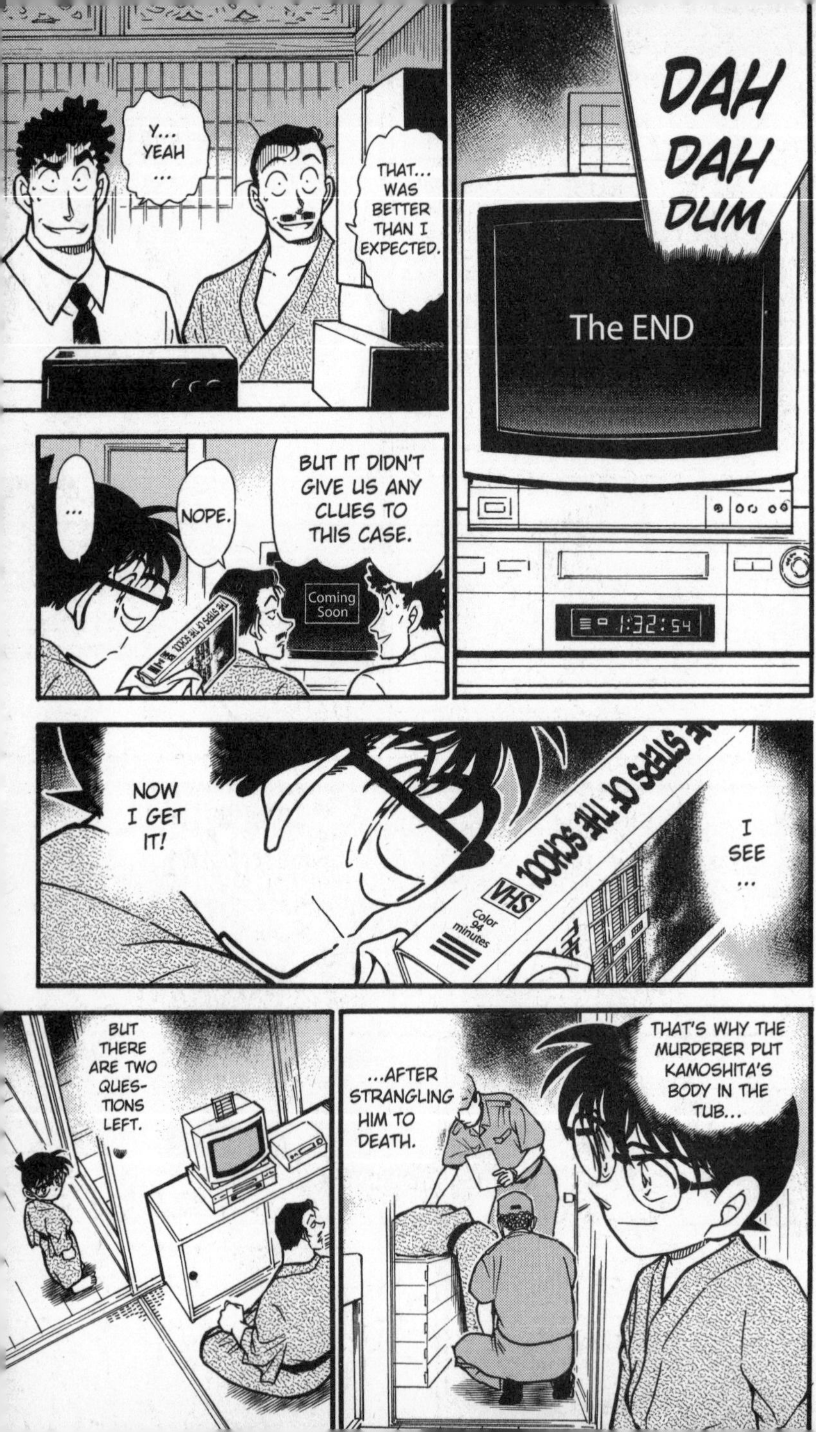
DAH DAH DUM
The END
1:32:54
THAT... WAS BETTER THAN I EXPECTED.
Y... YEAH ...
BUT IT DIDN'T GIVE US ANY CLUES TO THIS CASE.
NOPE.
...
Coming Soon
I SEE ...
THE STEPS OF THE SCHOOL
VHS
Color 94 minutes
NOW I GET IT!
THAT'S WHY THE MURDERER PUT KAMOSHITA'S BODY IN THE TUB...
...AFTER STRANGLING HIM TO DEATH.
BUT THERE ARE TWO QUES-TIONS LEFT.

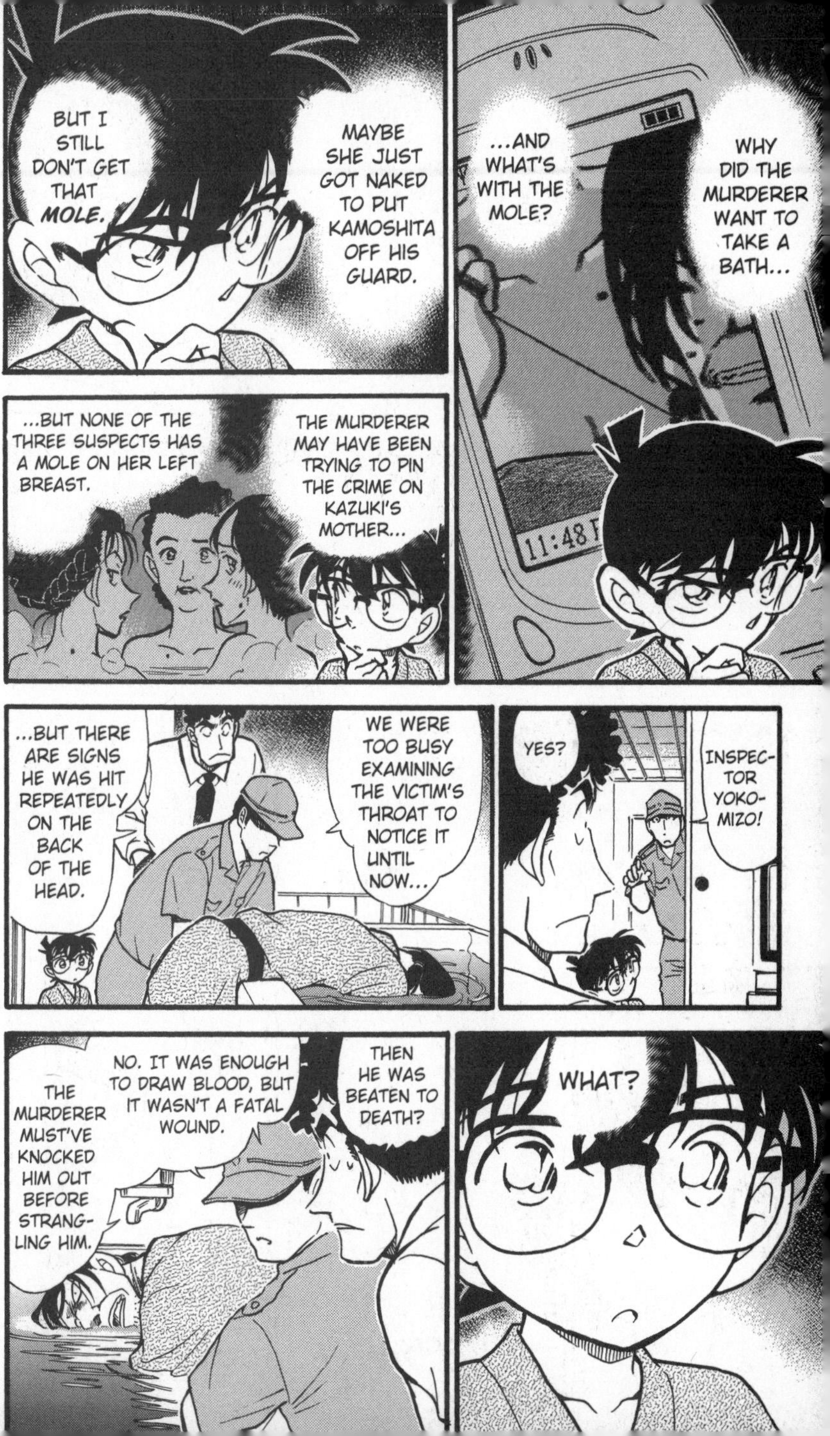
WHY DID THE MURDERER WANT TO TAKE A BATH...
...AND WHAT'S WITH THE MOLE?
MAYBE SHE JUST GOT NAKED TO PUT KAMOSHITA OFF HIS GUARD.
BUT I STILL DON'T GET THAT *MOLE.*
THE MURDERER MAY HAVE BEEN TRYING TO PIN THE CRIME ON KAZUKI'S MOTHER...
...BUT NONE OF THE THREE SUSPECTS HAS A MOLE ON HER LEFT BREAST.
INSPECTOR YOKOMIZO!
YES?
WE WERE TOO BUSY EXAMINING THE VICTIM'S THROAT TO NOTICE IT UNTIL NOW...
...BUT THERE ARE SIGNS HE WAS HIT REPEATEDLY ON THE BACK OF THE HEAD.
WHAT?
THEN HE WAS BEATEN TO DEATH?
NO. IT WAS ENOUGH TO DRAW BLOOD, BUT IT WASN'T A FATAL WOUND.
THE MURDERER MUST'VE KNOCKED HIM OUT BEFORE STRANG-LING HIM.

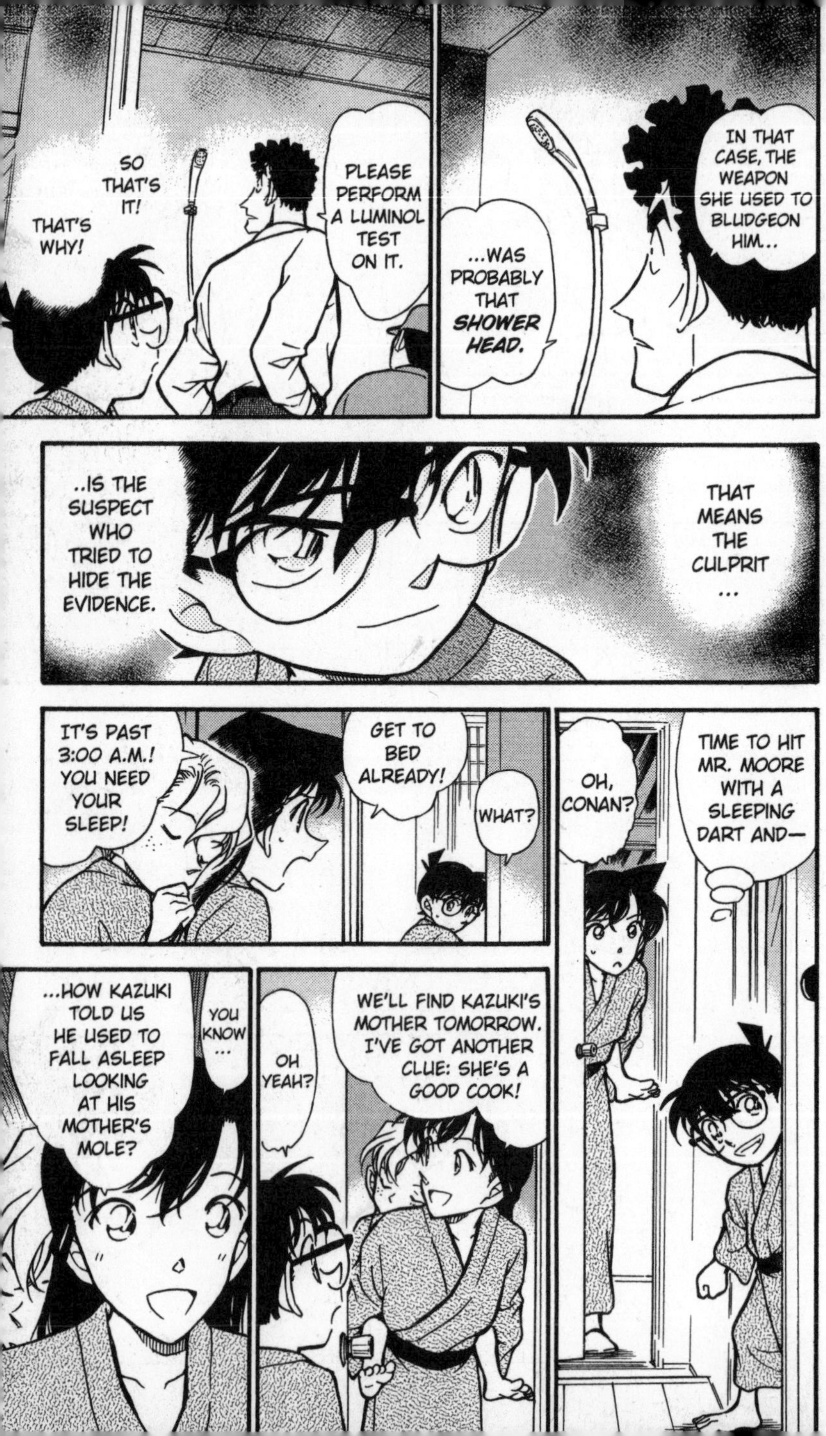
IN THAT CASE, THE WEAPON SHE USED TO BLUDGEON HIM...
...WAS PROBABLY THAT SHOWER HEAD.
PLEASE PERFORM A LUMINOL TEST ON IT.
SO THAT'S IT!
THAT'S WHY!
THAT MEANS THE CULPRIT ...
..IS THE SUSPECT WHO TRIED TO HIDE THE EVIDENCE.
TIME TO HIT MR. MOORE WITH A SLEEPING DART AND—
OH, CONAN?
IT'S PAST 3:00 A.M.! YOU NEED YOUR SLEEP!
GET TO BED ALREADY!
WHAT?
WE'LL FIND KAZUKI'S MOTHER TOMORROW. I'VE GOT ANOTHER CLUE: SHE'S A GOOD COOK!
OH YEAH?
YOU KNOW ...
...HOW KAZUKI TOLD US HE USED TO FALL ASLEEP LOOKING AT HIS MOTHER'S MOLE?

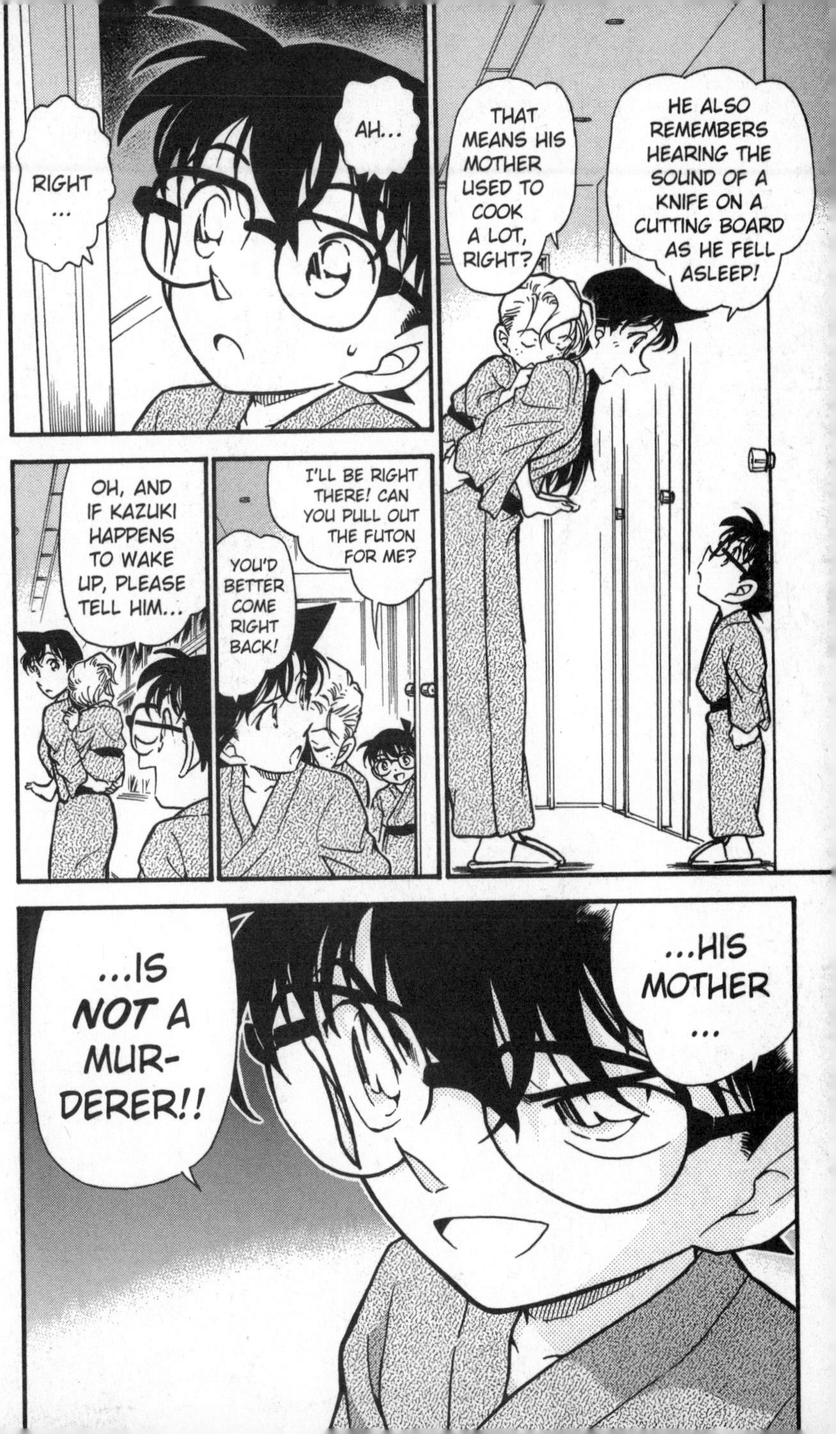
HE ALSO REMEMBERS HEARING THE SOUND OF A KNIFE ON A CUTTING BOARD AS HE FELL ASLEEP!
THAT MEANS HIS MOTHER USED TO COOK A LOT, RIGHT?
AH...
RIGHT ...
I'LL BE RIGHT THERE! CAN YOU PULL OUT THE FUTON FOR ME?
YOU'D BETTER COME RIGHT BACK!
OH, AND IF KAZUKI HAPPENS TO WAKE UP, PLEASE TELL HIM...
...HIS MOTHER ...
...IS *NOT* A MUR-DERER!!

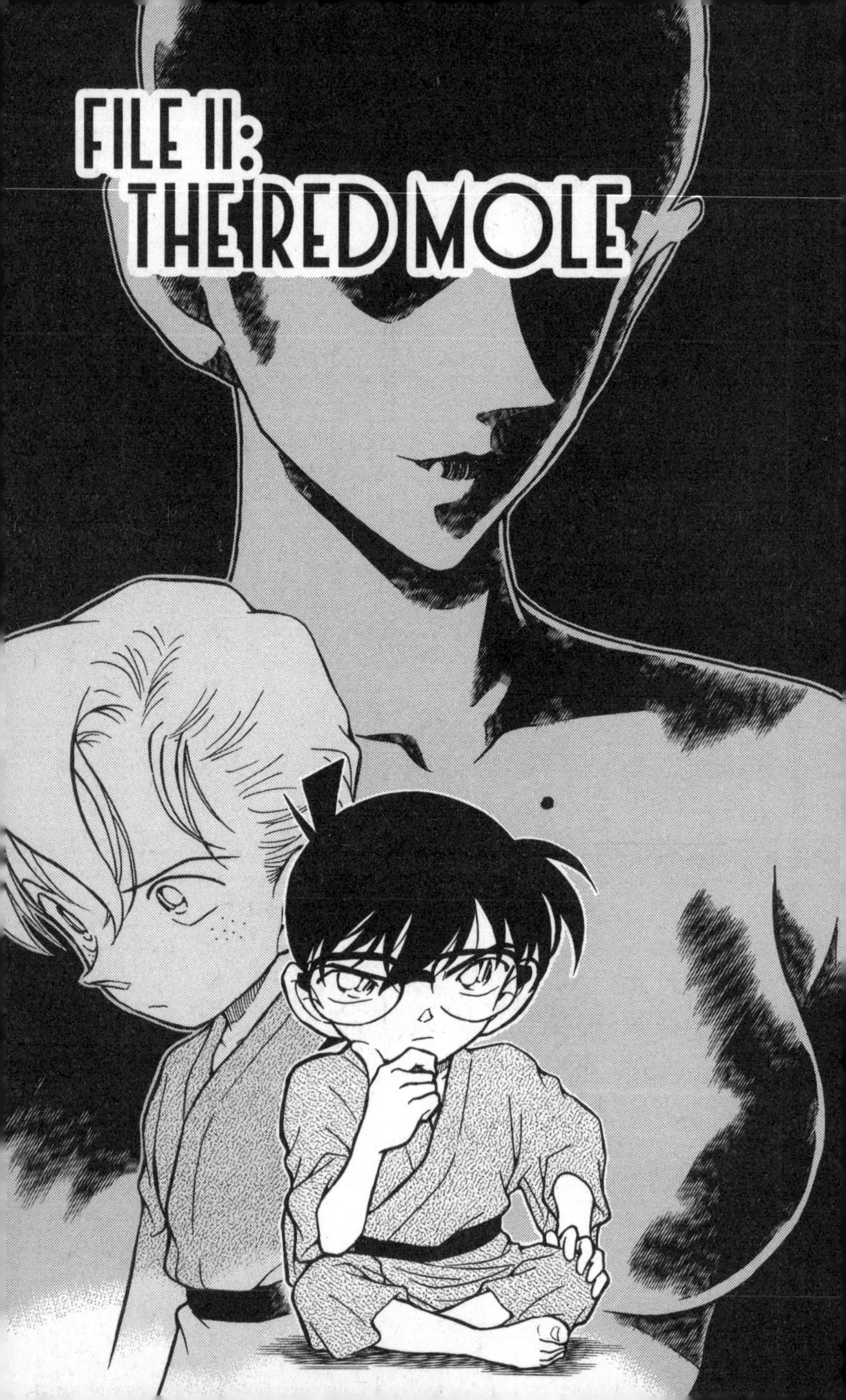
FILE 11:
THE RED MOLE

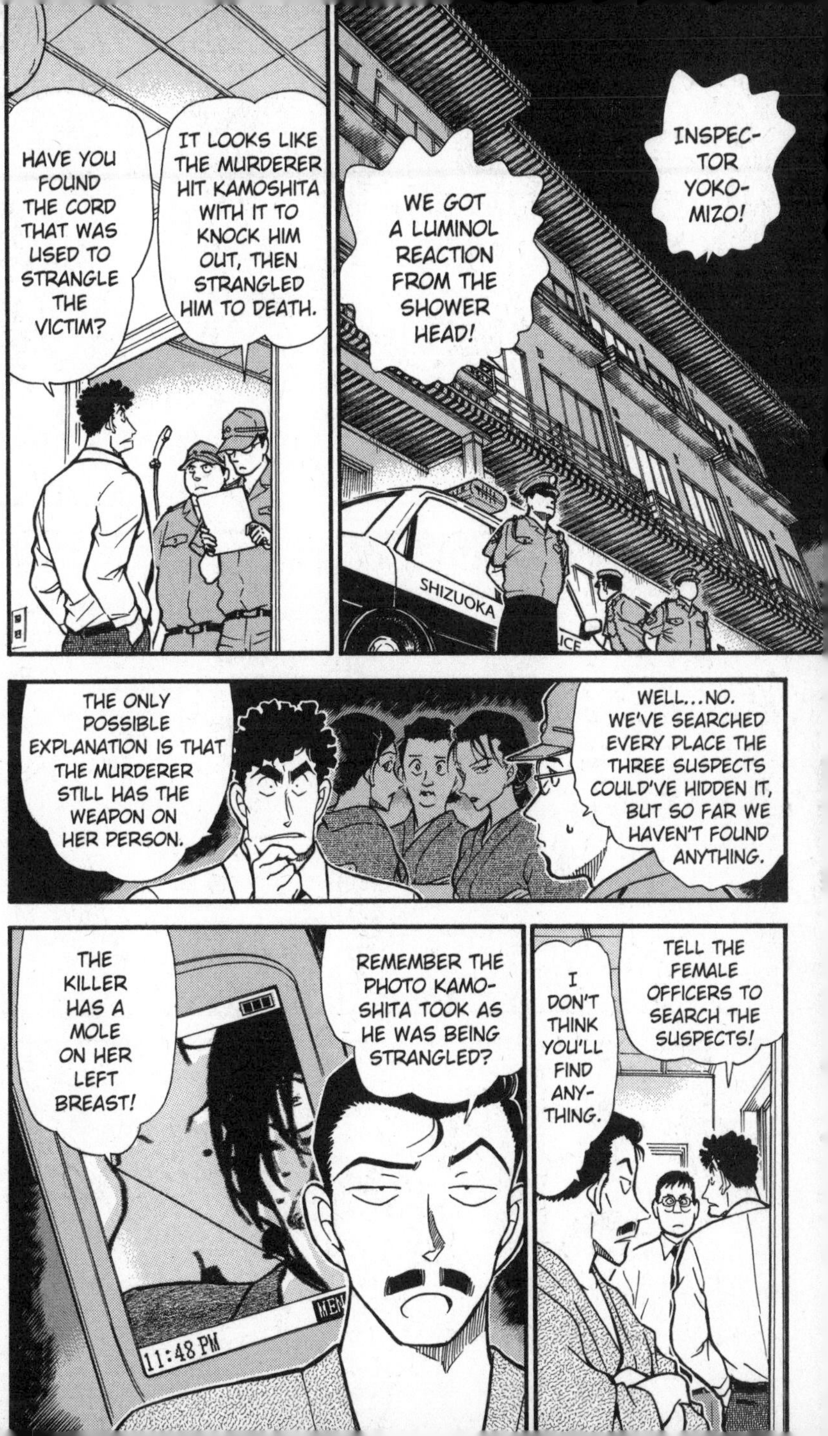
INSPECTOR YOKOMIZO!
WE GOT A LUMINOL REACTION FROM THE SHOWER HEAD!
SHIZUOKA
IT LOOKS LIKE THE MURDERER HIT KAMOSHITA WITH IT TO KNOCK HIM OUT, THEN STRANGLED HIM TO DEATH.
HAVE YOU FOUND THE CORD THAT WAS USED TO STRANGLE THE VICTIM?
WELL...NO. WE'VE SEARCHED EVERY PLACE THE THREE SUSPECTS COULD'VE HIDDEN IT, BUT SO FAR WE HAVEN'T FOUND ANYTHING.
THE ONLY POSSIBLE EXPLANATION IS THAT THE MURDERER STILL HAS THE WEAPON ON HER PERSON.
TELL THE FEMALE OFFICERS TO SEARCH THE SUSPECTS!
I DON'T THINK YOU'LL FIND ANYTHING.
REMEMBER THE PHOTO KAMOSHITA TOOK AS HE WAS BEING STRANGLED?
THE KILLER HAS A MOLE ON HER LEFT BREAST!
11:48 PM

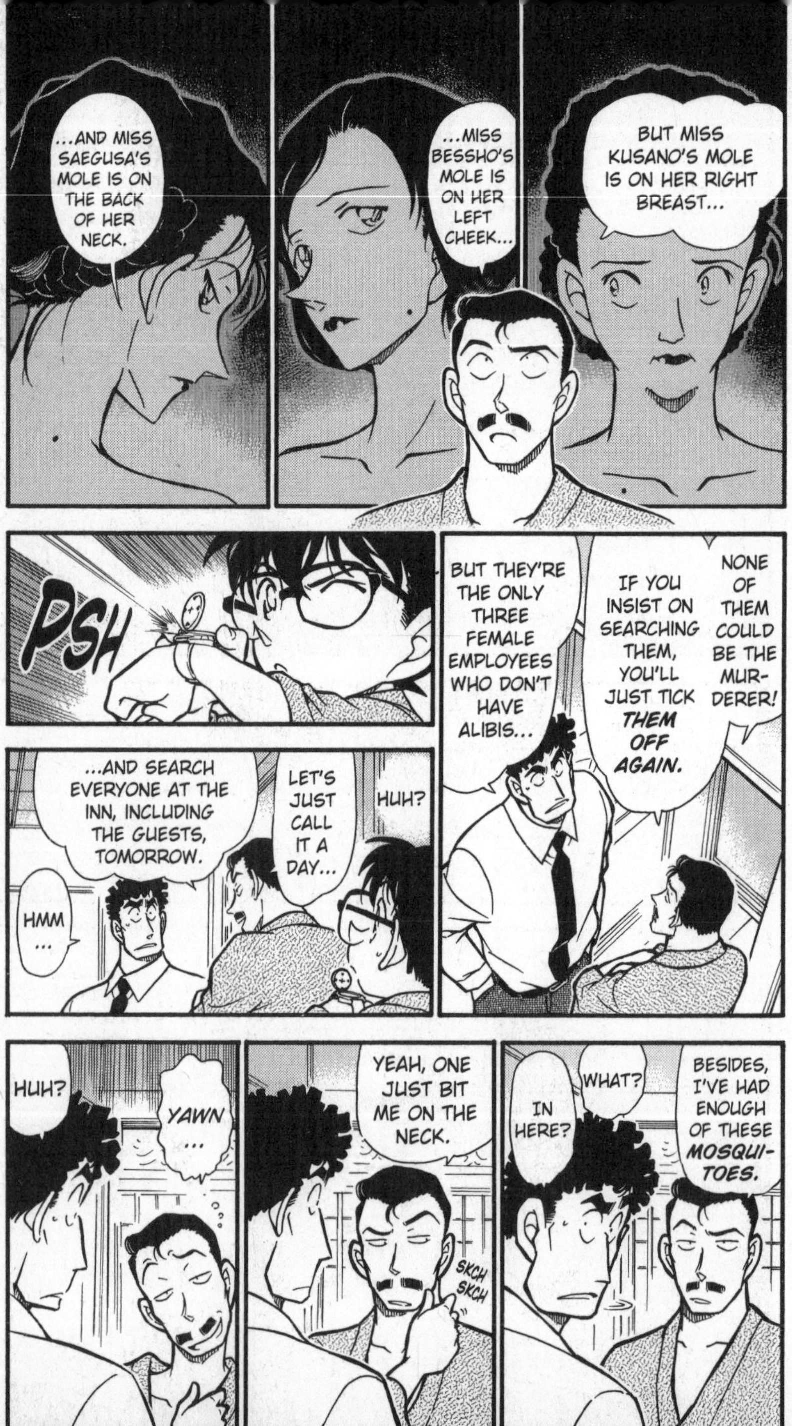
BUT MISS KUSANO'S MOLE IS ON HER RIGHT BREAST...
...MISS BESSHO'S MOLE IS ON HER LEFT CHEEK...
...AND MISS SAEGUSA'S MOLE IS ON THE BACK OF HER NECK.
NONE OF THEM COULD BE THE MUR-DERER!
IF YOU INSIST ON SEARCHING THEM, YOU'LL JUST TICK ***THEM OFF AGAIN.***
BUT THEY'RE THE ONLY THREE FEMALE EMPLOYEES WHO DON'T HAVE ALIBIS...
PSH
HUH?
LET'S JUST CALL IT A DAY...
...AND SEARCH EVERYONE AT THE INN, INCLUDING THE GUESTS, TOMORROW.
HMM...
BESIDES, I'VE HAD ENOUGH OF THESE ***MOSQUI-TOES.***
WHAT?
IN HERE?
YEAH, ONE JUST BIT ME ON THE NECK.
SKCH SKCH
YAWN...
HUH?

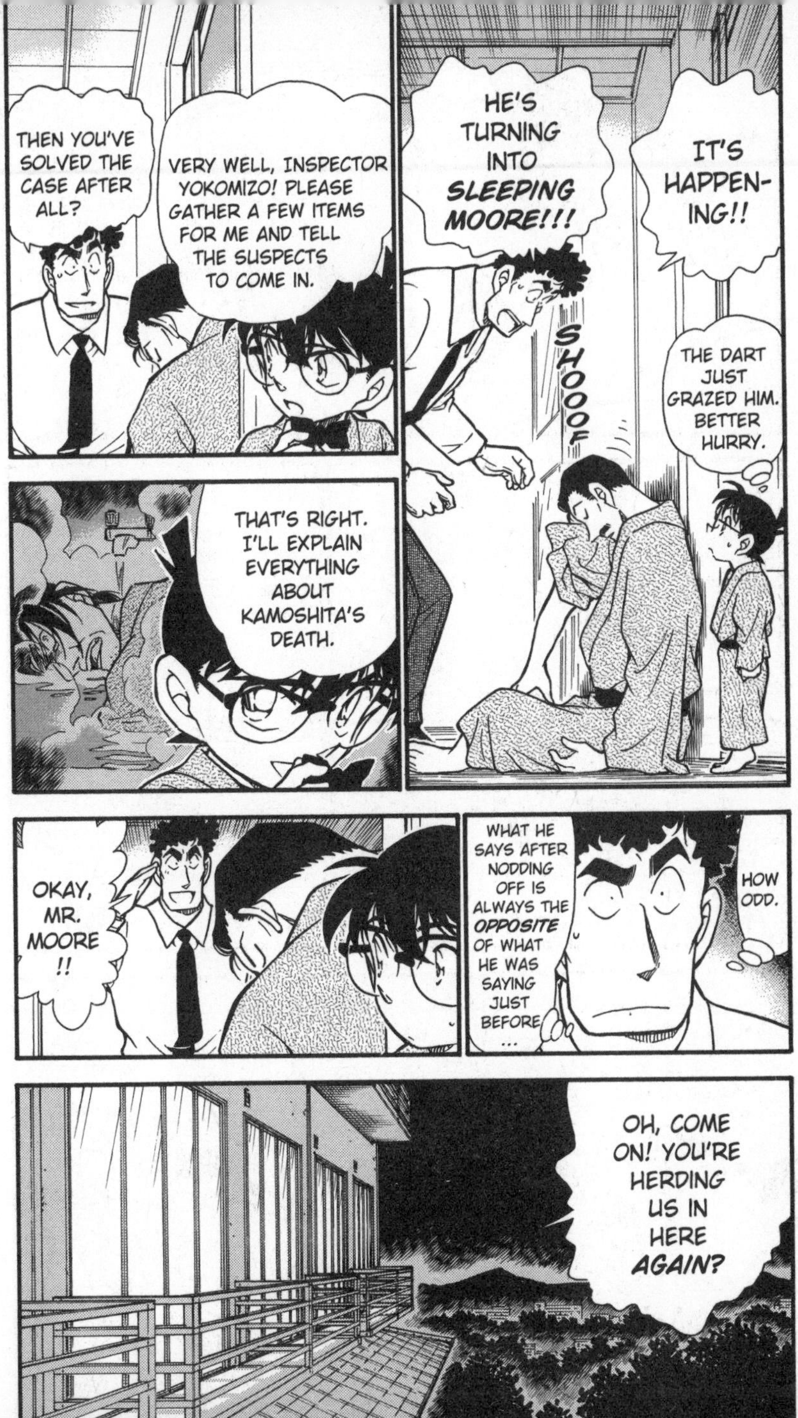
IT'S HAPPEN-ING!!
HE'S TURNING INTO SLEEPING MOORE!!!
SHOOOOF
THE DART JUST GRAZED HIM. BETTER HURRY.
THEN YOU'VE SOLVED THE CASE AFTER ALL?
VERY WELL, INSPECTOR YOKOMIZO! PLEASE GATHER A FEW ITEMS FOR ME AND TELL THE SUSPECTS TO COME IN.
THAT'S RIGHT. I'LL EXPLAIN EVERYTHING ABOUT KAMOSHITA'S DEATH.
WHAT HE SAYS AFTER NODDING OFF IS ALWAYS THE OPPOSITE OF WHAT HE WAS SAYING JUST BEFORE ...
HOW ODD.
OKAY, MR. MOORE !!
OH, COME ON! YOU'RE HERDING US IN HERE AGAIN?

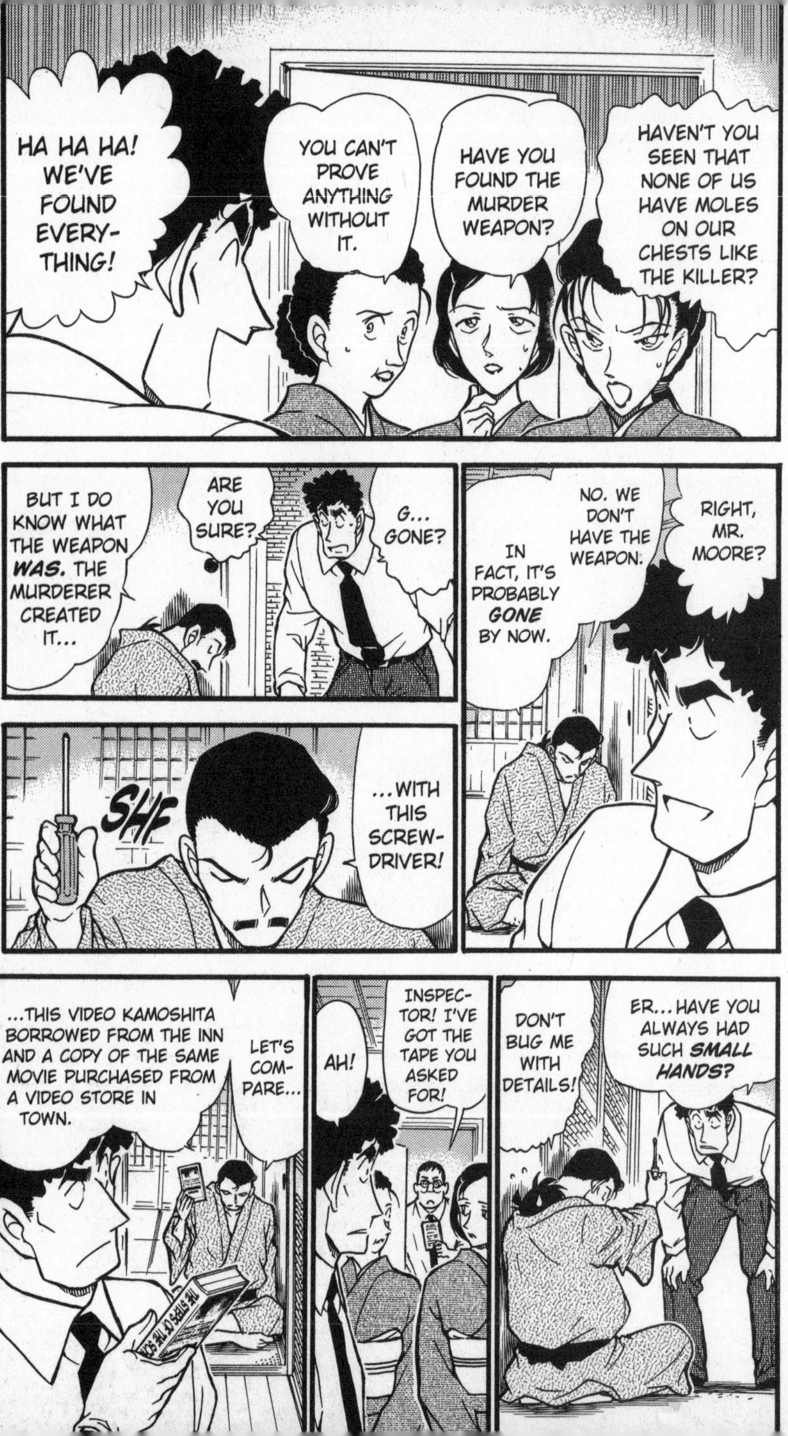
HAVEN'T YOU SEEN THAT NONE OF US HAVE MOLES ON OUR CHESTS LIKE THE KILLER?
HAVE YOU FOUND THE MURDER WEAPON?
YOU CAN'T PROVE ANYTHING WITHOUT IT.
HA HA HA! WE'VE FOUND EVERY-THING!
RIGHT, MR. MOORE?
NO. WE DON'T HAVE THE WEAPON.
IN FACT, IT'S PROBABLY **GONE** BY NOW.
G... GONE?
ARE YOU SURE?
BUT I DO KNOW WHAT THE WEAPON ***WAS.*** THE MURDERER CREATED IT...
...WITH THIS SCREW-DRIVER!
SHF
ER... HAVE YOU ALWAYS HAD SUCH ***SMALL HANDS?***
DON'T BUG ME WITH DETAILS!
INSPECTOR! I'VE GOT THE TAPE YOU ASKED FOR!
AH!
LET'S COM-PARE...
...THIS VIDEO KAMOSHITA BORROWED FROM THE INN AND A COPY OF THE SAME MOVIE PURCHASED FROM A VIDEO STORE IN TOWN.

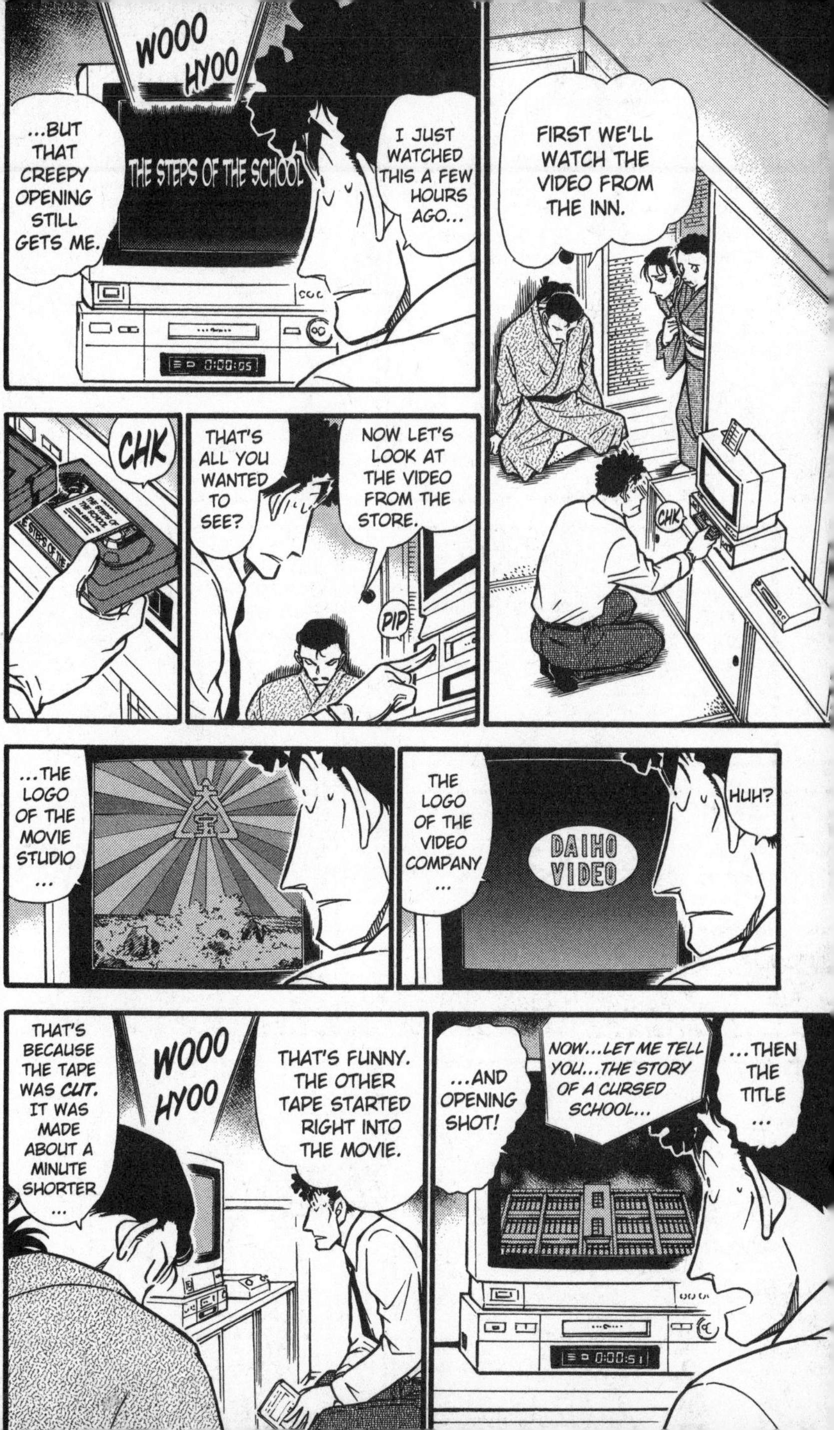
FIRST WE'LL WATCH THE VIDEO FROM THE INN.
CHK
WOOO HYOO
THE STEPS OF THE SCHOOL
I JUST WATCHED THIS A FEW HOURS AGO...
...BUT THAT CREEPY OPENING STILL GETS ME.
0:00:05
NOW LET'S LOOK AT THE VIDEO FROM THE STORE.
THAT'S ALL YOU WANTED TO SEE?
PIP
CHK
HUH?
THE LOGO OF THE VIDEO COMPANY...
DAIHO VIDEO
...THE LOGO OF THE MOVIE STUDIO...
...THEN THE TITLE...
NOW...LET ME TELL YOU...THE STORY OF A CURSED SCHOOL...
...AND OPENING SHOT!
0:00:51
THAT'S FUNNY. THE OTHER TAPE STARTED RIGHT INTO THE MOVIE.
WOOO HYOO
THAT'S BECAUSE THE TAPE WAS *CUT*. IT WAS MADE ABOUT A MINUTE SHORTER...

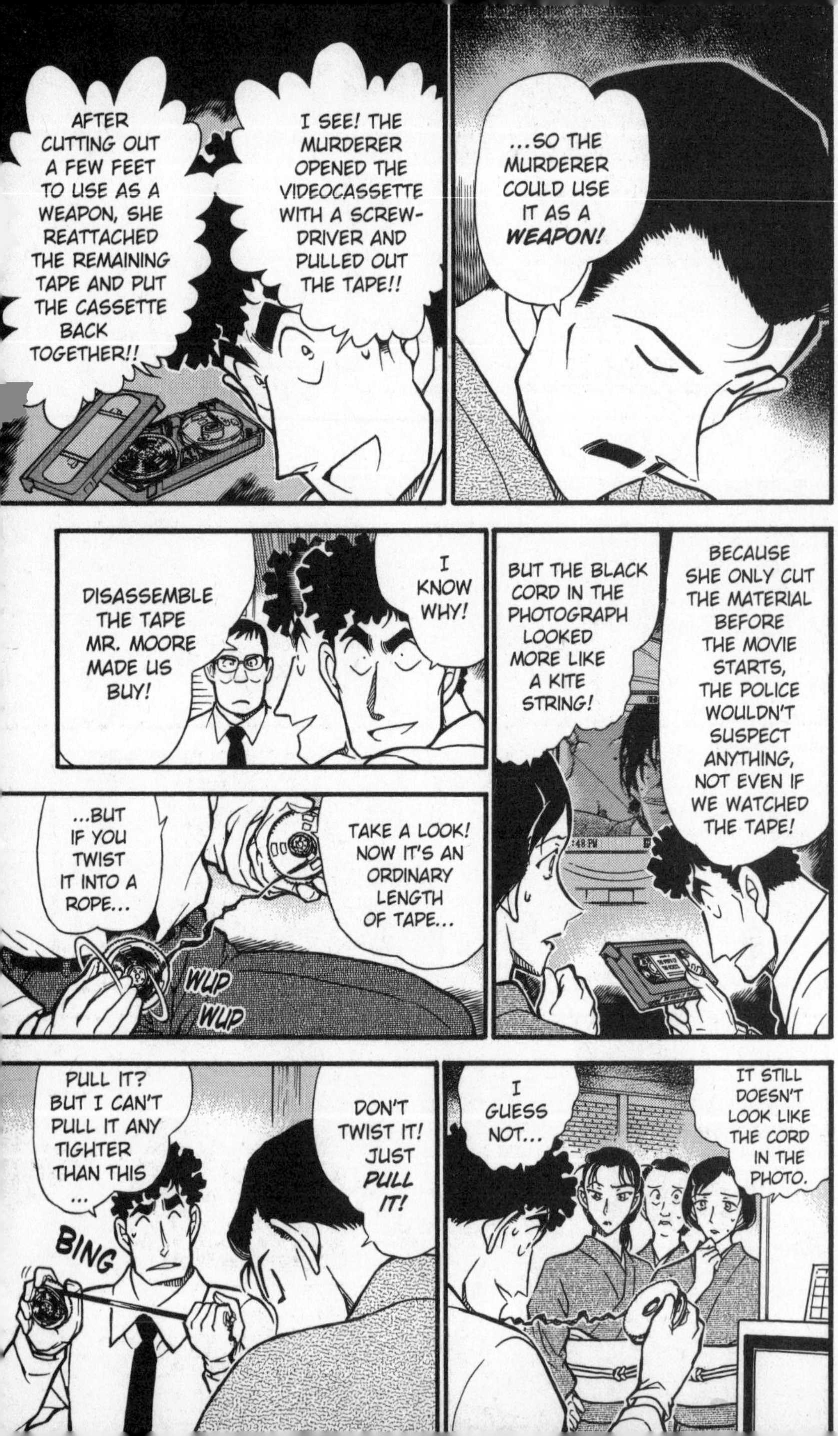
...SO THE MURDERER COULD USE IT AS A WEAPON!
I SEE! THE MURDERER OPENED THE VIDEOCASSETTE WITH A SCREW-DRIVER AND PULLED OUT THE TAPE!!
AFTER CUTTING OUT A FEW FEET TO USE AS A WEAPON, SHE REATTACHED THE REMAINING TAPE AND PUT THE CASSETTE BACK TOGETHER!!
BECAUSE SHE ONLY CUT THE MATERIAL BEFORE THE MOVIE STARTS, THE POLICE WOULDN'T SUSPECT ANYTHING, NOT EVEN IF WE WATCHED THE TAPE!
BUT THE BLACK CORD IN THE PHOTOGRAPH LOOKED MORE LIKE A KITE STRING!
I KNOW WHY!
DISASSEMBLE THE TAPE MR. MOORE MADE US BUY!
TAKE A LOOK! NOW IT'S AN ORDINARY LENGTH OF TAPE...
...BUT IF YOU TWIST IT INTO A ROPE...
WUP WUP
IT STILL DOESN'T LOOK LIKE THE CORD IN THE PHOTO.
I GUESS NOT...
DON'T TWIST IT! JUST PULL IT!
PULL IT? BUT I CAN'T PULL IT ANY TIGHTER THAN THIS ...
BING

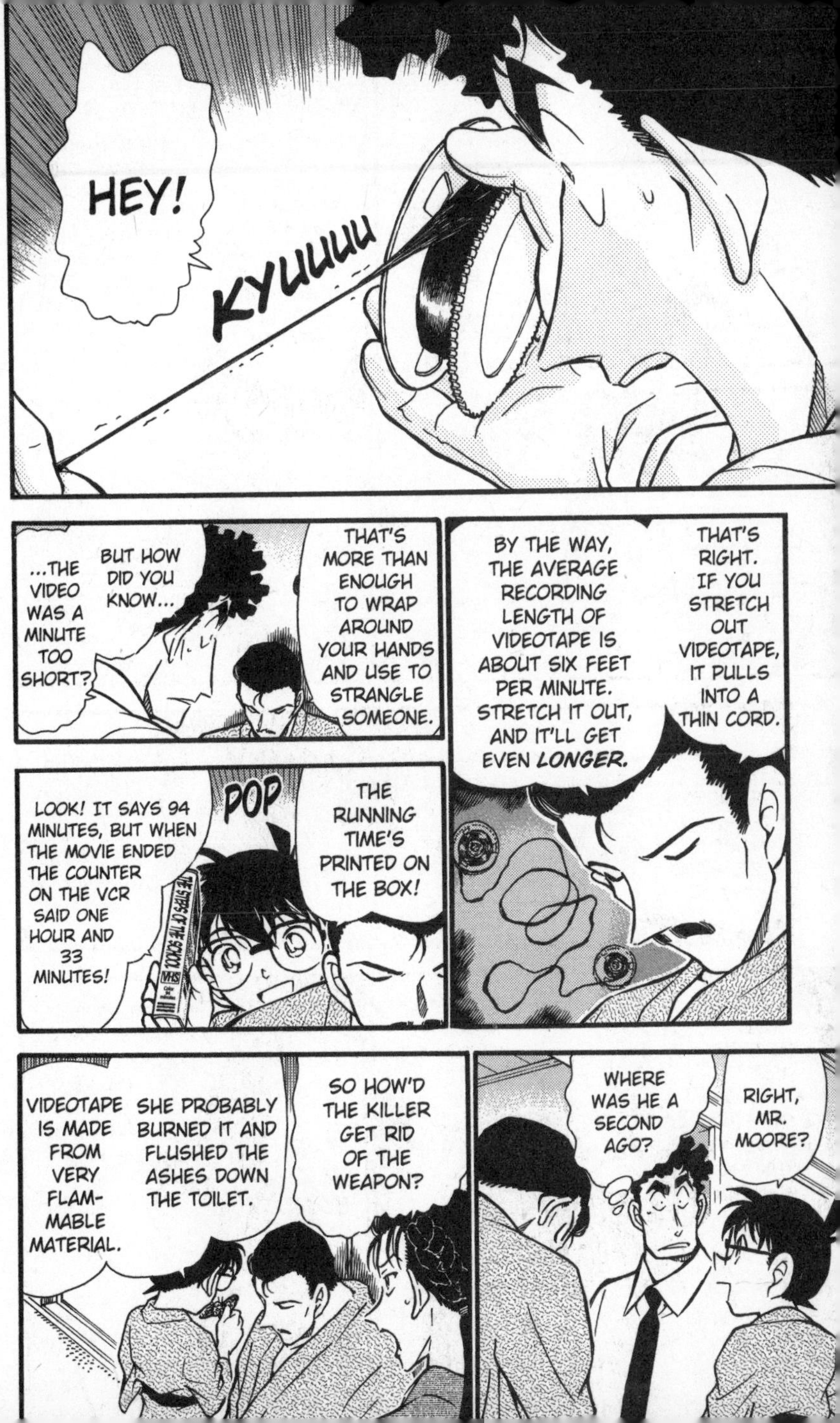
KYUUUU
HEY!
THAT'S RIGHT. IF YOU STRETCH OUT VIDEOTAPE, IT PULLS INTO A THIN CORD.
BY THE WAY, THE AVERAGE RECORDING LENGTH OF VIDEOTAPE IS ABOUT SIX FEET PER MINUTE. STRETCH IT OUT, AND IT'LL GET EVEN ***LONGER.***
THAT'S MORE THAN ENOUGH TO WRAP AROUND YOUR HANDS AND USE TO STRANGLE SOMEONE.
BUT HOW DID YOU KNOW...
...THE VIDEO WAS A MINUTE TOO SHORT?
THE RUNNING TIME'S PRINTED ON THE BOX!
POP
LOOK! IT SAYS 94 MINUTES, BUT WHEN THE MOVIE ENDED THE COUNTER ON THE VCR SAID ONE HOUR AND 33 MINUTES!
THE STEPS OF THE SCHOOL
VHS
RIGHT, MR. MOORE?
WHERE WAS HE A SECOND AGO?
SO HOW'D THE KILLER GET RID OF THE WEAPON?
SHE PROBABLY BURNED IT AND FLUSHED THE ASHES DOWN THE TOILET.
VIDEOTAPE IS MADE FROM VERY FLAM-MABLE MATERIAL.

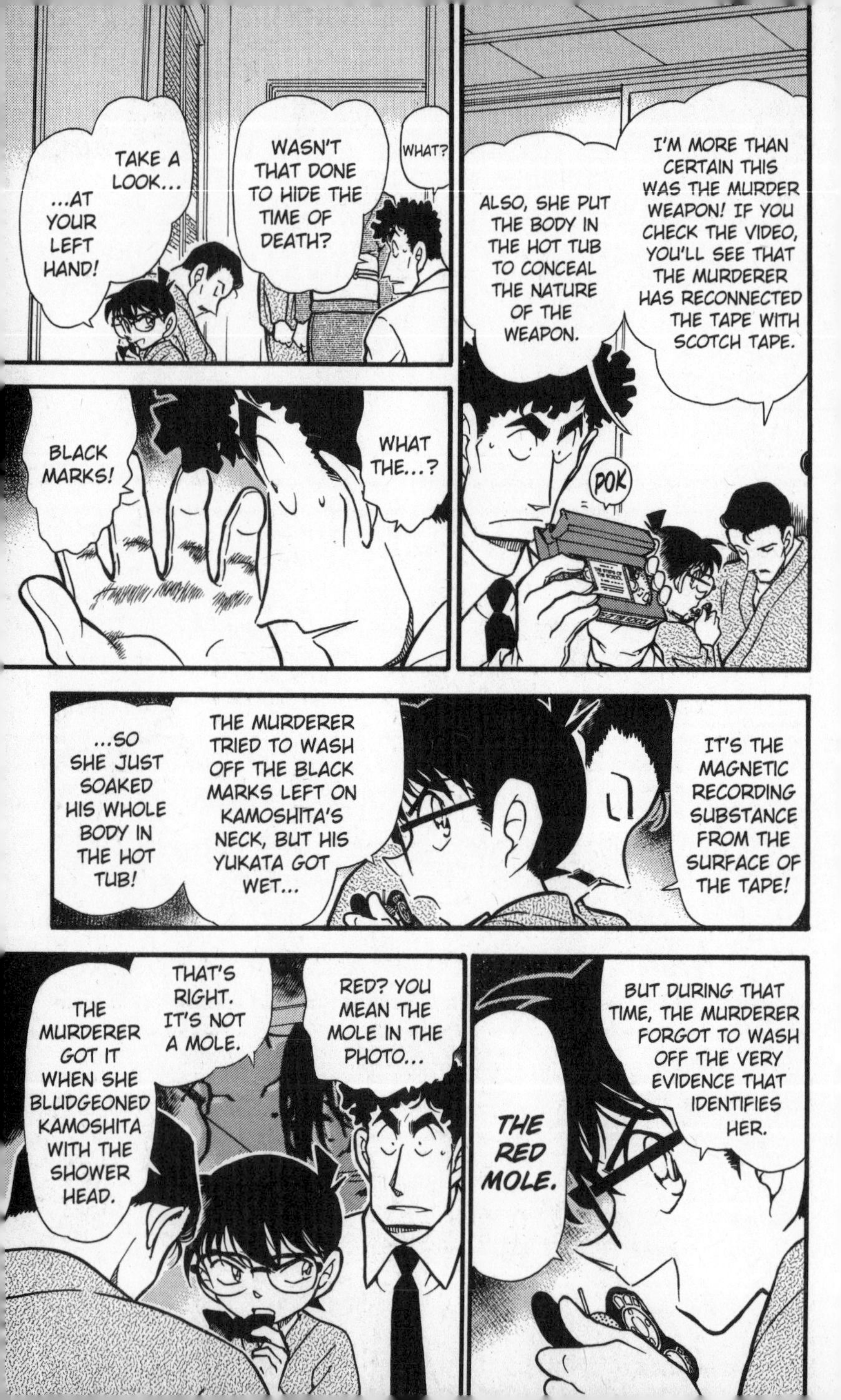
I'M MORE THAN CERTAIN THIS WAS THE MURDER WEAPON! IF YOU CHECK THE VIDEO, YOU'LL SEE THAT THE MURDERER HAS RECONNECTED THE TAPE WITH SCOTCH TAPE.
ALSO, SHE PUT THE BODY IN THE HOT TUB TO CONCEAL THE NATURE OF THE WEAPON.
POK
WHAT?
WASN'T THAT DONE TO HIDE THE TIME OF DEATH?
TAKE A LOOK...
...AT YOUR LEFT HAND!
WHAT THE...?
BLACK MARKS!
IT'S THE MAGNETIC RECORDING SUBSTANCE FROM THE SURFACE OF THE TAPE!
THE MURDERER TRIED TO WASH OFF THE BLACK MARKS LEFT ON KAMOSHITA'S NECK, BUT HIS YUKATA GOT WET...
...SO SHE JUST SOAKED HIS WHOLE BODY IN THE HOT TUB!
BUT DURING THAT TIME, THE MURDERER FORGOT TO WASH OFF THE VERY EVIDENCE THAT IDENTIFIES HER.
THE RED MOLE.
RED? YOU MEAN THE MOLE IN THE PHOTO...
THAT'S RIGHT. IT'S NOT A MOLE.
THE MURDERER GOT IT WHEN SHE BLUDGEONED KAMOSHITA WITH THE SHOWER HEAD.

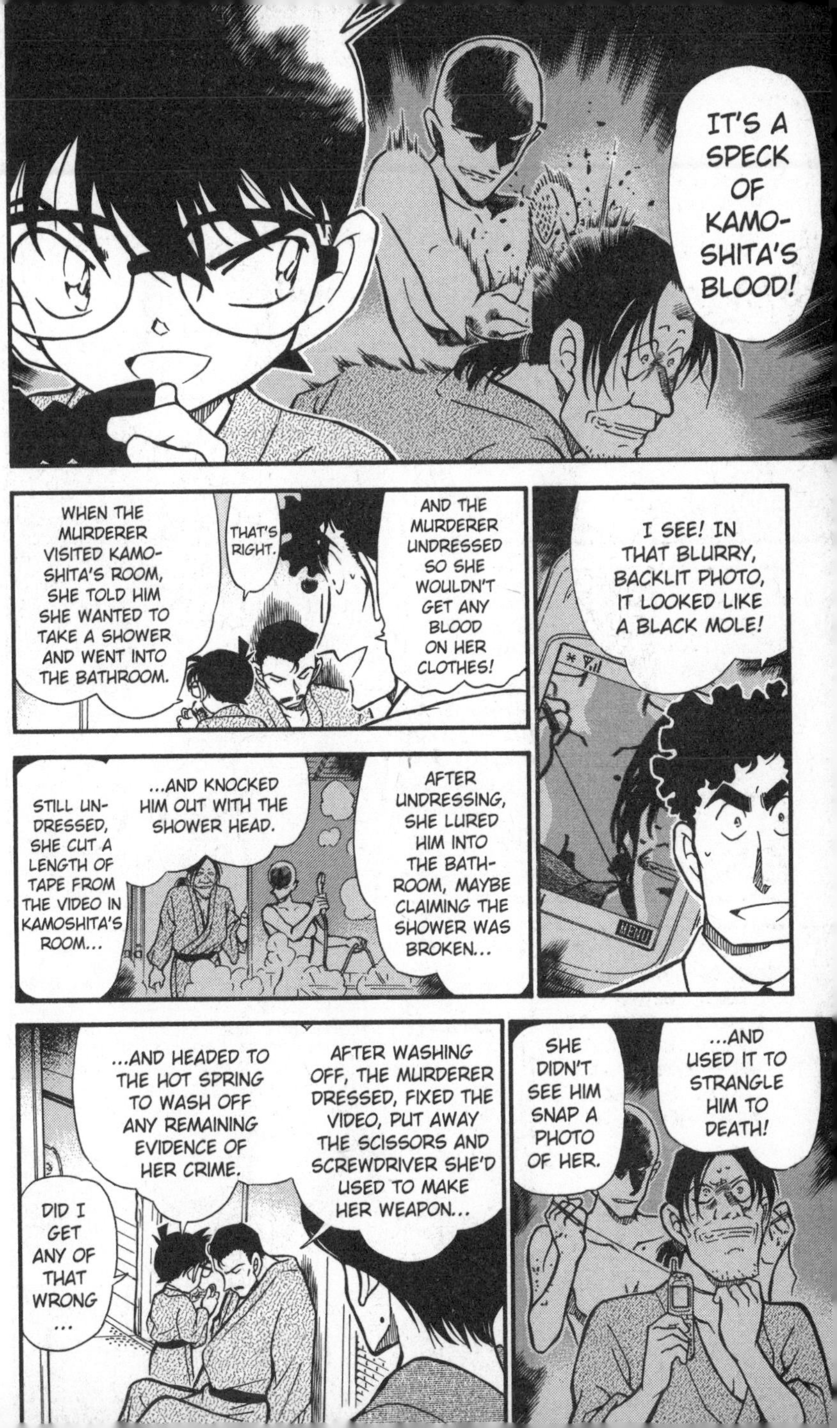

IT'S A SPECK OF KAMO-SHITA'S BLOOD!
I SEE! IN THAT BLURRY, BACKLIT PHOTO, IT LOOKED LIKE A BLACK MOLE!
AND THE MURDERER UNDRESSED SO SHE WOULDN'T GET ANY BLOOD ON HER CLOTHES!
THAT'S RIGHT.
WHEN THE MURDERER VISITED KAMO-SHITA'S ROOM, SHE TOLD HIM SHE WANTED TO TAKE A SHOWER AND WENT INTO THE BATHROOM.
AFTER UNDRESSING, SHE LURED HIM INTO THE BATH-ROOM, MAYBE CLAIMING THE SHOWER WAS BROKEN...
...AND KNOCKED HIM OUT WITH THE SHOWER HEAD.
STILL UN-DRESSED, SHE CUT A LENGTH OF TAPE FROM THE VIDEO IN KAMOSHITA'S ROOM...
...AND USED IT TO STRANGLE HIM TO DEATH!
SHE DIDN'T SEE HIM SNAP A PHOTO OF HER.
AFTER WASHING OFF, THE MURDERER DRESSED, FIXED THE VIDEO, PUT AWAY THE SCISSORS AND SCREWDRIVER SHE'D USED TO MAKE HER WEAPON...
...AND HEADED TO THE HOT SPRING TO WASH OFF ANY REMAINING EVIDENCE OF HER CRIME.
DID I GET ANY OF THAT WRONG ...

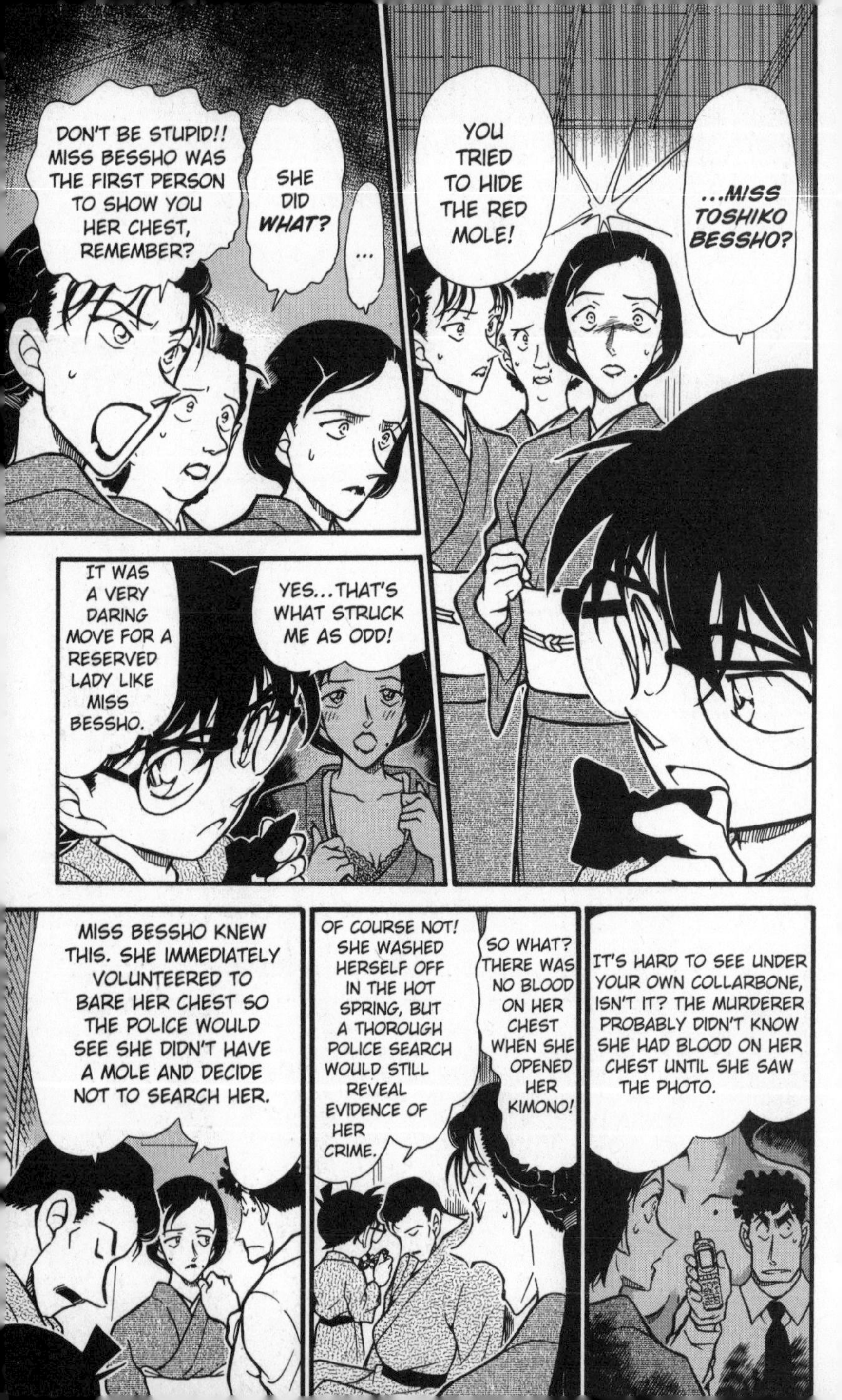
...MISS TOSHIKO BESSHO?
YOU TRIED TO HIDE THE RED MOLE!
SHE DID WHAT?
...
DON'T BE STUPID!! MISS BESSHO WAS THE FIRST PERSON TO SHOW YOU HER CHEST, REMEMBER?
YES...THAT'S WHAT STRUCK ME AS ODD!
IT WAS A VERY DARING MOVE FOR A RESERVED LADY LIKE MISS BESSHO.
IT'S HARD TO SEE UNDER YOUR OWN COLLARBONE, ISN'T IT? THE MURDERER PROBABLY DIDN'T KNOW SHE HAD BLOOD ON HER CHEST UNTIL SHE SAW THE PHOTO.
SO WHAT? THERE WAS NO BLOOD ON HER CHEST WHEN SHE OPENED HER KIMONO!
OF COURSE NOT! SHE WASHED HERSELF OFF IN THE HOT SPRING, BUT A THOROUGH POLICE SEARCH WOULD STILL REVEAL EVIDENCE OF HER CRIME.
MISS BESSHO KNEW THIS. SHE IMMEDIATELY VOLUNTEERED TO BARE HER CHEST SO THE POLICE WOULD SEE SHE DIDN'T HAVE A MOLE AND DECIDE NOT TO SEARCH HER.

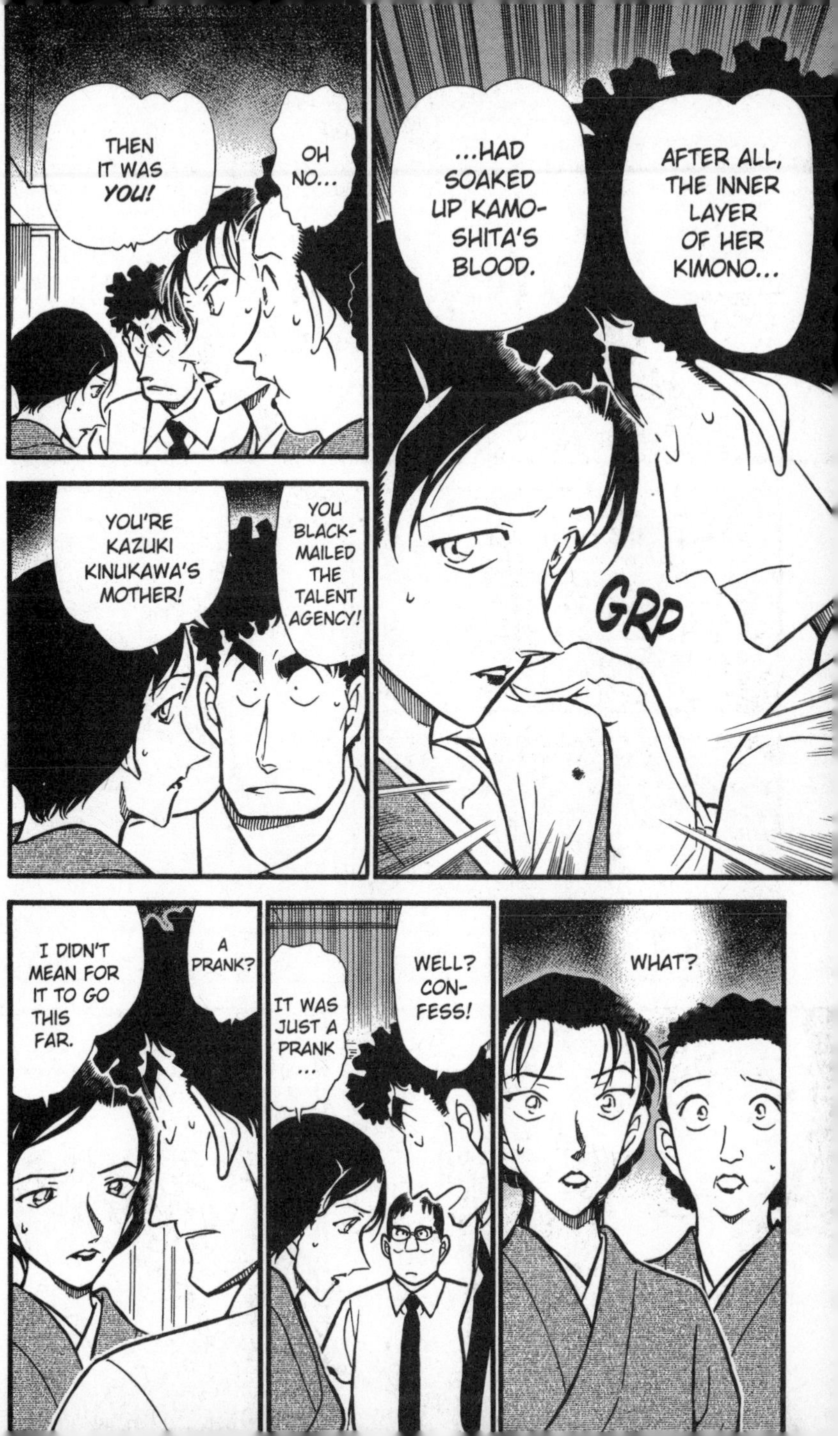
AFTER ALL, THE INNER LAYER OF HER KIMONO...
...HAD SOAKED UP KAMO-SHITA'S BLOOD.
GRP
OH NO...
THEN IT WAS YOU!
YOU BLACK-MAILED THE TALENT AGENCY!
YOU'RE KAZUKI KINUKAWA'S MOTHER!
WHAT?
WELL? CON-FESS!
IT WAS JUST A PRANK...
A PRANK?
I DIDN'T MEAN FOR IT TO GO THIS FAR.

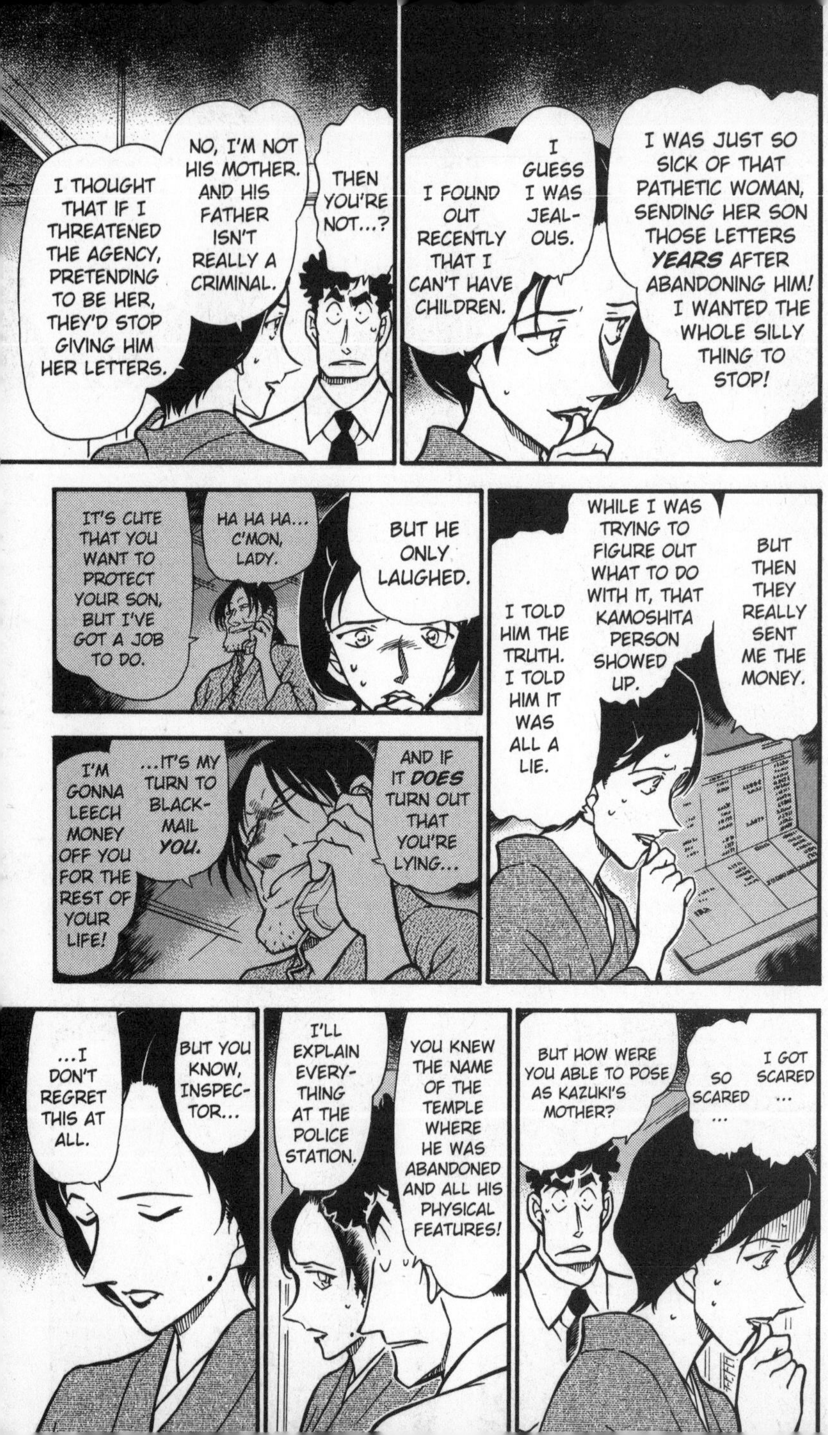
I WAS JUST SO SICK OF THAT PATHETIC WOMAN, SENDING HER SON THOSE LETTERS ***YEARS*** AFTER ABANDONING HIM! I WANTED THE WHOLE SILLY THING TO STOP!
I GUESS I WAS JEAL-OUS.
I FOUND OUT RECENTLY THAT I CAN'T HAVE CHILDREN.
THEN YOU'RE NOT...?
NO, I'M NOT HIS MOTHER. AND HIS FATHER ISN'T REALLY A CRIMINAL.
I THOUGHT THAT IF I THREATENED THE AGENCY, PRETENDING TO BE HER, THEY'D STOP GIVING HIM HER LETTERS.
BUT THEN THEY REALLY SENT ME THE MONEY.
WHILE I WAS TRYING TO FIGURE OUT WHAT TO DO WITH IT, THAT KAMOSHITA PERSON SHOWED UP.
I TOLD HIM THE TRUTH. I TOLD HIM IT WAS ALL A LIE.
BUT HE ONLY LAUGHED.
HA HA HA... C'MON, LADY.
IT'S CUTE THAT YOU WANT TO PROTECT YOUR SON, BUT I'VE GOT A JOB TO DO.
AND IF IT ***DOES*** TURN OUT THAT YOU'RE LYING...
...IT'S MY TURN TO BLACK-MAIL ***YOU.***
I'M GONNA LEECH MONEY OFF YOU FOR THE REST OF YOUR LIFE!
I GOT SCARED...
SO SCARED...
BUT HOW WERE YOU ABLE TO POSE AS KAZUKI'S MOTHER?
YOU KNEW THE NAME OF THE TEMPLE WHERE HE WAS ABANDONED AND ALL HIS PHYSICAL FEATURES!
I'LL EXPLAIN EVERY-THING AT THE POLICE STATION.
BUT YOU KNOW, INSPEC-TOR...
...I DON'T REGRET THIS AT ALL.

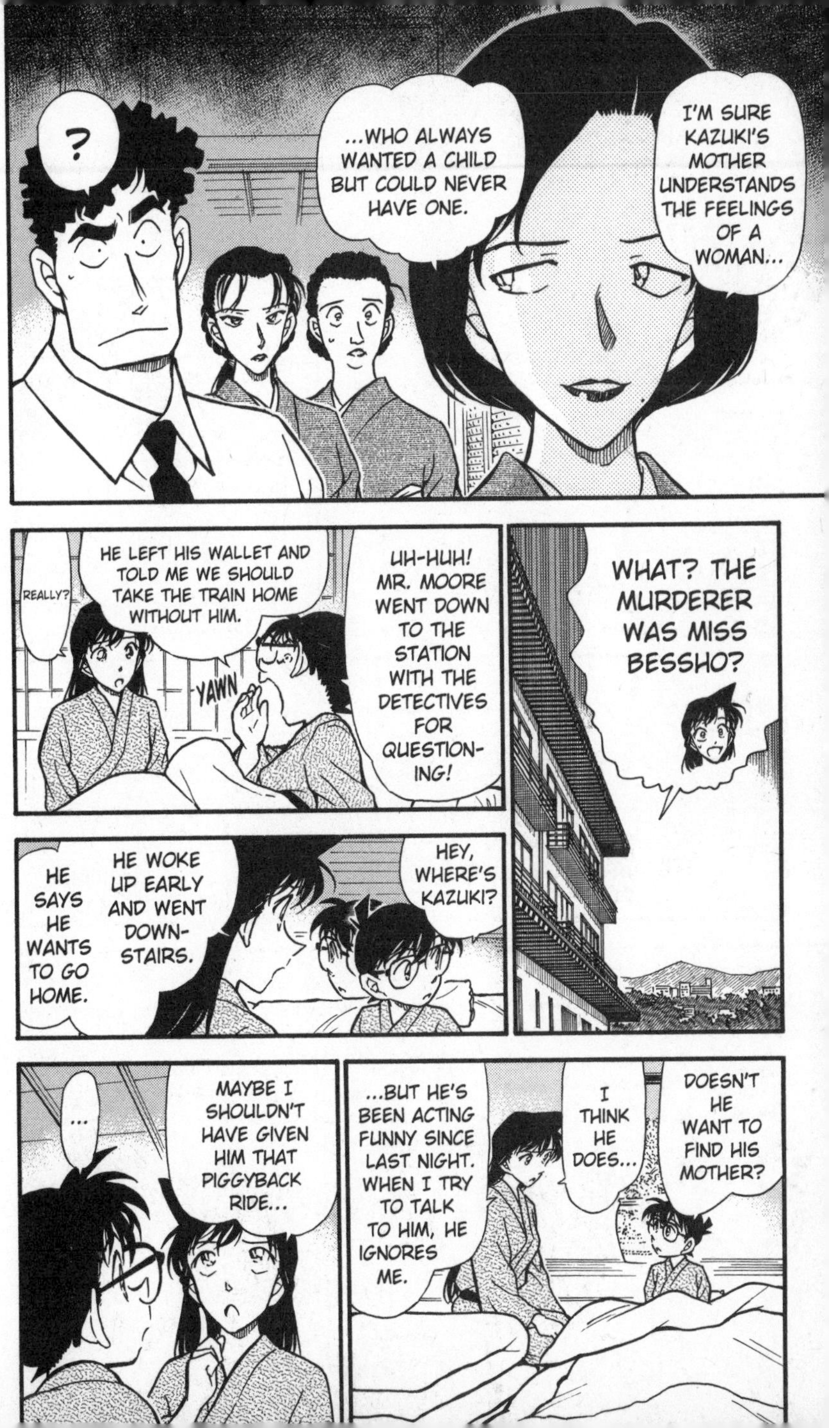
I'M SURE KAZUKI'S MOTHER UNDERSTANDS THE FEELINGS OF A WOMAN...
...WHO ALWAYS WANTED A CHILD BUT COULD NEVER HAVE ONE.
?
WHAT? THE MURDERER WAS MISS BESSHO?
UH-HUH! MR. MOORE WENT DOWN TO THE STATION WITH THE DETECTIVES FOR QUESTION-ING!
HE LEFT HIS WALLET AND TOLD ME WE SHOULD TAKE THE TRAIN HOME WITHOUT HIM.
YAWN
REALLY?
HEY, WHERE'S KAZUKI?
HE WOKE UP EARLY AND WENT DOWN-STAIRS.
HE SAYS HE WANTS TO GO HOME.
DOESN'T HE WANT TO FIND HIS MOTHER?
I THINK HE DOES...
...BUT HE'S BEEN ACTING FUNNY SINCE LAST NIGHT. WHEN I TRY TO TALK TO HIM, HE IGNORES ME.
MAYBE I SHOULDN'T HAVE GIVEN HIM THAT PIGGYBACK RIDE...
...

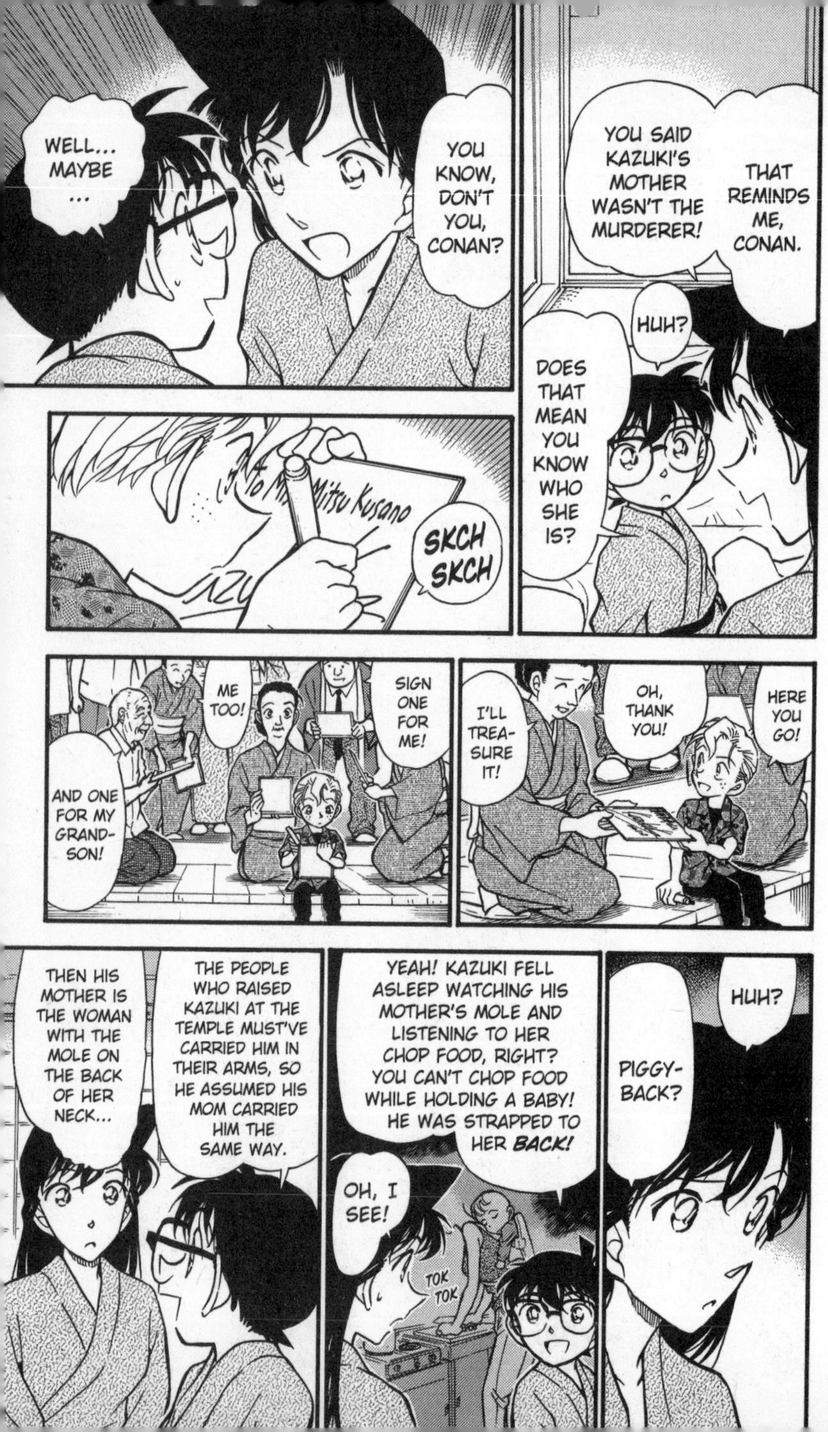
THAT REMINDS ME, CONAN.
YOU SAID KAZUKI'S MOTHER WASN'T THE MURDERER!
HUH?
DOES THAT MEAN YOU KNOW WHO SHE IS?
YOU KNOW, DON'T YOU, CONAN?
WELL... MAYBE ...
Mitsu Kusano
SKCH SKCH
HERE YOU GO!
OH, THANK YOU!
I'LL TREASURE IT!
SIGN ONE FOR ME!
ME TOO!
AND ONE FOR MY GRANDSON!
HUH?
PIGGY-BACK?
YEAH! KAZUKI FELL ASLEEP WATCHING HIS MOTHER'S MOLE AND LISTENING TO HER CHOP FOOD, RIGHT? YOU CAN'T CHOP FOOD WHILE HOLDING A BABY! HE WAS STRAPPED TO HER BACK!
OH, I SEE!
TOK TOK
THE PEOPLE WHO RAISED KAZUKI AT THE TEMPLE MUST'VE CARRIED HIM IN THEIR ARMS, SO HE ASSUMED HIS MOM CARRIED HIM THE SAME WAY.
THEN HIS MOTHER IS THE WOMAN WITH THE MOLE ON THE BACK OF HER NECK...

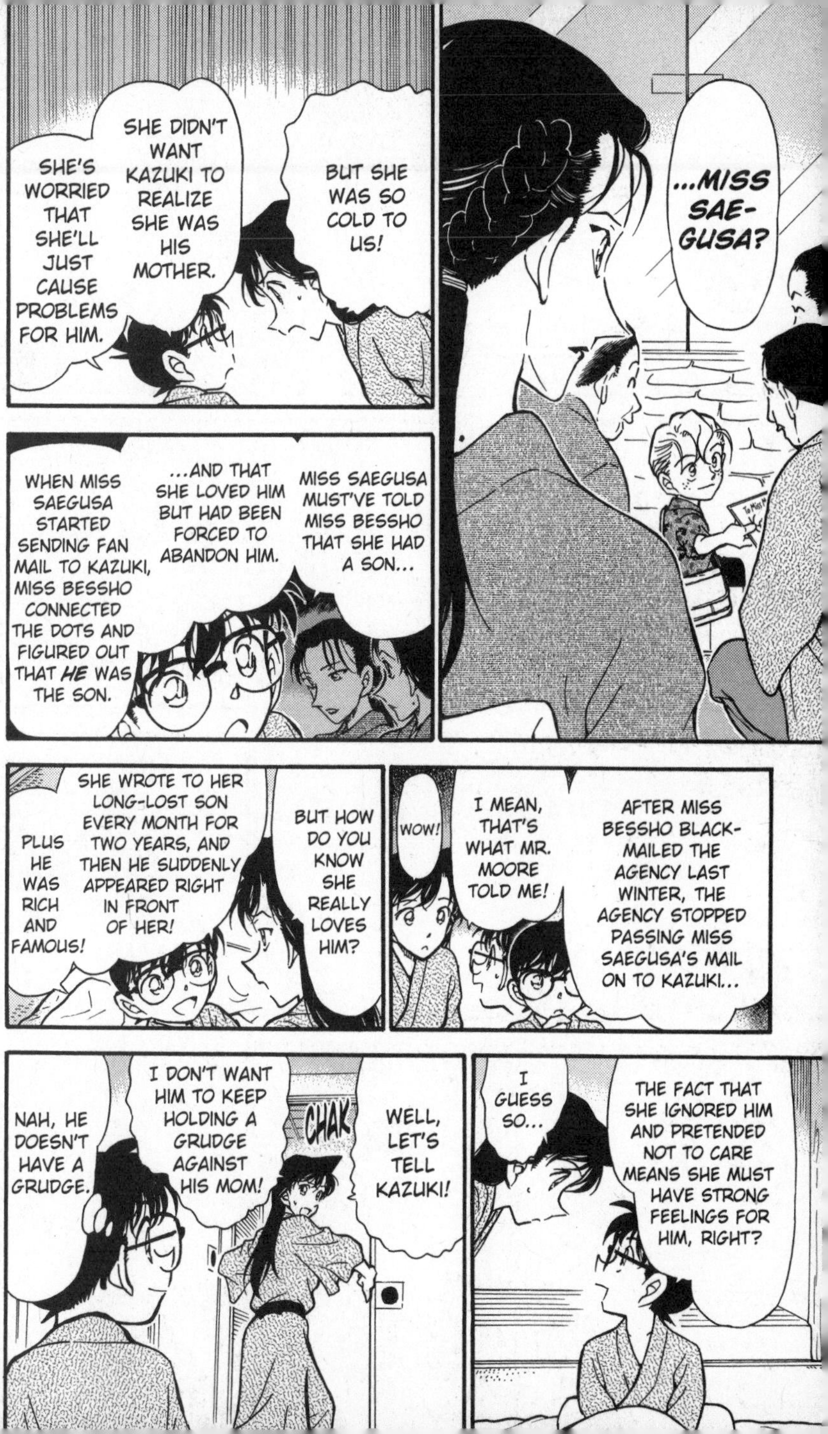
...MISS SAEGUSA?
BUT SHE WAS SO COLD TO US!
SHE DIDN'T WANT KAZUKI TO REALIZE SHE WAS HIS MOTHER.
SHE'S WORRIED THAT SHE'LL JUST CAUSE PROBLEMS FOR HIM.
MISS SAEGUSA MUST'VE TOLD MISS BESSHO THAT SHE HAD A SON...
...AND THAT SHE LOVED HIM BUT HAD BEEN FORCED TO ABANDON HIM.
WHEN MISS SAEGUSA STARTED SENDING FAN MAIL TO KAZUKI, MISS BESSHO CONNECTED THE DOTS AND FIGURED OUT THAT HE WAS THE SON.
AFTER MISS BESSHO BLACK-MAILED THE AGENCY LAST WINTER, THE AGENCY STOPPED PASSING MISS SAEGUSA'S MAIL ON TO KAZUKI...
I MEAN, THAT'S WHAT MR. MOORE TOLD ME!
WOW!
BUT HOW DO YOU KNOW SHE REALLY LOVES HIM?
SHE WROTE TO HER LONG-LOST SON EVERY MONTH FOR TWO YEARS, AND THEN HE SUDDENLY APPEARED RIGHT IN FRONT OF HER!
PLUS HE WAS RICH AND FAMOUS!
THE FACT THAT SHE IGNORED HIM AND PRETENDED NOT TO CARE MEANS SHE MUST HAVE STRONG FEELINGS FOR HIM, RIGHT?
I GUESS SO...
WELL, LET'S TELL KAZUKI!
CHAK
I DON'T WANT HIM TO KEEP HOLDING A GRUDGE AGAINST HIS MOM!
NAH, HE DOESN'T HAVE A GRUDGE.

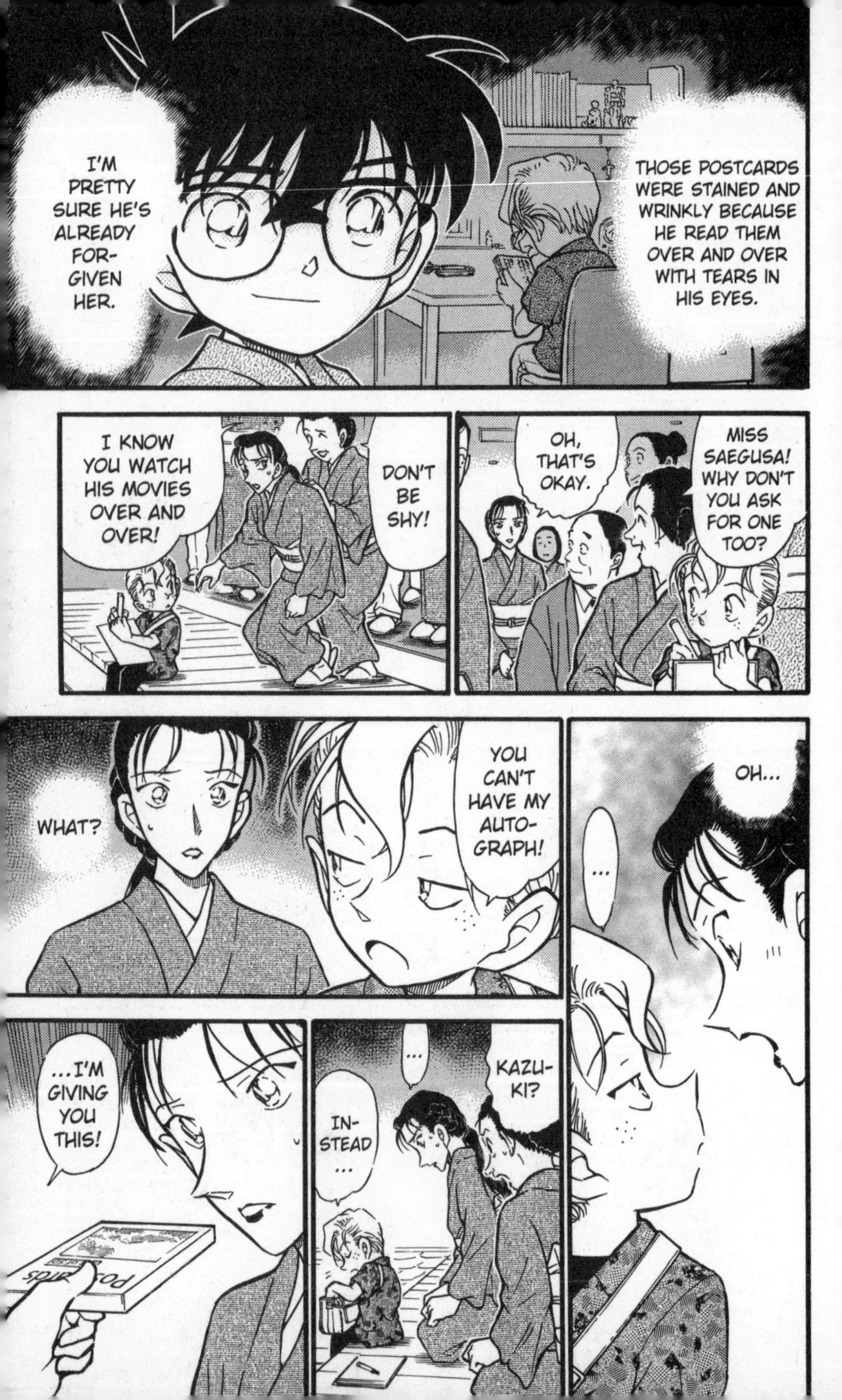
THOSE POSTCARDS WERE STAINED AND WRINKLY BECAUSE HE READ THEM OVER AND OVER WITH TEARS IN HIS EYES.
I'M PRETTY SURE HE'S ALREADY FOR-GIVEN HER.
MISS SAEGUSA! WHY DON'T YOU ASK FOR ONE TOO?
OH, THAT'S OKAY.
DON'T BE SHY!
I KNOW YOU WATCH HIS MOVIES OVER AND OVER!
OH...
...
YOU CAN'T HAVE MY AUTO-GRAPH!
WHAT?
KAZU-KI?
...
IN-STEAD ...
...I'M GIVING YOU THIS!

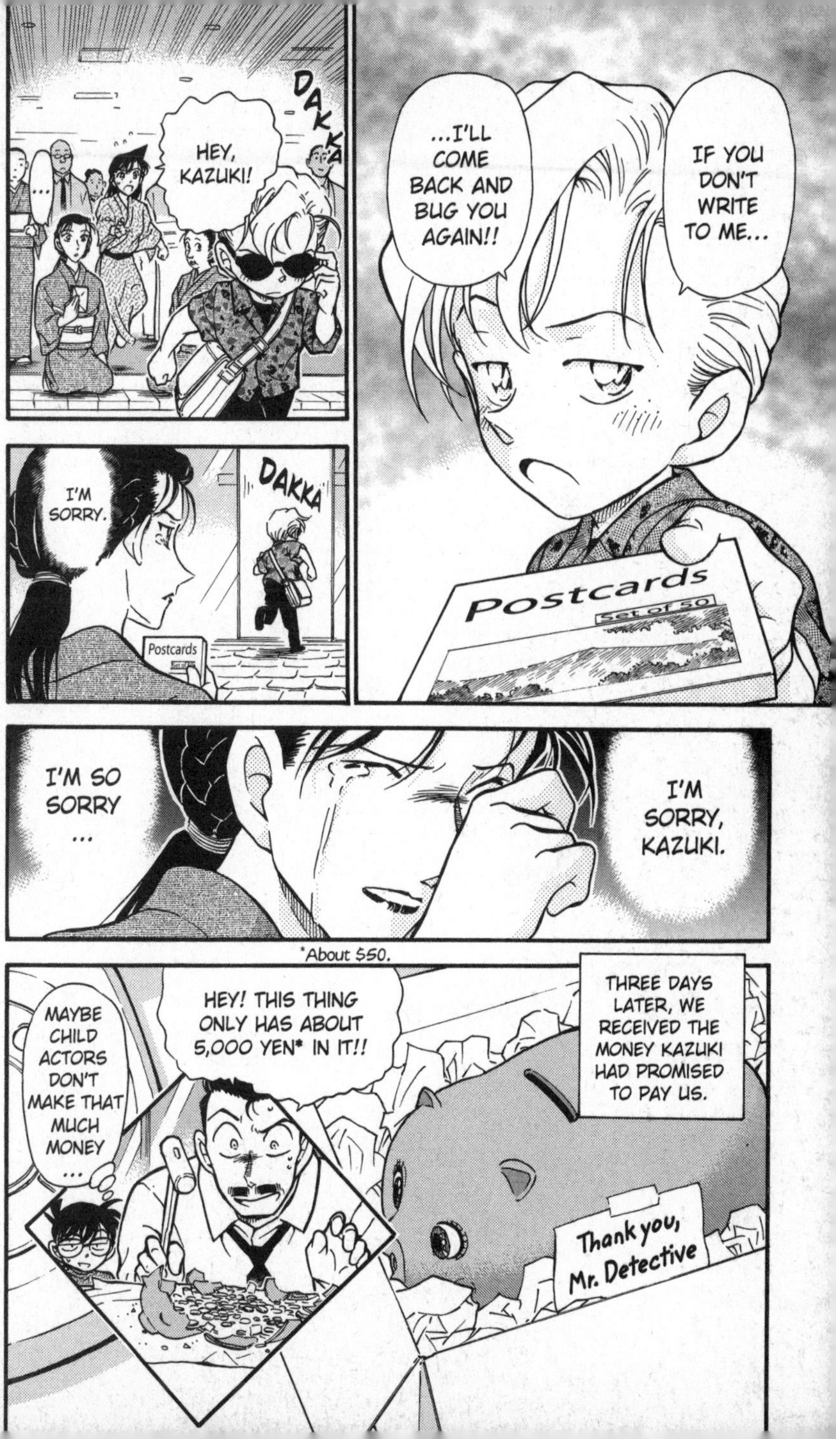
IF YOU DON'T WRITE TO ME...
...I'LL COME BACK AND BUG YOU AGAIN!!
Postcards
Set of 50
DAKKA
HEY, KAZUKI!
...
DAKKA
I'M SORRY.
Postcards
I'M SORRY, KAZUKI.
I'M SO SORRY ...
*About $50.
THREE DAYS LATER, WE RECEIVED THE MONEY KAZUKI HAD PROMISED TO PAY US.
Thank you, Mr. Detective
HEY! THIS THING ONLY HAS ABOUT 5,000 YEN* IN IT!!
MAYBE CHILD ACTORS DON'T MAKE THAT MUCH MONEY ...

Hello, Aoyama here.

While I was working on the Red Horse storyline, one of my assistants commented, "Wow, Rachel knows a lot about the *Romance of the Three Kingdoms*. That's pretty interesting."

I was so surprised to hear that! Isn't the *Romance of the Three Kingdoms* a popular book? Everybody at my studio is a *Three Kingdoms* fan, so I guess I can't blame myself for thinking the story was common knowledge. It's a great novel. You should all read it!

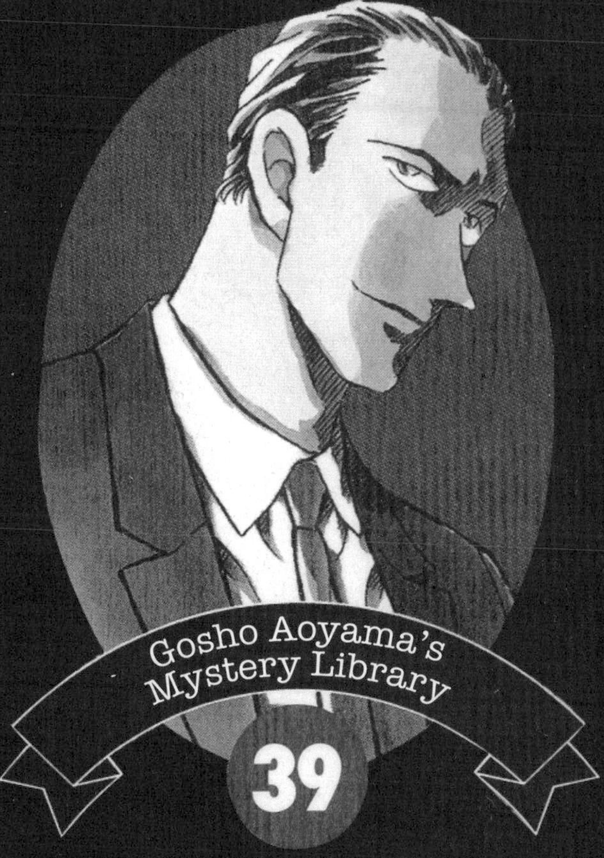
Gosho Aoyama's
Mystery Library
39

LEW ARCHER

Detectives do more than solve baffling murder cases. Infidelity investigations, background checks, disappearances...and "mostly divorce work," sneers grim, hard-boiled detective Lew Archer. Archer lives in California. He's 6'2", 190 pounds, currently single but formerly married (heh). A cool, handsome man, he self-deprecatingly claims, "I look like a coyote when I smile." He was once a police officer but quit after becoming disgusted by the corruption in the police force. He also worked in intelligence during WWII.

When it comes to investigating a case, Archer never jumps to conclusions. He "observes people, then makes a decision." His method is to contact people one at a time and gradually get closer to the truth. He drags himself through all the bloody complications that lie in wait for him with his natural toughness...and sometimes with the aid of a gun. Archer is the creation of Ross MacDonald, whose wife, Margaret Miller, is also a famous mystery writer.

I recommend *The Moving Target*.

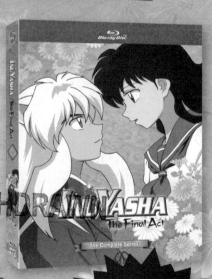

MAGI
The labyrinth of magic
Story & Art by
SHINOBU OHTAKA

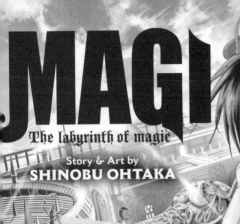

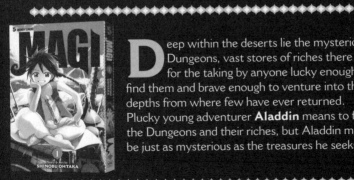

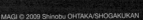

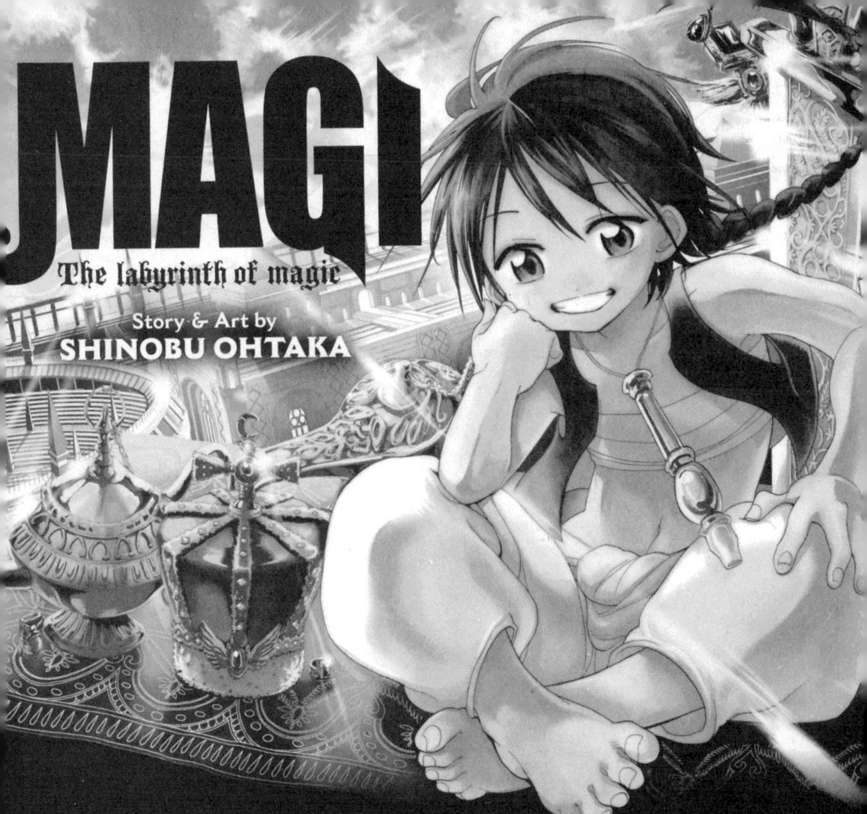

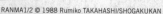

Hey! You're Reading in the Wrong Direction!

This is the ***end*** of this graphic novel!

To properly enjoy this VIZ graphic novel, please turn it around and begin reading from ***right to left.*** Unlike English, Japanese is read right to left, so Japanese comics are read in reverse order from the way English comics are typically read.

1
2
1
3
4
2
5
6
3
7
8
4
9
5
142

Follow the action this way

This book has been printed in the original Japanese format in order to preserve the orientation of the original artwork. Have fun with it!

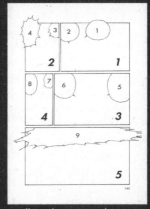